THE WORLD COPPER INDUSTRY

The World
COPPER INDUSTRY

Structure and Economic Analysis

RAYMOND F. MIKESELL

Published for Resources for the Future
by The Johns Hopkins University Press
Baltimore and London

The Johns Hopkins University Press, Baltimore, Maryland 21218
The Johns Hopkins Press Ltd., London

Library of Congress Catalog Card Number 79-4581
ISBN 8-8018-2257-2 cloth
ISBN 0-8018-2270-X paperback

Library of Congress Cataloging in Publication data will be found
on the last printed page of this book.

In memory of Orris C. Herfindahl, who was the inspiration for this book.

Contents

TABLES

FIGURES

Preface

THIS BOOK is a survey of the world copper industry and of the problems with which policy makers and students of the industry are currently concerned. My interest in the copper industry arose out of research on foreign investment in minerals, an interest that dates from my association with the President's Materials Policy Commission, as director of the commission's foreign resources division in 1951–52. Hence, readers will find a rather heavy emphasis on foreign investment in mining, especially in the Third World copper producing countries.

Although this book reflects information and suggestions from many individuals, I am solely responsible for all but two of the chapters. Chapter 2, which deals with the physical characteristics of the copper industry, including a description and evaluation of new metallurgical processes, is authored by John W. Whitney who is both a geologist and Ph.D. in mineral economics. Chapter 5, which is authored by Kirkor Bozdogan and Raymond S. Hartman, reflects the work of these economists on an econometric model of the copper industry prepared at Arthur D. Little, Inc. for the U.S. Environmental Protection Agency. This chapter, together with my own chapter 6 on the quantitative analysis of copper supply, is designed to provide the reader with an introduction to, and evaluation of, econometric commodity modeling techniques which have been applied to the copper industry. In preparing chapter 6, I received substantial assistance from Jos Bruggink, now with the Energy Study Center, Petten, the Netherlands.

The decision to undertake this study grew out of conversations with Orris C. Herfindahl and Sam Schurr of Resources for the Future. A large number of individuals have assisted me in dealing with various topics treated in this book. I would like first of all to acknowledge help from Hans Landsberg and John J. Schanz, Jr. of Resources for the Future, who reviewed the initial draft of my manuscript. Comprehensive critical reviews of my manuscript were undertaken at the request of RFF by Wolfgang Gluschke, United Nations Centre for Natural Resources, Energy and Transport; Roger Sedjo of RFF; Simon Strauss, vice chairman of ASARCO; Gerhard Theibach of the World Bank; and John E. Tilton, professor of mineral economics, Pennsylvania State University. The detailed criticisms and suggestions by these reviewers were immensely valuable in preparing the final edition of the manuscript, and although they are in no way responsible for the errors and weaknesses that remain, their comments contributed greatly to improving the quality of this study.

In addition to the assistance from the reviewers, I gained important insights on exploration from Merwin Bernstein and Thomas N. Walthier of St. Joe Minerals. I obtained numerous ideas and encouragement from Charles F. Barber of ASARCO; Walter Chudson of the United Nations; Alun G. Davies of Rio Tinto-Zinc; Ross Garnaut of the Australian National University; Sacha Gueronik and Peter Parkinson of CIPEC; Taylor Ostrander of AMAX; Sir Ronald Prain, formerly Chairman of Roan Selection Trust; Marian Radetzki of the Institute for International Economic Studies (Stockholm); Harold J. Schroeder, U.S. Bureau of Mines; Milton Stern of Kennecott Copper Corporation; Alexander Sutulov, Centro de Investigacion Minera y Metalurgica, Santiago, Chile; Kenji Takeuchi and Bension Varon of the World Bank; George R. Westby, Southern Peru Copper Corporation; Stephen A. Zorn, Commodities Research Unit; and my colleagues at the University of Oregon, Eaton H. Conant and Robert E. Smith.

Research assistance, including preparation of some of the appendixes for this book, was provided by Jos Bruggink and Steve Staloff, former graduate students in economics at the University of Oregon who have since received their doctorates. My wife, Irene, provided constructive criticism and countless hours in reading the manuscript for preliminary editing. Without her patience and encouragement this book could never have been written. Finally, my secretary, Letty Fotta, rendered competent and tireless service beyond what any author has the right to ask.

March 1979   Raymond F. Mikesell
                                                    University of Oregon

THE WORLD COPPER INDUSTRY

Introduction

OVER THE PAST decade, events relating to the world copper industry have generated widespread public interest, and hundreds of books have been written by economists, political scientists, environmentalists, commodity specialists, business executives, geologists, and engineers on topics of general interest concerned with this industry. In recent years more has been written about copper than about any other nonfuel mineral. The reasons are easy to understand. The prices of this important industrial commodity gyrated widely during the 1970s, and fears of inadequate copper supplies in 1973 and early 1974 quickly shifted to concerns about the effects of excessive copper supplies and low prices on employment and the financial welfare of the copper industry in the United States and Canada, and the impact on the economies of the principal copper producing countries in the Third World. Copper smelters constitute a serious environmental problem and current and proposed regulations by the Environmental Protection Agency have generated a heated debate between EPA and the environmentalists on the one hand, and industry spokesmen on the other. Foreign investments by large U.S. and European copper mining companies in Africa and Latin America have been expropriated by the governments of host countries to an extent not equaled for any other industry except petroleum. The justifications for the nationalization of American and European companies in Chile, Peru, Zambia, and Zaire, among others, have been the subject of intense debates among social scientists, politicians, and business leaders the world over. U.S. diplomatic relations with some of these countries have been considerably influenced by the treatment of U.S. investments in the copper industry. The 1978 invasion from Angola of Shaba Province in Zaire might not have generated the same degree of international concern and intervention if it had not threatened the bulk of the copper output from one of the world's leading copper producers. The debate within the United Nations Conference on Trade and Development (UNCTAD) in Geneva over methods for stabilizing the prices of

1

international commodities has centered in considerable measure on the stabilization of world copper prices. The establishment of the Inter-Governmental Council of Copper Exporting Countries (CIPEC) led to widespread concern in the developed countries that nonfuel mineral producing countries would be able to create cartels with market power similar to that exercised by OPEC. Finally, the U.S. copper industry has been the subject of a number of administration and congressional studies relating to the competitive structure of the industry, the need for import protection, and the creation of a national copper stockpile.

In light of these varied interests centered on copper, it seemed appropriate to write a book which would not simply review the major topics related to copper, but would provide a largely nontechnical basis for understanding them. An effort has been made to integrate the subject matter by showing the relationship between the physical characteristics of the industry and its market and industrial structure. These in turn are essential for understanding several policy issues relating to copper, including: (1) assuring adequate supplies at reasonable prices for meeting future world demand; (2) the role of foreign investment and measures for promoting it; (3) protecting the environment without endangering domestic supplies; (4) maintaining competition and an efficient price system; (5) encouraging resource conservation through recycling; and (6) moderating uneconomic price fluctuations.

Much of the analysis of the copper industry in this book also applies directly to other nonfuel minerals industries. This is particularly the case in the discussion of the economics of mining investment; measures for international price stabilization; foreign investment and its promotion; the economics of exhaustible resources; investment requirements for meeting future demand; and recycling. Even the physical characteristics, industrial structure, and market organization of copper have a great deal in common with such nonfuel minerals as iron ore, lead, zinc, and nickel.

Since this book covers a broad spectrum of disciplines ranging from geology and engineering to the economics of price stabilization and cartels, it is not intended to make an original contribution of interest to specialists in any area of the applied physical or social sciences. Rather, it is designed to acquaint the reader who may not be a specialist in mineral economics, geology, or mine engineering with the physical characteristics of the copper industry; to acquaint the reader who is not a mining company official or commodity specialist with the structure and operation of the world's copper markets; and to provide the reader who is not an econometric commodity model builder with the elements of quantitative analysis of the demand for and supply of copper.

The material in this book is in considerable measure oriented to policy issues rather than to description and theoretical analysis. However, the conclusions summarized in chapter 14 are more in the nature of findings than recommendations for specific policy actions. Special emphasis is given to the following policy issues: (1) the competitiveness of the U.S. copper industry; (2) the adequacy of world copper resources for meeting the long-run requirements of the market economies; (3) the possibilities for modifying sharp fluctuations in copper prices; (4) the likelihood of an effective world copper producers' cartel that would raise prices significantly above long-run equilibrium levels; (5) the outlook for the development of sufficient copper producing capacity for meeting world demand over the next two decades and the measures for assuring an adequate level of capacity; and (6) the role of foreign investment and measures for encouraging it. Our conclusions are broadly optimistic in terms of the long-run ability of the industry to supply world requirements and the feasibility of finding solutions to the industry's problems.

1

Overview

Brief History of Copper

THE DISCOVERY and use of copper dates from prehistoric times when Stone Age people in the Mediterranean beat the red stones found on the island of Cyprus (from which copper gets its name) into implements. Copper was first used in its pure, natural form without benefit of metallurgy, just as it was used by the native Africans who were visited by Dr. David Livingston,[1] and by the American Indians in the Lake Superior region long before the arrival of the Europeans. Some of the ancient copper ore bodies, such as those in the Timna Valley in Israel—believed to have been the site of King Solomon's mines—have been worked intermittently to the present day. The famous Cyprus mines which supplied the Phoenicians and the Greeks and later the Romans were rediscovered by the American engineer-geologist, D. A. Gunther, early in the twentieth century.[2]

Another copper region that has been mined intermittently, at least since the second millenium B.C. to the present, is the Rio Tinto in southern Spain—first by the Phoenicians and later by the Romans, who were followed by the Moors, and today by the European company that bears its name, Rio Tinto-Patino. The Romans extracted millions of tons of ore from the Rio Tinto mines, which went to a depth of 1,000 feet. But while their smelting technique was sufficient for oxide ore, it was the Moors who developed the metallurgy for recovering pure copper from the more accessible copper sulfides.[3] The Rio Tinto mines

[1] The David Livingston Museum in Livingston, Zambia has a remarkable collection of native copper instruments and utensils in use during the time of Livingston.

[2] In 1922 Cyprus Mines, Inc. began shipping copper from the Cyprus mines last worked by the Romans 1,600 years before. See Ira B. Joralemon, *Copper* (Berkeley, Howell-North Books, 1973) for a fascinating history of copper mining.

[3] Joralemon, *Copper*, pp. 31–32.

were rediscovered by the Spanish in 1556, but owing to bureaucratic delays and poor management, profitable production did not begin until nearly 200 years later. Modern development of the Rio Tinto mines on a substantial scale was initiated by a group of private British capitalists who purchased the mines from the Spanish government in 1873 and organized the Rio Tinto Company.[4]

During the Middle Ages and in the early Modern Period, copper mining, metallurgy, and fabricating were carried on in Europe and the Germans in particular developed new technology for this industry. The use of copper in the manufacture of brass cannon and other military supplies greatly increased the consumption of copper. In the eighteenth century, the center of the world's copper industry shifted to Britain and by the end of the century Britain was the world's largest copper producer, supplying three-fourths of all metal produced. Much of this copper came from the Cornish and Devon ores, trade in which had been organized by the Phoenicians as early as 1500 B.C.; later the industry was developed by the Romans. The demand for copper exceeded the capacity of British ores so that Britain began importing copper from various parts of the world for smelting. Advances in British smelting technology helped to establish a monopoly which continued until the middle of the nineteenth century, by which time foreign producers began to set up their own smelters, employing such British inventions as the reverberatory furnace.[5] Today Britain imports most of her refined copper requirements.

In Latin America, both the Aztecs and the Incas used copper and bronze tools, while in North America copper mining began with the Indians, whose copper tools and ornaments were noted by the early explorers. But it was not until the mid-nineteenth century that the rich deposits in northern Michigan from which the Indians obtained their copper were rediscovered, and a modern copper industry established. For several decades northern Michigan was the world's largest source of copper, but later on in the century the output of the Lake Superior region was exceeded by the mines discovered at Butte, Montana. During the 1870s Chile became the world's most important copper exporter, but these early mines tended to be small.

During the second half of the nineteenth century, the growth of electrical energy for power, lighting, and communications led to a doubling of the world demand for copper every few years. In 1860 the annual

[4] For an interesting history of the Rio Tinto mines, see David Avery, *Not on Queen Victoria's Birthday: The Story of the Rio Tinto Mines* (London, Collins, 1974).

[5] Sir Ronald Prain, *Copper: The Anatomy of an Industry* (London, Mining Journal Books, 1975) chapters I and II.

output of the world's copper mines was only about 100,000 metric tons (mt). By 1912 it had reached a million mt and by 1929, 2 million mt. By 1960 it had doubled again to 4 million mt and by 1974 the world's primary copper production was nearly 8 million mt.[6] As long as the supply of copper depended upon mining rich vein deposits, world reserves were quite limited in relation to the millions of tons of refined copper per year that would be required to meet industrial demand in the twentieth century. But there were vast quantities of copper in the form of low-grade porphyry deposits[7] which require large-scale mining methods for profitable operation. Porphyry copper deposits tend to occur in the earth's crust in discontinuous belts, the best known being the belt that runs from northern Canada down through southwestern United States, Mexico, Central America, and western South America through Peru, Chile, and western Argentina. Another belt runs through the Philippines and Papua New Guinea (PNG), and a third belt passes through southeastern Europe, Iran, and Pakistan (see figure 2-1).[8]

Porphyries constitute over 60 percent of presently known copper reserves and account for 45 percent of presently mined copper.[9] Although the existence of large porphyry ore bodies has been known for a long time, they were not developed until the early 1900s when an American engineer, Daniel C. Jackling, first applied the techniques of mass production to copper mining in 1905 at the Bingham Canyon open-pit mine in Utah where he showed that 2 percent copper porphyry ore could be mined profitably. Since that time, the grade of copper that can be profitably mined has declined to well under 0.5 percent in open-pit mines in the United States and elsewhere. Mass production mining requires large shovels, trucks, and ore crushers, but the development of large-scale mining was also facilitated by technological improvements in concentrating, one of the most important being flotation. In this process the crushed ore is reduced by rotating mills to a powder which is fed into flotation cells where the particles of copper-bearing materials are separated from the noncopper-bearing rock.[10] The flotation process of concentration was developed in Britain about the same time that large-scale mining of porphyries first took place. Technological developments in smelting and refining have also occurred in step with those in

6 Prain, *Copper: The Anatomy of an Industry,* pp. 8–9.

7 See chapter 2 for a systematic discussion of copper ores.

8 Alexander Sutulov, *Copper Porphyries* (Salt Lake City, University of Utah, 1974) pp. 19–21.

9 Sutulov, *Copper Porphyries,* p. 10.

10 The flotation process is described in chapter 2.

mining and milling to permit large-scale mining and processing of the low-grade copper ores. These developments have tended to hold down the real cost of producing copper in the face of a steadily declining average grade of mined ore.

Jackling's large-scale mining technique was again employed in Ely, Nevada in 1908; and later in 1910 at Miami, Arizona, and subsequently at the other great Arizona mines of Ray, Inspiration, New Cornelia, and Copper Queen; and at Chino in New Mexico. The porphyry copper belt in the southwestern United States extended across the Mexican border and by 1905 the great Cananea mine had been developed in Sonora, Mexico. The rapid development of large copper mines in the southwestern United States greatly increased U.S. production so that by 1910 three-fifths of the world's copper was produced in this country. At about the same time, large-scale copper mining was initiated in South America, largely under American leadership, and in Africa under British and Belgian leadership. Canadian copper mining began in the late nineteenth century in the Lake Superior region and later mines were found in northeastern Canada. By the 1930s Canada was the world's third largest producer behind the United States and Chile. With the opening of the large porphyry mines in British Columbia, Canadian output rose above Chile's in 1972 and 1973, but Canada declined to fourth place behind Chile and the U.S.S.R. in 1974.

Chile and Peru

The Jackling revolution in mine technology led American mining engineers to look for large ore bodies in other countries. Chile was a natural place for exploration since copper had been produced there in colonial times. Prior to the surge in U.S. copper output with the opening of the Butte, Montana and other western mines, Chile was the world's principal source of copper.[11] The pioneer in the development of large-scale mining in Chile was the American mining engineer, William Braden, who first went to Chile in 1903 to explore some of the ore bodies that had been worked decades before. In 1904 he obtained an option on El Teniente in central Chile and formed the Braden Copper Corporation (later acquired by the Kennecott Copper Corporation) to develop the mine, which had been abandoned earlier because of the exhaustion of high-grade ore and because of the difficulties encountered

[11] Between 1851 and 1880 Chile produced 1.2 million mt of copper, or 40 percent of the world's output (Corporacion del Cobre, *El Cobre Chileno*, Santiago, Editorial Universataria, 1975) p. 25.

in mining at the 12,000 foot level in the Andes. El Teniente began producing in 1910 and was the first large-scale mine to use the flotation
process for concentration. Shortly thereafter another Chilean mine,
Chuquicamata (which is located in the desert of northern Chile and
which had been worked on a modest scale for many years), was developed by the Chilean Exploration Company. This mine, which was
initially financed by the Guggenheims and later sold to Anaconda,
became the largest in the world and remains so today, with a production
capability of over 400,000 mt per year. Chile's mine production rose to
over 1 million mt in 1976.

In 1902 an American group formed the Cerro de Pasco Mining Company to develop a copper mine in the Cerro de Pasco district of Peru
where silver had been mined for generations. There were many production difficulties and, although the mine was successful, Peruvian output
was small compared with that of the mines of the Chilean Gran Mineria
(Chuquicamata, El Salvador, and El Teniente) until the completion of
the great Toquepala mine in Southern Peru in 1960. In 1961 Peru's
copper mine output reached 181,000 mt per year, and with the completion of the Cuajone mine in 1977, Peru became the seventh largest
producer in the world; it is the second largest producer in Latin
America.

Central African Development

Mineral exploration in Central Africa was initiated toward the end of
the nineteenth century by British interests led by Cecil J. Rhodes who
organized the British South African Company (BSAC) in 1889 for exploration in northern Rhodesia (now Zambia) and by Belgian interests
financed by King Leopold II in the Belgian Congo (now Zaire). A number of prospectors operated in northern Rhodesia under licenses granted
by the BSAC, which had administrative control and ownership of mineral rights in the entire region. BSAC granted mineral rights to others
in exchange for royalties and shareholdings in the mining companies.
The ore grades in northern Rhodesia tended to be low and initially the
lack of rail transportation hindered development. Small operations
were not profitable, so that there occurred an amalgamation of the
smaller mines. Eventually virtually all of the mines came under the
control of two groups: Anglo-American Corporation of South Africa,
with majority British ownership (and minority American ownership);
and Rhodesian Selection Trust, with majority American ownership.

The rich ore bodies in the Katanga region of the Congo came under
the control of Union Miniere du Haut-Katanga, with majority Belgian

ownership and minority British ownership.[12] Copper production in Katanga was 10.7 thousand mt in 1914, rising to over 90,000 mt in 1925. Copper output of northern Rhodesia remained quite small until 1927 when it rose to about 3.3 thousand mt and by 1933 output exceeded 100,000 mt. However, with the opening up of the large Rhodesian mines, for example, Roan Antelope, Mufulira, Nchanga, and Rhokana, Rhodesian production exceeded that of the Congolese mines in the 1930s, rising to 255,000 mt in 1938, more than double the output of the Belgian Congo in that year. Output in both of these countries continued to expand so that by 1974 production in Zambia (formerly northern Rhodesia) and Zaire (formerly the Congo) was 700,000 mt and 500,000 mt respectively (table 1-1). However, Zaire apparently has the greater mineral potential in terms of undeveloped, rich ore bodies, so that in another decade or so their relative positions may be reversed.

Developments Since World War II

Prior to World War II five countries—the United States, Chile, Canada, Zambia, and Zaire—produced about three-fourths of the world's copper and only the first two countries had an annual output in excess of 300,000 mt. The average annual world production during the 1923–35 period was only 1.9 million mt, of which nearly 1.8 million mt was produced in the Western world. After World War II these same five countries increased their production substantially, but by 1976 they accounted for only 55 percent of total world output and about 71 percent of Western world output. The Soviet Union increased its annual output from 115,000 mt in 1938 to 1.1 million mt in 1976, while world output grew to 7.9 million mt in 1976, of which 6.2 million mt was produced in the market economies (table 1-1).

The major new large producers in the Western world after World War II were Peru, Yugoslavia, the Philippines, South Africa, Australia, and Papua New Guinea (PNG), while in the Communist world Poland and China became large producers. U.S. foreign investment was mainly responsible for the growth in Philippine and Australian[13] output, while the expansion of PNG[14] output was sparked by Australian and British

[12] See Francis L. Coleman, *The Northern Rhodesia Copper Belt, 1899–1962* (Manchester, Manchester University Press, U.K., 1971).

[13] The principal Australian copper producer is the Mt. Isa mine in which ASARCO formerly had a majority equity interest, but ASARCO currently holds a 49 percent equity interest.

[14] The Bougainville mine in PNG was developed by Conzinc Riotinto of Australia, a subsidiary of Rio Tinto-Zinc. RTZ also developed South Africa's largest mine, Palabora, while another large South African mine, O'okiep, is controlled by the U.S. mining firm, Newmont.

Table 1-1. Copper Mine Production by Major Country and Region, Selected Years

(*000 metric tons*)

	1925	1929	1938	1950	1960	1974	1976
United States	761	905	506	825	994	1,489	1,462
Canada	51	113	267	240	399	821	747
Latin America	359	476	448	481	798	1,208	1,323
Chile	243	320	351	363	533	902	1,005
Mexico	55	87	42	62	61	83	89
Peru	37	56	38	30	182	212	219
Other	24[a]	13[a]	17[a]	26[a]	22[a]	11[a]	10[a]
Western Europe	120	129	160	97	111	281	315
Finland	1	5	12	16	29	37	42
Germany	24	26	30	1[b]	2[b]	2[b]	2[b]
Norway	32	19	22	16	15	23	32
Spain	48	58	30	6	8	45	46
Sweden	c	1	9	16	17	41	47
Yugoslavia	10	15	50	40	33	112	137*
Other	5	5	7	2	7	21[d]	9[d]
Asia	76	94	151	95	209	475	488
Cyprus	4	6	30	23	35	12	8
India	5	7	6	7	9	21	25
Indonesia	—	—	—	—	—	65	67
Japan	66	75	102	39	89	82	82
Philippines	—	—	4	10	44	226	227
Turkey	—	—	2	13	24	48	39
Other	1	6	7	3	8	21[h]	30[h]
Africa	109	164	395	520	978	1,448	1,447
South West Africa	8	11	5	11	20	28	39
Union of South Africa	8	9	11	34	47	179	197
Zaire	90	137	124	176	303	500	445
Zambia	2	6	255	297	578	698	709
Other	1	1	c	2	30	52[e]	57[e]
Oceania	13	13	20	15	107	435	391
Australia	12	13	20	15	107	251	214
Papua New Guinea	1	—	—	—	—	184	177
Total market economies	1,489	1,894	1,947	2,273	3,596	6,157	6,173

Table 1-1 (continued)

	1925	1929	1938	1950	1960	1974	1976
Communist countries	7	43	115	237	548	1,520	1,716
China	1	4	c	4	40	130	150
Bulgaria	1	2	c	c	11	52*	57*
Poland	c	c	c	c	11	185	267
U.S.S.R.	5	37	115	218	461	1,060	1,130
Other	c	c	c	15ᶠ	25ᵍ	107	112
Total world	1,496	1,937	2,062	2,510	4,144	7,677	7,889

Sources: Data for the years 1925, 1929, 1938, and 1950 were taken from *Minerals Yearbook*, U.S. Bureau of Mines, various issues. Data for 1964 from the American Bureau of Metal Statistics *Yearbook* 1964. Data for years 1974 and 1976 from *Metal Statistics, 1966–1976* (Frankfurt, Metalgesellschaft, 64th ed., 1977).
* Estimate.
a Largely Cuba and Bolivia.
b West Germany.
c Less than 0.5.
d Ireland, Austria, Portugal, and Italy.
e Rhodesia and Uganda.
f Includes estimates for East Germany and Bulgaria.
g Mainly East Germany.
h Iran, Israel, Republic of Korea, Taiwan.

capital. U.S. and British capital developed the South African copper industry.

World Copper Resources and their Locations

The world's copper resources include all the naturally occurring copper-bearing materials in or on the earth's crust in such form that economic extraction of copper is currently or potentially feasible. Most geologists divide copper resources into "identified resources" and "undiscovered resources." That portion of "identified resources" from which copper can be economically extracted at the time of determination is called a copper reserve, or a copper ore deposit. An "identified" copper reserve is a body of copper-bearing material whose location, quality, and quantity are known from geologic evidence supported with engineering measurements, while an "undiscovered" copper resource is a body of copper-bearing materials surmised to exist on the basis of broad geologic knowledge and theory. Identified copper resources are divided into

Table 1-2.   World Copper Resources
(*million metric tons of copper*)

	Reservesᵃ	Otherᵇ	Total
North America			
United States	85	291	376
Canada	31	109	141
Other	30	27	57
Total	146	427	574
South America			
Chile	85	118	203
Peru	32	36	68
Other	20	64	84
Total	137	218	355
Europe: Total	6	36	43
Africa			
Zaire	25	27	53
Zambia	29	64	93
Other	9	18	27
Total	63	109	173
Asia: Total	27	64	91
Oceania: Total	18	55	73
Centrally planned economies	60	173	233
Sea nodulesᶜ	—	692	692
World total	457	1,774	2,234

Source: H. J. Schroeder, *Copper*, Bureau of Mines (Washington, D.C., U.S. Department of the Interior, June 1977) p. 6.

ᵃ Of the listed reserves, approximately one-third of the copper contained in the U.S. and market economy country totals is located in undeveloped deposits. These deposits can move between reserve and resource classifications, depending on prevailing legal and economic conditions.

ᵇ Includes undiscovered (hypothetical and speculative) deposits.

ᶜ Estimate based on average of 1 percent copper per dry ton of nodules.

three classes, namely, measured, indicated, and inferred, depending upon the amount of information existing about the materials. Undiscovered copper resources are divided into "hypothetical" resources in known copper-bearing districts, and "speculative" resources in undiscovered districts.[15] The method of estimating copper reserves in identified resources is discussed in chapter 2.

[15] The above definitions are taken from *Geological Survey Bulletin* 1450-A (published jointly by the U.S. Bureau of Mines and the U.S. Geological Survey, Washington, D.C., 1976).

As is shown in table 1-2, total world copper reserves were estimated at 458 million mt as of 1977, but this amount constituted only about 20 percent of the world's copper resources (2,232 million mt). Estimates of both reserves and resources have been increasing every year. Only recently has the copper in deep sea nodules been included in total resources, but as more is learned about sea nodules and the economics of their extraction, some portion of these materials may be added to reserves and the total amount of copper in sea nodules listed as resources will also undoubtedly expand.

World Copper Consumption

World copper consumption grew from an estimated 50,000 mt per year in the mid-nineteenth century to about a half million mt in 1900, following which it grew at an average annual rate of about 4.5 percent to approximately 8.5 million mt in 1973–74.[16] This growth was a product of the electrical age, but the volume and pattern of copper consumption has been greatly affected by changes in the composition of industrial output, by changes in technology involving its use in particular industries, and by competition from substitutes, such as aluminum and plastics. Although per capita consumption of copper in the United States rose by some 47 percent between 1920 and 1929, it rose by only 30 percent between 1929 and 1950 and declined between 1950 and 1960. It rose again between 1960 and 1970 to about the 1950 level.[17] In 1960–64 U.S. average annual per capita consumption of copper was 17.1 pounds, but in 1970–74 average annual copper consumption was 20.8 pounds. British and German per capita consumption of copper was higher than in the United States during the 1960s, but Japanese per capita consumption, which was less than half of U.S. consumption in 1963, rose to an annual average of 20.5 pounds per capita in 1972–74.

Over the 1961–74 period, the ratio of the index of copper consumption to the index of industrial production declined by over 15 percent in the United States and by an even larger percentage in the United Kingdom, West Germany, France, and Italy. Declining intensity of use of copper may reflect one or more of the following developments: (1) the substitution of other materials either because of a rise in the relative price of copper in relation to prices of substitutes, or because substitute materials have more desirable properties, for example, lower weight;

[16] Prain, *Copper: The Anatomy of an Industry*, pp. 42–43.

[17] Consumption data include inventories so that in periods of rapid inventory build-up, "apparent" consumption will be larger than actual use by fabricators.

Table 1-3.   Breakdown of Copper Consumption by End Uses,
United States, Europe, and Japan, 1973
(*percent*)

	Electri-cal[a]	General engineering	Trans-port	Con-struction[a]	Consumer goods	Other
United Kingdom	38.3	12.5	11.9	32.0	3.8	1.5
Germany	50.0	12.1	10.2	23.6	2.7	1.4
France	39.2	17.6	8.1	26.9	4.3	3.7
Italy	40.0	16.5	12.0	18.0	10.0	3.5
United States	31.1	14.2	12.6	19.0	16.1	7.0
Japan	51.1	11.0	5.1	19.2	9.6	4.0

Source: "End-Use Investigation of the World Copper Market with Emphasis on the Prospects for Recycling and Substitution," Commodities Research Unit, January 1976 (prepared for the Centre for Natural Resources, Energy and Transport, United Nations) p. 21.

[a] Adjusted—tertiary wiring and cables attributed to construction, not electrical engineering.

(2) technological changes resulting in greater economy in use of copper; (3) or changes in product composition in favor of commodities requiring less copper or copper substitutes. Of the three factors, substitution of other materials, mainly aluminum and plastics, has been the most important in explaining the reduction in the intensity of copper use.

In 1973, 31 percent of U.S. copper consumption was used in electrical equipment as contrasted with 48 percent in 1929 and 40 percent in 1938. This development largely reflected encroachments of aluminum and plastics. On the other hand, the share of total U.S. copper consumption used in the construction and consumer goods industries was 19 and 16 percent respectively in 1973, compared with 11 percent and 6 percent respectively in 1938. The share of copper consumption in electrical uses in Germany, Japan, and Western Europe in 1973 was much higher than in the United States, but the share of copper consumption in the consumer durable goods industries in Europe and Japan was much lower than in the United States (see table 1-3).

The U.S. share of copper consumption has varied widely. In 1929 it was 46 percent of total world consumption. During the same year Western Europe accounted for 47 percent of total world consumption, and Japan 5 percent, leaving less than 3 percent for the rest of the world (see table 1-4). During the 1930s copper production and consumption declined sharply and in 1938 apparent consumption in the United States was only 24 percent of world consumption, while Western European

Table 1-4. World Consumption of Refined Copper, 1929, 1957, 1965, 1973, and 1976
(000 metric tons)

	1929	%	1957	%	1965	%	1973	%	1976	%
United States	687	46	1,163	37	1,688	35	2,221	32	1,783	28
Canada	13	1	107	3	205	4	231	3	206	3
Western Europe	708	47	1,538	48	2,114	44	2,650	38	2,654	41
Japan	75	5	177	6	429	9	1,201	17	1,050	16
Australia, South Africa, New Zealand	15	1	37[a]	1	80[a]	2	198	3	168	3
Developed countries	1,498	99	3,022	95	4,516	95	6,501	94	5,861	91
Developing countries	10	1	149	5	258	5	435	6	555	9
Total market economies	1,508	100	3,171	100	4,774	100	6,936	100	6,416	100
Communist countries	n.a.		466		905		1,817		2,092	
Total world	n.a.		3,637		5,679		8,753		8,508	

Sources: American Bureau of Metal Statistics Yearbook, 1964 and 1970. 1929 data from Resources for Freedom, Report of President's Materials Policy Commission, June 1952, vol. II, p. 192. 1973 and 1976 data from Metal Statistics, 1966–1976 (Frankfurt, Metalgesellschaft, 64th ed., 1977).

n.a. = not available.
[a] Australia only.

consumption represented 58 percent. In 1950 when European recovery was just getting under way, consumption figures were also distorted, with apparent U.S. consumption 54 percent of world consumption. By 1957 European recovery had been largely achieved and Western Europe consumed 48 percent of the world's total, contrasted with 37 percent for the United States.[18]

As a proportion of Western world consumption, U.S. consumption declined from 37 percent in 1957 to 28 percent in 1976, and consumption in Western Europe declined to 41 percent by 1976. Japan's share nearly tripled between 1957 and 1973. Consumption by the developing countries rose from 5 percent of the world total in 1957 to 8 percent in 1976; this percentage will probably continue to increase as their fabricating industries expand. Consumption in the Communist countries increased fourfold since 1957, accounting for nearly one-fourth of world consumption in 1976. Consumption data are given in terms of refined copper and tend to be higher than estimates of world mine production because a substantial portion of refined copper represents refining of scrap or secondary refining.

World Copper Production

Stages of Copper Production

The production of copper involves distinct stages, and there are several principal types or grades of copper sold on the market. The production process is dealt with in some detail in chapter 2, but we present here a few elementary aspects of the industry's structure. The four principal stages of the copper industry are (1) *mining* in which ore is extracted from the ground either by underground operations or from open pits; (2) *milling,* which includes crushing and grinding the ore and removing the bulk of the waste material to produce *concentrates* which may contain 12 to 30 percent or more of copper; (3) *smelting,* which involves feeding the concentrate into furnaces from which flow molten material that is about 98.5 percent copper, or *blister*; and (4) *refining* either by an electrolytic process or by a pyrometallurgical process, with the former having somewhat higher purity than "fire refined" copper. The last two stages have been combined in some of the new chemical smelting-refin-

[18] Apparent consumption of an individual country is equal to production plus net imports or minus net exports. Consumption also includes changes in stocks so that if inventories are building up, consumption is overstated and if inventories are being drawn down, actual consumption is understated.

ing processes. Most of the world's primary or mined copper is electrolytically refined. Refined copper may also be produced from copper
scrap, of which there are many grades ranging from virtually pure copper to alloys with a relatively low copper content. Copper produced
from scrap is referred to as secondary refined copper, but its quality may
be just as high as copper produced from newly mined ore.

Distribution of World Production

In 1925 the United States produced 51 percent of the world's mine
copper output and the developing countries about 31 percent, the vast
bulk of which came from Latin America. The U.S. proportion gradually declined and by 1976 the United States produced only 19 percent
of the world's mine copper while the developing countries produced 40
percent. In 1925 recorded production in the Communist countries was
only about one-tenth of 1 percent of the world's total, but by 1976 the
Soviet Bloc plus the People's Republic of China produced 22 percent of
the world's copper output. In 1976 the remaining 21 percent was produced by Canada (9 percent), Western Europe (4 percent), Australia
(3 percent), South Africa (2 percent), and Japan (1 percent) (see table
1-1). Within the developing world, Latin America's relative position
declined from 78 percent in 1925 to 42 percent in 1976, while the African
developing countries produced 40 percent and Asian countries plus
Papua New Guinea accounted for 19 percent in 1976. Although the
developing countries produced about 50 percent of the mine copper
output of the market economies in 1976, over 73 percent of the refined
copper was produced in the developed countries. A substantial portion
of the refined copper produced in the developed countries is derived
from scrap—15 to 20 percent—but only a small amount of the refined
output of the developing countries represents secondary production.
Although the developing countries smelt the bulk of their mine output,
a portion is exported in the form of concentrates to the developed countries. About 59 percent of the smelted production of the market economies in 1976 was in the developed countries (table 1-5).

World Trade Patterns for Copper

Since world trade in copper involves ores and concentrates, unrefined
metal (mainly blister), and refined copper, total trade and its allocation
among countries involves considerable duplication of metal values. For
example, Belgium accounted for about 12 percent of the world's exports
of refined copper in 1976, but Belgium mines no copper and imports

Table 1-5.   World Smelter and Refinery Production of Copper, 1976
(*000 metric tons*)

	Smelter	Refinery
Developed countries		
United States	1,392	1,715
Canada	489	511
Western Europe	541	1,503
Austria	2*	31
Belgium	6	425
Finland	50	38
West Germany	194	447
France	—	—
Norway	24	17
Italy	—	—
Spain	93	142
Sweden	47	60
Yugoslavia	122	137
United Kingdom	—	137
Other	3[a]	3[a]
Japan	770	864
Australia	167	189
South Africa	159	90
Total developed countries	3,518	4,872
Developing countries		
Latin America	1,129	886
Chile	856	632
Peru	188	140
Mexico	85	83
Brazil	—	31
Other	—	—
Africa	1,196	785
Zaire	408	66
Zambia	706	695
Rhodesia	38*	24*
South West Africa	36	—
Other	8*[b]	—

Table 1-5 (continued)

	Smelter	Refinery
Asia	90	96
India	25	21
Iran	7*	7*
Philippines	—	—
Turkey	28	28
Other	30c	40
Total developing countries	2,426	1,740
Total market economies	5,944	6,640
Planned economy countries		
Bulgaria	60*	53
U.S.S.R.	1,130*	1,460*
East Germany	16*	50*
Poland	270	270
Romania	50*	50*
China	160*	240*
Other	39*d	55*d
World total	7,674	8,831

Source: Metal Statistics, 1966–1976 (Frankfurt, Metalgesellschaft, 64th ed., 1977).
* Estimate.
a Portugal.
b Uganda.
c Taiwan and Republic of Korea.
d Albania, Czechoslovakia, and North Korea.

mainly blister copper for refining. The United States exports some refined copper, but is a net importer of refined copper, blister, and concentrates. Of the developed country producers of mine copper, only
Australia, Canada, and South Africa are important exporters of concentrates and unrefined copper. A substantial proportion of Canada's
mine output is exported to the United States for smelting and refining.
In 1976 just over half of Australia's copper exports took the form of
refined copper, while the bulk of South Africa's copper exports in that
year took the form of blister copper. Ignoring the duplications, in 1976
developing countries (excluding Yugoslavia) exported 62 percent of the
total exports (market economies) of ores and concentrates; 88 percent of
total exports of unrefined metal; and 60 percent of total exports of refined copper. Developing countries contributed 65 percent of total copper exports in 1976 (table 1-6).

Table 1-6. World Copper Exports (Market Economies)
(000 mt Cu content)

Ores & concentrates	1967	1970	1972	1973	1974	1975	1976
CIPEC total	<u>73</u>	<u>113</u>	<u>307</u>	<u>455</u>	<u>536</u>	<u>441</u>	<u>501</u>
Chile	<u>30</u>	<u>39</u>	<u>75</u>	<u>109</u>	<u>156</u>	<u>104</u>	<u>156</u>
Indonesia	—	—	—	38	64	61	67
Peru	31	40	48	34	18	24	13
Zaire	—	—	6	28	32	29	35
Zambia	—	7	10	—	—	—	—
Australia*	12	27	39	46	49	47	49
Mauritania*	—	—	11	20	25	6	7
PNG*	—	—	118	180	192	170	174
Canada	117	163	270	346	344	315	309
Philippines	86	160	201	210	221	210	248
Total developing countries	147	246	469	619	708	604	700
Total developed countries	<u>201</u>	<u>278</u>	<u>363</u>	<u>491</u>	<u>522</u>	<u>448</u>	<u>431</u>
Total market economies	348	524	832	1,110	1,230	1,052	1,131
% of total							
CIPEC	21	22	37	41	44	42	44
Developing countries	42	47	56	56	58	57	62
Developed countries	58	53	44	44	42	43	38

Unrefined							
CIPEC total	616	629	594	572	592	541	652
Chile	241	190	150	160	215	180	231
Peru	127	138	138	141	134	89	46
Zaire[a]	161	190	211	219	199	240	346
Zambia	80	104	88	43	32	19	21
Australia*	7	7	7	9	12	13	8
South Africa	147	102	105	92	90	93	95
Total developing countries	609	622	587	563	580	528	644
Total developed countries	250	165	196	196	201	180	84
Total market economies	859	787	783	759	781	708	728
% of total:							
CIPEC	72	80	76	75	76	76	90
Developing countries	71	79	75	74	74	75	88
Developed countries	29	21	25	26	26	25	12
Refined							
CIPEC total	1,094	1,290	1,426	1,404	1,568	1,524	1,573
Chile	361	440	406	388	488	504	595
Peru	34	33	32	34	35	40	130
Zaire[b]	161	180	215	229	252	224	67
Zambia	527	578	623	627	650	627	712
Australia*	10	31	60	48	71	89	69
Yugoslavia*	1	28	90	78	72	46	n.a.
Belgium	266	295	266	219	289	249	290
Canada	250	265	293	290	283	320	313

(*continued*)

21

Table 1-6 (continued)
(000 mt Cu content)

Ores & concentrates	1967	1970	1972	1973	1974	1975	1976
United States	147	201	166	173	113	156	104
Total developing countries	1,084	1,259	1,366	1,356	1,497	1,435	1,504
Total developed countries	1,058	1,089	1,036	1,142	1,292	1,060	999
Total market economies	2,142	2,348	2,402	2,498	2,789	2,495	2,503
% of total:							
CIPEC	51	55	59	56	56	61	63
Developing countries	51	54	57	54	54	58	60
Developed countries	49	46	43	46	46	42	40
Total exports							
CIPEC	1,783	2,032	2,327	2,431	2,696	2,506	2,726
Chile	632	669	631	657	859	788	982
Indonesia	—	—	—	38	64	61	67
Peru	192	211	218	209	187	153	189
Zaire	322	370	432	476	483	493	448
Zambia	607	689	721	670	682	640	733
Australia*	29	65	106	103	132	149	126
Mauritania*	—	—	11	20	25	6	7
PNG*	—	—	118	180	192	170	174
Yugoslavia*	1	28	90	78	72	46	n.a.
Philippines	86	100	201	210	221	210	248

Total developing countries	1,840	2,127	2,422	2,538	2,785	2,567	2,848
Total developed countries	1,509	1,532	1,595	1,829	2,015	1,688	1,514
Total market economies	3,349	3,659	4,017	4,367	4,800	4,255	4,362
% of total:							
CIPEC	53	56	58	56	56	59	62
Developing countries	55	58	60	58	58	60	65
Developed countries	45	42	40	42	42	40	35
Market economies total							
Ores and concentrates	348	524	832	1,110	1,230	1,052	1,131
%	10	14	21	26	26	25	26
Unrefined metal	859	787	783	759	781	708	728
%	26	22	19	17	16	17	17
Refined	2,142	2,348	2,402	2,498	2,789	2,495	2,503
%	64	64	60	57	58	58	57

Source: Statistical Bulletin 1976 (Paris, CIPEC, June 1977).

Note: Total trade involves double counting since concentrates or blister exported by one country may be reexported by another country as refined copper.

* Associate members.
a Cathodes included.
b Cathodes excluded.

Since a number of the copper exporting countries are members of the Intergovernmental Council of Copper Exporting Countries (CIPEC), it is customary to group these countries together in analyzing copper export trade. Five developing countries—Chile, Indonesia, Peru, Zaire, and Zambia—are full members of CIPEC, while four other countries—Australia, Mauritania, Papua New Guinea, and Yugoslavia—are associate members whose governments are not bound by the decisions of the full members with respect to export and pricing policies. It would be a mistake to regard CIPEC as a cartel since thus far members have been unable to exercise a significant influence on copper prices through export restrictions. Their capacity to do so is analyzed in chapter 7. In 1976 the CIPEC members, including associate members, accounted for 44 percent of total exports (market economies) of ores and concentrates; 90 percent of exports of blister copper; and 60 percent of exports of refined copper. CIPEC countries' overall share of copper exports in 1976 was 62 percent (table 1-6).

The principal importers of ores and concentrates in 1976 were Japan, Germany, the United States, and Spain; the principal importers of unrefined metal were Belgium, Germany, the United Kingdom, the United States, and Japan; and the principal importers of refined copper were Germany, the United States, France, the United Kingdom, Italy, Belgium, Japan, and Brazil (table 1-7).

Trade in refined copper as a percentage of total copper trade declined from 68 percent in 1955 to 57 percent in 1976. This decline was entirely the result of an increase in world exports of concentrates[19] from very small amounts in 1955 to 26 percent of total copper exports in 1976. Exports of unrefined copper declined from over 30 percent of total exports in 1955 to 17 percent in 1976. The increase in exports of concentrates reflected in considerable measure the development of new producing areas, for example, Bougainville, western Canada, Indonesia, and the Philippines, which had not established smelters, and the increased smelting capacity of Japan and certain Western European countries which mine little of their own copper. The relative importance of exports of both refined and blister copper is likely to increase in the future as the developing countries smelt and refine more of their own copper.

The copper industries in the developing countries and in Australia, Canada, and South Africa were mainly established by U.S. and European integrated copper companies. Hence, prior to 1970 much of the

[19] International trade in copper ore is very small.

Table 1-7. World Copper Imports (Market Economies)
(000 mt Cu content)

	1967	1968	1969	1970	1971	1972	1973	1974	1975	1976
Ores and concentrates										
United States	35	25	35	31	28	50	39	51	67	82
Japan	191	244	292	391	461	608	832	875	730	725
West Germany	72	94	92	83	82	150	238	174	166	197
Spain	14	28	26	20	29	36	29	37	29	44
Unrefined metal										
United States	244	246	216	204	142	143	140	189	79	40
Japan	116	128	150	137	116	120	81	62	40	30
Belgium	—	—	157	198	204	197	224	201	214	229
West Germany	165	146	145	133	156	118	121	98	120	131
United Kingdom	32	42	45	41	33	53	66	84	83	66
Refined copper										
United States	300	363	119	120	149	172	181	276	132	346
Brazil	36	49	50	51	73	85	94	137	126	148
Japan	159	157	200	165	153	173	314	230	168	201
Belgium	313	377	186	183	189	197	214	188	188	209
France	235	258	323	315	302	366	377	375	350	338
Germany	272	352	362	400	375	404	414	450	405	405
Italy	199	199	236	270	257	280	270	303	282	288
United Kingdom	420	416	417	410	366	395	399	381	369	368

Source: Statistical Bulletin 1976 (Paris, CIPEC, June 1977).

trade in copper was determined by ownership ties. Smelters were established at the larger mines in Chile, Zaire, and Zambia, but refineries tended to be concentrated in the industrialized countries. Since the copper content of blister is very high (99 percent or more), there is virtually no savings in transportation costs in shipping refined copper (99.9 percent purity) over blister. There are some advantages in locating refineries close to the fabricating plants so that the types of refined copper produced can readily be adjusted to the demand.

There are important economies of scale in both smelting and refining. Only the largest mines have their own smelters, but a smelter may be established for processing the concentrates of several mines. The number of refineries is considerably less than the number of smelters both in the United States and in the rest of the world, and refineries usually process the output of several smelters. Prior to the nationalization movements in Chile, Zaire, and Zambia in the late 1960s, much of the trade in blister copper was the result of intrafirm shipments by integrated copper producers. This relationship explained the blister trade between Belgium and Zaire, and between the United States and U.S. affiliates in Chile and Peru. Much of the blister trade between the African countries and the European refineries is carried on under long-term contracts which have replaced intrafirm shipments by integrated producers as a means of assuring supplies and markets.[20]

In 1976 Japan accounted for nearly 70 percent of all imports of copper concentrates, with Germany accounting for another 19 percent. The concentrates came mainly from the newer copper producing areas— western Canada, the Philippines, Papua New Guinea, and Indonesia. Japan also imports concentrates from the Japanese-owned Sodimiza mine in Zaire. Most developing countries want to increase the value added of their exports and therefore are increasing their smelter and refining capacity. In time, most of the copper mined in the developing countries may be exported in the form of refined copper. The Philippines has plans for a smelter and Papua New Guinea hopes to have one once the Ok Tedi mine is developed. Chile, Peru, and Zaire are expanding their refinery capacity.

Transportation costs as reflected by distance have not had a significant effect on the pattern of refined copper trade.[21] Ownership ties between producing and consuming countries have been declining as a determinant of trade relationships and, where such ownership ties exist, the

[20] See John W. Whitney, "An Analysis of Copper Production, Processing and Trade Patterns, 1950–1972" (Ph.D. dissertation, Pennsylvania State University, Department of Mineral Economics, May 1976) p. 136ff.

[21] Whitney, ibid., p. 135.

governments of producing countries have taken a more active role in marketing and are attempting to diversify their markets. Other non-price factors, such as strikes, transportation problems, natural disasters in the producing countries, and recessions in the consuming countries, frequently affect the pattern of trade in copper.

International trade in refined copper is for the most part based on annual contracts which provide for deliveries of specified amounts at prices related to market prices at the time of delivery. (This subject is discussed in chapters 3 and 4.) For example, it is reported that 80 to 85 percent of Chile's refined and blister copper output is sold through annual contracts, with the remaining 15 to 20 percent sold by means of spot sales. When Chile nationalized the large mining companies in 1971, its state mining enterprise, CODELCO, employed some of the same agents in Europe to negotiate contracts for Chile's output as had been used by Anaconda and Kennecott prior to nationalization. A number of nonprice factors play a role in the negotiation of copper contracts, including long-standing buyer-seller relationships, the confidence of buyers in the performance of the sellers in meeting delivery commitments and maintaining quality standards, transportation costs, and in some cases ownership ties.

When new mines are financed by medium- and long-term borrowing from banks and other financial institutions and by suppliers' credits, the creditors frequently require the mining company, whether privately owned or a government enterprise or of mixed ownership, to negotiate long-term contracts for the purchase of the mine output for a period covering the maturity of the loans and credits. This was true, for example, in the case of the Bougainville mine, for which external financing was obtained in 1969 and for the Cuajone mine in Southern Peru, the external financing for which was negotiated in 1974–75. In the case of the Bougainville mine, contracts for the delivery of concentrates to firms in Japan, West Germany, and Spain were negotiated for the bulk of expected production over the first fifteen years. In the case of the Cuajone mine, Southern Peru Copper Corporation (SPCC) was unable to negotiate outside contracts for a substantial portion of Cuajone's output, which the Peruvian government refines in the government-owned refinery. Hence, the principal equity holders of SPCC— ASARCO, Phelps Dodge, Newmont, and Cerro—had to commit themselves to take a portion of the refined output.

Until 1975, Zambia's copper output was marketed by the minority stockholders, AMAX and Anglo-American, while the output of Zaire's wholly owned government mining enterprise, Gecamines, was marketed by the Belgian company Société Generale des Minerais (SGM). In 1975 the governments of both countries undertook to market their own output, largely through agents appointed for various countries whose function is to negotiate annual contracts with buyers in accordance with policies established by the government marketing agencies.[22]

Ownership Status of the World Copper Industry

The introduction of large-scale technology in mining, milling, smelting, and refining early in the twentieth century led to the creation of large international copper firms that achieved control over the bulk of the world's copper output. These large firms are vertically integrated from mine production through refining, and, in some cases, semifabrication—the production of wire, cable, tube, brass, bronze, copper alloy castings, and so on. The large amounts of capital required for optimum scale production, the advantages of vertical integration, the high cost of exploration involving high-risk expenditures, the great variety of technical knowledge and managerial experience which has tended to be concentrated in a few international companies, and the special experience and large financial outlays required for operations in the developing countries have all contributed to the concentration of the industry. The bulk of the Western world's copper is produced in a small number of developing countries, and a few large international copper companies have developed the major producing regions of Latin America and Africa.

Concentration in Mining

Orris Herfindahl estimated that in 1947 four mining firms accounted for about 60 percent of world output (excluding the U.S.S.R.) and eight firms accounted for 77 percent of world output. By 1956 these percentages had declined to 49 and 70 percent respectively.[23] All of these companies were privately owned and most of the stock was held by residents of the United States, Canada, and the principal Western European countries. Since 1956 there has been a major change in the structure of the world copper industry. In 1974 the four largest private copper producers—Kennecott, Newmont, Phelps Dodge, and Rio Tinto-Zinc—had a majority ownership interest in less than 19 percent of the mine copper output of the market economy countries, and ten privately owned companies had a majority interest in less than 35 percent of the world's mine copper output from the market economy

---

[22] In 1976 Zaire again turned to SGM for assistance in marketing.

[23] Orris C. Herfindahl, *Copper Costs and Prices: 1870–1957* (Baltimore, Johns Hopkins University Press for Resources for the Future, 1959) p. 165.

countries.[24] Ten other privately owned companies (see table 1-8) are majority owners of an additional 10 percent of the copper output of the market economy countries.[25]

The majority or wholly owned government mining enterprises in Chile, Peru, Zaire, Zambia, Turkey, India, Uganda, and Yugoslavia accounted for about 34 percent of world mine output for the countries outside the Soviet Bloc and China in 1974. According to Sir Ronald Prain, at the beginning of the 1960s governments had an interest in only 2.5 percent of the copper producing capacity of the market economies, but in 1970 about 43 percent of copper producing capacity in the non-Communist world was owned in whole or in part by governments.[26] Moreover, government ownership of the copper industry is heavily concentrated in the copper exporting countries—mainly the CIPEC countries. In some countries, including Zambia, Mexico, and Australia (Mt. Isa), large international mining companies have reduced their equity holdings from a majority to a minority position in recent years. To summarize, twenty-one private companies have a majority interest in mines producing about 44 percent of total copper production in the market economies (including Yugoslavia), and another 34 percent is produced by majority-owned government enterprises in eight important copper producing countries. Most of the remaining 22 percent is produced by a fairly large number of privately owned companies, some of which have a minority government participation. In the centrally planned economies, which accounted for about 20 percent of total world mine production in 1974 (see table 1-4), 75 percent is produced in the U.S.S.R. and most of the remainder in Poland, China, and Bulgaria. Between 1973 and 1976 Poland doubled its mine production to an estimated 310 million mt in 1976.

Firms that refine copper produced by nonaffiliated firms are referred to as "custom smelters," while the integrated primary producers largely supply their smelters and refineries with company-mined ores. The three firms that do most of the custom refining and smelting in the United States are American Smelting and Refining (ASARCO), Phelps Dodge, and American Metal Climax (AMAX). ASARCO mines some

[24] The ten companies are Anaconda, ASARCO, Cyprus, Duval, International Nickel, Kennecott, Mt. Isa (owned by M.I.M. Holdings of Australia), Newmont, Phelps Dodge, and Rio Tinto-Zinc (RTZ). RTZ controls the Bougainville mine through its Australian subsidiary, Conzinc Riotinto of Australia, the Palabora mine (South Africa), and the Lornex mine (Canada). ASARCO formerly had a 52 percent equity interest in Mt. Isa, but now has a minority (49 percent) interest. By 1978 ASARCO was the second largest producer of copper.

[25] These companies include Atlas, Falconbridge, Freeport, Hudson Bay, Inspiration, Marcopper, Noranda, Rio Tinto-Patino, Texasgulf, and White Pine.

[26] Prain, *Copper: The Anatomy of an Industry,* pp. 222–223.

Table 1-8.   Mine Copper Production of Twenty-One Leading
Privately Owned Mining Companies in 1974[a]
(*000 metric tons*)

Companies	Output	
U.S. companies		
Anaconda	179	
ASARCO[b]	194	
Cyprus	100	
Duval	120	
Freeport[c]	65	
Inspiration	51	
Kennecott	366	
Newmont[d]	215	
Phelps Dodge	256	
White Pine	61	
Total		1,574
Canadian companies		
Falconbridge	49	
Hudson Bay	49	
International Nickel	172	
Lornex	58	
Noranda	45	
Texasgulf	53	
Total		426
Other companies		
Rio Tinto-Zinc (U.K.)[e]	307	
Atlas Consolidated (Philippines)	87	
Marcopper (Philippines)	47	
Mt. Isa (Australia)	160	
Rio Tinto-Patiño (Spain)	74	
Total		675
Grand total, all 21 companies		2,675
Total world output (market economies)		6,064
Leading private companies as percentage of world output		44.1

Source: *American Bureau of Metal Statistics Yearbook, 1975.*

[a] Includes output of majority-owned subsidiaries. There may be some under-statement because of lack of knowledge regarding all subsidiaries.

[b] Includes output of Southern Peru Copper Corporation (owned jointly with Phelps Dodge, Newmont and Cerro).

[c] Output of Freeport, Indonesia.

[d] Includes Canadian and South African subsidiaries.

[e] Includes output of Bougainville mine and Palabora mine in South Africa.

copper domestically and also refines a portion of the blister produced by the Southern Peru Copper Corporation (SPCC) of which it is the majority owner. Phelps Dodge is a fully integrated firm which buys some of the concentrates or blister from other domestic producers. It should be mentioned that the degree of integration of U.S., Canadian, and European firms with mines in the developing countries has declined in recent years, both because of forward integration of the foreign mines and the growing independence of foreign mines from the international companies that initially established them.[27]

The degree of integration into copper fabricating is much less than in the case of mining, refining, and smelting. Nevertheless, in 1966 it was estimated that approximately one-third of the U.S. copper fabricating capacity (mainly wire mills and brass mills) was owned by subsidiaries of the major copper producers, including Anaconda, Phelps Dodge, and Kennecott. These subsidiaries include Anaconda American Brass, Anaconda Wire Cable, Phelps Dodge Products Corp., and Kennecott Wire and Cable. There is apparently less forward integration into the fabricating stage in the case of foreign producers.[28]

Government Marketing Control

Majority private ownership in copper mines does not necessarily carry with it full control over production and marketing. For example, although the majority of Peruvian output is produced by a foreign-owned firm, SPCC, Peru's mineral output is marketed by MINPECO, a government agency. In the five CIPEC member countries—Chile, Indonesia, Peru, Zaire, and Zambia—the government exercises control over marketing.

Organization of the Copper Industry in the Major Producing Countries

United States

Copper production in the United States is highly concentrated, with three companies—Anaconda,[29] Kennecott, and Phelps Dodge—

---

27 For a discussion of vertical integration, see *Economic Analysis of the Copper Industry*, Charles River Associates, Inc. (prepared for the General Services Administration, Washington, D.C., March 1970) pp. 48–62.

28 Ibid., p. 60.

29 In 1977 Anaconda became a wholly owned subsidiary of Atlantic Richfield Company (ARCO).

Table 1-9.   Domestic Mine Copper Production of Leading U.S. Mining Companies, 1974

(*000 metric tons*)

Companies	Output
Anaconda	173
Anamax Mining Co.[a]	41
ASARCO	74
Cities Service	31
Duval	120
Inspiration	51
Kennecott	366
Magma Copper (Newmont)	136
Phelps Dodge	256
Cyprus	94
White Pine	61
Total	1,403
Other companies	48
Total United States	1,451

Source: *American Bureau of Metal Statistics Yearbook, 1975*, p. 22.
[a] Owned jointly by Anaconda and AMAX.

accounting for 55 percent of total U.S. mine production in 1974 and eight companies accounting for 88 percent of U.S. mine production (see table 1-9). The eleven companies shown in table 1-9, which are responsible for 97 percent of U.S. copper mine output, do not indicate the full extent of concentration of control. Anamax is partly owned by Anaconda, and Anaconda also owns about a fifth of the stock of Inspiration Copper, a medium-sized company included among the eleven. Most of the eight companies also smelt all of their own output. Copper refining in the United States is even more concentrated, with six companies—ASARCO, Kennecott, Phelps Dodge, Anaconda, AMAX, and Newmont—accounting for nearly 90 percent of U.S. refining capacity in 1974. U.S. smelting and refining companies also process a limited amount of foreign concentrates and large tonnages of imported blister copper. The United States is currently about 90 percent self-sufficient in copper; it imports substantial amounts of blister copper, mainly from Latin America, and refined copper, mainly from Canada and Latin America. The three largest U.S. mine producers are vertically integrated into the fabricating stage. Approximately one-third of the copper output of

U.S. refineries is sold to downstream affiliates, and U.S. firms export a substantial amount of refined copper.

Petroleum companies have become increasingly important in the U.S. copper mining industry. Duval (owned by Pennzoil), the Cities Service Company, and recently Atlantic Richfield Company, which acquired Anaconda, are examples of petroleum companies that have important interests in copper mining. In 1978, the EXXON Corporation, which has important mining interests in the United States, acquired Disputada, a medium-sized mine in Chile.

Canada

There are about twenty important companies producing mine copper in Canada, with seven companies producing about 56 percent of the total output in 1974. Only 61 percent of Canada's mine production was smelted in Canada in that year. However, Canada's refinery production exceeded smelter output in 1974 and 1976. Canadian smelting capacity is concentrated in four firms—Falconbridge, Noranda, Hudson Bay, and International Nickel. Refining capacity is controlled by two firms—Canadian Copper (a Noranda subsidiary) and International Nickel.

Chile

In 1974 Chile was the world's second largest copper producer and the vast bulk of the copper output is produced by the large mines operated by the governmental body, Corporacion Nacional de Cobre de Chile (CODELCO-Chile). CODELCO-Chile operates the large mines that were established and formerly owned by Anaconda (Chuquicamata, El Salvador, and Exotica); Kennecott (El Teniente); and Cerro Corporation (Andina). A few medium and small mines are privately owned, producing about 15 percent of Chile's mine output in 1974. Chuquicamata, El Salvador, and El Teniente smelt and refine a substantial portion of their own output with much of the remainder treated at other government plants. Most of Chile's mine output is smelted in Chile and about 60 percent of her output is refined in the country. Under the new foreign investment law of July 1974, foreigners are permitted to invest in Chilean mining, but they must first negotiate an agreement with the Committee on Foreign Investment. In 1977 several foreign companies, including EXXON, Noranda, Falconbridge, and St. Joe Minerals negotiated investment agreements for copper and other mineral production in Chile.

Peru

Three-fourths of Peru's mine and smelter capacity—totaling about 400,000 mt in 1978—is in the hands of SPCC (majority owned by ASARCO with minority interests held by Phelps Dodge, Newmont, and Cerro Marmon). SPCC holds 100 percent of the equity in the Toquepala mine and 88.5 percent in Cuajone, the remaining 11.5 percent being held by Billiton B.V., a Royal Dutch Shell subsidiary. Peru's second largest mining company, Centromin, is a government enterprise which operates the mining properties formerly held by Cerro de Pasco before the company was nationalized in 1974. (Cerro de Pasco was owned by Cerro Corporation of the United States.) There are also several privately owned medium and small mines. The Peruvian government agency, Mineroperu, controls a number of large undeveloped ore bodies formerly owned by large international companies, including Anaconda and ASARCO. Mineroperu is in the process of exploring and developing some of these copper deposits. Most of Peru's mine output is smelted in the country and by 1977 the government had established refining capacity for half of the blister output.

Zaire

In 1976 the government-owned mining company, Gecamines (which expropriated the properties of the Belgian firm, Union Miniere), produced about 92 percent of Zaire's output, with the remainder being supplied by a Japanese firm, Sodimiza. Zaire encourages foreign investment in mining and Sodimiza has under way the development of another mine, Kinsenda. Sodimiza expects to be producing a total of 80,000 mt by 1979. Societe Miniere de Tenke-Fungurume, which is owned by a consortium of U.S. and European firms, plus 20 percent equity holding by the Zairian government, was for several years exploring and developing the Tenke-Fungurume mine, which constitutes perhaps the richest large ore body in the world. However, early in 1976 construction was indefinitely suspended because of a rise in the capital cost estimate to over $900 million from an initial estimate of $300 million. Gecamines has smelter capacity for all of its output, but currently refines less than half of its production. Sodimiza's output is in the form of concentrate, all of which is shipped to Japan.

Zambia

All of Zambia's copper is produced by Roan Consolidated Mines (RCM) and Nchanga Consolidated Copper Mines (NCCM), both of which are owned 51 percent by the government, while foreign interests, mainly AMAX in the case of RCM, and Anglo-American in the case of NCCM, own the remainder. RCM and NCCM were formed to take over the mining assets of the Zambian subsidiaries of two foreign companies, Roan Selection Trust and Anglo-American Corporation of South Africa, whose Zambian properties were nationalized in 1969. However, until 1974 AMAX had a management and marketing agreement for RCM while Anglo-American had a similar arrangement for NCCM. These arrangements were terminated and foreign companies have virtually no control over operations or sales. Two foreign companies, Noranda of Canada and Geomin, a Romanian state enterprise, are undertaking exploration under joint ventures with the Zambian government enterprise, Mindeco. Zambia has smelter and refining capacity for nearly all of its mine output.

Australia

In 1976, 65 percent of Australia's mine copper output was accounted for by the privately owned Mt. Isa mine, and the second largest mine, Mt. Lyell, produced 12 percent of total copper output. (Mt. Isa is owned 49 percent by ASARCO.) Mt. Isa has smelting and refining capacity for all of its copper output, but less than half of the concentrates produced by other copper mining companies are processed in Australia. In 1972 foreign interests owned approximately 40 percent of the total Australian production of copper concentrates, 43 percent of smelter production, and 47 percent of refined copper output. (In each case these percentages were arrived at by weighting production tonnages by the foreign equity ownership share.)[30]

South Africa

Nearly 85 percent of South Africa's mine copper output is produced by three firms: Palabora (owned by Rio Tinto-Zinc); O'okiep (owned by Newmont Mining); and Prieska (joint venture involving U.S. Steel and South African companies). South Africa has smelter capacity for over 80 percent of its mine output and refining capacity for less than half.

The Philippines

The bulk of the Philippine copper mine output is produced by five privately owned mining companies—Atlas Consolidated, Lepanto,

[30] R. B. McKern, *Multinational Enterprise and Natural Resources* (Sydney, Australia, McGraw-Hill, 1976) p. 86.

Marcopper, Marinduque, and Philex—with Atlas producing about 40 percent of the total. Philippine investors control these companies, but there are some foreign equity holdings. Currently there are no smelters or refineries, but two smelters and a refinery are planned.

Papua New Guinea (PNG)

PNG's output is produced solely by the majority foreign-owned firm, Bougainville Copper Ltd. (a subsidiary of Conzinc Riotinto of Australia which in turn is a subsidiary of RTZ). The PNG government owns 20 percent of Bougainville Copper Ltd. All output is shipped abroad in the form of concentrates. The Bougainville mine is one of the largest in the world (184,000 mt in 1974). In 1976 an agreement was reached with a consortium headed by Broken Hill Pty. for the exploration and eventual development of the Ok Tedi mine, which had been explored by Kennecott Copper and abandoned by that company when it could not reach a development agreement with the PNG government.

Mexico

Mexico was once one of the leading Western Hemisphere copper producers, but in recent years its mine output has been less than the level reached in 1929. The Mexican government's Mexicanization program induced foreign investors to reduce their equity in the mines to 49 percent or less. For example, ASARCO has reduced its equity in Industria Minera Mexico (formerly ASARCO Mexicana) to 34 percent, and IMM turned over its La Caridad ore body to Mexicana de Cobre, a company controlled by the same group of Mexican investors that control IMM. Anaconda reduced its equity in Minera de Cananea (currently Mexico's largest copper producer) to 49 percent. Mexicana de Cobre, in which the Mexican government has a minority equity, expects to bring the La Caridad mine into production by 1979; it will eventually have an annual capacity of 180,000 mt. The Mexican government is anxious to develop the country's copper mining potential, but is having difficulty in interesting foreign investors to come in as minority stockholders. Mexico has smelter and refining capacity for most of its present mine output.

Indonesia

Indonesia has just one copper mine in operation, the Ertsberg in Irian Jaya, owned and operated by Freeport Indonesia, a subsidiary of Freeport Minerals Company of the United States. Indonesia has other copper ore deposits, but no agreement has been made to develop these deposits, although negotiations have been conducted by other foreign companies. All of Ertsberg's output is shipped abroad in the form of copper concentrates.

Importance of Copper Exports for the Developing Countries

In terms of export value, copper is by far the most important nonfuel export of the developing countries. For example, the average combined value of exports of bauxite, iron ore, manganese, lead, tin, and zinc by the developing countries over the 1970–72 period was $2.2 billion, as contrasted with $2.4 billion for the average value of copper exports by developing countries over this period.[31] In 1970 copper constituted 7.7 percent of the commodity share of total export earnings (excluding petroleum) of the developing countries.[32] The total value of export earnings from copper by the developing countries in 1974 was $5.3 billion; this value declined sharply to $2.8 billion in 1975 and rose by an estimated 25 percent in 1976, but was still well below the 1974 level,[33] even in current dollars.

The bulk of the copper exports of developing countries is concentrated in Chile, Indonesia, Papua New Guinea, Peru, the Philippines, Zaire, and Zambia. In 1974 copper exports constituted 65 percent of Chile's total export income and 20 percent of that country's gross domestic product. For Zaire the corresponding figures were 74 percent and 41 percent; for Zambia, 93 percent and 69 percent; and for Peru, 23 percent and 4 percent.[34] In 1974, copper exports accounted for 14 percent of total exports for the Philippines, and 55 percent of the total exports for Papua New Guinea.

[31] Rex Bosson and Bension Varon, *The Mining Industry in the Developing Countries* (Washington, D.C., World Bank, 1977) p. 253.

[32] *Price Prospects for Major Primary Commodities* (Washington, D.C., World Bank, June 1977) p. 37.

[33] "Copper Statistics" (mimeo, United Nations Conference on Trade and Development, TD/B/IPC/Copper/AC/L.5, Geneva, January 1977) table 14.

[34] *Statistical Bulletin 1976* (Paris, CIPEC, June 1977) table 23.

Appendix 1-1
Profiles of Selected Major Private Copper Producing Companies

I. U.S. Companies

American Metal Climax, Inc. (AMAX)

AMAX is one of the world's largest diversified mineral resource companies. Its principal products are molybdenum, aluminum, iron ore, coal, copper, lead, zinc, and potash. It has a large copper refining and smelting capacity through its subsidiary, the U.S. Metal Refining Company at Carteret, N.J., but its copper mining interests are mainly in the form of 50–50 partnership and minority equity holdings in copper mining companies in the United States and foreign countries. In 1975 AMAX sought to acquire 100 percent of Copper Range Company, but the merger was opposed by the U.S. Justice Department.

Principal Affiliates in the Copper Industry

Anamax Mining Company—50–50 partnership between AMAX and Anaconda. Operates Twin Buttes copper mine in Arizona.

Copper Range—owns 20 percent.

Roan Consolidated Mines Ltd.—owns 20 percent. RCM is owned 51 percent by the Zambian government.

O'okiep Copper Company, Ltd.—17 percent. O'okiep is a major South African producer owned 56 percent by Newmont Mining.

Tsumeb Corporation—owns 30 percent. Tsumeb mines copper in Southwest Africa (Namibia). It is a joint venture involving Newmont Mining, 30 percent; Selection Trust, 14 percent; and other mining companies.

Botswana RST—owns 30 percent. Botswana RST has controlling interest in a nickel-copper mining and milling company in Botswana.

The Anaconda Company

Anaconda is the third largest U.S. producer of primary copper, the largest producer of brass mill products in the United States, and an important producer of wire mill products. In addition to mining and processing copper, it produces aluminum, uranium, and other resource products. Domestic output of its own mines was 179,000 mt in 1974, over half of which comes from the Butte Mines in Montana. In addition to smelting virtually all its copper concentrates, Anaconda had copper refining capacity of nearly 270,000 mt at the end of 1974. In 1977 Anaconda became a wholly owned subsidiary of Atlantic Richfield Company (ARCO).

Principal Affiliates in the Copper Industry

Anamex Mining Company—50–50 partnership with AMAX.
Inspiration Consolidated Copper Company—owns 20 percent.
Compania Minera de Cananea—49 percent. Fifty-one percent of Cananea is owned by Mexican private and governmental interests. It operates an open-pit mine in the state of Sonora, Mexico and produced 44,000 mt of blister in 1974.

ASARCO

ASARCO is a major nonferrous metal mining, smelting, and refining company with substantial foreign equity ownership. In 1974 the output of its U.S. copper mines was about 74,000 mt, but at the end of 1974 ASARCO's copper refining capacity was about 584,000 mt, and its smelter capacity was 346,000 mt.

Principal Affiliates in the Copper Industry

Revere Copper and Brass, Inc.—33 percent plus convertible debentures.
Southern Peru Copper Corporation—51.5 percent. SPCC owns and operates the large open-pit Cuajone and Toquepala mines in Peru with a combined capacity of 275,000 mt.
Industrial Minera Mexico—34 percent (formerly ASARCO Mexicana).

MIM Holdings—49 percent. MIM Holdings owns the Mt. Isa copper and zinc mine in Australia.

Granduc Mine Ltd.—50 percent owned. Operates in British Columbia, Canada.

Cities Service Company

Cities Service is principally an oil, gas, and chemical products producer and marketer, but it has extensive copper-producing operations in Copperhill, Tennessee and Miami, Arizona. In 1974 it produced 31,000 mt of mine copper.

Copper Range Company

Copper Range operates the White Pine copper mine and smelter-refinery complex in northern Michigan and in 1974 produced 61,000 mt of mine copper. The company's Hussey Metals Division is an important copper fabricator.

Cyprus Mines Corporation

Cyprus Mines is a diversified company producing a number of metallic minerals, including copper, lead, zinc, iron ore, silver, and aluminum, and is integrated into the manufacture of wire cable, tubing, and related products. In 1974 its copper mine output was 100,000 mt, produced mainly by its majority-owned subsidiaries, the Cyprus Pima and Cyprus Bagdad companies operating in Arizona.

Duval Corporation

The Duval Corporation is a wholly owned subsidiary of Pennzoil and is engaged in mining and processing ores and minerals, principally copper, molybdenum, potash, and sulfur. (Pennzoil is engaged mainly in oil and gas exploration and production, refining, and marketing.) Duval produced 120,000 mt of mine copper in 1974, mainly from open-pit mines in Arizona and Nevada. ASARCO currently smelts and refines about 80 percent of Duval's copper concentrates; the remainder is handled by Duval's CLEAR process.

Inspiration Consolidated Copper Company

Inspiration's mine copper production totaled 51,000 mt in 1974, mainly from its open-pit operations in Arizona. Anaconda and the Anglo-American group collectively own the majority of Inspiration's stock. It has substantial smelting and refining capacity.

Kennecott Copper Corporation

Kennecott is the largest domestic producer of copper, producing 366,000 mt in 1974, virtually all of which was processed in its own smelters and refineries. It is also integrated into fabricating and its subsidiaries include the Chase Brass and Copper Company and Kennecott Wire and Cable. Since the loss of its Chilean holdings, Kennecott has no foreign copper production, but conducts exploration in Canada and Australia.

Newmont Mining Corporation

Newmont's principal U.S. copper mining subsidiary is the Magma Copper Company, which produced 136,000 mt of mine copper in 1974, principally in Arizona. Its output is smelted and refined in Magma's own smelter and refinery. As indicated below, Newmont has important investments in foreign copper mining companies.

Principal Affiliates in the Copper Industry

O'okiep Copper Company—56 percent owned and managed in South Africa.

Tsumeb Corporation—30 percent owned and managed company. Operates in South West Africa (Namibia).

Sherritt-Gordon Mines Ltd.—38 percent owned and operates in Canada.

Palabora Holdings Ltd.—42 percent. Palabora is an open-pit mine in South Africa and that country's largest copper producer.

Southern Peru Copper Company—10 percent.

Granduc Mine Ltd.—50 percent owned and operating in British Columbia, Canada.

Phelps Dodge

In 1976 Phelps Dodge U.S. mines produced approximately 300,000 mt of copper, 380,000 mt of smelter output, and 490,000 mt of refinery output. Phelps Dodge foreign investments in copper production are small compared with its large domestic operations. It holds a 16 percent equity interest in Southern Peru Copper Corporation, and has several foreign mining projects under development. These include the Wood-lawn project for the development of a zinc-lead-copper-silver deposit in New South Wales, Australia in a joint venture with St. Joe Minerals Corporation and Conzinc-Riotinto of Australia, and the Aggeneys project in South Africa for the development of a lead-zinc-copper-silver mine.[35]

II. Canadian Companies

Falconbridge Nickel Mines Ltd.

Falconbridge mines nickel-copper ore in the Sudbury, Ontario area and produces copper concentrates from mines in Quebec and western Canada. Quebec production is shipped to Noranda plants for smelting and refining, while that of western Canada is exported. Falconbridge produced about 49,000 mt of copper in 1974.

International Nickel Company of Canada Ltd. (INCO)

INCO is the world's leading nickel producer, but is also a large copper producer by virtue of the copper contained in the company's ore mined at Sudbury, Ontario and elsewhere in Canada. In 1974 it produced 172,000 mt of mine copper for which it has both smelting and refining capacities.

Noranda Mines Ltd.

Noranda is the leading copper smelting and refining company in Canada and has majority or minority ownership of a number of copper

[35] *Phelps Dodge Annual Report,* 1976.

mining firms, most of which ship concentrates to Noranda smelters. It also has copper fabricating capacity in Canada and elsewhere through subsidiaries.

Other Canadian Copper Producing Companies

Other copper producing companies include Hudson Bay Mining and Smelting (controlled by the Anglo-American group) which produced 49,000 mt of mine copper in 1974 and which has substantial mining and smelting capacity; Lornex Mining Corporation (controlled by Rio Tinto-Zinc) whose mine produced 58,000 mt of copper in 1974; and Texasgulf Canada, Ltd., a subsidiary of the U.S. company, Texasgulf, Inc., which produced 53,000 mt of mine copper in 1974.

III. Companies in Other Countries[36]

Anglo-American Corporation of South Africa

Anglo-American is a diversified holding company with investments in a wide range of mining enterprises as well as manufacturing, engineering, and commercial enterprises. The company is closely associated with De Beers Consolidated Mines and Charter Consolidated of London. The Anglo-American group originally had controlling interest in several of the principal Zambian copper mines until partial nationalization in 1969. Anglo-American interests are held through a complex network of holding and operating companies which we will not attempt to identify.

Principal Affiliates in the Copper Industry

Nchanga Consolidated Copper Mines—49 percent. Majority interest is held by the Zambian government.

Roan Consolidated Mines—12 percent interest. Majority interest is held by the Zambian government, while a 20 percent interest is held by AMAX.

---

[36] Large privately owned and controlled companies that have been mentioned as subsidiaries of the companies listed, such as Mt. Isa Mines of Australia, the Palabora Mining Company of South Africa, the Bougainville Mining Ltd. in PNG, and Southern Peru Copper Company have not been listed separately.

Hudson Bay Mining and Smelting of Canada—owns 35 percent.
Botswana RST nickel-copper company—owns 30 percent.

Rio Tinto-Zinc Corporation of London (RTZ)

RTZ is a large holding company with investments in the production and processing of zinc, lead, potash, aluminum, and gold. Subsidiaries in which RTZ has an equity interest produced over 300,000 mt of mine copper in 1974.

Principal Affiliates in the Copper Industry

Palabora Mining—owns 39 percent and manages company.
Conzinc Riotinto of Australia—owns 85 percent. CRA in turn owns 80 percent of Bougainville Mining Ltd. in PNG.
Cia Espanola de Minas de Riotinto (Spain)—owns 33 percent.
Lornex Mining Company (Canada)—owns 50 percent.

2

The Physical Characteristics of the Copper Industry

John W. Whitney

THIS CHAPTER provides a brief description of each phase of the copper industry: the identification of ore reserves and copper deposits, exploration, mining, metallurgy, smelting, and refining.

Nature and Location of the World's Copper Deposits and Reserves

Ore Deposits

In contrast to iron and aluminum, copper is a geochemically scarce element. Whereas iron and aluminum are estimated to constitute 5.80 percent and 8.00 percent, respectively, of the earth's continental crust, the continental crust contains only about 0.0058 percent copper.[1] Commercial iron ore deposits generally contain from 22 to 55 percent iron; bauxite deposits from 22.5 to 27.5 percent aluminum; and copper deposits from 0.5 to 6 percent copper. This indicates that the copper in a copper deposit must be between a hundred and a thousand times more concentrated than the crustal average, whereas iron and aluminum need to be only three to ten times as concentrated. A copper deposit is a localized zone in the earth's crust that contains copper-bearing minerals in unusual quantities.

[1] Brian J. Skinner, "A Second Iron Age Ahead?" *American Scientist* vol. 65 (May/June 1976) pp. 258–269.

Table 2-1. Most Commonly Occurring Copper Minerals

Mineral	Elemental components (weight percent)					
	Cu	Fe	S	CO_2	SiO_2	H_2O
			Sulfides			
Chalcopyrite	34.5	30.5	35.0	—	—	—
Bornite	63.3	11.2	25.5	—	—	—
Chalcocite	79.8	—	20.2	—	—	—
Covellite	66.4	—	33.6	—	—	—
			Carbonates			
Azurite	55.3	—	—	25.6	—	5.2
Malachite	57.4	—	—	19.9	—	8.2
			Silicates			
Chrysocolla	36.1	—	—	—	34.3	20.5
Dioptase	Chemically similar to chrysocolla					

Source: Cornelius S. Hurlbut, Jr., ed., Dana's Manual of Minerology (New York, Wiley, 17th ed., 1966) p. 609.

Copper occurs in three different types of minerals—sulfides, carbonates, and silicates—with sulfides being most important and silicates least important. The sulfide minerals are composed of copper, sulfur, and iron. The most important copper-bearing minerals and their composition are listed in table 2-1. Since copper metal is more easily extracted from the carbonate and sulfide minerals, mining companies have a preference for exploiting these minerals.

Copper mineral deposits occur only under special geological conditions and consequently their geographical distribution is limited. Most copper mineral deposits have definable boundaries; in some these are gradational whereas in others they are sharply defined (fixed). A copper mineral deposit is classed as an ore deposit or reserve if the copper-bearing minerals are sufficiently concentrated to be extracted at a profit. Many ore deposits have zones within them that are subeconomic. This subeconomic material is referred to as protore, but it may become ore if the price of metal increases (or the cost of extraction declines) sufficiently to make exploitation profitable. Ore deposits with gradational boundaries often contain large quantities of protore, whereas those with fixed boundaries generally do not. Hence, significant increases or decreases in perceived ore reserves may occur for deposits with gradational boundaries as a result of cost or price changes.

Classes of Copper Deposits

Copper deposits are generally divided into three classes: (1) porphyry type deposits; (2) strata-bound deposits in sedimentary rocks; and (3) massive sulfide deposits. Porphyry deposits generally contain the largest ore reserves, have the lowest grade or copper content, and have gradational boundaries. The ore reserves in strata-bound deposits are usually smaller and of higher grade, and generally have distinct boundaries. The massive sulfide deposits usually have the smallest ore reserves although they may be quite high grade, and these deposits often have fixed boundaries. The geographic occurrence of each class of deposit and some of their important physical characteristics are discussed below.

Porphyry Deposits. This class of deposit occurs most commonly and contains the largest portion of the Western world's copper metal reserves. These deposits occur as bodies of igneous intrusive rocks with copper sulfide minerals disseminated in them. Most deposits of this type which are economical to mine occur in Chile, Peru, southwestern United States, northern Mexico, western Canada, Papua New Guinea, and the Philippines (figure 2-1).

The grade and size of porphyry copper deposits vary. Typical deposits in Chile and Peru contain 1.0 to 2.0 percent copper and 500 million to 1 billion tons of ore. The deposits in the southwestern United States and northern Mexico contain 200 to 500 million tons of 0.4 to 0.8 percent copper ore. Those in the Philippines and Canada contain from 0.3 to 0.5 percent copper and generally from 50 to 200 million tons of ore.

Strata-Bound Deposits. These deposits are less common in occurrence, but are the second most important in terms of metal reserves. The copper-bearing minerals, typically silicates, carbonates, and sulfides, occur in old marine sediments, including shales and sandstones. Most strata-bound copper reserves are located in Zambia and Zaire. The size of strata-bound deposits varies widely, ranging from 1 million to 100 million tons of ore. The Zambian deposits commonly contain 2.0 to 4.0 percent copper in sulfide minerals. The Zairian deposits characteristically contain 4.0 to 6.0 percent copper in carbonate and silicate minerals.

Massive Sulfide Deposits. Copper is found in many other types of deposits, a large portion of which contain the copper as massive concentrations of sulfide minerals. Included in this category are vein deposits, massive replacements in limestone, and massive sulfides which occur in volcanic rock sequences. Massive sulfide copper reserves are

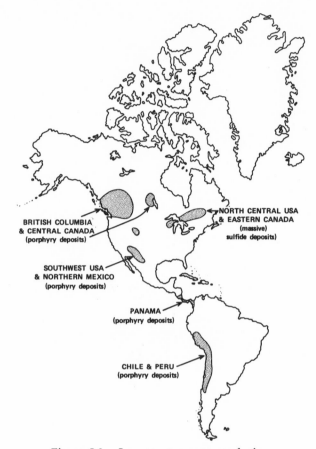

Figure 2-1.   Important copper producing

most important in eastern Canada, Australia, South and Southwest Africa, the Philippines, and Cyprus. (Included in this class are the massive copper-nickel deposits in eastern Canada.) These deposits are typically small with well-defined boundaries and commonly have a copper content from 1.0 to 5.0 percent. The volume of ore reserves ranges from several hundred thousand to several million tons.

*Measurement and Distribution of
Copper Reserves*

Copper reserves constitute those portions of known copper mineral deposits that can be technologically and economically extracted at the

regions of the non-Communist world.

time of determination. The criteria for the measurement of copper reserves have not been standardized, so that totaling (or comparing) reserves on the basis of published reports from various companies and governments will almost inevitably involve heterogeneity. Economic feasibility of extraction necessarily implies that the amount of per-ceived reserves is a function of price and of extraction costs, and that the net return on producing them will be sufficient to attract the required investment, including an allowance for risk. However, mini-mum acceptable rates of return or discounted cash flow rates will differ between government enterprises and private international companies. Even when there is agreement on the economic feasibility of extraction, reserve categories indicate different degrees of knowledge regarding the quantity of reserves in an ore body. These categories include measured (or proved) reserves; indicated (or probable) reserves; and inferred (or possible) reserves. Determination of measured reserves requires extensive drilling of the ore body, and the existence of a minimum volume of ore must be proved in order to prepare a feasibility study for a potential mine. However, indicated and inferred reserves may be a far larger figure since extensive drilling is costly and companies may not undertake drilling beyond what is required for the feasibility study. Nevertheless, in many cases published figures on reserves will include not only measured reserves, but indicated and inferred reserves as well.

A study prepared by the U.S. Bureau of Mines based on 1970 data showed that total known U.S. domestic copper reserves available at a price of $2.00 per pound and assuming a 12 percent return on the capital investment required to mine, concentrate, smelt, and refine the material are about 164 million mt. However, only 76 million mt could be recovered economically assuming a copper price of 50 cents per pound and a 12 percent return on capital investment. This quantity would be increased to 84 million mt at 50 cents per pound if we assumed a 6 percent return on the investment.[2] It should also be mentioned that what constitutes economically recoverable copper may depend in part on the by-products or co-products associated with it in the ore. For example, it may be economically feasible to mine a deposit with a fairly low grade of copper provided the ore also contains a substantial percentage of gold or molybdenum or other valuable metal.

In the absence of a standard methodology for determining copper reserves for all deposits and of frequent adjustments to reflect changes in technology, costs, prices, and new information derived from exploration, not much confidence may be placed in global estimates or even national estimates of copper reserves as indicators of how many years of output can be maintained at present levels or how long it will be before the world runs out of copper. Nevertheless, it is useful to obtain some idea of total reserves by simply adding up what various companies or governments have reported their reserves to be. A recent UN report, which is described in some detail in chapter 12 of this study, estimates world reserves (copper content) to be 451 million mt, of which the developing countries hold nearly 59 percent. This estimate of copper reserves at the end of 1976 is nearly the same as the 458 million mt

    [2] *An Economic Appraisal of the Supply of Copper from Primary Domestic Sources,* Bureau of Mines Information Circular No. 8598 (Washington, D.C., U.S. Department of the Interior, 1973) p. 36.

of measured copper reserves estimated by the U.S. Bureau of Mines for 1976 (table 1-2). In addition, the U.S. Bureau of Mines estimates hypothetical copper resources located near known deposits to be 436 million mt.[3] World copper resources that are potentially recoverable (hypothetical and speculative) were estimated by the Bureau of Mines in 1977 to be about 1.8 billion mt of copper metal, including 0.7 billion contained in sea nodules (table 1-2).

Recoverable Reserves of Other Metals Occurring with Copper

Many copper deposits contain more than one valuable product. These are classed as co-products or by-products, depending on their relative value. If the deposit is economically viable on the basis of copper production alone, then copper is the main product and any other metals are by-products. If the economic viability of the deposit depends on the production of both copper and one or more additional metals, then copper and the other metal or metals are co-products.

Each class of copper deposit is characterized by a different set of co-product and by-product metals. Consistent estimates of co-product and by-product reserves are not published so that only a qualitative description is possible. Important by-products contained in porphyry deposits are molybdenum, silver, and gold. Molybdenum is a by-product present in some of the North and South American deposits, and for some of the Canadian deposits it is actually a co-product. Some Philippine deposits have an unusually high gold content, and molybdenum is generally absent. The Bougainville deposit in Papua New Guinea also has a high gold content, and since the rise in the price of gold in the 1970s, gold can almost be characterized as a co-product.

The strata-bound deposits in Central Africa commonly have cobalt as a by-product and the deposits in Zaire generally have a higher cobalt content. These Central African deposits are the Western world's most important source of cobalt.

The massive sulfide deposits generally contain appreciable amounts of copper, lead, and zinc. Other metals of less importance contained in massive sulfide deposits are silver, gold, bismuth, cadmium, and cobalt. The copper-nickel deposits in Canada are a special case, with copper generally a by-product.

[3] *Commodity Data Summaries 1977*, Bureau of Mines (Washington, D.C., U.S. Department of the Interior, 1978) p. 47.

Exploration

Methods of Exploration

Modern exploration methods are sophisticated and expensive in contrast to those employed in the past. Historically, the near-surface, high-grade deposits were found first. New discoveries of surface deposits were easily made in areas that had not been previously explored. Discoveries were often made by lone prospectors with very little technical training. Today most of the world's land surface has been examined for easily recognizable surface occurrences. Consequently, new methods are being developed to explore the subsurface. Each succeeding discovery becomes more difficult and more costly to make because of a declining supply of undiscovered near-surface deposits.

Modern exploration activities include geologic, geochemical, and geophysical investigations; three-dimensional sampling by core drilling or other methods; laboratory analyses, including ore treatment, concentration, and recovery tests; economic appraisal; and evaluation of transportation, water, and energy requirements. Favorable results must be obtained from these studies before a mineral deposit can be considered for development.

Geology is the principal discipline used in mineral exploration and a thorough understanding of the physical and chemical characteristics of the mineral deposit is essential. Geochemical exploration uses the systematic measurement of one or more chemical properties of a naturally occurring material to discover and delineate abnormal chemical patterns that may be related to potentially economic mineral deposits. The chemical property most commonly measured is the concentration of an element, or of a group of elements, found in rocks, soil, or streambed sediments; in vegetation, streams, lakes, or ocean water; and in glacial debris or airborne volatile materials. Exploration geophysics applies the principles of physics to the search for mineral deposits that occur in the earth's subsurface. Most geophysical work is done with sophisticated electronic equipment that can detect subtle contrasts in such physical properties as specific gravity, electrical conductivity, heat conductivity, seismic velocity, and magnetic susceptibility. The common techniques used, either singly or in combination, are gravity, magnetic, electrical, electromagnetic, seismic, and radioactivity methods. Measurements may be made from aircraft, at the earth's surface, or in bore-holes.

In recent years, a variety of "telegeologic" or "remote sensing" techniques—measurements of various geologic or related properties from aircraft or satellites—have provided insights into complex structures of some regions where much of the bedrock is concealed. Side-looking radar imagery or photography has provided useful base maps in areas where conventional photographic methods are inadequate. LANDSAT (formerly Earth Resources Technology Satellite) imagery of many areas provides information on potential mineral and mineral-fuel deposits and is proving to be valuable for understanding groundwater conditions and water-management problems. Preliminary results in Alaska and elsewhere suggest that LANDSAT data may have significant value in monitoring the environmental effects of mineral and fuel production activities.

Modern laboratory techniques are applied in exploration projects. Electron microprobe, X-ray microanalysis, rapid chemical analysis, visual color-comparison techniques, and neutron-activation analysis have been found particularly useful.

Modern exploration is now most commonly carried on by teams of experts backed by large exploration budgets. These experts include geologists, geochemists, and geophysicists, many of whom have a Ph.D. in their respective fields. The increasingly intensive education required to prepare the explorationist for his career is further evidence that ore deposits are becoming much more difficult to find.

Stages in Exploration

The first step in the exploration sequence is often a review of geological and mining literature on an area and a survey of the records of mining claims and of past mining and prospecting activity in order to identify old mining districts, existing prospects, and areas thought to be favorable but which have not been systematically explored. The second level of the sequence is general geological reconnaissance and orientation surveys. The techniques include aerial photogeology and ground geological reconnaissance for data concerning the distribution of mineral deposits. Small-scale geologic mapping may be carried out and geophysics and regional geochemical drainage survey methods may be employed. At this level of exploration, the area covered may range from 10,000 to 50,000 km². Such exploration is often referred to as "grass roots" exploration. Successively smaller areas may be delineated for geologic mapping, aerial geophysical surveys, geochemistry, and other methods for locating an ore deposit within a target area. This work sometimes leads to the identification of a potential prospect, which will then be examined by physical exploration, including exploratory drilling. If the results of such exploration are positive, development drilling designed to outline the projected ore body will follow.

Some companies prefer to do "grass roots" exploration, whereas others prefer to buy into an exploration endeavor at a more advanced stage. The stage of exploration usually determines the size of the area for which an exploration permit, or an exploration concession giving the holder exclusive mining rights over the area, will be required. Frequently, mining companies may obtain exploration rights over a very large area and agree to relinquish a portion each year as exploration proceeds, with the right to obtain mining concessions on relatively small areas within the larger exploration concession.

After the ore body is delineated, shafts may be sunk to permit underground exploration to confirm drill results and to obtain bulk samples. These samples will be assayed to confirm drill assay results. Then, metallurgical tests will be run to determine the amenability of the ore to flotation or other techniques designed to separate the valuable minerals from the unwanted material.

All of the information obtained in the detailed exploration and sampling phase is used to determine the feasibility of establishing a mining operation on the deposit. The feasibility study requires information about the ore reserves of the deposit, the average grade of the ore reserves, the cutoff or minimum grade used to delimit the ore reserves, and the metallurgical characteristics of the ore. The cost of acquiring this information for a large porphyry copper deposit today ranges up to $30 million.

Although point estimates are commonly used for tonnage, grade, and metallurgical recovery, in practice they are variables. Statistical estimation techniques, particularly geostatistics, are becoming more widely used. These techniques permit estimation of sample reliability in probabilistic terms so that the degree of certainty of grade and tonnage can be estimated. This information provides a clearer picture of expected variability once mining begins and contributes to more realistic feasibility statements. As ore deposits become lower grade, increased reliability of tonnage and grade estimation is essential because small differences can have important financial effects in large-scale mining operations.

Organization of Exploration Activity

The actual physical exploration for copper deposits in the United States, Canada, Australia, South Africa, and the Philippines is generally carried on by private individuals and companies. Exploration for copper in Chile, Mexico, Peru, Zaire, and Zambia is carried on by both companies and the governments of the respective countries. The United Nations Development Program (UNDP) has provided direct assistance to copper exploration in Iran, Mexico, Panama, Colombia, and more recently Pakistan. UNDP exploration activities in Mexico contributed to the discovery of the La Caridad deposits; in Panama they contributed to the identification of the prospect that eventually became the Cerro Colorado deposit; and in Iran they contributed to the finding of the Sar Chesmeh mine. So far, two copper mineral deposits have been identified by UNDP efforts in Pakistan.

Companies active in exploration may be divided into three classes: (1) small exploration companies; (2) mining companies; and (3) petroleum companies. Small exploration companies often start out with a specific prospect. The financing, which may involve the sale of stock to the public, is conducted in stages from exploratory drilling to development drilling, and then to mine development. New stock may be issued to finance each stage, and, if the early stages are successful, a mining company may take an option on a block of stock in the exploration company and help finance the development of the mine. The small exploration companies have been confined primarily to Canada, the United States, Australia, Mexico, and the Philippines.

The traditional mining companies maintain exploration staffs and many conduct exploration activities in a number of countries. The mining companies pursue both grass roots exploration and detailed evaluation of prospects discovered by others. The preferences of individual companies may vary greatly. Companies such as ASARCO, Kennecott, and Phelps Dodge have historically conducted extensive grass roots exploration, whereas Newmont, Noranda, and Rio Tinto have preferred to acquire deposits that were already partially explored.

Petroleum companies have played an increasing role in nonfuel mineral exploration. For example, Conoco and EXXON have conducted grass roots explorations that were successful in identifying copper ore bodies. Other companies, such as Occidental, Getty, and Superior have preferred to participate in exploration at a more advanced state on a joint venture basis.

Historically, government agencies in the Western countries have not been especially active in exploration. The U.S. Geological Survey and the Canadian Geological Survey have provided regional geological mapping, topographic mapping, and detailed mapping and evaluation of known deposits and known mining districts. The latter studies are designed to provide a better understanding of the mechanisms of ore formation; some of their subtle alteration and geochemical patterns may serve as guides to the discovery of new deposits in similar environments. The Mexican Department of Natural Resources provides regional mapping and detailed mapping in known districts, but also conducts actual exploration.

Since the copper industries in a number of countries are now partly owned by the government, government agencies will probably play a greater role in exploration in the future. In addition, government agencies of several developed countries are actively involved in international copper exploration and development.[4] The French government agency, Bureau de Récherches Géologique et Minières (BRGM), is active in copper development in Bolivia, Jordan, Saudi Arabia, and Zaire. The Rumanian state-owned company, Geomin, has joint ventures for copper exploration and development in Peru and Zambia. The Canadian International Development Agency and the Soviet Union provide exploration, mapping, and other types of natural resource assistance in developing countries.

The Nature of Mining Activities

Alternative Mining Processes

There are two basic types of mining operations used to extract the copper-bearing ore: open-pit or surface mining, and underground mining. An open-pit mine is largely a quarrying operation that handles huge volumes of material; open-pit mining consists of drilling and blasting the rock and then hauling it out of the pit in large trucks, with capacities ranging from 60 to 150 tons, or in ore trains. Underground mining is more selective, although large tonnages of rock must still be moved. The task is more difficult than in open-pit operations because the material is normally moved through underground passageways to a centrally located shaft through which it is lifted to the surface. The ore must still be drilled and blasted, but there are numerous mining techniques that are used, depending to a large degree on the nature of the underground ore body. Open stoping, shrinkage stoping, sublevel stoping, and block caving are the techniques most commonly used in underground copper mines.[5] Block caving is used for mining the underground porphyry deposits whereas the other underground

---

[4] Michael Chender, "Copper Exploration Restrained by Resource Nationalism and Low Metal Prices," *Engineering and Mining Journal* (August 1976) pp. 77–80.

[5] For brief descriptions of these techniques, see appendix 2-1.

methods are used for mining the strata-bound and massive sulfide deposits.

Most porphyry deposits are mined by large-scale open-pit methods, although some deep deposits must be mined by block caving. They tend to be low-grade deposits that are capable of being accurately measured and sampled at an early stage in the operation, and are of such a size and shape that they lend themselves to low-cost bulk mining methods. Mines built on the porphyry deposits are operated with a high capital investment and a high output per worker. Returns are very sensitive to changes in input costs, operational efficiency, and taxation.

The strata-bound deposits are mined by both underground and surface methods. Underground mining is predominant in Zambia, whereas open-pit mining has prevailed in Zaire. The underground mines in Zambia are quite labor intensive, and some must pump large amounts of water and contend with unstable ground. Some of the ores in Zambia and Zaire have a high content of copper silicate minerals from which metal extraction is more difficult than for sulfides, and copper recovery is not as complete. Therefore, the strata-bound deposits usually have higher costs per ton of ore removed, but because of the high grade of the ore, some of the Central African mines produce copper at a relatively low cost per pound. Recently, however, costs in Zaire and Zambia have been relatively high because of transportation difficulties.

Deposits of the strata-bound type must be selectively mined to maintain a profitable grade, and the ore reserves for such deposits are difficult and expensive to evaluate. Normally, the prospects for additional reserves remain high long after mining has begun. Mines built on strata-bound deposits usually require a high labor input, a high level of technical expertise, and complex engineering.[6] These mines are generally moderate- to high-risk operations,[7] and are decreasing in relative importance.

The massive sulfide deposits must be selectively mined by underground methods. The deposits are relatively small, occurring as veins, pods, and lenses, and are intermediate to high grade. Because of their high grade, they tend to yield substantial operating profits, even though the cost per ton of ore extracted is generally high because of overhead and labor requirements.[8] Because of the high grade of ore produced, the

[6] Eugene P. Pflieder, "Merits of Open Pit versus Underground Mining in the Future," *Mining Congress Journal* vol. 58, no. 1 (January 1972) pp. 25–29.

[7] Michael West, "Capital Requirements of the World Wide Mining Industry," *Mining Congress Journal* vol. 57, no. 11 (November 1971) pp. 84–87.

[8] Arthur L. English, "The Changing Nature of Mine Finance in Canada," *Proceedings of the Council of Economics* (American Institute of Mining and Metallugical Engineers, Annual Meeting, February 25–March 1, 1973) pp. 7–14.

first sulfide ores extracted were sometimes shipped directly rather than as concentrates.

Factors Affecting Costs of Mine Development

Differences in costs determine to a large measure the relative development of mining capacity for each country or region that has ore reserves. The physical factors determining mining costs include the size and grade of the deposit and its depth from the surface, the content of by-products and/or co-products, and the location. Location affects both operating and capital costs since mines in remote areas usually require large capital outlays for transportation and other infrastructure.

Open-pit mining, and to a lesser extent underground mining, is subject to economies of scale. The size and grade of a deposit determines the scale of operations, and low-grade deposits usually require a large-scale operation to be economical. The deposit must be large enough to amortize the investment over the life of the mine and the grade must be high enough to cover the operating, processing, and transportation costs and taxes, plus a risk-weighted return on investment. Capital requirements increase substantially with the scale of operation, but capital costs per unit of output are maintained at acceptable levels through high operating rates.

The more selective mining techniques required for the strata-bound and massive sulfide deposits are the most costly per ton of ore mined, and usually call for underground mines. The shape of a deposit and its location below the surface also affect costs. An underground mine is more costly to operate than an open-pit mine of the same capacity. Hence, underground mining is usually not feasible for extracting low-grade ores.

Capital requirements tend to be lower for mines constructed in an existing mining district than for those in undeveloped areas. The location of mines in new and more remote areas increases the capital requirements for transport, water, power, and communications facilities. Cost estimates provided by Gordon Driver[9] of Noranda for a typical capital-intensive North American open-pit mining operation indicate that new mine construction in a remote area such as northern Canada may increase the capital requirements as much as 75 percent above those for mines in a more developed area. Mine expansion requires less capital than new mine construction, and data provided

---

[9] R. Gordon Driver, "Copper in the Seventies," *Mining Congress Journal* vol. 58, no. 2 (February 1972) pp. 65–70.

by Prain[10] indicate that capital requirements for new mine construction are about 40 percent greater than for mine expansion.

In the 1950–75 period, new mine construction was focused on porphyry copper deposits because of their near-surface occurrence and their suitability for open-pit mining. This development has resulted in an increased proportion of world copper production being derived from open-pit mines. For example, in 1955 open-pit mines produced 42 percent of the world's primary copper; in 1960, 47 percent; in 1965, 50 percent; in 1969, 58 percent; and in 1975, more than 60 percent.[11]

In recent years, the creation of new copper mining capacity has tended to take the form of new mine development rather than the expansion of existing mines. This is illustrated by the fact that in 1962 an estimated 400,000 tons of new productive capacity were scheduled to be constructed, of which 16 percent was to come from new mines and the remainder from extensions to existing mines. In contrast, by 1970, 2,193,000 tons of new capacity were scheduled for construction during the 1970–75 period, of which 58 percent was to come from new mines and 42 percent from expansion of existing mines. However, there are indications that this pattern may be reversed, with greater emphasis on the expansion of existing mines in the United States and Canada, and less on the creation of new mines in the developing areas.[12] This shift is encouraged by the exceedingly high cost of new mines, especially in remote areas, and by the political risks incurred by investment in the developing countries.

Copper Metallurgy

Once copper ore has been mined, the copper-bearing minerals must be separated from the rock, and the copper extracted from the minerals. As was noted earlier in this chapter, most copper occurs in three different types of copper minerals: sulfides, carbonates, and silicates.

[10] Sir Ronald Prain, *Selected Papers,* vol. III, 1961–1964; vol. IV, 1964–1967 (London, Batsford). See also Sir Ronald Prain, "The International Outlook for Copper," a paper presented at the American Metal Market Forum, London, 1971.

[11] Author's estimates.

[12] In its *Annual Report* (March 1977) Kennecott Copper Corporation stated that its present strategy is to expand its copper producing capacity by increasing the capacities of the company's operating mines in the United States—principally the Chino mines, the Ray mines, and Utah Copper Mine—rather than to develop new mines. The report stated that the capacity of these properties can be increased at a capital cost of less than $5,000 per annual short ton, as contrasted with the capital cost of new copper capacity which is approaching $7,000 per annual short ton.

Most of the copper ore bodies that are in production carry their copper in copper sulfide minerals. However, the ore bodies in Zaire, the southwestern United States, and in Chile carry varying amounts of copper in carbonates and silicates. The separation of copper from different kinds of copper minerals requires different metallurgical techniques.

Sulfide Ores

Most copper-bearing sulfide minerals can be easily separated from the other rock minerals by selective flotation. The ore is crushed and finely ground so that the individual mineral grains are separated from the rock, and the copper-bearing minerals are then removed by flotation to produce copper concentrate. This is a process that relies on the ability of certain minerals to attach themselves to bubbles of air in water. Chemicals called frothers are used to condition the minerals to be separated. Frothers reduce the wettability of certain minerals and cause them to adhere to air bubbles, thus enabling them to be floated. The metallurgy of flotation is complex and different reagents are used to produce different types of mineral separation.

Copper concentrates produced today usually contain from 22 to 32 percent copper metal by weight. In those deposits where concentrations of other sulfide minerals, such as lead or zinc, are sufficiently large, they are separated from the copper minerals by selective flotation. However, most of the gold and silver recovered from copper deposits are carried in the copper concentrate.

Copper oxide minerals, the carbonates and silicates, present special recovery problems. They are difficult to separate from the other rock-forming minerals and, in the case of silicate minerals, the copper is more difficult to extract from the minerals themselves. Ores in which it is difficult to separate the metal from the other mineral components are called refractory ores and present special problems that have been only partially solved. Most copper ores are not refractory, although some deposits do have refractory ore in them.

Leaching Technology

Copper oxide minerals are quite common, especially the carbonates. Deposits containing these minerals were first mined in Zaire. They were often high grade, so that the ore could be smelted directly, but the lower grade ore required special technology to separate the copper from the rock. Certain deposits in Arizona and in Chile present similar problems. The desire to mine these ore bodies led to the development of leaching technology.

In leaching, the copper is separated from the copper-bearing minerals while they are still mixed with other rock components. The ore may be crushed prior to leaching, or it may be leached without crushing. Four different leaching methods have been developed: (1) vat leaching, (2) heap leaching, (3) dump leaching, and (4) *in situ* leaching. Some mines combine leaching with flotation for mixed oxide–sulfide ores. In this latter process, the ore is first leached, and the leach residue is treated by flotation to remove the sulfide minerals.

Historically, vat leaching has been the most commonly used method. In this process, the ore is crushed and placed in tanks or vats where it is immersed in a weak acid solution which is circulated until most of the copper has been extracted from the ore. The copper is then extracted from the copper-bearing solution by precipitating it on scrap iron, or by recovering it directly as copper metal in electrolytic cells. A relatively new recovery technology which is coming to be widely employed involves the use of ion exchange resins.[13]

During the past two decades leaching technology has been developed for application to low-grade ores and to mineralized rock that is too low grade to run through the flotation plant or to vat leach. Both heap leaching and dump leaching were developed to recover copper from low-grade ores. Heap leaching, which is normally used to process low-grade oxide ores, is performed by piling the ore as it is mined on specially prepared pads; a sulfuric acid solution is then pumped onto the surface through hoses or pipes placed on top of the ore. This solution percolates down through the pile, dissolving the copper-bearing oxide minerals and picking up the copper ions. The copper-bearing liquor flows from the bottom of the pad into a collecting pond from which it is pumped to the recovery plant where the copper is recovered electrolytically, or by precipitation on iron.

Dump leaching derives its name from the fact that many of the large waste dumps generated in the process of mining porphyry deposits can be leached to obtain some additional copper. Many waste dumps contain both oxide and sulfide copper minerals. At some of the larger mines which have been operated for many years, the waste dumps are quite large; material that was waste fifteen or twenty years ago may now be suitable for processing by the leaching method.

---

[13] Ion exchange resins are used to effect a chemical extraction of the metal from the metal-bearing solution. Separation is a two-step process: the copper is captured by the resin and then it is extracted from the resin and recovered electrolytically.

Dump leaching is performed the same way as heap leaching, except that the dumps are made as a result of waste haulage in the general course of mining and consequently they are not placed on specially prepared bases. The dumps may contain very large tonnages of material, and ponds are often made on top of them to contain the weak sulfuric acid solution. The solution is recovered by building a dike around the base of the dump if it is on flat ground. If it is built on a slope, clays soon coat the surface so that the solution runs out of the downhill side of the dump, where it is collected in a pond for recycling over the dump, or it is sent to the recovery circuit where the copper is extracted. Bacteria may be used for breaking down the sulfide minerals; this process is called bacterial leaching. Dump leaching is likely to become more widespread as the technology improves and as the supply of by-product acid from copper smelters increases.

In situ leaching is a low-cost alternative to other forms of copper mining and processing, and one deposit in the southwestern United States is now being leached in place. An important advantage is that it minimizes visible environmental disturbance. *In situ* leaching is only used in special situations because it results in lower copper recovery from a deposit and only copper is recovered. Other problems with *in situ* leaching are containment of the leach liquors beneath the deposit and the formation of minerals that prevent ready percolation through the deposit. Containment of the leach liquor is an especially difficult problem because many copper deposits are highly fractured rock bodies. If the ore body is deeply buried, it is difficult to devise a means for sealing the base of the deposit. Leakages result in large solution losses and ground water contamination. *In situ* leaching is still in the experimental stage, but it may be used for certain deposits in the future.

Dump leaching and heap leaching eliminate the need for complex and expensive mill facilities and for smelting copper concentrate. Two products are derived from the copper-bearing leach liquor, cement copper and electrowon cathode. Cement copper is produced by precipitating the copper from the leach solution on iron scrap that has been detinned. Electrowon cathode is produced by electroplating copper cathodes directly from the leach liquor. Special high quality cathodes are made by using ion exchange resins to strip the copper from the leach solution, and then putting the copper back into solution by stripping the ion exchange resin, and electroplating the copper from this solution. Use of this latter method produces copper that is sufficiently pure to be used for copper wire production without further refining.

In the United States about 223,000 tons of copper (14 percent of production) were produced by leaching methods in 1974. Of this amount, 193,000 tons were precipitated with iron and 30,000 tons were electrowon. About 146,000 tons were produced by *in situ* and dump leaching. This copper was mainly recovered by precipitation on iron.[14]

Copper Smelting

In contrast to the hydrometallurgical methods used to extract copper from oxide minerals described in the previous section, pyrometallurgical methods are generally used to extract copper from sulfide minerals. However, hydrometallurgical technology is also being developed for the extraction of copper from sulfide minerals.

Although some of the pyrometallurgical techniques used today were developed late in the eighteenth century, large-scale copper smelting is a twentieth century development. Traditionally, three steps are involved in smelting sulfide concentrates: roasting; smelting with appropriate fluxes to produce copper matte; and converting the matte to blister copper. Roasting reduces the sulfur content of the concentrate, while smelting breaks down the crystalline structure of the sulfide minerals so that the constituent elements—copper, iron, and sulfur—can be separated. Smelting produces: (1) a slag bearing minor amounts of copper and iron, and nonmetal impurities such as calcium, aluminum oxide, and silicates; and (2) a copper matte containing iron, sulfur, precious metals, and minor amounts of metals such as lead, arsenic, antimony, selenium, tellurium, bismuth, and nickel. The copper matte is transferred to a converter where fluxes are added along with oxygen to separate the iron and to drive off the sulfur.

Both chemistry and economics determine the optimum composition of the matte which is produced in the smelting furnace. An optimum concentration for many converter operations is 30 percent copper, 39 percent iron, and 26 percent sulfur. This composition minimizes the time required to oxidize the iron and sulfur in the converting stage. Early smelting operations often used the roasting step before smelting to control the sulfur content of the feed material. Today many smelters use a mixture of concentrate and precipitate to achieve the same result more economically. Some mines produce ore that is deficient in sulfur for smelting purposes. At these mines pyrite concentrate is sometimes added to bring the sulfur content up to the required level.

[14] Harold J. Schroeder and George J. Coakly, preprint of the "Copper" chapter from the 1974 Bureau of Mines *Minerals Yearbook*, p. 3.

Four types of furnaces have been used for smelting : (1) blast, (2) reverberatory, (3) electric, and (4) flash. The reverberatory furnace and the blast furnace were developed at about the same time. However, the blast furnace required high-grade lump ore as feed and so was not widely adopted. The reverberatory furnace became the workhorse of the copper industry because of its ability to handle large volumes of concentrate efficiently. Later, electric furnaces were developed and used where low-cost electric power was available. Flash furnaces were developed by Inco in Canada and by Outukumpu Oy in Finland. The flash furnaces produce an off-gas that is ideal for the manufacture of sulfuric acid. The Inco process requires pure oxygen to sustain the smelting process, whereas the Outukumpu process uses preheated air. Both processes were initially employed where there were nearby markets for sulfuric acid. The Outukumpu technology has been widely adopted in Japan and Western Europe.

The reverberatory furnace was widely adopted in the United States, South America, and Africa, but has several disadvantages relative to electric furnaces and flash furnaces. The two most important disadvantages are the low concentration of SO_2 in the outlet gases, and low thermal efficiency. Off-gases contain from 0.5 percent to 1.0 percent SO_2. This concentration is too low for efficient sulfuric acid recovery, and the volume of gas is so large that SO_2 removal from the stack gases on an economical basis is almost impossible. Both of these disadvantages are critical in a period when energy has become very expensive, and when environmental regulations require the removal of most of the particulate matter and SO_2 from smelter off-gases. For these reasons, reverberatory furnaces are being phased out in the United States and being replaced by either flash furnaces or electric furnaces, or by entirely new technology.

Two types of converters are commonly used by the copper industry: the Peirce–Smith converter and the Hoboken converter. The converters are cylindrical vessels which rest horizontally on a foundation and which can be rotated vertically to decant slag and blister copper. Oxygen is blown into the converters through side vents called tuyeres, and the gases produced are given off through the mouth of the Peirce–Smith converter and through the side of the Hoboken siphon-type converter. The Peirce–Smith converter is considered to be more efficient in handling large volumes of material, but SO_2 concentration of the off-gases is difficult to control. The Hoboken converter, on the other hand, is somewhat less efficient because of its smaller size, but its design permits careful control of SO_2 concentration in the off-gases at an average of about 8 percent compared to 2 to 6 percent for the Peirce–Smith converter. Both types of converters produce blister copper that is 97.0 to 98.5 percent pure.

Utilization of the Outukumpu flash furnace–Hoboken converter technology, or the electric furnace–Outukumpu converter technology requires careful control of copper concentrate composition because the furnace works best with a specific composition of feed material and is relatively intolerant of concentrates of varying composition. Because of this, custom smelters using the newer technologies require careful blending of toll material before it is fed to the furnace. Varying amounts of copper concentrate and precipitate from different mines may be required to achieve the proper composition of feed material.

New pyrometallurgical smelting technology has focused on continuous processes to achieve smelting and converting in the same or in connecting vessels. The two best-known processes are the Noranda and the Mitsubishi. Both have been tested in the pilot stage, and the Noranda Company has completed a full-size installation at its smelter at Noranda, Quebec. The Mitsubishi process has been tested on a pilot scale, and a small commercial plant has been constructed. A third process developed by Conzinc Riotinto of Australia—the WORCRA process—was also designed for smelting and converting in a single vessel. The process was tested extensively on a pilot basis, but problems were apparently encountered in maintaining the proper degree of separation of slag and metal within the smelter vessel. No plans are currently known for commercial development of this process.

Both the Mitsubishi and the Noranda processes produce off-gases that have an SO_2 concentration adequate to ensure recovery in a sulfuric acid plant. Both processes also offer advantages of increased efficiency and lower cost operation by being able to operate continuously rather than on a batch basis, and by offering semiautomatic operation that can be computer controlled. Both systems are said to reduce capital costs because smelting and converting are done in integrated units, one reactor in the case of the Noranda process and three connected reactors in the case of the Mitsubishi process. Kennecott Copper Corporation is planning to use the Noranda process at its Utah Mines Division, and Texasgulf Sulfur is planning to use the Mitsubishi process at its Kidd Creek mine in Canada.

Hydrometallurgical Processing of
Sulfide Concentrates

In recent years, a considerable amount of attention has been given to hydrometallurgical processing of sulfide concentrates. Mixed oxide–

sulfide ores have been processed for years in Zaire and Zambia by the roast–leach–electrowin (RLE) process. In this process the oxide material is separated from the sulfide material and sent directly to leach vats. The sulfides are then concentrated and roasted to drive off the sulfur and produce an oxidized iron–copper sinter. This sinter is also sent to the leaching vats where the copper is leached. If the copper is recovered directly from the leach solution, a low-grade copper cathode is produced which must be refined electrolytically. If ion exchange resins are used, a product suitable for shipment directly to wire and brass mills can be produced. The above RLE technology has one major drawback: the precious metals and nickel by-products are not recovered.

The Lakeshore mine in Arizona has an RLE process that enables recovery of by-product precious metals. The copper deposit is mixed oxide-sulfide, but the oxide ore and the sulfide ore are mined separately. The oxide ore is sent directly to leach vats and the sulfide ore is concentrated and roasted, and then sent to the leach vats. The copper-bearing sinter is leached separately from the oxide ore so that the remaining iron-bearing residue that contains the by-product metals can be pelleted and then converted to sponge iron. Copper leached from the sinter is recovered electrolytically and shipped directly to wire and brass mills. The copper leached from the oxide ore is recovered by precipitating on the iron sponge. This latter material, which carries the precious metals, is sent to a smelter for processing. Sulfuric acid used for leaching is obtained at the mine from SO_2 produced by roasting the sulfide concentrate. This plant is the first of its kind to be constructed in North America.

Three purely hydrometallurgical methods of processing sulfide ores have been developed in the United States. The CLEAR and Cymet processes use a chloride leaching method that is an outgrowth of concepts developed by the U.S. Bureau of Mines. The Arbiter process was developed by Anaconda and uses an ammonia leach followed by solvent extraction and electrowinning. All three processes have been pilot tested and two of them—CLEAR and Arbiter—are now operating on a commercial basis.

One key advantage of hydrometallurgical processing is that it is environmentally clean. The leaching process extracts only the copper from the concentrate, leaving the iron, sulfur, and by-product metals in the leach residues. These plants can be built on a smaller scale than pyrometallurgical smelters and still operate efficiently, thus enabling smelters to be constructed at medium- or even small-sized mines in the future. The sulfur can be extracted as elemental sulfur, the iron can be recovered as iron oxide, and the precious metals can also be recovered. Environmental problems created by large volumes of waste are to a great extent eliminated.

The principal disadvantage at the present time appears to be a relatively high operating cost. The CLEAR process requires electricity as a power source, whereas the Arbiter process uses oxygen, ammonia, and lime. The high cost of oxygen and ammonia may preclude wide adoption of the Arbiter process, and adoption of CLEAR will be determined partially by relative energy costs.

The Cymet process was developed by Cyprus Mines Corporation and was originally planned for use at the Bagdad mine in Arizona. However, Cyprus decided not to go ahead with a commercial plant, suggesting that the Cymet process might not be economical. The CLEAR process, on the other hand, was developed by Duval Corporation and is now in commercial production at Duval's Esperanza mine in Arizona. This process produces copper crystals that are equivalent in quality to blister copper and so must still be refined electrolytically. Very little information is available as to Duval's future plans for this process. However, it seems likely that if the commercial plant works as expected, Duval will build similar plants at its other mines.

Pollution Abatement

Most air pollution problems in the copper industry occur at the smelting stage. Air pollution arises primarily from the particulate matter and SO_2 gases given off during the pyrometallurgical smelting process. Although other pollution, such as water contamination and visual alteration of the landscape, is associated with mining, these effects have been less serious than air pollution. In contrast with many U.S. smelters, Japanese smelters have historically recovered the SO_2 produced by copper smelting. Although the Central African and South American producers use pyrometallurgical smelting techniques, the remote location of the smelters has reduced the concern for environmental pollution. In recent years environmental regulations requiring SO_2 recovery have been legislated in the United States and in other industrial countries.

Both the location of the smelting enterprises and the availability of low-cost sulfur from other sources have influenced the recovery of SO_2 from smelter stack gases and the type of smelting technology employed. The isolation of western U.S. copper producers from the industrial markets in the East and the availability of low-cost Frasch sulfur made SO_2 recovery uneconomic in the United States, except in special cases.[15] On the other hand, both Western Europe and Japan have had to import sulfur, and the smelting enterprises were often located close to industrial markets. European and Japanese smelters commonly recover more than 90 percent of the SO_2 gas produced in smelters, from which they make sulfuric acid that is sold in local markets.

Sulfuric acid is a relatively low-value bulk product and transportation charges may be prohibitive if it must be moved over long distances. The available means of transportation also affects the cost. Barge transportation is lowest cost, whereas truck transportation is most costly, and rail is intermediate. A factor that has affected sulfur economics in very recent years is the rapidly escalating cost of energy. Frasch sulfur is produced with steam generated by natural gas or oil furnaces. The rise in the cost of energy has raised the cost of Frasch sulfur to the point where by-product sulfur recovered from smelting has become competitive with Frasch sulfur in some areas in the United States.

Smelters located near a sulfuric acid market may benefit from the sale of sulfuric acid recovered during the smelting process, provided the revenues from sulfuric acid sales cover the cost of acid production and sale, and partially offset smelting charges. The development of leaching technology has changed the character of the sulfuric acid market in the southwestern United States, since some of the acid can now be used locally for leaching oxide ores and waste dumps. The amount of acid used for this latter purpose can be expected to increase in future years as the technology becomes more widely adopted.

The implications of pollution abatement regulations for the future supply of copper are discussed in chapter 13.

Pyrometallurgy versus Hydrometallurgy

Will pyrometallurgical or hydrometallurgical processes dominate future generations of copper smelting plants?[16] It seems likely that no single process will be dominant in the near future and diversification of processing equipment will be the trend for at least the next decade.

---

[15] The Cities Service Company's Copperhill, Tennessee smelter has manufactured sulfuric acid for sale in the local market for years.

[16] I. C. Herbert, "New Copper Extraction Processes," *Journal of Metals* (August 1974) pp. 16–24; and W. A. Gow, "Hydrometallurgy in Mineral Processing," *Canadian Mining Journal* (June 1974) pp. 70–71.

Pyrometallurgical processes will remain attractive because the huge capital investments in existing equipment and the relatively slow growth of copper demand slant the choice of technology toward adaptation rather than revolution. The gradual introduction of improved pyrometallurgical techniques may be the safest way to maintain profits. Moreover, some hydrometallurgical processes are still plagued by unsolved technical problems. Corrosion controls may be difficult and expensive and the gaseous waste disposal problem is replaced by a sometimes equally troublesome liquid waste disposal problem for some processes. Other problems in liquid solid separation and reagent regeneration also remain.

It is likely, however, that these technical problems will be solved within the next decade and that hydrometallurgy will gradually penetrate the industry, first in auxiliary operations and hybrid processes and later, independently. Two factors facilitate this penetration. First, hydrometallurgical plants can be operated efficiently with small mines. Second, capital costs are low and operation costs are similar to those of pyrometallurgical plants of the same size.

It will take longer than a decade, however, for hydrometallurgical plants to form a substantial part of industry capacity. The pyrometallurgical processes have been demonstrated to work well for large-scale operations whereas hydrometallurgical processes have not. Thus, pyrometallurgical processes will most likely be preferred for large-scale operations, at least until more is known about scale efficiencies of the hydrometallurgical plants.

For the more distant future, it is tempting to conclude that one process will become dominant because it is found to be the minimum cost process. However, this may not be the case. First, local conditions of mining and smelting will be more varied in the future than they have been in the past. Copper ores of differing composition may call for different processes, especially since the recovery of by-products which formerly were discarded may become economical. Energy supply conditions vary considerably from region to region and will, therefore, help dictate the choice of technology. Second, although hydrometallurgical processing may prove to be the minimum-cost method for small-scale plants, it is not known if any economies of scale can be expected. The most likely result of the availability of a rather broad range of technological choice will be that the particular technology chosen will be the one that is best suited to local conditions at the time the construction decision is made. The availability of efficient technology suited for small- to medium-scale plants may mean that more smelting will be done at the mine site in the future than has been done in the past.

Refining

Blister copper and, in some cases, electrowon cathodes produced by leaching must be refined before the copper is suitable for use in final products. Blister copper often contains oxygen, sulfur, and minor amounts of other metals. Electrowon cathodes may also contain minor amounts of other metals, especially lead. A large percentage of primary copper is used for wire manufacture and consequently must be quite pure. High purity requires that the oxygen content be reduced to a controlled amount, the sulfur driven off, and the minor amounts of other metals removed.

Two refining processes are used: fire refining and electroyltic refining. Fire refining is most often used for blister copper which has a low by-product metal content and where the most important impurity is oxygen and sulfur. The refining is accomplished in a reverberatory furnace where the metal is kept in a molten state while it is treated with air, oxygen, hydrocarbon gas, or pine logs to remove impurities. Very little Western world copper is fire refined. The rise in precious metal prices in the 1970s has increased their value to a point where it pays to remove very small amounts of these metals. For this reason, electrolytic refining is most commonly used.

In electrolytic refining the unrefined copper in the form of anodes is placed in tanks along with thin sheets of pure copper called starter sheets. Starter sheets are the cathodes and are placed so that every other sheet is a cathode. The electrolyte is commonly a sulfuric acid solution. The process involves dissolving the copper from the anodes and plating it on the cathodes. The impurities contained in the unrefined copper drop to the bottom of the tank as a sludge.

Modern electrolytic refineries are designed to handle very large volumes of copper. For example, the new ASARCO refinery at Amarillo, Texas is designed to handle up to 420,000 mt of copper per year. In the Amarillo refinery, the blister copper is melted in furnaces, cast into anodes, and the cathodes are cast into refinery products such as wirebars, billets, cake, and rod.

Historically, refineries have been built near industrial centers where refined copper is consumed. The United Kingdom, Germany, and Belgium have been the principal Western European copper refining countries, although the importance of the United Kingdom is declining. Western European refineries and associated smelters are located with access to water transport. Most of the refineries in the United States were built on the eastern seaboard with access to both ocean and land transport. Refining is now being undertaken in the southwestern United States because the market for refined copper products is shifting westward.

The mining districts of Zambia and Zaire are landlocked and their copper production must be shipped over long land distances. Both of these countries have refining capacity. However, the saving in transporting refined copper as contrasted with blister copper (98 percent pure) is rather small and there are advantages in having refineries near the copper markets. The copper-producing centers of Chile, Peru, Zaire, and Zambia desire to integrate forward so that an increasing proportion of their copper exports is refined.

In Canada, the Inco refinery is located in the Sudbury, Ontario mining district, whereas Noranda's refinery is located in Montreal and has access to both water and land transport. Much of the Japanese refinery capacity has been constructed since World War II and is located with access to water transport.

Refinery Products

Copper is shipped from the refinery in five different shapes: cathodes, wirebars, continuous cast rod (CCR), billets, and cakes. Historically the most common shape has been the wirebar, but important changes are occurring in the product mix that is shipped from refineries. This change is due in considerable measure to the development of the shaft furnace designed by ASARCO and commonly referred to as the ASARCO furnace. This furnace is cylindrical in shape, stands upright, and is between 25 and 30 feet high. It can be fired by natural gas, oil, or propane and permits melting under controlled conditions so that the oxygen content of the copper can be carefully regulated. Cathodes are fed into the furnace from the top and the molten copper is tapped from the bottom. The furnace can be started up quickly and shut down just as quickly without damage. It provides a low-cost, efficient alternative to the reverberatory or blast furnace. The shaft furnace permits efficient melting on a relatively small scale and can be connected to a casting wheel for continuous casting. Modern plants use a shaft furnace, a casting wheel, and a rolling mill hooked together in series to produce continuous cast rod (CCR). Four U.S. refineries, in addition to the Southwire Company which developed the process, now have CCR capacity.

Wirebars have a distinctive shape; they commonly measure up to 4 3/8 inches wide, and have a thickness ranging from 3 5/8 to 4 3/8 inches.

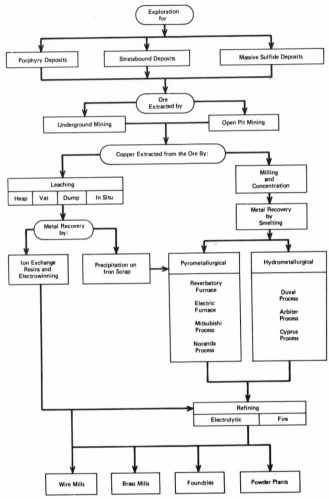

Figure 2-2.   Technology of primary copper production.

Standard wirebars weigh 265 pounds each, but bars are also produced in weights from 200 to 300 pounds. Wirebars have been used mainly for the manufacture of wire and rod. However, wirebars are being rapidly displaced by cathodes and CCR as the principal products of international copper trade, and in the future the cathode will probably become the standard product of copper trade.

Most CCR measures 5⁄16 of an inch in diameter and is produced in coils that range from 5,000 to 15,000 pounds. The coils may contain as much as 15 miles of rod in a single strand. The coils are easily damaged during shipment and so do not enter international trade in large quantities. The packaging and shipping technology is still being developed, however, so that large international shipments in the future are not precluded.

Copper billets are solid, cylindrical shapes up to several inches in diameter and 4 to 6 feet long. Their weights range from just over 100 pounds to more than 400 pounds each. Almost all seamless copper tubing is manufactured from billets. Now special alloys of copper are available which impart special drawing characteristics to the copper, making it possible to manufacture thin-walled tubing.

Copper cake is the largest of the basic copper shapes. Copper cakes are large slabs of copper and may range up to more than 3 feet wide, 35 feet long, and a foot thick, and weigh more than 30 tons. Cake is used by manufacturers to make plates, sheets, strips, and bars.

Other copper products available from refineries include copper powder, which is used in bearings, bushings, brake linings, conductive parts, and circuits; copper sulfate, which is used in fertilizer production; and copper anodes, which are used in copper plating.

The several stages and alternative procedures employed in the copper industry which have been described in this chapter are summarized in the flow sheet, figure 2-2.

Copper Fabrication

Semifabricators are the principal consumers of copper. The two most important types of semifabricating plants are wire mills and brass mills. The wire mills use primary refined copper exclusively, whereas the brass mills use a large proportion of copper scrap, both unrefined and refined. Powder plants and foundries account for less than 2 percent of total U.S. copper consumption.

Factors affecting the location of semifabricating plants are labor availability, transportation costs, and tariffs. Semifabricating is a low profit margin operation and the value added is low. It is also capital intensive.[17] Transportation costs for semifabricated products are high relative to transport costs of the copper inputs. Hence, semifabricating plants are generally located close to industrial markets. Another factor that encourages the location of semifabricating plants in industrialized countries rather than in the less developed producing countries is the

[17] Martin S. Brown and John Butler, *The Production, Marketing and Consumption of Copper and Aluminum* (New York, Praeger, 1968).

tariff structure of the industrialized countries. The United States, Japan, and Western European countries impose a tariff on semifabricated copper products ranging from 5 to 22 percent *ad valorem*, but unwrought copper is admitted either free of duty or at a very low rate.

Semifabricating plants are generally small to medium sized and so scale economies do not appear to be important.[18] It is estimated that in 1969 about 15 companies supplied 75 percent of the world's refined copper, but there were more than 500 semifabricating company groups.[19] The semifabricating plants are often subsidiaries of primary copper producers.

End Uses of Refined Copper

The most important uses for copper, in order of their importance, are electrical and electronic goods, construction, general engineering, transportation, consumer goods, military applications, and coinage. Electrical applications account for about half the copper consumed. Wire and cable are used in telecommunications, electrical wiring, electric motor and generator coil winding, and electronics applications, including computers. Construction is the largest market for brass mill products, although some wire mill products are also used. Major applications include plumbing and heating, as well as wire and cable systèms in building construction. General engineering uses both brass and wire mill products in fittings, valves, bearings, screws, pumps, and so on. Many of these parts are machined from extruded rod. Copper and brass tubing are used for heat exchangers in refrigeration, air conditioning units, freezers, and water coolers. Condenser tubing used in power and other utilities represents a major market for copper alloy tubing. Copper is used in transportation for automobile manufacture, especially radiator construction. It is also used as brass for shipbuilding and in railway equipment. About half of the copper employed for consumer goods is used in durables such as washing machines, refrigerators, radios, televisions, phonographs, tape recorders, and cutlery. Another important application is coinage, especially in the United States. During wartime, copper consumption increases dramatically because of its use in ammunition as shell casings and in other military hardware.

---

[18] Brown and Butler, *Production, Marketing and Consumption of Copper and Aluminum,* chapter 4.

[19] B. R. Stewardson, "The Nature of Competition in the World Market for Refined Copper," *The Economic Record* (June 1970) pp. 169–181.

Substitution and Other Demand-Reducing Developments

There are three types of activities that have a demand-reducing effect: (1) direct substitution, (2) technological substitution, and (3) more efficient use of copper.

Direct substitution is most easily identified and its impact is easier to gauge. The materials that are most commonly substituted for copper are aluminum, stainless steel, certain types of alloys, and plastics. Aluminum has had the largest impact because of its wide adoption for use in high voltage cross-country transmission lines. Attempts have been made to use aluminum in automobile radiators, but its lack of weldability has prevented widespread adoption. Plastic pipe used for household plumbing has replaced copper for some applications. However, with the rise in the cost of petroleum products, it is uncertain how far this trend will proceed. Stainless steel and certain types of specialized alloys have also been substituted for copper in certain applications.

Probably the largest impact on copper demand has come about as a result of technological developments. Undersea cables have been large copper consumers, but the development of microwave technology and communications satellites has substantially reduced the demand for copper in this area. A large amount of copper is still used by intracity communications systems, but if the fiber optics transmission technology proceeds to the commercial stage, a large portion of the existing market for copper in transmission lines will be eliminated.[20]

Efforts to increase the efficiency of copper in its various uses, some of which have been promoted by the copper industry itself, cut both ways. On the one hand they reduce the demand for copper in a specific application, while on the other hand by reducing the relative cost of copper they avoid substitution of other materials; in some cases, copper may become the substitute material. For example, improved copper alloys have made it possible to make thinner walled copper tubing, with the result that it requires substantially less copper to produce a foot of copper tubing of the same diameter today than it did ten or fifteen years ago. To take another example, the copper fins in automobile radiators have been made thinner in recent years, thus reducing both the cost and the weight of copper radiators.[21]

---

[20] "Bell Hopes to Cut Copper Consumption With Increased Use of Fiber Optics," *American Metal Market* (January 24, 1977) p. 28.

[21] See W. Stuart Lyman, "Copper—An Available Resource for the Future," a paper presented to the Society of Automotive Engineers, Automotive Engineering Congress, Detroit, Michigan, February 24–28, 1975, p. 8.

Taken together, these technological developments are undoubtedly reducing the intensity of copper use in the more advanced industrial economies. On the other hand, in the less advanced countries copper-using products are becoming more abundant and copper intensity may be increasing with time. However, the developing countries have displayed a strong preference for advanced technology, a prime example being Indonesia's utilization of a satellite as an integral part of its developing interisland telephone communication network. Thus, the uncertainty regarding the course of these technological developments constitutes one of the major difficulties in projecting the long-run demand for copper. Detailed information on long-run substitution for copper is provided in appendix 5-1.

Secondary Copper

Secondary copper is derived from scrap, of which there are two major categories: "new scrap," a by-product of fabricating operations; and "old scrap," which arises from discarded copper-containing goods and equipment. New scrap does not constitute a net addition to copper supply, and its amount is largely determined by the level of current consumption. Indeed, some new scrap generated by machining and cutting processes is simply reprocessed by the semimanufacturing firm generating it for reuse and is never statistically recorded. In other cases, the new scrap may be sold or treated on toll for reuse by the generating firm. The refining and resale of new scrap takes time, and although the ratio of new scrap production to total copper consumption tends to remain fairly constant, it does change from year to year with the ratio tending to vary directly with the price of copper. Over the period 1964–74 the ratio for the United States averaged about 0.25.

Old scrap is graded into categories related to the composition of the scrap. There are five classifications of unalloyed copper scrap and over thirty classifications of copper base or alloyed scrap. However, a large portion of the scrap consumed falls into four categories: (1) No. 1 wire and heavy copper; (2) No. 2 wire, mixed heavy and light copper; (3) yellow brass; and (4) low-grade scrap and residues. The first category includes all unalloyed copper scrap that is clean, uncoated, and 99.9 percent pure copper. The second category covers unalloyed copper scrap that is relatively free of contaminants and contains between 92 and 96 percent copper. The third category contains copper base scrap that is about 65 percent copper. The fourth category may contain as little as 10 percent copper.[22]

Category (1) scrap is regarded as interchangeable with refined copper in many uses and does not require further refining. However, even the purest copper scrap is not ordinarily used by wire mills in the United States, but category (1) scrap is used directly by ingot makers and brass mills. Category (2) copper is usually treated in a refinery since its copper content is generally lower than that of blister; in some cases, however, it is used directly by brass mills and ingot makers. Many refineries use both primary and secondary feeds as a matter of course. Category (2) scrap can be smelted in an anode furnace and then put through the tankhouse to emerge as electrolytic cathode. Secondary refined copper sells in roughly the same market as primary copper, but with a relatively larger volume of metal being supplied as cathode to brass mills, including producers of copper sheet, strip, and tube. Lower grade copper scrap (categories 3 and 4 above) is normally both smelted and refined. In the United States there are several copper smelters that are referred to as secondary smelters. These smelters are generally small and handle only secondary copper materials. However, the primary smelters also handle copper scrap, and scrap is becoming more widely accepted as a part of normal smelter feed. One effect of this has been the improvement of the eastern U.S. market for copper scrap and a reduction in the demand for primary copper. Both the European and Japanese smelters have historically used large amounts of copper scrap, and it appears that U.S. primary smelters are moving in the same direction. The future role of scrap in the world's supply of copper is discussed in chapter 13.

[22] John E. Tilton and Elizabeth S. Bonczar, "An Economic Analysis of the Determinants of Metal Recycling in the United States: A Case Study of Secondary Copper" (final report to the Bureau of Mines, Department of Interior, Washington, D.C., 1975) p. 9.

Appendix 2-1
Definitions of Common
Underground Mining Techniques

Open Stoping: Consists of extracting the ore from a steeply inclined or vertical tabular ore body, leaving openings behind. It is accomplished by mining downward in successive steps or horizontal slices while standing on unbroken ore (underhanding), or by mining upward (overhead) in successive cuts while standing on timbers. The opening where ore is being extracted is called a stope.

Shrinkage Stoping: In this type of mining, enough broken ore is left in the mined-out space to enable the miners to stand on it in order to drill and blast the ore above. Enough ore is withdrawn from below to maintain an open working space.

Cut and Fill: Similar to shrinkage stoping except that all broken ore is removed after each round of drilling and blasting and waste rock is introduced as fill material. This procedure is used where walls are too weak to stand unsupported.

Sublevel Stoping: This method is used for large inclined or vertical tabular ore bodies that are found in rock that will stand with large openings. This method is used for mechanized mining; haulage levels are rather far apart vertically and intervening blocks are penetrated longitudinally by sublevels at intervals of from 30 to 100 feet. From these sublevels miners drill long holes that permit blasting the ore off in vertical transverse slices which fall into chutes just above the haulage level below.

Block Caving: With this method, large bulk ore bodies are divided into rectangular blocks with a long vertical dimension. The blocks are undercut to induce caving under their own weight and the ore is usually drawn from them at the same rate so as to prevent dilution from waste rock on the margins of the ore body.

3

World Markets for Copper:
An Institutional Analysis

Types of Coppers Traded and their Markets

COPPER IS NOT a homogeneous commodity. The American Society for Testing Materials has classified some forty distinct types of refined copper by metal content, shape, and so on. There is a high degree of substitutability among refined coppers in many uses, and, given time, refiners can shift output among these types. However, some consumers are limited to certain types of coppers while individual refineries cannot produce all types. Nevertheless, over time the prices of all refined coppers tend to move together and to be quoted in terms of a differential from the price of one of the coppers traded on the principal copper exchanges. Until now, the most important has been electrolytic wirebar.[1] In addition to refined coppers, including secondary refined, there is trade in five classifications of unalloyed copper scrap and in over thirty classifications of copper base or alloyed scrap. In 1974 about 70 percent of the total U.S. copper supply consisted of refined copper, of which 83 percent represented primary refined copper and the remainder was refined from scrap. About 60 percent of total copper supplied in the United States normally comes from newly mined ore and the remainder from scrap. About 30 percent of the total supply of copper represents scrap that is consumed directly by semimanufacturers without further refining. Of the total scrap supplied to the market, about one-third is used to make refined copper and the remainder is used directly.

From the standpoint of market behavior in the United States, there is an important distinction between the primary copper industry and

1 Cathode copper may replace wirebar as the most significant product in the future.

the secondary copper industry since the members of the former sell at U.S. producers' prices, while members of the latter tend to sell at prices reflecting those in the "outside market," which at times may differ considerably from primary producers' prices. Members of the primary copper industry include firms integrated from mining through the refining stage (e.g., Anaconda, Kennecott, Phelps Dodge, Inspiration, Magma, and Copper Range); and independent mining firms only partially integrated through the concentrating or smelting stage. These deliver their output to the smelters or refineries of the integrated firms or to a custom smelter or refiner such as ASARCO,[2] which sells at producers' prices. A portion, normally less than 25 percent, of the secondary refined copper is also produced by the primary copper industry. The secondary copper industry not only uses primarily scrap for producing refined copper, but their output is sold at prices related to the outside market of which they form a part. Secondary producers are in a sense "price takers" rather than "price makers," which characterizes the market behavior of the members of the primary producing industry.

It is estimated that the primary producing industry has accounted for 88 percent of the refined copper produced in the United States over the 1949–74 period. This percentage may vary from year to year, and in 1974 was only 83 percent. It should be kept in mind, however, that refined copper normally represents about 70 percent of total copper supplied in the United States, so that the primary producing sector accounts for only about 60 percent of total copper supply. This fact, together with the growing importance of imported refined copper, should be taken into account in appraising the degree of market control by the U.S. primary copper sector.

Since 1945, about 76 percent of U.S. consumption of refined copper has been sold at domestic producers' prices; about 13 percent of annual consumption has been marketed by the principal secondary refiners at prices which generally reflect outside market prices or the prevailing prices for copper scrap plus an operating margin. The remaining 11 percent of U.S. consumption consists of imports from foreign producers and copper handled by U.S. metal merchants which is sold at prices reflecting commodity exchange quotations. It may be said that about one-fourth of refined copper consumption in the United States is marketed on the basis of commodity exchange prices and prices of domestic scrap which also tend to follow closely movements in the commodity exchanges, the most important of which is the London Metal Exchange (LME).

---

[2] ASARCO is also partially integrated into mining and is regarded as a part of the primary copper industry.

Mines selling their concentrates to custom smelters in the primary producing sector are generally paid producers' prices for copper, less smelting and refining charges, freight costs, and other costs connected with selling the copper. If the mine has its own smelter, it will sell the blister to a custom refiner at the producers' price less refining and sales costs. Some sales of concentrates and blister are made to secondary refiners. In such cases the seller will receive a price related to the outside market price, less refining and other charges. Mining firms operating abroad that sell their concentrates or blister to smelters or refiners outside the United States generally receive a price based on the LME price, less smelter and refining charges.

World Pricing Systems for Copper

There are two major categories of pricing systems for refined copper. First, there are the free market prices quoted on the two major exchanges, the London Metal Exchange (LME) and the New York Commodity Exchange (Comex), on which standard copper grades and shapes are bought and sold on a competitive basis, with prices changing continuously. Second, there are the domestic producers' prices charged by copper refineries to local fabricators with prices changing infrequently at the initiative of the sellers. There are also prices quoted by dealers (merchants), such as the New York dealer price; the latter usually fluctuates at a small premium above the prices on the two exchange markets. Outside the United States most sales, whether spot or on contract, are based on the LME price quotations. This applies to a variety of contracts such as those between mining companies selling concentrates and smelters and refineries; those between refineries and fabricators; and those between merchants and fabricators. Quotations by national organizations such as the French Groupement d'Importation et de Repartition des Metaux (GIRM), a nonprofit cooperative that buys copper for the French industry, and other national price quotations such as German Del Notiz price,[3] the Japanese producers' price,[4] the Australian price,[5] and the South African price,[6] are fixed for certain periods of time, but they all tend to follow LME quotations. There are

[3] The Del Notiz price is a weighted average based on reports of German refinery selling prices and German dealer prices.

[4] The Japanese producers' price is fixed every two weeks and is related to the average LME prices during the previous two weeks.

[5] The Australian price is announced periodically by the leading producer, and generally followed by other Australian producers.

[6] The South African price is set at the beginning of each month by the South African producers.

also Canadian producers' prices with some of these tending to follow U.S. producers' prices.

U.S. fabricators buy the bulk of their copper from U.S. and Canadian producers at the U.S. and Canadian producers' prices. Most U.S. producers sell all or a part of their refined production under annual contracts with a specified monthly tonnage. But some producers sell on a month-to-month basis.[7] Fabricators may also purchase copper from secondary refiners or from dealers (merchants), or they may even buy overseas at a price based on the LME price which, with certain exceptions, tends to govern sales of copper outside the United States and Canada. Prices on the Comex and on the LME tend to move together and to influence one another. Prices charged by merchants tend to follow (at a premium) the Comex and LME prices. Merchants obtain their supplies of copper, including scrap, from both domestic and foreign sources at prices governed by the Comex or the LME, or they may operate directly on the Comex and the LME. Merchants have the flexibility to meet short-term changes in demand as well as to supply special requirements. They will also undertake to hedge for producers and consumers who cannot perform the function as effectively through the futures market on the commodity exchanges because of the small tonnages with which they work. Merchants may also act as agents for producers who are selling outside the producers' market.

The Copper Exchanges

Since the bulk of the world's refined copper is sold directly by the refiners to the fabricators, or handled through merchants as described above, only marginal amounts are sold through the LME and the Comex. Of the two exchange markets on which copper is quoted, the LME is more important in terms of volume of transactions, physical deliveries, and influence on world copper prices generally. Prices quoted by producers outside the United States tend to follow LME quotations rather closely and long-term contracts employ a variety of formulas for pricing copper related to LME prices. However, in the case of both LME and Comex, an important function is to provide hedging facilities for both producers and fabricators rather than to act as markets for

---

[7] A month-to-month sales contract permits the consumer to reduce his monthly purchases, but when he does so he lowers his "book position" with the producer. In periods of shortage, producers allocate according to the "book position" so that in such periods the customer might be better off with an annual contract unless his book position remains high. Usually on long-term contracts prices are fixed at the time of delivery on the basis of the producers' price. However, in November 1975 Kennecott introduced a new contract that allows customers to fix the currently ruling producers' price for three months ahead.

spot sales and physical deliveries. Although there is frequently a price differential of several cents per pound for the same type of copper between the two markets as a consequence of the time and cost of shipping copper, government price controls, and other factors, arbitrage transactions between the Comex and the LME tend to limit the amount of the differential. There are a number of important differences in the two markets that require explanation.

The London Metal Exchange (LME). The London Metal Exchange deals exclusively in nonferrous metals—copper, lead, zinc, tin, and silver. Two copper contracts are traded on the LME: one for electrolytic wirebar, and one for electrolytic cathode. Cathodes normally trade at a discount under wirebar, reflecting conversion costs. (See appendix 3-1 for LME contract rules.) Contracts may be traded for "spot," "ninety days," and any market day in between. The minimum contract is for 25 tons and dealings are conducted in multiples of 25 tons. Dealings on the LME are not simply paper transactions. Purchasers can always obtain delivery of metal on the day agreed upon (and in the case of spot transactions, the following day) at any of the registered LME warehouses at the seller's option. Copper for delivery on contract terms is held in warehouses in London, Birmingham, Liverpool, Manchester, Hull, or Glasgow in the United Kingdom; Rotterdam in the Netherlands; Hamburg in Germany; and Antwerp in Belgium. Contracts may not contain any *force majeure* provisions.

Trading on the LME takes place through representatives of member firms who are seated in a circle around the exchange floor and who make bids and offers to each other across the ring. Deals are made when a bid or offer is accepted and contracts are issued promptly. Dealing members accept the responsibility of honoring their own contracts. (This differs from the Comex where the Clearing Association has responsibility for honoring transactions.) Two rings operate daily, Monday through Friday. Trading commences at noon and at 3:45 p.m. Copper, like the other metals on the Exchange, is traded for a period of 5 minutes with two 5-minute sessions. During each trade period or ring, one 5-minute session is devoted to copper wirebar and the other to cathode. Closing prices in the noon session become the official prices and form the basis for the major share of long-term contracts on which LME quotations are based.[8] No official prices are announced as a result

8 The LME daily quotation is based either on the last transaction entered into or on the closing bids and offers made in the short period in which dealings occur. Despite the fact that these prices reflect business involving only small tonnages of copper, these same quotations are used as a basis for pricing the vast bulk of the world's transactions in copper metal outside the United States. Regulations for trading on the LME are reproduced in appendix 3-1.

of the afternoon session. Dealings outside the market ("kerb" dealings) are permitted both in the morning and in the afternoon, and trading is allowed outside regular market hours.

Hedging on the LME. Although the LME provides a market on which consumers may obtain immediate possession of copper or possession at a desired date in the future, a major function is that of a hedging market for the international copper industry. Hence, the forward market is more important than the spot market. In the language of the commodity exchanges, a "contango" occurs when the three-month forward price is at a premium over the "cash" or nearby delivery price, while a "backwardation" is just the opposite—when the "cash" or nearby price is higher than the three-month forward price. In the case of a contango, the price differential between the cash and the forward price rarely exceeds the total cost of warehousing and financing the metal, but there is no limit for backwardation, which generally reflects a market shortage and a heavy demand for copper in the short term.

Hedging provides protection for both producers selling copper for delivery in the future and for fabricators making contracts for the delivery of their products in the future, the prices of which tend to reflect the then current prices of their raw materials. Some of the uses of hedging may be illustrated as follows:

1. Assume a refinery sells copper for delivery three months in the future at the price prevailing on the exchange on the day of delivery. Let us assume that at the time the refiner makes the contract he makes a futures contract on the LME for the delivery of the same amount of copper in three months at 60 U.S. cents per pound. If three months later when he delivers the copper the spot price is 50 cents, he buys on the LME at 50 cents to liquidate his futures contract. Thus, what he loses on the sale of his copper as compared with the price at the time the contract was made, he recoups on the futures transaction.

2. A manufacturer of copper wire may cover his future copper requirements on the LME for the manufacture of wire contracted for sale at a price based on the LME quotation at the time the contract is made.

3. A manufacturer with a stock of 1,000 tons of copper finds the demand for his products slackening and anticipates a decrease in the price of copper. To prevent a decline in the value of his inventory, he can hedge by selling 1,000 tons of copper on the LME for future delivery, thereby maintaining a balanced position of 1,000 tons in inventory against 1,000 tons of copper sold forward on the LME.

The New York Commodity Exchange (Comex). The Comex copper contract calls for delivery of 25,000 pounds of either electrolytic wire-bar, high conductivity fire-refined copper (HCFR), Lake Copper, electrolytic cathode, or 99.88 percent fire-refined copper, all specified according to American Society for Testing Materials (ASTM) standards. Trading on the Comex is conducted by floor brokers working in a ring through bid and offer procedures daily from 9:45 a.m. to 2:10 p.m. At the end of the day purchases and sales on the Comex are "cleared" through the Clearing Association composed of commission houses and trading firms. The association guarantees fulfillment of all contracts handled by its members. (This procedure differs from that of the LME, which is a market of "principals," i.e., the participating brokers underwrite the performance of each contract.) All members of the Clearing Association maintain guarantee funds and fixed original margins within the association. Trading takes place for delivery in seven specified months—January, March, May, July, September, October, and December. Delivery on Comex contracts may be made on any day during these months, at the seller's option, to any registered Comex warehouse. Warehouses are located in Chicago; St. Louis; and Franklin Park in Illinois; Amarillo and El Paso, Texas; Reading, Pennsylvania; New York City; and Tacoma, Washington. Price movements on the Comex have a daily limit of 2 cents per pound for all trading months except the spot months. This limitation, together with the system of trading for delivery in seven selected months and at any day during the month at the seller's option, is designed to prevent the price from being disproportionately affected by a few large transactions. However, this system complicates the use of Comex as a hedging medium and as a basis for establishing prices for contracts outside the market. It also complicates the problem of comparing LME and Comex spot and forward prices and of arbitrage between the two exchange markets. However, formulas have been adopted to compare the prices in the two markets in a manner which will eliminate to the maximum degree possible the distortions arising from the different trading and delivery arrangements.

The Merchants Market. Merchants markets operate in both the United States and in Europe. Merchants deal in a variety of coppers, including scrap, which they sell to secondary refiners. In turn they buy various grades of refined copper for the secondary sector of the copper industry, and sell copper to fabricators who do not have contracts with the primary producers, or to large fabricators when copper from primary producers is in short supply and rationed. Merchant copper is traded at prices related to the Comex or LME prices and many of the physical deliveries of purchases on the Comex or LME result from merchants' transactions. They also carry out arbitrage operations on a worldwide basis. Merchants are usually busiest when the demand for copper is highest. During such times fabricators build up inventories in anticipation of a shortage of supply from primary producers and of higher prices. They look to the merchants for supplies beyond the amounts which they have contracted to buy from the primary producers. Also at such times marginal mines may begin producing which have not committed their production to any given refinery.

Scrap

Prices of scrap vary with the grade and tend generally to move in the same direction as prices in the primary market. The market for scrap is highly competitive and constitutes a significant obstacle to any attempt to control the price of copper. No. 1 (wire) scrap is virtually pure copper which needs only to be melted down and cast into suitable shapes for it to be directly substitutable for primary cathode or billet. Hence, No. 1 scrap follows the free market price rather closely. No. 2 scrap is also new scrap, but must be refined before it is used for making copper wire and other purposes. Since it takes several weeks to collect and refine No. 2 scrap, its price tends to be related to the forward price of refined copper rather than to the spot price. Also, the price of No. 2 scrap reflects the tightness of refining capacity so that when refining capacity is ample for meeting all demands, the margin between No. 2 scrap and the LME three-month wirebar price will be substantially less than when refining capacity is tight. As shown in the table in the following section, in April 1974 the differential between the three-month LME and U.S. No. 2 scrap was 25.1 cents per pound, while in December 1975 when refining capacity was ample, the differential was only 11.6 cents per pound.

Comparison of Copper Prices

U.S. producers' prices are quoted by the primary producers for delivery of wirebar, ingot, and ingot bars to any destination within the continental United States. Most U.S. producers sell at the price prevailing on the date of shipment, but some sales are made at the seller's price prevailing on the date of sale. In addition, there are some sales at the average weekly or monthly producers' quotations for wirebar published in *Metals Week* (E/MJ) or the *American Metal Market*. (As has already been noted, Kennecott in November 1975 introduced a system of contracts for sales at prices fixed for three months.) U.S. producers' prices are usually fairly uniform among the major primary producers, but they sometimes differ for short periods of time, especially when they are substantially higher or lower than the LME. In mid-1975 some U.S.

producers' prices were lower than others for a period of about six weeks. When changes occur either way, one U.S. producer has to initiate the change and they do not all change on the same day, or in the same pattern.[9] In May 1978 Kennecott introduced a major change in its pricing system by setting its price for electrolytic cathode at the spot closing price of the previous Comex trading session plus 2.5 cents per pound. This action was followed by substantial adjustments in the producers' prices of other U.S. primary producers and in July 1978 Anaconda announced that beginning August 1, 1978 it would adopt Kennecott's pricing system.

Although prices in the outside market, including those established by the secondary refiners,[10] the merchant prices, and prices of copper purchased directly from foreign producers, are by no means uniform as indicated in the table below, they tend to move with the prices on the LME and the Comex. Because secondary refiners depend heavily on the copper scrap market for their inputs, their prices tend to reflect prices of copper scrap. Although scrap prices have a cycle of their own, depending on demand and supply conditions, nevertheless they tend to move with the prices on the copper exchanges (see figure 3-1).

The following average prices prevailed during the months of April 1974, June 1974, and December 1975 in the LME, U.S. producers', New York dealers, Comex, and U.S. scrap markets (in U.S. cents per pound):

	April 1974	June 1974	December 1975
LME cash	137.5	110.6	52.2
LME 3-months	129.4	107.4	54.0
U.S. producers'	68.6[a]	86.2	63.8
New York dealers'	129.1	107.4	55.4
Comex first (nearest month)	129.1	103.0	53.7
Comex second	118.5	98.0	54.5
Comex third	113.0	94.5	58.9
U.S. No. 2 scrap	104.3	78.8	43.4

Source: CIPEC, The Copper Market, 2nd quarter, 1974 and 4th quarter 1975.

[a] Maximum price permitted under U.S. government price ceiling.

[9] The extent to which producers discriminate among buyers by shading from the announced producers' price is not known to the author.

[10] ASARCO, AMAX, and Cerro are the principal refiners of scrap in the United States. However, ASARCO uses a substantial proportion of primary ore and blister inputs in its smelting and refining operations. ASARCO sells on a producers' price basis.

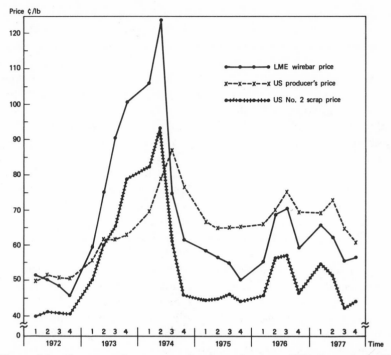

Figure 3-1. Copper prices: quarterly data, January 1972–December 1977. (Data for January 1972–December 1974 from CIPEC annual reports; data for January 1975–December 1977 from CIPEC quarterly review.)

The above quotations are not wholly comparable, for reasons indicated in the above discussion, but they are sufficiently so to reveal the trend in the relationships among the various markets. The first point to be noted is that all three of the relatively free markets for refined copper—the LME, the Comex, and the New York dealer (merchants)—tended to move in harmony without excessively large differentials.[11] However, the Comex nearest month delivery price was lower than the LME cash price when copper prices were near their peak in April 1974, while just the opposite was the case when copper prices had fallen to about their lowest level in December 1975. Also, the New York dealer price tends to be at a premium above the Comex. On the other hand, the U.S. producers' price did not exhibit the wide variations of the free

---

[11] LME prices are quoted in pounds sterling per metric ton. Hence, arbitrage transactions between the LME and the Comex involve the spot and futures markets for dollars and sterling.

market prices, but adjusted moderately with the LME and Comex movements and with a considerable lag. The U.S. producers' price was only half the LME cash price in April 1974 (in part as a result of the U.S. government price ceiling), but was 11.6 cents higher than the LME cash price in December 1975. Finally, it may be noted that during the period of very high copper prices in the first half of 1974, forward prices on both the LME and the Comex were lower than the cash prices (or Comex price for the nearest month), indicating a "backwardation," while during the period of low prices in December 1975, forward prices were above the spot prices, thus indicating a "contango."

The U.S. primary copper industry is frequently characterized by economists as an oligopoly and producers' prices as oligopoly prices. This definition of oligopoly does not imply the absence of competition, the existence and nature of which is explored in chapter 4 of this book. Rather the term oligopoly means that each seller takes into account the effects of his own pricing policies on those of other sellers—a condition which does not exist under pure competition where all sellers are price takers rather than price makers.

Contracts for the Sale of Copper

Producer Contracts and the LME Price

Except for some transactions between the United States and Canada,[12] most international sales by copper producers are based on LME prices. There are, however, a variety of contractual arrangements involving such factors as the date corresponding to the LME price which applies to a particular delivery, the price for the particular grade of refined copper (e.g., cathode versus wirebar), and the smelting and refining charges deducted in sales of concentrate and blister copper. Changes in these arrangements often reflect competitive conditions in the world copper market when the contracts are negotiated or when spot sales are made. The pricing formula may be quite specific as to the date on which the LME price shall apply, e.g., the delivery date or the average price during a particular month or, more commonly, the producer may give the buyer 60 or 90 days over which to price his copper. In the case of contracts providing the buyer with an option to employ any LME price prevailing between the date of shipment and, say, three months

[12] Noranda usually exports refined copper to the United States at U.S. producers' prices.

following shipment, the buyer obviously has considerable advantage in being able to choose the date on which the LME price is lowest. Sometimes only a portion, say, 25 percent, of the amount of the shipment can be priced on the basis of the LME quotations during any particular period, for instance, a week. When pricing is established for a particular day or the average LME price for a given month, the buyer may be given the right to price his copper before the market opens on that day on the basis of quotations on the previous day—a practice known as back-pricing. In the CIPEC countries, producers' contracts for refined copper typically grant the consumer a two-month period over which to price his copper—the month preceding shipment and the month of shipment. In addition, the consumer has the right to price his copper before the market opens based on the quotations from the previous day. However, the back-pricing privilege may be restricted to 25 percent of the monthly shipment being priced on any one day or 50 percent during one week. Recently, CIPEC producers have been discussing the adoption of a uniform contract which would give the buyer less leeway in selecting the quotational period, for example, reducing the period to 30 days.

Contracts for the Sale of Concentrates

Many copper mines, even large ones such as the Bougainville mine in PNG or the Sodimiza mine in Zaire, do not smelter their own ore; they may not even be affiliated with firms that do smelting and refining. In such cases the mining company usually negotiates long-term contracts with smelters and refineries, running from five to fifteen years. The contracts call for the delivery of a certain tonnage each month at prices for contained metal based on the LME price to destinations outside the United States, and the *Metals Week* U.S. producers' price quotations for delivery to the United States. Typically for contracts outside the United States, the base price will be the LME wirebar settlement of the month following the month of arrival at the smelter. The smelting and refining charges are subtracted from the base price for the metal content; freight from the mine to the smelter is also subtracted unless the freight is paid directly by the mine. When the concentrates contain gold or other recoverable metals, the contracts usually provide for payments to the mine for a fixed percentage (generally 90 to 98 percent) of the quoted market price of the by-product metal. Long-term contracts sometimes contain a floor price with a provision that if the market price falls below the floor price for a time, the seller must compensate the buyer for the difference when the market price rises above the floor price.

Contracts differ widely with respect to the determination of the smelting, refining, and transportation charges. Sometimes the refining charges are a fixed percentage of the price of the metal; in other cases a fixed amount (usually in U.S. cents) is charged, or some combination of the two. Smelter charges may take the form of a portion of the concentrates.

Most long-term contracts contain escalation clauses according to which treatment charges are tied to costs of wages, fuel, and so forth, at the smelter. Alternatively, there may be a fixed rate of escalation, that is, a certain percentage increase in treatment cost each year. Contracts may also include "participation" clauses which grant the smelter a share of the copper price above a certain level, for example, 10 percent of the difference between 60 U.S. cents per pound and the equivalent LME quotation at the time of delivery to the smelter.

Costs of smelting, refining, and transportation have been rising very rapidly in recent years. In the early 1960s treatment and refining charges were in the neighborhood of 5 to 6 cents per pound, but by 1975 they had more than tripled to a range of 19 to 21 cents per pound, mainly as a consequence of increased fuel prices, environmental regulations, and other factors raising costs. Long-term contracts made in earlier years with modest escalation provisions (principally by Japanese smelters) have been renegotiated at the request of the buyer. A demand for renegotiation of long-term contracts by the buyer may occur when the demand for copper declines. This occurred in 1975 in the case of some of the Japanese contracts for the purchase of concentrates.

Force majeure clauses are generally written into contracts to prevent either party to a contract from being liable to the other for inability to meet contract terms due to circumstances beyond their control. The typical *force majeure* clause spells out the conditions under which *force majeure* shall apply, such as labor difficulties, mine accidents, inability to secure transportation or fuel, plant breakdowns, and so forth. Shipments may be postponed for a time, but if the *force majeure* continues, say, beyond three months, the contract may give the buyer the right to cancel the contract. Contracts also differ with respect to the obligation of the seller to make up delays in shipments after the conditions giving rise to the *force majeure* have disappeared.

Exchange Rates and Copper Contracts

Buyers and sellers of copper face not only a risk of loss arising from changes in the price of copper, but also of a loss arising from changes in currency values since their future receipts and obligations may involve two or more currencies. This has always been a problem even under the Bretton Woods system when the values of the major currencies tended to remain relatively stable in terms of dollars, with parities changing only infrequently. But with the present system of floating exchange rates, the problem of operating under contracts, and even of properly interpreting changes in quotations on the LME or Comex, has become quite complex.

Take the case of an Australian producer selling concentrates to a Japanese smelter with payments made in U.S. dollars based on LME quotations. The Australian producer's local wages and other costs are in Australian dollars while debt service and external purchases may be in U.S. dollars, sterling, or Australian dollars. (Conceivably the contract may call for smelter charges tied to the exchange value of the yen, in which case the seller would bear the exchange risk arising from a change in the Australian dollar-yen rate.) Japanese smelter costs, on the other hand, are in yen, except for certain external costs which may be in dollars or in other currencies. At least four currencies are involved in the operation of the contract, all of which may be changing in relation to one another over a given period. Some of the risks arising from changes in exchange rates can be avoided through hedging in the foreign currency markets, but it is usually not practical to hedge all of them.

LME quotations are in sterling, but the dollar equivalent of the spot price depends upon the daily sterling-dollar exchange rate. Contracts made by an American firm to buy copper at the three-month forward LME price would require the American to buy forward sterling if he were to avoid a possible loss arising from an appreciation of sterling in terms of the dollar. Likewise, the sale of copper for delivery against sterling three months hence would require the American to sell sterling forward in terms of dollars to avoid a loss arising from a depreciation of sterling in terms of the dollar. The same problem is faced by buyers and sellers in other countries where different currencies are involved in their contracts.

Prior to August 1971, the U.S. dollar was the universally recognized international standard of value and it was convertible by foreign central banks into gold at $35 an ounce. However, in the present period of floating exchange rates, a change in the LME price of sterling or the dollar equivalent as determined by the dollar-sterling rate may reflect in part a change in the exchange relationships among the world's leading currencies rather than simply a change in the fundamental demand and supply forces in the world market for copper. For example, if both the dollar and sterling declined sharply in relation to most of the other leading international currencies, a rise in the LME sterling (or the dollar price) of copper might reflect in large part the depreciation of sterling (or the dollar) in relation to other currencies, rather than a *real* rise in the world price of copper.

In the spring of 1976 speculation on the currency markets probably had a direct effect on the price of copper. With sterling weak and expected to decline further, there is evidence that some British traders (who are restricted by British exchange controls from taking speculative positions in foreign currencies) bought copper as a hedge against a decline in the value of the pound sterling. Such purchases are believed to have been responsible for a substantial portion of the rise in the LME copper price in the spring of 1976. With the improvement in the outlook for sterling in early 1977, this speculative support for copper disappeared.

Appendix 3-1
LME Contract Rules (as of 1973)

Contract Rules

Rule A—Members of the London Metal Exchange, in their dealings with other Members, shall be responsible to and entitled to claim against one another, and one another only, for the fulfillment of every Contract for Metals.

Rule B—In these Rules the expression "Members of the London Metal Exchange" include firms and Companies who, although not themselves Subscribers to the Exchange, are represented and deal thereon by and through "Representative Subscribers" to the Exchange acting as the representatives or Agents of such Firms or Companies.

Rule C—If any Member of the Metal Exchange fails to meet his engagements to another Member, whether by failing to provide on the due date documents (i.e. Bills of Lading, Warrants or Delivery Orders according to the metals dealt in) to meet sales made or money to pay for metals bought, or by making default in fulfilling any other obligation arising out of dealings made subject to the Rules and Regulations of the London Metal Exchange, notice of the default shall be given at once in writing to the Committee of the Exchange and the Committee shall immediately fix and publish a settlement price or prices as at the date of such communication to them for all contracts which the defaulter may have open under these Rules, whether with Members or with parties who are not Members. All such contracts shall forthwith be closed and balanced, by selling to or buying from the defaulting Member such metals as he may have contracted to deliver or take, at the settlement prices fixed for this purpose by the Committee, and any difference arising whether from or to the party in default shall become payable forthwith notwithstanding that the prompt day or other day originally stipulated for the settlement of the transaction may not have arrived. In fixing settlement price under this Rule, the Committee may in their discretion take into consideration the extent and nature of the transaction which the defaulting Member has open and any other circumstances which they may consider should affect their decision. In any case where the Committee shall be of opinion that the default is not due to the insolvency of the defaulter the Committee shall by resolution negate the application of this rule. Any claim arising out of a default not due to insolvency shall be settled by arbitration in the usual manner. This rule shall apply to cases in which at or after the decease of a Member the engagements entered into by him are not duly met.

Rule D—If any Contract made subject to the Rules and Regulations of the London Metal Exchange between a Member and a Non-Member in the event of the Non-Member failing to meet his engagements arising out of any such contract whether by failing to provide on the due date documents to meet sales or money to take up documents (as the case may be) or otherwise howsoever or of his failing to supply or maintain such margin (if any) for which the Member is entitled to call and has called, or in the event of the Non-Member suspending payment or becoming bankrupt or committing any act of bankruptcy or (being a Company) in the event of its going into liquidation whether voluntary or otherwise, the Member shall have the right to close all or any such Contracts outstanding between them by selling out or buying in against the Non-Member (as the case may be) and any differences arising therefrom shall be payable forthwith notwithstanding that the prompt day or other day originally stipulated for settlement may not have arrived.

Rule E—Payments for Warrants or other documents (when deliverable under the Contracts), unless otherwise stipulated on the contract, shall be made by cash in London, or by cheque on a London clearing bank, either made in Seller's option. The documents shall be rendered in London against the cash or cheque, as the case may be, and not later than 2:30 p.m. on the prompt or settling day.

Rule F—Contracts wherein Buyer or Seller (as the case may be) has the option to uplift or to deliver, prior to the prompt or settlement date by giving previous notice of his intention, shall have the notice reckoned by market days, such notice, unless otherwise stipulated at time of purchase or sale, shall be as follows: On a Contract with the option to uplift or to deliver during one calendar month or less, one day's notice shall be given, and on a contract with the option beyond two and up to three calendar months, three days notice shall be given previous to the date on which delivery is required, or will be made. Notice shall be given for the whole quantity stated in the contract and shall be tendered in writing and delivered at the office of the seller of the option not later than noon on the day of notice. Rent shall only be allowed to Buyer to the actual day of settlement, and there shall not be any allowance of interest for a payment made prior to the prompt date.

Rule G—Prompt or settlement dates falling on Saturday, Sunday, or a Bank Holiday, which days are not market days, shall be settled as follows: Prompts falling on Saturday shall be settled on the Friday previous, but should the preceding Friday be a Bank Holiday the prompt shall be extended to the Monday following, should both the Friday preceding and the Monday following be Bank Holidays, the prompt shall be settled on the Thursday previous. Prompts falling on Sunday should be extended to the Monday following, but should that Monday be a Bank Holiday the prompt shall be extended to the Tuesday following, should both the following Monday and Tuesday be Bank Holidays, the prompt shall then be extended to the Wednesday following. Prompts falling on a Bank Holiday shall be extended to the day following, and if the Bank Holiday falls on Friday the prompts shall be extended to the Monday following, but should the Friday be Good Friday, prompts falling on that day shall be settled on the Thursday previous. If Christmas Day falls on Monday, prompts falling on that day shall be extended to the Wednesday following but if Christmas Day falls on Tuesday, Wednesday, Thursday, or Friday, prompts falling on that day shall be settled on the day previous.

Rule H—The establishment, or attempted establishment of a "corner" or participation directly or indirectly in either, being detrimental to the interests of the Exchange the Committee shall, if in their opinion a "corner" has been or is in the course of being established, have power to investigate the matter and to take whatever action it considers proper to restore equilibrium between supply and demand. Any member or members may be required to give such information as is in his or their possession relative to the matter under investigation.

Rule J (Option)—On the day on which notice is due, the holder of the option shall, except in cases to which Rule C applies, declare in writing before 12 o'clock noon whether he exercises or abandons the option, and if he fails to make such declaration the option shall be considered as abandoned. Options (subject to Rule F above) may be declared for less than the total optional quantity in quantities of 25 tons for, Copper-Electrolytic Wirebars, H.C.F.B. Wirebars, Cathodes, or Fire Refined, 5 tons for Standard Tin, 25 tons for Standard Lead, and 25 tons for Standard Zinc or multiples thereof, only one declaration against each contract being allowed. In cases to which Rule C applies the prices fixed by the Committee, at which outstanding contracts are to be closed, shall equally apply to all option contracts, and all options shall be automatically determined, and be deemed to have been either exercised or abandoned according as the prices may be in favour of or against the defaulter and whether the defaulter be the Seller or the Buyer of an option, and the option money shall be brought into account. In contracts with optional prompts, the price which shall be taken as the basis of settlement shall be the settlement price fixed by the Committee under Rule C for the prompt most favourable to the holder of the option.

Rule K (Clearing)—All contracts made between Members of the London Metal Exchange who are entitled to deal in the Ring, either for Copper-Electrolytic Wirebars, H.C.F.R. Wirebars, Cathodes or Fire Refined, Standard Tin, Standard Lead, or Standard Zinc, shall be settled through the Clearing, except when a Member insists on his right to receive cash instead of cheque from the Member to whom he has sold, in which case the Seller shall give notice to his Buyer before noon on the market day preceding the settling day, and such transaction shall then be exempted from settlement through the Clearing. The rules governing the Clearing of all Contracts shall be those in existence at the time fixed for the fulfillment of the contract. Copies of such rules may be obtained from the Secretary of the Exchange.

Rule L—In the case of strikes, lock-outs, or other unforseen contingencies, in London, or other authorised port, which prevent or delay the discharge and or warehousing of Copper-Electrolytic Wirebars, H.C.F.R. Wirebars, Cathodes, or Fire Refined, Standard Tin, Standard Lead and/or Standard Zinc, the Seller may be allowed to postpone delivery if he can prove to the satisfaction of the Committee (of which proof the Committee shall be the sole judge) that he does not hold available metal in warehouse with which to fulfill his contracts and that he has metal of the requisite quality which has arrived in London or any other authorized port at least ten days prior to the earliest prompt for which relief is asked, or has metal of the requisite quality in his works, but the delivery, discharge and/or warehousing of which is prevented or delayed, as aforesaid. He must also deposit with the Secretary of the Exchange such sum as the Committee may require but not exceeding £5 per ton in the case of Copper, Lead and Zinc, and £10 per ton in the case of Tin. No interest will be allowed on deposits, which will be returned after delivery of Warrants. Should his application be passed by the Committee he shall deposit documents or other proof to the satisfaction of the Committee with the Secretary of the Exchange, who shall issue Certificates for Copper, Lead and Zinc in quantities of 25 tons, and Certificates for Tin in quantities of 5 tons. The Seller shall deliver these Certificates to his Buyer. The Certificates will then constitute a good delivery on the Clearing within the period stated thereon and differences must be settled on the prompt day. The holder of a Certificate must present it to the firm named thereon not later than 2:30 p.m. on the day following that on which he receives notice in writing from his Seller that the Warrant for the actual Copper, Tin, Lead or Zinc, is ready. He must take up the Warrant against payment at the settlement price fixed on the preceding market day, receiving or paying any difference between this and the price mentioned on the Certificate. In the event of the price on the Certificate being above or below the settlement price operative on the day of delivery the receiver shall pay or be paid the amount of any difference. No other payment shall pass except against delivery of the actual Warrant in case of any dispute, the Committee's ruling to be final. A fee of 5/– to be paid by the Applicants for each Certificate issued.

Arbitration

1. All disputes arising out of or in relation to contracts subject to the Rules and Regulations of the London Metal Exchange shall be referred to two arbitrators, one to be appointed by each party to the difference from the Arbitration Panel of the London Metal Exchange, such arbitrators having power to appoint a third arbitrator from the Panel and having all the powers conferred on arbitrators by the Arbitration Act 1950 or any statutory modification thereof for the time being in force. The Secretary of the Committee of the London Metal Exchange (hereafter called "the Secretary") shall be notified in writing by each party of the appointment of the arbitrators. The arbitration shall take place at the London Metal Exchange.

2. Persons eligible for appointment to the Arbitration Panel shall be members of the Exchange, their partners, or co-directors (as the case may be) or members of their staff. Appointment to and removal from the Panel shall be made, at their sole discretion, by the Committee of the London Metal Exchange who will also be responsible for maintaining a panel of sufficient size.

3. In the event of either party to the difference (a) failing to appoint an arbitrator, or (b) failing to give notice in writing or by cable of such appointment to reach the other party within 14 days after receiving written or cabled notice from such other party of the appointment of an arbitrator (any notice by either party being given to the other by cable or by registered post addressed to the usual place of business of such other party), or (c) in the case of death, refusal to act, or incapacity of an arbitrator, then, upon written or cabled request of either party an arbitrator shall be appointed from the said Arbitration Panel by the Committee of the London Metal Exchange.

4. In case the two arbitrators appointed as aforesaid, whether originally or by way of substitution, shall not within three calendar months after the appointment of the arbitrator last appointed deliver their Award in writing, or

choose a third arbitrator, then the said Committee on the written request of either party shall appoint a third arbitrator selected from the said Arbitration Panel to act with the two aforesaid arbitrators.

5. The Award in writing of the arbitrators or any two of them shall be made and delivered in triplicate to the Secretary within a period of three calendar months from the date of the acceptance of the appointment by the arbitrator last appointed.

6. Every Award made pursuant to any provision of this Rule shall be conclusive and binding on the parties to the arbitration, subject to appeal as hereinafter mentioned.

7. The procedure upon arbitration shall be as follows:–

(a) Within a period of 21 days after the appointment of the second of the two arbitrators so appointed, each party shall deliver to the arbitrators and to each other a statement of case in writing with the originals, or copies, of any documents referred to therein. All such documents to be in the English language or accompanied by certified translations into English.

(b) If either party shall make default in delivery such statements and documents (due consideration being given to time occupied by mails), the arbitrators shall proceed with the case on the statement before them, provided always that, in the sole discretion of the arbitrators, an extension of time may be allowed for the delivery of such statements and documents.

(c) The arbitrators shall appoint a day for a hearing within 28 days, or such further time as the arbitrators shall in their sole discretion allow, after the expiry of the 21 days in accordance with Section 7(a), and shall give due notice in writing thereof to the parties, who may, and if required by the arbitrators shall, attend and shall submit to examination by the arbitrators and produce such books and documents as the arbitrators may require. Each party shall be entitled to produce verbal evidence before the arbitrators.

(d) Neither Counsel, nor Solicitor shall be briefed to appear for either party without the consent of the arbitrators.

(e) The arbitrators may engage legal or other assistance.

(f) The arbitrators may adjourn the hearing from time to time, giving due notice in writing to the parties of the resumed hearing, and the arbitrators may, if they think fit, proceed with such a resumed hearing in the absence of either party or of both parties.

(g) Where any change takes place in the constitution of the tribunal of arbitrators, either by substitution or otherwise, the new tribunal shall appoint a day for the hearing which shall not be later than 28 days, nor earlier than 7 days, after the change. Each party, if desiring to do so, may submit an Amended Statement of Case, with a copy to the other party, which must reach the new tribunal within seven days of its appointment.

(h) In the event of a third arbitrator being appointed, the provisions contained in Section 9 Sub-Section 1 of the Arbitration Act 1950 shall not apply to any reference.

(i) The cost of the arbitration shall be at the sole discretion of the arbitrators. The arbitrators shall fix the amount of their remuneration. The

Award shall state separately the amount of such costs and remuneration and by whom they shall be paid in the event of either or both parties having been granted permission by the arbitrators to be legally represented at the hearing, the arbitrators may take into consideration any legal costs which have been incurred.

(j) The Award shall be deposited with the Secretary who shall forthwith give notice of receipt thereof in writing to both parties, and a copy of such Award shall be delivered to both parties on payment by either party of the costs specified in the Award, which payment shall not affect any provision of the Award.

(k) At the time of issuing their Award, all statements and all documents lodged with the arbitrators, shall be delivered by them to the Secretary, by whom they shall be retained until the expiration of the time for giving notice of appeal, as hereafter mentioned, after which the Secretary shall, unless there shall be such appeal, return them to the parties concerned.

8. Either party shall have the right to appeal against the Award to the Committee of the London Metal Exchange.

9. The method of appeal against the award shall be as follows:–

(a) The party making the appeal shall (i) within 21 days of the date of the Award give notice in writing of such appeal to the Secretary, and to the other party and shall at the same time state the grounds for appeal, (ii) deposit with the Secretary the sum of £200, and in addition the sum, if any, which shall be payable under the Award by the Appellant.

(b) Upon the receipt of such Notice of Appeal the Committee shall within 4 weeks nominate not less than five members, (hereinafter called "the Appeal Committee") to hear the Appeal. Members of the Appeal Committee shall be members of the Committee of the London Metal Exchange and/or members of the Board of the Metal Market & Exchange Co. Ltd.

(c) The procedure on appeal shall as far as possible be similar to that above provided for the original hearing, except that all statements and documents delivered to the Secretary under Section 7(k) shall be laid before the Appeal Committee, who may, however, require such further statement or statements or other information or documents from either or both of the parties, as the Appeal Committee may think necessary.

(d) The decision in writing of the majority of the Appeal Committee (which latter shall not at any time number less than five) shall be final and binding on all parties, and the Appeal Committee shall also decide whether the whole or any part of the said deposit of £200 shall be returned to the Appellant or be forfeited.

(e) The Appeal Committee shall have the same discretion regarding costs as is given to the arbitrators under Section (7)(i) and shall fix the amount of their remuneration and direct by whom it shall be paid.

(f) All statements and all documents lodged with the Appeal Committee shall, together with the Award, be deposited by them with the Secretary by whom they shall be retained until the costs and fees specified in the Award have been paid by either party. On payment, which shall not affect any provision of the Award, a copy of the Award shall be delivered to both parties and all documents returned to the parties concerned.

LME Copper Rules

Contract

25 Tons (56,000 lbs.) or multiples thereof.

Quotations

Pounds sterling and quarters (5/-d) thereof per long ton.

Minimum Fluctuation

5/-d per ton – £6 5s Od per contract.

Special Rules

1. *Quality*

   i *Wirebars* The Copper delivered under this contract must be in the form of wirebars of standard dimensions in the weight range 200 lbs. to 275 lbs. and may be either –
   (a) Electrolytic Copper or
   (b) High Conductivity Fire Refined Copper.
   In the latter case (b) a deduction of £20 per ton shall be allowed on the invoice.

   All Copper delivered must be of brands approved by and registered with the Committee, and must conform with the current appropriate standard of either the B.S.I. or the A.S.T.M.

   ii *H.C.F.R.* The Copper delivered under this contract must be High Conductivity Fire Refined Copper in the form of wirebars of standard dimensions in the weight range 200 lbs. to 275 lbs. All Copper delivered must be of brands approved by and registered with the Committee and must conform with the current appropriate standard of either the B.S.I. or the A.S.T.M.

   iii *Cathodes* The Copper delivered under this contract must be Electrolytic Copper in the form of cathodes assaying not less than 99.90 per cent of copper (silver being counted as copper). All Copper delivered must be of brands approved by and registered with the Committee, and must conform with the current appropriate standard of either the B.S.I. or the A.S.T.M.

   iv *Fire Refined* Sellers under this contract have the option to deliver each 25 tons, either in: –

   Class A—High Grade Fire Refined Copper assaying not less than 99.88 per cent of copper (silver being counted as copper) in the form of ingots or ingotbars, at contract price.

   Class B—Fire Refined Copper assaying not less than 99.70 per cent of copper (silver being counted as copper) in the form of ingots or ingotbars, at contract price less £7 per ton.

   All Copper delivered must be of brands conforming to the appropriate class as approved by and registered with the Committee.

2. *Settlement*

Contracts shall be settled on exact quantities of 25 tons at the official Settlement price quoted by the Committee operative on the prompt date. Buyer and Seller paying or receiving, as the case may be, the difference, if any, between the Settlement price and the contract price.

3. *Delivery*

The Copper shall be delivered on the prompt date in warehouse, either London, Birmingham, Manchester, Liverpool, Birkenhead, Hull, Newcastle-on-Tyne, Glasgow, Avonmouth, Swansea, Rotterdam, Hamburg (free port area) or Antwerp in seller's option. In all cases the warehouse must be one approved by and registered with the Committee. Warrants tendered in fulfillment of contracts shall be invoiced at the Settlement price mentioned in Rule 2 above in parcels each of 25 tons or a multiple thereof (each 25 tons to be treated as a separate contract). Warrants shall be for 25 tons each (two per cent either more or less), each parcel of 25 tons shall be of one brand, shape and size, and shall lie at one warehouse. Rent shall be allowed on the invoice.

4. *Weights*

The word "TON" wherever appearing in this contract shall be a long ton of 2240 lbs. In the case of warrants where the weights are shown in kilogrammes conversion shall be at the rate of 1016 kilogrammes to one long ton. Warrant weights in all cases shall be accepted as between buyer and seller.

5. *Warrants*

   i *Wirebars and H.C.F.R.*   Each warrant must state the brand and whether Electrolytic or H.C.F.R. and the wirebars comprising each parcel of 25 tons shall be uniform weight subject to the usual tolerances, and the wirebar weight and the number of wirebars comprising each parcel must be shown on the Warrant.

   ii *Cathodes*   Each Warrant must state the name of the producer and the number of plates comprising each parcel.

   iii *Fire Refined*   Each Warrant must state the brand.

6. *Exchange Control Regulations*

If Rotterdam, Hamburg or Antwerp Warrants are delivered to a resident of the United Kingdom not participating in the Bank of England Metals Scheme in fulfillment of the contract, the seller must issue a C.M. form in accordance with the procedure currently in force under the Scheme. The buyer must conform with the requirements expressed on those parts of the C.M. form which he receives from the seller.

7. *Disputes*

Any dispute under this contract to be settled by arbitration in accordance with the Rules and Regulations of the London Metal Exchange.

(In the above Rules "The Committee" means the Committee of the London Metal Exchange.)

4

Copper Prices and Costs:
An Historical Review

Brief Review of Copper Prices

FROM THE analysis of the world market structure for copper given in chapter 3, it is obvious that the market for copper is not purely competitive and that there are significant price differentials for virtually the same product both within the United States and between the United States and the rest of the world. This does not mean that there is a strong collusive group of sellers that is able to keep prices well above competitive levels for long periods of time. For the years 1954–77, average annual U.S. producers' prices for refined copper were higher than the average annual LME price during only thirteen years; in the remaining eleven years, average annual U.S. producers' prices were less than the LME price (see figure 4-1). The reasons why U.S. producers' prices have been frequently below the LME price and the outside market prices in the U.S. are to be found in a combination of U.S. government and industry policies that will be examined in a later section in this chapter.

Clearly U.S. producers' prices have been less volatile and sensitive to speculative pressures and to short-run shifts in copper demand and supply. This has sometimes been given as an argument for eliminating LME quotations as the basis for most transactions in copper in the world outside the U.S. primary copper sector, and adopting a world producers' price. We shall examine this argument critically (and then reject it) in a later chapter, but the following discussion of copper prices and cartel activities designed to maintain prices has considerable relevance for this argument.

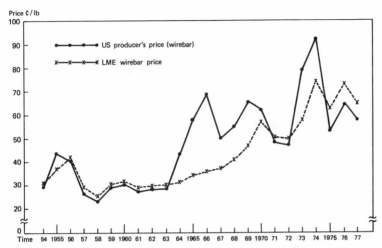

Figure 4-1.   Copper prices: annual data, 1954–77. (Data from CIPEC quarterly and annual reports and Orris Herfindahl, *Copper Costs and Prices: 1870–1957*, Baltimore, Johns Hopkins University Press for Resources for the Future, 1959, pp. 188–189.)

Copper Prices Before World War II

Orris Herfindahl has provided a detailed history of U.S. and world copper prices over the 1870–1957 period and of the numerous private collusive arrangements and government activities designed to control prices. These activities occurred during much of this entire period.[1] I shall not repeat this material except to summarize briefly the results on prices. Cartel action, whether limited to U.S. producers or world wide, has tended to be of short duration. When prices rose above world competitive levels, increased investment and production were encouraged and it became impossible to hold prices in the face of expanding inventories. Collusive efforts of U.S. producers in the early 1870s managed to achieve a substantial price differential between U.S. and foreign prices for a few years, and international cartels, such as the Secrétan operation based in France in the late 1880s, also raised world prices above competitive levels. Similar short-lived successes were achieved by the U.S. Amalgamated Copper Company for the period 1889–1901, which had the cooperation of some foreign copper producers, but the U.S. producers bore the brunt of sales restrictions that resulted in large

---

[1] Orris C. Herfindahl, *Copper Costs and Prices: 1870–1957* (Baltimore, Johns Hopkins University Press for Resources for the Future, 1959) chapters 4, 5, and 6.

inventory accumulations. Two U.S. copper export associations organized under the Webb–Pomerene Act, the first operating in 1918–23
and the second in 1926–32 (the latter including both U.S. and foreign firms), also managed to affect U.S. and to some extent world prices,
but again the brunt of the restrictions was on U.S. firms. U.S. domestic
prices were maintained at higher levels than foreign prices in the face
of U.S. exports. The depression of the 1930s was marked by the levying
of a 4-cent per pound U.S. tariff in 1932 and government encouragement
of U.S. copper industry collusion to control prices and production under
the National Recovery Administration. In 1935 an international cartel
was formed which included the foreign subsidiaries of U.S. companies
in Chile and Africa and the British and Belgian mining subsidiaries in
Africa. The effects of the cartel on world prices were apparently not
very great, but the U.S. price was higher than the London price most of
the period from 1936 to 1939, despite the fact that the United States was
a net exporter of copper.[2]

Prices After World War II

During World War II, private cartel arrangements were replaced by
direct government controls nearly everywhere and the LME remained
closed until August 1953. Following the war, copper prices tended to
decline, reflecting the sharp drop in demand, until the Korean War,
when they rose sharply. During the early 1950s, U.S. prices were held
below foreign prices by U.S. price controls, and production and prices
were influenced in the late 1950s by quantitative controls on U.S. exports, the operations of the U.S. copper stockpile, and the encouragement to production provided by the Defense Production Agency. U.S.
producers' prices tended to remain below the LME price until 1956. In
that year they declined less than the LME price, which broke sharply,
and thereafter average annual U.S. producers' prices were above the
LME price until 1964 when the LME price rose by 50 percent.

Prior to the mid-1960s, a substantial portion of non-U.S. copper output was not sold at the LME price, but at prices related to the U.S.
producers' prices. Prior to 1966 a major portion of Chile's copper output was sold to the United States at U.S. producers' prices. The Chilean
government was anxious to sell at a higher price and in 1965 raised its
export price to the United States from 36 to 38 cents per pound, resulting in a similar rise in U.S. producers' prices. The U.S. government then
brought pressure on U.S. producers to decrease their price to 36 cents

[2] Ibid., pp. 121–122.

per pound. Accompanying this pressure was a release of copper from
the national stockpile and a suspension of the 1.7 cents per pound im-
port tax. There was also an agreement made with the Chilean government to permit the export of 100,000 tons of copper to the United
States at the domestic price of 36 cents per pound. This agreement
included a $10 million low-interest U.S. government loan to Chile.[3]
Nevertheless, Chile began raising its export prices by stages toward the
LME price which in April 1966 reached 88 cents per pound as against
U.S. producers' prices of 36 cents per pound. In July 1966 the Chilean
Copper Corporation announced an increase in the price of copper exports to 70 cents per pound, in line with the LME price at that time.
Meanwhile, the Zambian and Belgian Congo copper producers, which
had been selling at producers' prices since 1964, resumed selling at the
LME price so that after 1966 virtually all major foreign producers
(except Noranda in sales to the United States) sold at the LME price,
while U.S. producers continued to sell at domestic producers' prices
which from time to time were held down by the U.S. government by
sales from the U.S. stockpile, by direct price controls (which were initiated in 1971), or by jawboning.

CIPEC

By the late 1960s only the U.S. primary producing sector exercised any
degree of market power by retaining a pricing system that differed from
that of the rest of the world. However, with the fall in copper prices in
1966–67, there was created in June 1967 an intergovernmental organization consisting of four of the world's largest copper exporters—Chile,
Peru, Zaire, and Zambia—which called itself the Intergovernmental
Council of Copper Exporting Countries (CIPEC).[4] This intergovernmental effort was sparked not only by the fall in copper prices, but was
undoubtedly related to the Chileanization program initiated by President Frei which involved greatly increased participation of the Chilean
government in the copper industry, and to the recently won political
independence of Zaire and Zambia. CIPEC members debated for a long
time on how they should attempt to influence copper prices, but took
no overt action until after the sharp fall in copper prices beginning in

[3] Raymond F. Mikesell, "Conflict and Accommodation in Chilean Copper," in *Foreign Investment in the Petroleum and Mineral Industries* (Baltimore, Johns Hopkins
University Press for Resources for the Future, 1971) chapter 15.
[4] In 1975 Indonesia joined CIPEC as a permanent member while Australia and
Papua New Guinea and, more recently, Mauritania and Yugoslavia, became associate
members without vote.

mid-1974. Two actions were taken by CIPEC that year. First, there were
negotiations with the Japanese industry for an agreement whereby
Japan would cease exporting refined copper, coupled with a reduction
of 15 percent in shipments of concentrates to Japan from several mines
in nonmember countries. The second action was a voluntary agreement
among the CIPEC members to limit copper shipments in 1975 to 90
percent of the 1974 average. In April 1975, with the continuing fall in
copper prices, CIPEC members agreed to limit shipments to 15 percent
below the 1974 level and to cut back production in order to avoid continued accumulation of stocks. These agreements were not fully observed and, in any case, the actions taken did not have a significant effect
on copper prices. In fact, cutbacks by private U.S. and Canadian mines
were considerably larger than those of CIPEC members between 1974
and 1975. In 1976–77 CIPEC took part in the efforts of UNCTAD and
the Paris Conference on International Economic Cooperation (CIEC)
to establish some kind of international commodity stabilization agreement for copper which would be participated in by both copper-
producing and copper-importing countries. We discuss these efforts,
along with the economics of copper price stabilization, in chapter 7.

Competition and Market Power in the Copper Industry

There is no clear-cut answer to the question of whether the copper
industry is competitive, nor is there a satisfactory measure of the degree
of competition. The fact that the U.S. primary copper sector can maintain a common producers' price for several months in the face of higher
or lower prices in the outside market indicates that the primary sector
can exercise short-term market power, but this does not mean that, in
the absence of concerted intergovernmental action, the industry can
constrain the growth of capacity or maintain prices indefinitely above
long-term competitive levels. The conclusion reached by Herfindahl
in 1958 that, "other than during the well-defined periods of joint action,
competitive forces in this industry have been strong enough to induce
investment and production when profit over the necessary return to
capital appears" would seem to be valid today.[5]

As was noted in chapter 1, there exists a fairly high degree of concentration in the U.S. primary copper industry, and the larger primary
producers are integrated from mining into the fabrication stage. However, this degree of concentration has been declining with the emergence

[5] Herfindahl, *Copper Costs and Prices*, p. 238.

of several new mine producers since the 1950s, including Newmont, Duval, Cyprus, and ASARCO. Moreover, the primary copper sector represents only 60 percent of total U.S. copper consumption, and concentration of ownership of copper production in the rest of the world has declined substantially in the past twenty years. Not only is the U.S. primary copper sector faced with substantial competition from the secondary copper sector, but U.S. firms are not in a position to isolate the U.S. market for refined copper from imports from abroad through collusive action with large foreign copper firms and through control of their own foreign subsidiaries in Chile and Africa.

Copper mining is characterized by high fixed costs and even the variable costs such as labor are not as flexible as those for a manufacturing firm since unemployed workers are inclined to move from the mining communities rather than remain until they are rehired. In developing countries, it is often difficult for private mining firms to lay off workers, and government mining firms may be constrained by political factors from doing so. High startup costs also tend to discourage shutdowns, although sometimes mines reduce the number of days a week or month that they operate. On the other hand, it is not possible to expand output significantly beyond rated capacity for a mine without additional capital expenditures, which requires considerable time. All of this suggests that it is difficult to adjust production in the short run to changes in demand, especially at the mining stage. It is possible to produce for inventory if the price is expected to rise soon enough to cover the storage and interest costs of inventories. Also, large private mining firms can shut down marginal mines and smelters in some areas, while maintaining the output of their lower cost operations. These adjustments, along with producing for inventory, give them greater flexibility than smaller mining firms.

The large integrated U.S. firms in the primary copper industry do possess a considerable amount of short-term market power by reason of their dominance of the market for refined copper. Fabricators are heavily dependent upon the primary copper sector for supplies and primary copper prices are less subject to the sharp fluctuations of outside market prices. By being integrated into the refining stage, their own mine production is not subject to refinery bottlenecks and their fabricating affiliates have an assured supply of refined copper in periods of shortage. There are economies in integrated operations both in transportation costs and in planning capacities at several stages of production. They can adjust to a reduction in demand by shutting down high-cost mines and the nearby processing plants that serve them, and their financial strength enables them to produce for inventory at certain stages as an alternative to reducing production.[6] In periods of heavy demand they can supplement their mine output by using scrap or by importing concentrates and blister. The dominant integrated primary producers also have affiliate relationships with nonintegrated firms producing at various stages from mines to refineries.

It has been estimated that nearly half of the U.S. semifabrication industry is affiliated with the large, primary copper producers. Some aspects of the competitive advantage of integration into the fabrication stage are not altogether clear, but such integration has been the subject of antitrust suits. It has been alleged that integrated primary copper producers seek to keep prices of fabricated products low and rely on the sale of primary metal for the bulk of their profits, while the independent fabricators want to raise product prices and margins. On the other hand, independent fabricators would appear to suffer less in a recession since they benefit from lower raw materials costs, especially when outside market prices fall by more than the producers' prices; while the integrated producers with high fixed costs undergo an increase in total unit costs as output and earnings decline.

Barriers to Entry

J. S. Bain classified the U.S. primary copper industry as one having substantial barriers to entry.[7] The principal types include scale economies, capital costs, and control of ore reserves. There are no significant capital or technical barriers to entry into mining,[8] and a number of small mines have come on-stream in recent years. But as we move from mining to concentrating, smelting, and finally to refining, economies of scale become more and more important. Only medium-sized mines can afford to have concentrators and only large mines can support smelters. While refining is the most concentrated of the stages in the United States, it is usually done in locations close to the markets. Putting all the stages together requires large ore reserves in order to maintain a high level of mine production over long periods of time, and capital amounting to

---

[6] Between 1973 and 1975, U.S. mine production declined by 18 percent and refined copper production declined by 23 percent. In August 1977 Phelps Dodge announced a 15 percent cutback in mine output and there were also substantial cutbacks by other major U.S. producers. *Wall Street Journal*, August 1977, p. 4.

[7] J. S. Bain, *Barriers to New Competition* (Cambridge, Mass., Harvard University Press, 1956) pp. 192–195.

[8] An exception would be low-grade porphyry mines which require large capital outlays.

over a billion dollars for a completely integrated operation today. Most of the known reserves in the United States are held primarily by existing producers, but, in the absence of a lucky discovery, an accumulation of sufficient reserves properly located to sustain a large integrated operation would require large expenditures of high-risk exploration capital. Despite the existence of these barriers to entry, the dominant U.S. integrated firms, for example, Anaconda, Phelps Dodge, and Kennecott, have a smaller share of the U.S. market today than they did in the immediate post-World War II period. Many petroleum firms and conglomerates have ample resources to go into the copper mining industry on large scale, and many of the major petroleum companies have done so, both in the United States and abroad. In some cases it is more attractive to take over existing copper companies. Also of significance is the movement by the two major U.S. custom copper refiners, ASARCO and AMAX, to integrate backward into domestic mining operations.

Excess Capacity and Limit Pricing

In industries with a high degree of concentration, the large firms sometimes seek to maintain their share of the market by deliberately creating excess capacity, while relying on short-term market power to prevent prices from declining to the level of variable costs. They may combine this with "limit pricing" or deliberately holding down prices in periods of high demand in order to discourage new entrants.

In most periods since 1954, U.S. producers' prices for copper have been above the LME, and have not remained substantially below the free market price except for relatively short periods of time. Since the use of limit pricing to restrict new entrants seems to require long periods of price maintenance at levels below free market prices, this tactic cannot be very significant in pricing policies. Finally, there is little evidence that U.S. primary copper producers deliberately create excess capacity to forestall new entrants.

Competition from Scrap

New scrap is a product of the manufacturing process and, although its price and consumption vary in the short run in relation to prices and consumption of refined copper, the ratio of new scrap collected to current consumption should be constant over time. During the 1970–75 period, 25.5 percent of total U.S. copper consumption was derived from new scrap, with very little variation each year. In 1974, following the sharp rise in copper prices, the proportion rose to 27 percent.[9] Old scrap arisings, while somewhat lower than new scrap, are not dependent upon current copper consumption, but are drawn from an ever-rising pool of copper in use. Although old scrap arisings in the United States have not shown a definite upward trend in the past decade, the expected continued rise in the cost of producing primary copper should result in increased collection and utilization of old scrap. This is true because the copper content of old scrap does not change over time and, with improved collection and separation techniques, the relative cost of producing secondary copper should fall relative to that of primary copper.[10] This subject is discussed in greater detail in chapter 13.

Competition from Substitute Materials

The fact that copper is in competition with other materials such as aluminum and plastic probably affects the long-run price of copper, but the short-run elasticity of substitution is believed to be quite low. The elasticity of demand for copper is discussed in chapter 7. The question of whether competition from other materials has influenced competitive price policies of the primary copper industry in the United States is debatable. However, over the longer term, it seems likely that competition from substitutes has influenced copper prices and helped to limit copper producers in exercising market power.

Profitability

Although profitability comparisons are difficult, there is no evidence that the major copper companies are more profitable than the average for all manufacturing companies. A comparison of rates of return on stockholders' equity over the ten-year period 1965–74 reveals that pretax rates of return for major copper companies averaged 16.8 percent as against 20.0 percent for all manufacturing, but that after-tax rates of return were 11.9 percent for both groups. Taxes on resource companies are lower than for manufacturing companies mainly because of the depletion allowance (which is 15 percent for domestic copper). After-tax earnings of the copper companies were much more volatile than those of all manufacturing concerns, ranging from 4.2 percent in 1971

[9] *End Use Investigation of World Copper Market with Emphasis on the Prospects of Recycling and Substitution* (mimeo, Commodities Research Unit, prepared for the Center for Natural Resources, Energy and Transport, United Nations, New York, January 1976) p. 8.
[10] Ibid., p. 12.

to a high of 15.3 percent in 1969 for the major copper companies.[11] Profit margins as a percentage of sales were higher for the major copper companies than for the large industrial companies, but this reflects the greater capital intensity of the copper industry. Data on major copper companies are distorted because of the diversified nature of their operations. For example, aluminum production is an important part of Anaconda's and Phelps Dodge's earnings, while Kennecott and some of the other companies are large producers of coal and other minerals.

The Two-Price System

A Brief History

An important characteristic of the copper market during the postwar period has been the existence of U.S. producers' prices (and, at times, foreign producers' prices) which have been significantly higher or lower than the LME and other outside market prices. During the 1950–54 period, the divergence between U.S. producers' prices and outside market prices can be explained in part by U.S. government price controls during the Korean War. In 1954 there was a sharp rise in the LME price that was set off by a sudden increase in world demand, and in 1955 the average differential was nearly 11 cents and at times considerably wider (figure 4-1). The U.S. producers' prices were raised twice in January 1955 and again in March, and primary producers rationed copper to customers at their prices. In May 1955 Roan Selection Trust (RST), a major African copper producer, announced it would sell in line with U.S. producers' prices, but later reverted to the LME price.

After mid-1956 the world demand for copper declined and the two price series fluctuated closely together, but with U.S. producers' prices remaining slightly higher than the LME price. Early in 1964 there was another sharp rise in world demand and in the LME price so that in April 1966 there was a differential of 50 cents per pound between the two prices. However, some of the foreign producers, including RST, Anglo-American, and the major Canadian producers, refused to follow the increase in the LME price and sold at producers' price during the 1964–66 period. Throughout 1966 until late 1970, the LME price remained substantially above U.S. producers' prices and the U.S. primary sector rationed its supply. From August 1967 to April 1968 there was a

11 *Economic Impact of Environmental Regulations on the Copper Industry* (prepared for the U.S. Environmental Protection Agency, Washington, D.C. by Arthur D. Little, January 1978) chapter IV-10, table IV-5.

strike in the U.S. copper industry and the domestic producers' prices were suspended. In mid-1970 the LME price fell dramatically and for the first time since 1963 it was below U.S. producers' prices. However, in early 1973 a sharp increase in world demand led to a record rise in the LME price which reached an average of $1.38 per pound in April 1974. Due in part to U.S. government price ceilings, U.S. producers' prices were only 69 cents in April 1974, rising to an average of 89 cents by July 1974, following the lifting of U.S. price controls in May 1974. By this time the LME was coursing rapidly downward and by August 1974 reached 82 cents as against an average of 87 cents for U.S. producers' prices. The U.S. producers' prices declined to a low of about 63.6 cents per pound at the end of 1975 while the LME price declined to 52 cents and the New York merchants and Comex prices fell to a range between the LME and U.S. producers' prices. The LME price increased from 53.9 cents per pound at the end of December 1975 to 70.6 cents by April 1976, and U.S. producers' prices increased over the same period in two steps from 63 cents to 66 cents in mid-March and to 70 cents by mid-April, following which the two prices, together with the outside prices such as the merchant price and the Comex, maintained a fairly close relationship. However, in early August 1976 the U.S. producers' price for electrolytic wirebar was 74.6 cents per pound as against the LME price of 69.8 cents, and U.S. producers' prices remained above the LME price during the rest of 1976 and 1977 (see figure 4-1).

During the first five months of 1978, U.S. producers' prices remained well above the LME price. However, as was noted in chapter 3, in May 1978 Kennecott announced that its price for electrolytic cathode would be the spot closing price of the previous Comex trading session plus 2.5 cents a pound. This had the effect of narrowing substantially the difference between Kennecott's price and the open market prices. For a time other major primary copper producers held their prices above Kennecott's price for the same type of copper, but in early July most U.S. primary copper producers reduced their prices to levels more or less in line with Kennecott's price, thereby reducing the spread between U.S. primary producers' prices and the Comex and LME prices. At the time of writing, the future of U.S. producers' prices and their relationship to the open market prices are uncertain.

The Mechanism

The mechanism by which the producers' prices are maintained at levels significantly above or below the LME and other outside prices may be explained as follows. First, when the producers' prices are below the outside prices, existing contracts are honored (in the absence of strikes or other conditions giving rise to *force majeure*), but if demand exceeds production, the amounts available to buyers beyond the contracts depend on the level of past purchases or the "book positions" for the preceding year. It must also be kept in mind that nearly half of the output of the primary copper sector in the United States goes to fabricators that are affiliated with the large integrated copper producers. Nevertheless, it has been stated that rationing has also been applied to affiliated firms. Buyers at the producers' prices may be asked not to sell the refined copper in the outside market. Fabricators whose requirements are not met by purchases from the primary copper sector, including copper for inventories, must go to the secondary refiners, to the merchants, or in some cases to the Comex or the LME.

When the outside prices are lower than the U.S. producers' prices, the primary copper sector has a market for a large part of its output with its affiliates and with fabricators that have negotiated annual contracts. The latter are willing to honor these contracts even at the higher prices since they never know when the price relationship may be reversed and they are anxious to maintain their "book position" with the primary producers. Another important insulating factor for the U.S. market is the cost of delivery of copper from LME warehouses to U.S. destinations, which is currently about 5 cents a pound. It may be noted, however, that periods when producers' prices have exceeded the LME price by more than 5 cents per pound have usually been less than a year. When producers' prices are higher than the LME price, independent fabricators begin acquiring more of their copper from secondary refiners and other outside sources as their contracts expire, and the fabricating affiliates of the primary copper producers begin to feel the squeeze from competitors with substantially lower raw material costs. In addition, output of some primary copper producers is affected more than others, and there are ways of attracting customers other than by changing posted prices. For example, in the fall of 1975 the demand for Kennecott's refined copper declined relative to that of other major copper producers, with the result that Kennecott introduced a contract which it believed would be more attractive to buyers than the traditional one used in the industry.

Rationale for the Two-Price System

It is not too difficult to explain why the U.S. primary copper industry employs its market power to maintain producers' prices *above* outside market prices, but it is much more difficult to explain satisfactorily why the industry maintains producers' prices substantially *below* the LME and other outside prices for extended periods of time.

Although not all sellers are motivated by the same factors, two arguments for the producers' price system coupled with rationing of copper at the (lower) producers' prices are that (1) higher prices arising from temporary causes, such as strikes or speculative demand, will lead to substitution for copper by the users; and (2) price volatility and excessive price movements away from the long-term equilibrium level make for instability of the industry, either by encouraging excess capacity or by discouraging steady growth in capacity in line with long-term growth in demand. Objections have been raised to each of these arguments. Regarding the first argument, long-run substitution (LRS) is likely to take place only in response to a perception of long-run change in copper prices relative to prices of substitutes. This is true because it takes considerable time and expense to shift to other materials. It is argued that little substitution is likely to take place during a short period of high copper prices. It is further argued that rationing will tend to raise the prices of semifabricated coppers, even though raw material prices might be artificially low. Moreover, copper manufacturers are usually more afraid of material shortages than of high prices since, even in such uses as electrical transmission cables, the price of raw materials will be small compared with the total value of the product and the cost of delaying projects because of material shortages. If the copper industry could discriminate sufficiently to assure those end users of semifabricated products most susceptible to substitution that they would always have plenty of copper products at prices below the substitution threshold, a rationing scheme might achieve its objective.[12] Rationing takes place mainly at the fabricating level—wire, tubing, castings, and so forth—rather than at the level of the engineering, electrical, transport, construction, and consumer goods industries. How well the semifabricating firms ration and/or limit price increases to the end users who make the basic decisions for substitution is not known.

The second argument for the producers' price system, the general objective of achieving greater price stability, has been countered by the assertion that when a large portion of the total U.S. market is subject to rationing, the magnitude of the price fluctuations in the outside market will tend to increase. It is believed that the market taken as a whole would be subject to less price fluctuation if the primary producers would make both spot and forward contracts freely and in line with the

---

[12] Discriminatory rationing would very likely result in legal action against the discriminating firms either by the U.S. government or by buyers discriminated against.

Comex and LME prices. Moreover, sales of forward contracts by the primary copper industry would reduce the incentive of users to build up inventories of copper.

In May 1970 the Subcommittee on Copper to the U.S. Cabinet Committee on Economic Policy (the Houthakker Committee) criticized the two-price system in the copper industry on two major counts. First, the system results in unfair discrimination against some fabricators in favor of others which have close associations with the primary copper-producing sector. Second, the system tends to discourage the long-run expansion of the domestic copper industry.[13] Among the alternative courses of action, the subcommittee favored that of permitting the shipment of U.S. copper ores, concentrates, and scrap abroad for refining, with the refined copper returned to the United States without duty. This was favored as a means of increasing U.S. supplies of refined copper in the face of a shortage of U.S. smelter capacity.[14] The subcommittee rejected both the elimination of rationing and the institution of a government program to make rationing more equitable. It also could not agree on requiring the primary producers to make substantial amounts of copper available to the outside markets. It seems likely that some of the members of the subcommittee were heavily concerned with keeping down U.S. copper prices even if it required rationing for temporary periods.

David McNichol published an analysis of the two-price system in the copper industry in which he points out that rationing is a logical policy if the industry discriminates in favor of those end uses most susceptible to long-run substitution, for example, copper wire.[15] However, the evidence shows that at times the domestic industry has also rationed wire as well as brass mills and other semifabricating industries whose products are less susceptible to LRS, and that it has rationed output to both affiliated and nonaffiliated wire mills. McNichol then proceeded to show how a partially integrated copper producer employing a policy of discriminatory rationing might raise the price of semifabricated commodities, for example, copper wire, thereby increasing profits at the fabrication level. The gains would be derived from monopolistic restriction of copper supplies affecting both affiliated and nonaffiliated semi-fabricators. This explanation is scarcely consistent with the copper

13 "Report of the Subcommittee on Copper to the Cabinet Committee on Economic Policy" (mimeo, Washington, D.C., May 13, 1970).

14 With the increased pollution abatement regulations on smelters in Japan and Europe, it is doubtful whether there is significant excess smelter capacity anywhere.

15 David L. McNichol, "The Two Price System in the Copper Industry," *The Bell Journal of Economics and Management Science* (Spring 1975) pp. 50–73.

industry's alleged concern for LRS. McNichol admits that his explanations are not fully substantiated by the evidence, but he believes they are plausible.

The explanation for the existence of producers' prices alongside prices determined in commodity exchanges and in other markets is to be found more in the history and structure of the U.S. primary copper industry than in a collective determination on the part of the dominant copper companies that producers' prices would achieve certain agreed-upon objectives. Many students of the industry are convinced that a world producers' price which would react to longer run demand and supply forces but would not be subject to sharp month-to-month or year-to-year fluctuations would be beneficial to both producers and consumers. Others would put their trust only in world-wide free markets in which all sellers and buyers would be price takers. The action of Kennecott in May 1978 in tying its cathode price to the Comex indicates the absence of a unified position among large U.S. primary copper producers, while the current debate over whether and how international copper prices should be stabilized reflects widely differing opinions among economists, officials of governments, producers, and consumers. This subject will be taken up in chapter 7.

Production Costs

Information on costs of production in the copper industry is not available on a basis that would enable us to prepare a historical index of year-to-year changes in average operating or total costs. Costs differ widely from mine to mine in the same country, depending upon the grade of ore, including that of co-products, the method of extraction, the required metallurgy, the geographical location, the amount of infrastructure supplied by the producer, etc. Capital costs differ with the age of the mine, the method of financing, and the cost of borrowing. Production costs differ among countries as a consequence of differences in wages and fringe benefits, the cost of imports, and differences in tax regimes. Higher average ore grades in developing countries are often offset by the high cost of imported capital equipment and engineering services, higher transportation costs, and higher taxes. We find cases where it may be more profitable to mine 0.4–0.5 percent Cu ore in the United States than 3.0–4.0 percent Cu ore in Africa, even apart from different political risks.

Each of the four stages of production in the copper industry—mining, concentrating, smelting, and refining—is faced with variable and fixed costs. The principal variable costs are wages, materials, energy, fuel, maintenance (including replacement parts), taxes associated with production, transportation, and a portion of sales and administrative costs. Fixed costs in the sense of those that are independent of the level of output, so long as the mine is operating, include interest on debt, property taxes and insurance, depreciation, and general administration. In addition there is the economic cost of the capital funds supplied by the equity holders. Firms must anticipate a certain level of return before making an investment, which includes all of the outlays prior to the initiation of commercial production (including exploration) not covered by external borrowing. Once these expenditures are made, the mining operations will go on even if profit expectations are disappointed. Income taxes are, of course, a charge against before-tax revenues. The decision to reinvest a portion of the earnings, or, more properly, net cash flow including both accounting net income and depreciation allowances, also plays a role in the production process. In many operations additional investment may be needed to maintain a certain level of output or to increase the level of output. These include exploration and research directed to the operating mine itself, as well as additional equipment. For example, as the ore grade declines it may be necessary to expand mine capacity and to install additional ball mills and crushers to avoid a decline in output. Whether this investment is made will often depend upon a reassessment of expected earnings on the additional capital outlay.

The behavior of each of these categories of costs will affect decisions relating to production over time. For nonintegrated firms, downstream charges for concentrating, smelting, or refining constitute costs to the producers. Nonintegrated mines may shut down or reduce output if there is a sharp increase in smelting and refining charges not offset by an increase in the price of copper metal. Integrated firms with a number of different operations at each stage of production have a variety of options. They can break even or even lose money at one stage of production and make their profits at another, or they can shut down various operations. Firms may not continue to operate if they do not cover their variable costs although even in such cases they may produce for inventory on the expectation that copper prices will rise in the near future. Another consideration is the cost of reopening a mine once it is shut down. If firms cover their variable costs and there is something left over for fixed costs, they may continue producing indefinitely, depending on their financial ability to sustain losses. Companies that have sustained losses over several years may sell out or merge with companies with high profits and tax obligations. A high-cost mine in terms of overall economic cost may become a relatively low-cost mine if the external debts have been paid off and the capitalized value of the assets has been written down. However, it is the capital cost of new mines and of expanding the capacity of old mines that determines in considerable measure whether there is expansion of capacity. Given the assumption of a reasonably competitive industry without barriers to entry, long-run equilibrium price will be equal to total cost, including a rate of return on equity high enough to attract investors.

Production Costs and the Herfindahl Hypothesis

In his book on *Copper Costs and Prices: 1870–1957,* Herfindahl had to rely on a few case studies of U.S. government agencies for particular years and on statements of industry officials for absolute cost estimates. A few corporate annual reports give operating costs per pound of copper and in some cases they can be inferred from other information found in the annual reports. However, the coverage and the comparability of the data are insufficient to construct a reliable national or world average cost series for the copper industry.

Herfindahl advanced the hypothesis that the long-run price of copper tends to equal the price that is sufficient to induce continued investment at all stages of production from exploration through refining.[16] This price may be regarded as the long-run economic cost of copper. Long-run costs are determined by the technical conditions of production, the prices of the factor inputs, including the normal rate of return on equity investment, taxation, and the grade of ore mined.[17] Regional differences in costs are equated over time by differences in the rates of production. If there is a difference in cost between two regions, it will be eliminated by a slowing of investment in the higher cost region and an increase in investment in the lower cost region until the cost difference is eliminated.[18]

Using a deflated price series, Herfindahl found that the long-run equilibrium price (cost) of copper remained fairly steady between 1885 and World War I, after eliminating selected abnormal years. Largely as a consequence of changes in mining and processing of copper around World War I, the postwar equilibrium real price (cost) of copper declined by about 40 percent, but remained fairly stable, after excluding the abnormal years, between the early 1920s and 1957. The average price for the period 1923–25 was 14.1 cents per pound and the estimated long-run equilibrium cost in 1957 was 13.4–16.1 cents per pound, with

[16] Herfindahl, *Copper Costs and Prices,* chapter 2.

[17] By equating long-run price with long-run economic costs, Herfindahl evidently meant the total cost of producing copper from a marginal deposit.

[18] Herfindahl, *Copper Costs and Prices,* pp. 58–59.

the prices deflated by the GNP deflator (1926 = 100). The actual average (deflated) price in 1957 was 16.1 cents, but Herfindahl regarded 1957 as an abnormal year.[19]

According to Herfindahl, several opposing developments combined to maintain the real price (cost) of copper during the period between World War I and 1957. First, there was a decline in the grade of ore mined. In the United States the average grade of copper ore mined was 1.6 percent in 1921–30 and 0.8 percent in 1951–56.[20] Opposing the declining grade of ore were two factors: (1) technological advances and scale economies that tended to reduce real costs per pound; and (2) a decline in the rate of growth in production and demand, partly as a consequence of competition from scrap and substitute materials such as aluminum. The rate of growth in world production declined from 3.6 percent for the period 1905–14 to 1923–29 to 1.9 percent for the period 1936–39 to 1947–57 (continuously compounded annual rate).[21] There were also important changes in the rate of growth in production among regions and in the regional shares of world copper output. Between 1925–29 and 1955–57, U.S. output grew at a compound annual rate of less than 0.6 percent while the corresponding rate of growth for the world, excluding Communist countries, was about 2.0 percent.[22] According to Herfindahl's hypothesis, this reflected the higher U.S. costs relative to those abroad, and the relatively slow growth in U.S. output tended to restore equality of costs among regions. Partly offsetting higher U.S. costs, U.S. firms were given the benefit of depletion allowances and tariff protection not afforded prior to World War I.[23]

Copper Prices and Costs, 1957–77

Herfindahl estimated the range for the long-run equilibrium price of copper in 1957 to be 25–30 cents per pound (equivalent to 13.4–16.1 cents in 1926 prices). Table 4-1 shows average annual U.S. producers' and

[19] Ibid., table 22, pp. 208–209.
[20] Ibid., p. 224.
[21] Ibid., p. 225.
[22] Data derived from Joseph Grunwald and Philip Musgrove, *Natural Resources in Latin American Development* (Baltimore, Johns Hopkins University Press for Resources for the Future, 1970) p. 176.
[23] The U.S. depletion allowance on copper was 15 percent, but the duty was suspended in 1974. For most U.S. mining companies the corporate tax rate on income from domestic copper production was about 35 percent in 1976. Taxes in foreign copper-producing countries were relatively low until the 1930s when several countries, including Chile, raised effective tax rates on foreign copper companies to levels exceeding those in the United States.

Table 4-1.   Average U.S. Producers' and LME Prices of Copper in
1957 Prices, 1957–77

(*cents per pound*)

Year		U.S. GNP deflator 1957=100	Average U.S. prod. price	Average LME price	Average U.S. prod. price in 1957 prices	Average LME price in 1957 prices
1957		100	29.6	27.4	29.6	27.4
1958		102.6	25.8	24.8	25.1	24.2
1959		104.3	31.2	29.8	30.0	28.6
1960		105.9	32.1	30.8	30.3	29.1
1961		107.3	29.9	28.7	27.9	26.7
1962		108.5	30.6	29.3	28.2	27.0
1963		109.9	30.6	29.3	27.8	26.7
1964		111.7	32.0	44.0	28.6	39.4
1965		113.7	35.0	58.6	30.8	51.5
1966		116.8	36.2	69.1	31.0	59.2
1967		120.6	38.2	51.2	31.7	42.5
1968		125.4	41.8	56.0	33.3	44.7
1969		131.5	47.5	66.3	36.1	50.4
1970		136.7	57.7	63.9	41.6	46.1
1971		145.0	51.4	49.3	35.4	34.0
1972		149.8	50.6	48.5	33.8	32.4
1973		158.3	58.9	80.8	37.2	51.0
1974		174.6	77.3	93.1	44.3	53.3
1975		190.5	64.2	56.0	33.7	29.4
1976	1st qtr.	196.2	64.0	56.6	32.6	28.8
	2nd qtr.	199.4	70.1	69.1	35.2	34.7
	3rd qtr.	201.6	74.6	70.2	37.0	34.8
	4th qtr.	204.3	69.5	58.2	34.0	28.5
1977	1st qtr.	207.0	69.1	65.6	33.4	31.7
	2nd qtr.	210.5	72.7	62.2	34.5	29.5
	3rd qtr.	213.0	64.1	54.4	30.1	25.5
	4th qtr.	216.2	61.0	55.2	28.2	25.6

Source: Survey of Current Business for GNP deflator. American Bureau of Metal
Statistics, *Metal Bulletin,* and CIPEC *Quarterly Review* for copper prices.

LME copper prices for 1957–77 in 1957 prices (using GNP deflator).[24] In
most years during 1957–68, the deflated U.S. producers' prices were

[24] Herfindahl used the New York (Comex) price in his series, but U.S. producers'
prices are better indicators of the prices received by U.S. producers and the LME a
better indicator of the prices received by most foreign producers outside the United
States and Canada in recent years.

reasonably close to the upper range of Herfindahl's estimated long-run equilibrium price for copper, but the deflated LME price was substantially higher in most years between 1964 and 1970. After 1968 the deflated U.S. producers' prices were substantially higher than the upper range on Herfindahl's long-run equilibrium price, and in 1975 when prices were regarded as quite depressed, the deflated U.S. producers' price was 4 cents higher than Herfindahl's long-run equilibrium price, while the average LME price during 1975 was well within Herfindahl's range. In the second quarter of 1976, both the (deflated) U.S. producers' prices and the LME price were well above the 1957 prices, but in the fourth quarter of 1976 the (deflated) LME price was nearly equal to the 1957 price (table 4-1). There was a further weakening of copper prices in the third quarter of 1977, and in September of that year the LME price averaged 55.1 cents per pound, or 25.9 cents in 1957 prices, while U.S. producers' prices declined to 60.6 cents, or 28.5 cents in 1957 prices.

We must now relate these price developments to the information available on costs, with cost defined as the price that would justify new investment. In order to duplicate Herfindahl's approach, we should have estimates of total costs for different regions, including rates of return on capital that would justify investment in new capacity. We could then relate cost differentials to regional differences in rates of increase in output over time. Unfortunately, adequate cost data on a comparable basis are not available for this purpose. Nevertheless, it may be instructive to examine some cost estimates for recent years.

Gordon Driver, president of the Noranda Company, estimated North American production costs for new copper mines in 1971 to be 43 cents per pound (30 cents in 1957 prices), including an 8 percent return on capital. Driver's estimates for North American production costs per metric ton in 1971 were as follows:[25]

	U.S. $	U.S. ¢/lb
Mining and milling	396	18
Smelting, refining, freight	330	15
Capital depreciation	132	6
Return on capital (8 percent)	88	4
Total	$946	43

In a paper presented by Sheldon P. Wimpfen and Harold J. Bennett of the U.S. Bureau of Mines in October 1973, the authors estimated that

[25] Gordon Driver, "Copper in the Seventies," address to the American Mining Congress Convention, Las Vegas, October 13, 1971.

at a price of 50 cents per pound, U.S. mine production of copper could rise from 1.7 million short tons in 1973 to about 2.0 million short tons in the mid-1980s, following which it would decline rapidly (50 cents per pound is about 32 cents per pound in 1957 prices).[26] Alexander Sutulov estimated the cost of copper production in the United States, including a 12 percent return on capital and an allowance of 5 cents per pound for environmental controls, at about 50 cents per pound in 1973 (or about 32 cents in 1957 prices).[27] However, Sutulov suggests that the United States is probably a relatively high-cost producer and that foreign costs are probably lower.[28]

Each of the above total cost estimates (in 1957 dollars) is close to the upper range of Herfindahl's estimated long-run equilibrium price of copper in 1957, but was somewhat lower than average U.S. producers' prices (in 1957 dollars) for 1970–73. As is shown in the paragraphs below, there is considerable evidence that operating costs in the developing countries have tended to run somewhat lower than in the United States and Canada. Nevertheless, because of higher capital costs and higher taxes, total economic costs may be as high or higher in the developing countries, and in any case the flow of international capital into the mining industries of the developing countries has tended to decline in recent years.

Operating Costs in Different Regions

An unpublished (and restricted) study done for CIPEC by the Battelle Memorial Institute estimates production costs (excluding capital cost) in various countries for 1970, both on an average and marginal cost basis. (Marginal cost here refers to the additional cost of output from expanding the capacity of existing mines.) Marginal costs are estimated to be somewhat lower in the United States than for the CIPEC countries as a

[26] "Copper Resources Appraisal," National Research Council Committee on Mineral Resources and the Environment Appraisal Panel III meeting on mineral resources, Estes Park, Colorado, October 12, 1973.

[27] Alexander Sutulov, *Copper Porphyries* (Salt Lake City, University of Utah, 1974) p. 198.

[28] Sir Ronald Prain stated that in 1970, "United States costs were around the world average for competitive copper of 32 cents." However, Prain's estimate appears to be an average cost, including normal profits, for existing mine facilities and not an estimate of the price that would be required to induce investment. Prain's 32-cent copper in 1970 is equivalent to only 23 cents in 1957 prices (Sir Ronald Prain, *Copper: The Anatomy of an Industry*, London, Mining Journal Books, 1975, p. 194).

group, probably reflecting lower additional equipment costs. These estimates for the CIPEC countries and the United States are as follows:

Country	Average cost in U.S. dollars per metric ton	Marginal cost in U.S. dollars per metric ton
Chile	$680	$1,140
Peru	590	700
Zaire	550	860
Zambia	660	770
Total CIPEC	640 (29 U.S. cents)	1,140 (52 U.S. cents)
United States	700 (32 U.S. cents)	1,120 (51 U.S. cents)

The above figures are roughly comparable to those provided by *Copper Studies,* which estimates average net operating costs in the United States at 32.3 cents per pound in 1970 (23.2 cents in 1957 dollars) as contrasted with 29.8 cents in Latin America, 28.0 cents in Africa, and 30.2 cents in Asia and Australia.[29]

In 1971 production costs, including direct and indirect costs, refining and delivery, amortization, depreciation, depletion, but less credits for silver and molybdenum, were only 24.3 cents per pound at SPCC's Toquepala mine in Peru. This is less than 17 cents per pound in 1957 dollars, but does not include a return on equity. As late as 1973 operating costs at the Bougainville mine in PNG were less than 20 cents per pound (13 cents in 1957 dollars), largely as a consequence of the value of gold in the ore, which is deducted in calculating production costs.[30]

The annual report of Roan Consolidated Mines Ltd. (owned 51 percent by the Zambian government) gives the following data for production costs at the mines in recent years: 1970–71, 26 cents per pound; 1971–72, 29 cents per pound; 1973–74, 37 cents per pound; and 1974–75, 44 cents per pound. In 1957 dollars these costs were 18 cents in 1970–71; 22.3 cents in 1973–74; and 24.4 cents in 1974–75. Capital costs and transportation to ports (which today are very high) are not given, but they must add another one third to total costs.

The cost of production at Gecamines (in Zaire), according to the company's annual report for 1972 (including interest on borrowed capital and the management fee), was US$750 per metric ton (34 U.S. cents

---

[29] *Copper Studies* (August 5, 1977) p. 1.
[30] Information on operating costs in Toquepala and at the Bougainville mine was obtained from confidential sources.

Table 4-2.   Average Annual Compound Rates of Increase in Mine
Copper Production
(*percent*)

Area	1925–29 to 1955–57	1955–57 to 1971–73
United States	0.6	2.7
Market economies	2.0	4.2
World	2.5	4.6

Sources: See table 1-1. 1925–1929 data from Joseph Grunwald and Philip
Musgrove, *Natural Resources in Latin American Development* (Baltimore, Johns
Hopkins University Press for Resources for the Future, 1970) p. 176.

per pound, or 23.7 cents in 1957 dollars). Zairian mines apparently had
a lower total cost in 1972 than the Zambian mines.

Although the cost data given in the preceding paragraphs are not
wholly comparable, they suggest that prior to 1973 the real cost of copper had not risen significantly above Herfindahl's range of 25–30 cents
for 1957. The data given also suggest that U.S. production costs were
somewhat higher than those in Africa, Latin America, and Oceania.

Reasons for the Stability of Costs During 1957–72

Since 1957 both U.S. and world copper production have risen at rates
substantially greater than those between the 1920s and 1957 (see table
4-2). This reflects the higher rate of increase in world demand for copper
since 1957. Herfindahl had explained the relatively stable long-run real
cost of producing copper between World War I and 1957 in part by the
fact that the rate of growth in production during this period was substantially lower than the rate prior to World War I. In the absence of
major technological advances, or of important new discoveries, one
might have expected that the real cost of copper would have risen significantly since 1957. This did not appear to have been the case, at least
prior to 1973. However, there have been substantial changes in the
industry over the past two decades, including greater mechanization and
the increasing importance of large tonnage, open-pit porphyry mines. In
the case of some mines, the higher prices of co-products such as gold
reduced the net cost of copper production. But most important was the
rapid development of large-scale copper mines in Bougainville, Canada,
Chile, Peru, Zaire, and Zambia.

The share of U.S. production in world copper output declined from
28 percent in 1957 to 21 percent in 1973, thus continuing the decline

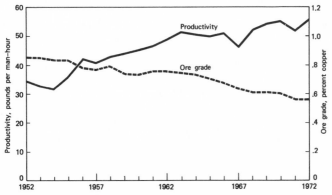

Figure 4-2. Copper ore grade and productivity in the United States. (From *Technologic and Related Trends in the Mineral Industries, 1972*, Bureau of Mines Circular 8603, Washington, D.C., U.S. Department of Interior, 1973, p. 8.)

which took place since the end of World War I when U.S. output constituted nearly 60 percent of the total world copper mine production. Although U.S. mine copper has been rising more rapidly since 1957 than it did between the mid-1920s and 1957, the rate of rise in U.S. output has been substantially less than that of the rest of the world. Between 1955–57 and 1971–73, U.S. mine production of copper rose at an average annual compound rate of 2.7 percent, while Western world production during this period rose at an average annual compound rate of about 4.2 percent. Total world production, including that of Communist countries, rose at an average annual compound rate of about 4.6 percent during this same period. According to Herfindahl's hypothesis, the slower rate of growth in U.S. output helped to maintain equality of long-run production costs between this country and other copper-producing regions of the world in Africa, Asia, Canada, and South America where reserves were less intensively developed.

The average copper content of the ore grade mined in the United States declined from about 0.85 percent in 1957 to 0.55 percent in 1972 (figure 4-2). Unfortunately, I have no data on the change in the copper ore grade outside the United States, but the average grade of ore mined outside the United States is undoubtedly higher than in this country at the present time.[31] During this same period productivity rose from about 41 pounds per man-hour in 1957 to about 54 pounds per man-hour in

31 For data on ore grades in various mines in the world, see Sutulov, *Copper Porphyries,* chapters 3 and 4.

1972, but productivity has not increased significantly since 1962 (figure 4-2). Unfortunately, we have no data on productivity in other countries. The rise in productivity in U.S. copper mines resulted mainly from increased use of mechanized equipment and automation in mines, mills, smelters, and refineries. This resulted in an increased need for skilled mechanics, technicians, and operators, while reducing the need for large numbers of unskilled laborers. Also, an increasing proportion of copper production came from the more efficient large-scale mines.

Copper Costs After 1972

The estimates cited above suggest that until 1973 Herfindahl's outside estimate of 30 cents per pound in 1957 prices as the long-run equilibrium price (cost) of copper was maintained, or did not significantly increase. However, there is considerable evidence that the equilibrium price of copper has risen in recent years. For example, a recent Bureau of Mines study sought to determine the sales price per pound of copper that would be necessary to provide a 12 percent discounted cash flow over a twenty-year period for a typical new open-pit copper mine in Arizona (operating at 100,000 tons per day of ore). If the mine were constructed at costs existing in mid-1973, the price of copper (in 1973 dollars) that would just make production economical under the above assumptions is calculated at 63 cents per pound (or 40 cents per pound in 1957 prices).[32] Since U.S. producers' prices in 1973 averaged 59 cents, it was suggested that the hypothetical Arizona porphyry copper mine would not have been economical at current copper prices.

Since 1972 both production and capital costs of the copper industry have increased dramatically. Between 1972 and 1975 prices of materials, parts, and other supplies used by the U.S. copper industry increased by 45 percent; purchased electric power by 45 percent; and fuels by 105 percent.[33] By mid-1976 these price increases were 5 to 10 percentage points higher. Between 1972 (average) and mid-1976, hourly wages in mining rose by about 45 percent.[34] We are, however, interested in the rise in real costs or the rise in the cost of producing copper in relation to other prices. When we compare these increases in money costs with the GNP

[32] Includes allowances for transportation, smelting, and refining charges and credits for co-products. *Comparative Porphyry Copper Mining and Processing Costs—Alaska and Arizona*, Bureau of Mines Information Circular 8656 (Washington, D.C., U.S. Department of the Interior, 1974) p. 12.

[33] Arthur D. Little estimates based on wholesale prices of items.

[34] *Survey of Current Business* (Washington, D.C., Department of Commerce) various issues.

deflator, which increased by about 36 percent between 1972 (average) and mid-1976, it seems evident that real operating costs in the copper industry rose significantly between 1972 and mid-1976. If we use whole-sale prices (which rose about 53 percent between 1972 and mid-1976) as a deflator, real operating costs in terms of purchased inputs were prob-ably about the same. However, there is some evidence that productivity in terms of output per man-hour has declined since 1972. Also, pollution abatement requirements have increased operating costs.

Copper Studies estimates that U.S. average net operating costs rose by 50 percent between 1970 and 1975, or by about 9 percent in deflated dollars. For Africa the rise in operating costs was 73 percent, to 48.5 cents (or by 26 percent in deflated dollars), but the increase for Latin America was only 26 percent to 37.5 cents, an actual decline in terms of 1957 dollars.[35] However, in the case of Peru's Toquepala mine, the rise in production costs between 1971 and 1974 was 79 percent to 43.5 cents in 1974—an increase of 48 percent in 1957 dollars.[36]

A recent study by the CIPEC staff published in November 1977[37] gave estimates of the percentage of the Western world's copper-producing capacity in 1977 that could cover total production costs at various prices. At 55 cents per pound for copper (26 cents per pound in 1957 prices), mines representing only 41 percent of the Western world's capacity in 1977 could have covered total production costs, but 55 percent of the capacity of the CIPEC countries could have covered production costs at the 55-cent price. At 70 cents per pound, 86 percent of the Western world's capacity could have covered total production costs in 1977, including 96 percent of the capacity of the CIPEC countries. However, 70 cents per pound is equivalent to 33 cents per pound in 1957 prices, well above Herfindahl's range of real costs in 1957.[38] The CIPEC study estimates the U.S. average cost of copper production in 1977 at 62–65 cents per pound (29–31 cents in 1957 prices)[39] and states that only those companies with the lowest cost could cover their costs at 58 cents per pound under the most favorable conditions. These figures suggest that since the U.S. producers' price during the fourth quarter of 1977 was only 61.0 cents and the LME price was 55.2 cents, well over half of U.S.

[35] *Copper Studies* (August 5, 1977) p 1.

[36] These production costs are not calculated on a comparable basis since the data for Toquepala include certain capital costs, but they do indicate the general trend in operating costs.

[37] *Outlook for Development in the World Copper Industry* (Paris, CIPEC, Novem-ber 1977).

[38] Ibid., p. 17, table 8.

[39] Ibid., p. 112. Based on an article in *Metals Week* (June 27, 1977).

output was sold at prices below total production costs in the last quarter of 1977. However, these estimates refer to existing mines. Production costs for new mines built at 1977 prices would be much higher.

The rise in capital costs during the 1970s has perhaps been even greater than the rise in operating costs. Sir Ronald Prain estimated the average capital costs of producing a ton of refined copper in 1970 at $3,000 per metric ton.[40] A recent unpublished study found that in 1972 new mine construction in Canada required $3,000 per metric ton of annual capacity; smelter construction, $640 per metric ton; and refinery construction, $190 per metric ton. Using these figures, a ton of annual capacity of refined copper in Canada in 1972 required about $3,830. Estimates of planned expansion of copper mines, smelters, and refineries published by the *Engineering and Mining Journal*[41] suggest capital costs of producing a ton of refined metal at around $5,000 in 1976. For example, the Cyprus Bagdad mine expansion, plus smelter, at Bagdad, Arizona is estimated to cost $4,800 per metric ton, but the addition of a refinery would bring the cost to well over $5,000 per metric ton. The Lakeshore, Arizona mine and concentrator project owned by Hecla and El Paso, which began production in 1976 with a capacity of 59,000 mt per year, is estimated to cost $195 million, or about $3,300 per metric ton.[42] The addition of a smelter and refinery would certainly boost that cost to $5,000 per metric ton. These figures suggest that capital costs per ton of output rose by more than 15 percent in real terms between 1970 and 1976. By 1977, capital costs per metric ton of output were estimated at $6,000, or a rise of 32 percent in real terms since 1970.

Several industry spokesmen have stated that a price of 90 cents to $1.00 per pound in 1975 prices will be necessary to induce the additional capacity required to meet projected copper demand in the 1980s.[43] This would represent a price of 46 to 51 cents in 1957 prices. These estimates indicate that the real cost of producing copper has risen well above the 1957 level and this increase has occurred largely since 1972.

The Cuajone mine in southern Peru, whose construction was initiated in 1969 and whose first full year of operation was in 1977, cost $726 million, of which $576 million was construction cost, $80 million interest on capital during the construction period; and $70 million working

[40] Prain, *Copper: The Anatomy of an Industry*, p. 187.

[41] "1976 Survey of Mine and Plant Expansion," *Engineering and Mining Journal* (January 1976) pp. 74ff.

[42] Hecla Mining Corporation, *Annual Report 1975*, p. 9.

[43] See for example, Simon D. Strauss (ASARCO), "Copper—Still An International Commodity?" an address before the Copper and Brass Warehouse Association, April 1, 1976.

capital, including warehouse stocks. Charles Barber estimated that an average price of 80 cents per pound of copper in 1977 dollars would be required for SPCC to recover its investment with interest, and a price of 97 cents per pound would be required to earn a 15 percent return on the investment after taxes. Barber further stated that the total cost of the Cuajone mine would have been $1.2 billion, or about $6,100 per annual metric ton of capacity, had it been constructed at 1977 prices. At this capital cost, an average price of $1.35 per pound of copper (in 1977 dollars) would be required for SPCC to earn a 15 percent return on its investment.[44] These estimates are especially impressive in light of the fact that the Cuajone mine has been rated as one of the lowest cost mines in the world. A copper price of $1.35 per pound in 1977 dollars is equivalent to nearly 64 cents in 1957 dollars and more than double Herfindahl's average long-run cost of copper over the 1926–57 period. Moreover, it may be noted that few, if any, mining companies would make a large mining investment in a developing country with the expectation of earning only a 15 percent return. In most cases, investors in developing countries target for a discounted cash flow (DCF) rate of 20 percent or higher.

Some Unanswered Questions

Chapter 3 and this chapter have reviewed the market structure of the world copper industry and the history of copper prices and costs of production. We have concluded that despite market imperfections, the world copper industry is essentially a competitive one, and that there exist parallel movements of prices over time for the standard grades of copper traded on the various national and world markets. The foregoing analysis provides little explanation for the short-run and long-run movements in the price of copper, even though there is some evidence that long-run prices are related to long-run marginal costs. More important, our analysis does not provide much guidance for dealing with the national and world policy issues relating to copper, such as the assurance of adequate future supplies at long-run equilibrium prices

---

[44] Charles F. Barber, "Economics of New Supplies of Copper," *Mining Congress Journal* (March 1978) pp. 33–37. Barber is Chairman of ASARCO, which has a majority interest in SPCC's Cuajone mine. The above figures do not include the Peruvian government's workers' participation tax of 10 percent of earnings before taxes and depletion. If this tax is included, the price of copper would have to be $1.43 per pound in 1977 dollars in order for the investors to earn a 15 percent return on their investment, assuming an actual cost of $1.2 billion for the mine.

for meeting long-run national and world demand, and the moderation of sharp short-run price fluctuations that may impair the welfare of both producers and consumers. For these purposes we need to know the structure of demand and the behavioral patterns of copper consumers; the possibilities for substituting other materials for copper in various uses; and the factors determining the short-run and long-run supplies of copper from a variety of sources. The following two chapters provide the empirical and theoretical bases for analyzing the factors responsible for the movements in copper prices and their interrelations with copper demand and supply.

5

U.S. Demand for Copper:
An Introduction to
Theoretical and Econometric Analysis

Kirkor Bozdogan and Raymond S. Hartman*

Introduction

IN THIS chapter we focus on patterns of copper consumption and the dynamics of demand for copper. In the first section we review copper consumption trends and patterns in the past, with emphasis on the following points: (1) key attributes of copper; (2) comparative copper consumption trends in the United States and the world; (3) consumption of refined and nonrefined (scrap) copper; (4) major direct users of copper; (5) consumption of copper by end-use industries; (6) the consumption and uses of copper versus the demand for copper; and (7) definition of the market for copper for demand analysis. The second section is designed to provide a simplified introduction to the theoretical and econometric analysis of the demand for copper, and in the third section we examine the findings of several econometric studies of the copper industry on short-run and long-run demand elasticities. Available econometric studies of demand for copper, including our own, generally

* Dr. Bozdogan is senior policy economist and head of the industry modeling and policy econometrics unit at Arthur D. Little, Inc. and Dr. Hartman is assistant professor of economics at Boston University, research associate at the MIT energy laboratory, and economic consultant to Arthur D. Little. In preparing this chapter the authors drew heavily on the ADL study, *Economic Impact of Environmental Regulations on the United States Copper Industry* (submitted to the U.S. Environmental Protection Agency, 1978).

indicate that in the short run demand is quite inelastic with respect to both price and activity variables. The long-run elasticity estimates are all greater than the short-run estimates, indicating that the response of demand to relative prices and activity is more sensitive in the long run. However, even the long-run estimates in about half of the studies examined fall in the inelastic range. The presence of long-run substitution in demand for copper is generally recognized as an important aspect of demand analysis for copper. In our own econometric work, we have focused the analysis of copper substitutes on aluminum because of its overriding importance as a competitor to copper, not only in the past, but also potentially in the future.

Patterns of Copper Consumption

Key Attributes of Copper

The physical properties of copper having major significance in determining commercial demand are its high electrical and thermal conductivity, corrosion resistance, ductility and malleability, durability, low melting point, and high strength. In addition, copper has a pleasing color, is nonmagnetic, and is easily finished by plating or lacquering; it can be welded, brazed, and soldered. Because it can be alloyed readily with many other metals to improve certain basic properties, the commercial brasses, bronzes, copper-nickel alloys, and nickel silvers have been developed. Copper has a wide range of uses in today's modern industrial economy, in pure or alloyed form, including such diverse products as plumbing fixtures, ship propellers, electrical wire, and car radiators. While aluminum and other materials can be substituted for copper and its alloys in many electrical, structural, and decorative applications, there are many other uses for which copper is the preferred and largely nonsubstitutable material.

Copper Consumption in the United States and the World: Comparative Trends

Table 5-1 shows comparative U.S. and world trends in refined copper consumption over the 1963–74 period. World consumption of refined copper was about 8.3 million mt in 1974. Of this, U.S. consumption accounted for nearly 2.0 million mt, or 23.5 percent. The U.S. share of world consumption of refined copper dropped from 28.8 percent in 1963 to 23.5 percent in 1974, reflecting a relatively higher growth in

Table 5-1.   U.S. and World Comparative Trends in Refined Copper
Consumption, 1963–74

(*000 metric tons*)

Years	U.S.	World	U.S. as percent of world
1963	1,590.0	5,519.3	28.8
1964	1,690.0	5,995.4	28.2
1965	1,845.6	6,193.2	29.8
1966	2,157.8	6,444.8	33.5
1967	1,797.5	6,194.8	29.0
1968	1,701.4	6,523.3	26.1
1969	1,944.3	7,148.0	27.2
1970	1,854.3	7,283.4	25.5
1971	1,830.5	7,309.9	25.0
1972	2,028.6	7,944.5	25.5
1973	2,218.6	8,791.6	25.2
1974	1,956.4	8,325.4	23.5
Average annual compound growth rate (percent)			
1963–73	3.39	4.77	—
1964–74	1.47	3.34	—

Source: Metallgesellschaft Aktiengesellschaft, *Metal Statistics 1963–1973* and *1964–1974*, pp. 32–33.

demand for copper in the rest of the world. Accordingly, while refined copper consumption in the United States has increased by only 1.9 percent per year during the 1963–74 period (1.5 percent per year over 1965–74 and 3.4 percent per year over 1963–73), world consumption has recorded a substantially higher rate of growth at 3.8 percent per year over the 1963–74 period (3.3 percent per year over 1964–74 and 4.8 percent per year over 1963–73).

Consumption of Refined and
Nonrefined (Scrap) Copper

Copper consumption trends in the United States since 1950 are shown in table 5-2. It can be seen that refined copper accounts for a large and increasing share of total U.S. consumption during this period, with directly consumed scrap constituting 31 percent by 1974. It should be noted, however, that during this same period the share of refined copper from scrap in total refined copper production has increased from 14.3

Table 5-2. Consumption of Copper in the United States, 1950–74
(*Cu content, 000 metric tons*)

Year	Total	Refined copper[a]	Scrap	Percent composition (%)		
				Total	Refined copper[a]	Scrap[b]
1950	2,067.5	1,348.8	718.9	100.0	65.2	34.8
1955	2,201.0	1,398.3	802.6	100.0	63.5	36.5
1960	1,892.2	1,248.7	637.6	100.0	66.0	34.0
1965	2,725.8	1,851.3	874.5	100.0	67.9	32.1
1970	2,666.8	1,860.0	806.7	100.0	69.7	30.3
1971	2,689.9	1,936.1	844.3	100.0	68.3	31.7
1972	2,972.2	2,034.9	910.0	100.0	68.5	31.5
1973	3,168.3	2,225.4	942.8	100.0	70.2	29.8
1974[c]	2,826.6	1,962.5	864.1	100.0	69.4	30.6
		(Average annual compound growth rate)				
1950–70	1.28	1.62	0.58	—	—	—
1950–74	1.31	1.57	0.77	—	—	—
1960–73	4.04	4.54	2.98	—	—	—
1960–74	2.91	3.28	2.13	—	—	—

Source: Copper Development Association, *Copper Supply and Consumption 1950–1969; 1955–1974.*
[a] Includes copper refined from scrap.
[b] Refers to directly consumed scrap.
[c] Preliminary.

percent in 1950 to 22.6 percent in 1974. Consequently, refined copper production from scrap plus directly consumed scrap, taken together, account for a larger share of total consumption (i.e., 46.1 percent in 1974) than in 1950. Over the 1950–74 period, the growth in total U.S. consumption of copper has been relatively slow at 1.3 percent per year. However, since the early 1960s, the growth rate has been significantly higher (4.0 percent per year over 1960–73 and 2.91 percent per year over 1960–74). The following table shows the change in U.S. refined copper consumption for the period 1973–76:

Year	U.S. refined copper consumption (thousands of metric tons)	Percent change
1973	2,218	—
1974	1,997	−9.96
1975	1,397	−30.07
1976	1,784	27.74

Major Direct Users of Copper

As shown in figure 5-1, there are six major groups of direct users of refined copper and scrap: four copper semifabricating industries—wire mills, brass mills, foundries, and powder mills; ingot makers; and a group of "other" industries such as chemicals, steel, and aluminum. Ingot makers are, in effect, intermediate processors of refined copper and scrap, producing copper alloy ingot, the bulk of which they sell to other semifabricating industries, principally brass mills and foundries. While ingot makers and "other industries" are not copper semifabricators as commonly defined, for convenience we shall refer to the aggregate demand schedule of the six consuming groups as the demand for refined copper and its equivalent on the part of semifabricators.

Wire mills and brass mills have traditionally been the largest consumers of refined copper and its equivalent, accounting for about 86 percent of total consumption in 1974 (table 5-3). Wire mills, which use only refined copper, consumed about 46 percent, while brass mills, which use refined copper and scrap in fairly equal proportions, consumed about 40 percent. Ingot makers, who use almost entirely scrap, were the third largest consumers at 7 percent. Foundries, which use mostly scrap, consumed about 5 percent of the total, with powder plants and "other industries" accounting for the remainder. Over the past two decades, brass mills have generally accounted for 39–42 percent of total consumption; wire mills, on the other hand, have gradually increased their proportion of total consumption from 37 percent in 1956 to the above-

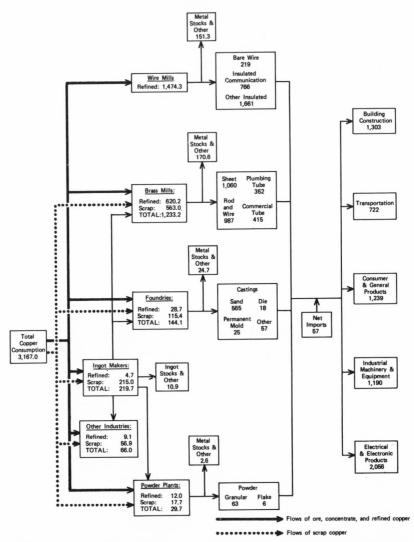

Figure 5-1.   Copper consumption in the United States, 1974. Semifabricator consumption is by copper content, thousands of short tons. The supply of semifabricated and fabricated products and end user consumption is by metal weight, millions of pounds. (From *Economic Impact of Environmental Regulations on the U.S. Copper Industry,* Cambridge, Mass., Arthur D. Little, 1978, p. VII–6.)

Table 5-3. Consumption of Copper Products by Domestic
Semifabricators, 1974[a]

(000 metric tons of Cu content)

	Refined copper[b]	Scrap[c]	Total	Percent breakdown (%)
Wire mills	1,304.3		1,304.3	46.1
Brass mills	609.9	512.3	1,122.3	39.7
Foundries	26.1	105.0	131.6	4.6
Powder mills	10.9	16.1	27.0	1.0
Ingot makers	4.3	195.6	199.9	7.1
Other	6.8	35.0	41.8	1.5
Total	1,962.3	864.0	2,826.9	100.0

Source: Copper Development Association, *Copper Supply and Consumption,* Annual Data, 1955–1974.
[a] Preliminary.
[b] Includes refined copper from scrap.
[c] Old and new scrap which is directly consumed.

mentioned 46 percent. The proportion of total consumption attributable to ingot makers and foundries has declined somewhat over the past two decades.

Table 5-4 provides a breakdown of the various products of the four semifabricating industries and gives production levels for 1966, 1970, and 1974 in terms of metal content. Although total output appears to have declined by 10 percent between 1966 and 1974, fluctuations in intervening years not shown make it difficult to discern any secular declining trend. Production of wire mill products increased in absolute terms and as a percentage of the total. Powder mill output remained fairly stable in both absolute and percentage terms, while total production of brass mill products and foundry products declined. Brass and wire mill products account for approximately 85 percent of total production by metal weight for the entire period. The right side of figure 5-1 illustrates the fact that semifabricating industries demand refined copper and its equivalent, not for final consumption, but as intermediate inputs in the production of semifabricated products. The demand for semifabricated products on the part of fabricators or end-use industries is, in turn, derived from the demand for final goods being produced by fabricators or end-use industries.

Table 5-4. Production of Semifabricated Copper Products, 1966, 1970, 1974
(000 metric tons)

	1966		1970		1974[a]	
	Metal content	Percent of total	Metal content	Percent of total	Metal content	Percent of total
Wire mill products						
Bare wire	122.4	3.9	102.8	4.0	99.6	3.5
Insulated communication	293.9	9.4	318.5	12.4	348.5	12.4
Other insulated	718.4	22.9	638.3	24.9	755.8	26.8
Total	1,134.7	36.2	1,059.6	41.3	1,203.9	42.7
Brass mill products						
Sheet	597.4	19.0	401.8	15.7	482.3	17.1
Rod and mechanical wire	474.1	15.1	365.8	14.3	449.1	15.9
Plumbing tube	215.2	6.9	171.9	6.7	160.1	5.7
Commercial tube	226.6	7.2	203.9	7.9	188.8	6.7
Total	1,513.3	48.2	1,143.4	44.6	1,280.3	45.4

Foundry products						
Sand castings	389.4	12.4	282.1	11.0	257.1	9.1
Permanent mold	20.9	0.7	22.3	0.9	11.3	0.4
Die castings	13.7	0.4	10.1	0.4	8.2	0.3
Other	33.7	1.1	27.3	1.0	25.9	0.9
Total	457.7	14.6	341.8	13.3	302.5	10.7
Powder products						
Granular	27.3	1.0	19.5	0.7	28.7	1.0
Flake	3.2	neg.	18.2	0.1	2.7	0.1
Total	30.5	1.0	21.7	0.8	31.4	1.1
Grand total	3,136.2	100.0	2,566.5	100.0	2,818.1	100.0

Source: Copper Development Association, *Copper Supply and Consumption, 1955–74.*
[a] Preliminary.

Table 5-5.   U.S. Copper Consumption by Broad End-Use Categories,
(*000 metric tons*)

	1960	1961	1962	1963	1964	1965
Building construction	435.4	490.9	566.9	589.7	682.9	709.3
Transportation	267.1	270.3	308.0	320.3	362.2	390.8
Consumer and general products	311.7	362.2	349.4	361.7	426.8	467.3
Electrical and electronic products	563.7	550.1	570.6	612.9	684.9	744.4
Industrial machinery and equipment	411.3	406.3	440.4	460.5	505.9	518.2
Total	1,989.2	2,079.8	2,235.3	2,345.1	2,662.7	2,830.0
	Percentage composition					
Building construction	21.9	24.0	25.4	25.1	25.6	25.1
Transportation	13.4	13.2	13.8	13.7	13.6	13.8
Consumer and general products	15.7	16.0	15.6	15.4	16.0	16.5
Electrical and electronic products	28.3	26.9	25.5	26.1	25.7	26.3
Industrial machinery and equipment	20.7	19.9	19.7	19.7	19.1	18.3
Total	100.0	100.0	100.0	100.0	100.0	100.0

Source: 1969–74: Copper Development Association, *Copper Supply and Consumption, 1955–1974;* 1960–68: Charles River Associates, Inc., *Economic Analysis of the Copper Industry,* March 1970, p. 12.

Consumption of Copper by End-Use Industries

Table 5-5 presents data on consumption of copper by end-use industries. The end-use (fabricating) industrial categories that predominate in the consumption of semifabricated copper are the following, in order of importance: electrical and electronics products, building construction, consumer and general products, industrial machinery and equipment, transportation, ordnance and accessories.

The electrical and electronics products group has grown to be the principal consumer of copper, accounting for somewhat less than one-third of all annual copper consumption. Building construction continues to be a significant consumer of copper for electrical wiring and pipe. The consumer products group grew significantly during the late 1960s; however, its use of copper declined after 1969. While economic conditions may explain part of this decline, substitution and product redesign may also have contributed to this change. The industrial machinery and equipment industry and the transportation industry increased their consumption of copper through 1966; however, by 1970 both industries returned to consumption levels found in 1960.

1960–74

1966	1967	1968	1969	1970	1971	1972	1173	1974[a]
709.8	589.2	580.1	647.0	575.1	633.3	682.3	746.6	570.2
411.3	319.4	364.4	376.8	303.5	344.8	374.0	417.6	345.0
674.3	684.8	739.4	713.9	547.4	534.2	604.2	637.9	549.6
862.2	725.3	723.4	818.5	759.8	776.6	890.8	1,017.8	915.4
577.4	472.3	494.2	481.8	440.4	436.3	504.6	533.3	455.9
3,235.0	2,791.0	2,901.5	3,038.0	2,626.2	2,725.2	3,055.9	3,353.2	2,836.1
Percentage composition								
21.9	21.1	20.0	21.3	21.9	23.2	22.3	22.3	20.0
12.7	11.4	12.5	12.4	11.6	12.7	12.2	12.5	12.1
20.8	24.5	25.5	23.5	20.8	19.6	19.8	19.1	19.3
26.6	26.0	25.0	26.9	28.9	28.5	29.2	30.3	32.5
18.0	16.9	17.0	15.9	16.8	16.0	16.5	15.8	16.1
100.0	100.0	100.0	100.0	100.0	100.0	100.0	100.0	100.0

[a] Preliminary.

Consumption and Uses of Copper versus Demand for Copper

The analysis of demand for copper requires a distinction among the consumption, the uses, and the demand for copper. First, the consumption and uses of copper are not definitionally identical. Similarly, uses of copper and the demand for copper differ conceptually. Of these three terms, "consumption" is the most straightforward. Next, while "uses of copper" refers to the disposition of copper on hand, "demand" is an economic concept which refers to the quantities the buyers are willing to purchase at different prices, everything else being equal. The problem typically encountered in demand analysis is to move from consumption data to a data base that more accurately approximates actual market conditions under which, at prevailing prices, producers are willing to supply a certain amount and the consumers are willing to purchase a certain amount (i.e., the market is cleared; supply and demand are equal at the prevailing price level). Data on copper flows are usually collected in terms of production, consumption, and inventories. Therefore, "demand" (i.e., point estimates of demand over time) must be estimated from these figures, by adjusting either overall production or consumption figures for changes in inventories and/or net exports. How this is actually accomplished depends on one's analytical objectives.

On the demand side, the principal use categories for refined copper and refined copper equivalent (e.g., unrefined scrap or copper alloy ingot) are consumption by semifabricators, net additions to inventories, and net exports.

The category of net inventory additions can be further subdivided into: (1) stock changes of primary refiners; (2) stock changes of secondary refiners; (3) changes in federal government stockpiles; and (4) stock changes of semifabricators.

Consumption by semifabricators dominates among uses of refined copper equivalent. Inventory changes at the semifabricator level have represented only a marginal proportion of total uses. Although in some years net exports and changes in primary producer inventories and government stockpiles have represented a somewhat larger proportion of total uses, their net impact on total quantities has been relatively small.

By definition, the total amount of copper supplied by the primary producers, secondary refiners, and scrap suppliers in any year must equal total uses of copper for that year. The "materials balancing" identity or accounting equation can then be represented as follows:

$$QPR + QSR + QSNR = QC + NE \\ + \Delta IGOV + \Delta IF + \Delta IRR + \Delta IRS \quad (1)$$

where QPR represents the quantity of primary refined copper produced, QSR is the quantity of secondary refined copper produced from scrap, and $QSNR$ represents the quantity of unrefined scrap supplied (and used directly); QC is consumption by semifabricators; NE is net exports; $\Delta IGOV$ is the change in government stockpiles; ΔIF is the change in semifabricator inventories; ΔIRR represents the change in inventories of primary refiners; and ΔIRS is the change in inventories of secondary refiners.

If demand is defined as the demand on the part of the domestic semifabricators (definition 1), the relevant figure (QD) can be derived from the consumption side as follows:

$$QD = QC + \Delta IF \quad (2)$$

Demand may also be defined, more broadly, to include net exports and changes in government inventories (definition 2):

$$QD^* = QC + \Delta IF + NE + \Delta IGOV \quad (3)$$

These two additional components, when positive, clearly represent additional demand for domestic supplies of refined copper equivalent. The

Table 5-6.   U.S. Semifabricator Demand for Refined Copper and
Scrap, 1954–74

(000 metric tons of Cu content)

	QC	+	ΔIF	=	QD
1954	1,744.0		−26.0		1,718.0
1955	2,201.0		24.0		2,225.0
1956	2,152.1		7.0		2,159.1
1957	1,916.8		−2.0		1,914.8
1958	1,796.9		4.0		1,800.9
1959	2,109.9		−39.0		2,070.9
1960	1,892.1		8.0		1,900.1
1961	1,974.7		4.0		1,978.7
1962	2,148.6		5.0		2,153.6
1963	2,334.7		−8.0		2,326.7
1964	2,525.2		10.0		2,535.2
1965	2,725.8		9.0		2,734.8
1966	3,065.4		63.0		3,128.4
1967	2,593.8		−49.0		2,544.8
1968	2,560.2		−14.0		2,546.2
1969	2,879.4		10.0		2,889.4
1970	2,666.7		64.0		2,730.7
1971	2,689.9		−13.0		2,767.9
1972	2,972.2		−62.0		2,910.2
1973	3,168.3		0.0		3,168.3
1974[a]	2,826.6		75.0		2,901.6

Source: Copper Development Association, *Copper Supply and Consumption,* 1954–
1973 and 1955–1974.

[a] Preliminary.

net result of adjusting semifabricator consumption figures for net exports and government stockpile changes, as well as semifabricators'
inventory changes, will be as follows: $QD^* > QD$ in years when net
exports and government stockpile changes are positive and $QD > QD^*$
when net exports and government inventory changes are negative.

Because we are concerned principally with the dynamics of demand
on the part of domestic semifabricators, we have chosen to focus directly
on the demand for refined copper equivalent on the part of domestic
semifabricators. Aggregate demand figures for the domestic semifabricator industries under definition 1 are presented in table 5-6. It should
be noted that in our construction of a simultaneous-equation econometric model of the copper industry, separate equations have been

constructed for the various types of inventory holders and for net exports, while changes in government inventory stocks enter the model exogenously.

Definition of the Market for Copper
for Demand Analysis

For purposes of analyzing market demand, it is generally accurate to think in terms of a unified market for refined copper, copper scrap, and copper alloy ingot. As pointed out earlier in this chapter, except for wire mills, semifabricators and fabricators use not only refined copper, but also various types of scrap and copper alloy ingot in their operations. Typically the difference between refined copper prices and prices of various types of scrap and copper alloy ingot would be roughly indicative of the added costs to the user of substituting the latter form of copper for the former. Since there are buyers for all possible combinations of products, arbitrage can be fully effective, especially since copper merchants stand ready to trade in virtually all types of copper.

Theoretical and Econometric Analysis of the Demand for Copper

Basic Considerations

There are a number of points that deserve emphasis in a discussion of the demand for copper. First, the demand for copper is negatively correlated with its price. Assuming all other variables are held constant, we may state the relationship between the total quantity demanded, Q, and the unit price for copper, P, as $Q = F(P)$ or linearly as $Q = \alpha_0 + \alpha_1 P$. The coefficient α_1 will have a negative sign. This equation can be represented graphically by a demand curve (schedule), which indicates the total quantity of copper that would be demanded by a group of users (in this case domestic semifabricators) at various price levels. Thus, the demand curve in figure 5-2 indicates that, if everything else is held constant and the price of copper (refined copper and its equivalent) is P_1, demand for copper would be Q_1 units. If the price were to fall to P_2, Q_2 would be demanded.

Second, the demand for copper is a "derived" demand, which arises from the final demand for the goods for which it is an input. The four semifabricating industries (i.e., brass mills, wire mills, foundries, and powder plants) plus other industries (i.e., chemical, steel, aluminum, and

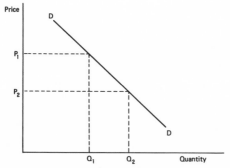
Figure 5-2.   General demand schedule for copper.

others) which directly use refined or scrap copper as inputs, buy copper, not for final consumption, but for use in their own immediate production. Their output of semifabricated products is, in turn, demanded by fabricators and end-use industries as intermediate inputs in the production of final durable goods for domestic consumption (i.e., personal consumption or government purchases), investment (i.e., as producers' durable equipment or construction), or exports to the rest of the world. Consequently, we should expect a causal relationship between the general utilization of copper and industrial production of durable manufactured goods, including construction materials. As industrial production of durable manufactured goods increases, the demand for copper would then increase. If greater specificity in demand analysis is sought, the demand for copper can be analyzed by relating it to the activity of the individual end-use industries. This requires a more differentiated examination of the dynamics of demand, since the share of copper's cost in total cost is different for different final products (e.g., in an automobile or a refrigerator its share is very small, whereas in power transmission lines its share is very large).

Third, the demand for copper is positively correlated with the price of substitute goods. For various products which use copper, there are other materials which could be used even though they are not perfect substitutes for copper in the manufacturing process. The most important substitutes for copper include aluminum, stainless steel, zinc, and plastics. Each substitute is a competitor to copper in limited situations. For example, aluminum is a substitute for copper mainly in wire products. For consumer products, plastics are the more important substitutes.

Substitution of aluminum or another material for copper may occur in either the short or the long run. Short-run substitution for copper may take place whenever an alternative material can be used without requiring major alterations in fixed plant and equipment, or changes in product design. The major instances of this sort of substitution are probably to be found in residential and nonresidential construction. For example, the leading substitutes for copper drainage pipe are plastic and cast iron pipe. Copper pipe is preferred on technical grounds, but if the price becomes too high or copper is simply unavailable, contractors can readily use plastic or cast iron. Decisions on what sort of pipe to use are made frequently, so substitution can take place in the short run in the sense that it requires no investment and that the effects of a change in price probably occur rapidly.

Short-run substitution may also take place through variations in the copper content of alloy semifabricated products. That is, a consumer who normally uses semis of pure copper or alloys with a very high copper content might switch to alloys with a lower copper content when prices are high. There are also many ways in which the quantity of copper used per unit of output can be reduced.

While in some cases there is a noticeable short-run response to changes in price, in many other situations the capital fixity of plant and equipment will limit the possibilities for substitution in the short run. Although copper and its substitutes may exhibit the same required physical properties in use, the capital equipment in place cannot generally be used for production with substitutes.

Speculative demand and speculators are often blamed for much of the copper market's instability. Although speculators may influence prices for a very short time, according to Prain, they do not alter long-run supply and demand.[1]

Specification and Functional Forms

The demand for refined copper and its equivalent is a function of macro-economic activity levels (driving the activity levels of the end-user industries), the price of refined copper, and the price of substitute products. In an econometric analysis of demand for copper, these would serve as the independent variables. Other factors, such as the prices of complementary commodities and factors of production, probably have some influence on quantities of refined copper demanded, but there is little *a priori* evidence to suggest a degree of influence substantial enough to require their inclusion as explanatory variables in an analysis of demand for copper. As economic activity and income increase, greater quantities

[1] Sir Ronald Prain, *Copper: The Anatomy of an Industry* (London, Mining Journal Books, 1975) p. 97.

of producers' durable goods and consumer durables using copper inputs will be demanded; this will, in turn, lead to a greater derived demand for copper on the part of semifabricators. Similarly, as copper prices increase, semifabricators and end-users will usually cut back their consumption, and when prices decrease, semifabricators and end-users will usually demand more. Accordingly, a demand equation for copper can be specified showing the relationship not only between the quantity (of copper) demanded and its own price, as given above, but also between the quantity demanded and all of the pertinent variables simultaneously. This is represented by the equation:

$$Q = F(P, P^s, Y) \tag{5}$$

This equation indicates that although the price of copper (P) affects the quantity demanded (Q), the quantity demanded is also a function of the prices of substitute commodities (P^s), and the income of activity levels (Y) of the users. The demand function suggested by equation (5) is not only static (i.e., time invariant), but also quite general; it indicates that the variables are causally related in some way to quantities demanded. In order to introduce greater specificity into the demand equation, it is necessary to look at the production function for semifabricators. This production function is simply a technical relationship indicating the maximum amount of output which can be produced by a producer or industry with each and every set of possible factor inputs (capital, labor, materials). The mathematical form of the demand schedule for refined copper equivalent will reflect the relationship expressed in the aggregate production function for semifabricators.[2] However, the form of the equation may be specified in different ways, each of which involves different assumptions concerning the price and income responses of semifabricators (and, by implication, fabricators and end-users) over time. For example, the demand equation introduced above may be specified in either a linear or a nonlinear form. The linear form of equation (5) can be written as follows:

$$Q_t = \alpha_0 + \alpha_1 P_t + \alpha_2 P_t^s + \alpha_3 Y_t + u_t \tag{5a}$$

where t refers to a given year, α_0, α_1, α_2, α_3 refer to econometrically estimated parameters (coefficients) and u_t is a stochastic (random) disturbance term. The requirements for u_t are that it be independent of the other explanatory variables, be free of autocorrelation, and have constant variance.

[2] Technically speaking, the derived demand schedule will fall out of the first-order conditions for cost minimization subject to the production constraint.

The general demand function in equation (5a) could be utilized to model the demand for refined copper equivalent for each semifabricating industry (wire mills, brass mills, foundries, powder mills, ingot makers, and other industries) separately or for the group of all semifabricating industries consuming refined copper equivalent. Demand analysis would be performed for each of the separate semifabricating "end-use" categories if the objective is to estimate detailed end-use specific movements in demand for copper in response to copper prices, prices of substitute products, and activity levels. While perhaps desirable, such disaggregated analysis is not necessary; an aggregate analysis of demand might prove generally sufficient for most industry-wide analytical purposes. It should be noted, in this connection, and not necessarily as a justification for aggregate analysis, that attempts in the literature to disaggregate demand analysis to individual industry end-use categories have not been successful.[3]

Equation (5) may also take a nonlinear form, such as

$$Q_t = \alpha_0 P_t^{\alpha_1} P_t^{s\alpha_2} Y_t^{\alpha_3} \tag{6}$$

which is normally transformed for estimation purposes into the following log-linear (log-log) form:[4]

$$\log Q_t = \log \alpha_0 + \alpha_1 \log P_t + \alpha_2 \log P_t^s + \alpha_3 \log Y_t + u_t \tag{6a}$$

The linear form requires the assumption that, whatever the initial price level, an *absolute* increase in price of a certain amount will lead

[3] See Charles River Associates, (CRA), *Economic Analysis of the Copper Industry* (March 1970) pp. 264–265. CRA reports that several alternative specifications of the disaggregated demand model were estimated; however, the results obtained were found generally unsatisfactory. The authors note that because the model was difficult to estimate, many possible sources of error could not be explored. Nevertheless, co-linearity among the variables of the model seemed to be at least one of the major difficulties. Each of the equations in the model satisfied the necessary conditions for its identification, but the excluded variables were found to be frequently highly correlated with one or more of the included variables (i.e., several of the equations may not have been identified in the sample). The disaggregated model was hence abandoned not only because there was some reason to believe that reasonable estimates of the disaggregated model could not be obtained but also because the techniques required to estimate the model were found to be so time consuming that additional work was deemed impractical. Consequently, the disaggregated model was replaced by a single equation for the total demand for copper.

[4] Other forms of logarithmic transformation for estimation purposes include the semilogarithmic

$$Q_t = \alpha_0 + \alpha_1 \log P_t + \alpha_2 \log P_t^s + \alpha_3 \log Y_t + u_t$$

and the inverse semilogarithmic

$$\log Q_t = \alpha_0 + \alpha_1 P_t + \alpha_2 P_t^s + \alpha_3 Y_t + u_t$$

to an *absolute* decline in the quantity demanded. Thus, a $1.00 increase in price will lower the quantity demanded by the same absolute amount whether the initial price is $10.00 or $100.00. The log-log form, on the other hand, imposes the assumption that a proportional (percent) increase in price from any initial price level will lead to a corresponding proportional (percent) decrease in quantity demanded. Consequently, in the log-log specification, a $1.00 price increase from a $100.00 price level (i.e., 1 percent) would have a much smaller absolute impact on the quantity demanded than a $1.00 increase from a $10.00 price level (i.e., 10 percent).

If a log-log form is used, and the equation is estimated on an annual basis, the nature of the log-log form will cause the estimated price and income elasticities to be constant annually over the entire sample period. This imposed constancy of the elasticity estimates may be undesirable if it is felt that in reality price elasticities change from year to year. The linear form requires no such assumption, and permits the estimation of differing elasticities as they may change from year to year. Hence, any model of demand applied to a body of data imposes certain inherent constraints. That is, the linear relationship is basically just as arbitrary and restrictive as the logarithmic relationship. If the range of price variation has historically been small, the assumption of a fixed absolute quantity response to an absolute price change (as in the linear form) may not be worrisome. In such a case, the ability of the linear formulation to estimate different elasticities over the sample period may be analytically useful. Following a review of existing econometric analyses of demand for copper and after having made some econometric analyses of our own, we found the linear functional form analytically satisfactory for our own modeling work.

Long-Run Substitution in Demand

Long-run substitution (LRS) has been a serious concern of the copper industry, especially since 1947 when the price of copper went above the price of aluminum for the first time. Although the relative price of copper has fallen sharply on occasion in the past (e.g., during 1957 and again during the last half of 1970), the upward trend was resumed shortly thereafter. Industry observers are not in complete accord on the importance of LRS. However, it is generally agreed that aluminum has been the most serious competitor to copper, having made the greatest inroads in electrical conductor and heat-exchanger applications. The most important potential instances of LRS are in telephone conductor cable and automobile radiators. Conductor cable and automotive radiators account for roughly 25–30 percent of total demand for primary copper in the United States. There is also clearly LRS in the demand for copper electric transmission cable where aluminum has almost completely displaced copper for overhead transmission, and the possibility of LRS in the demand for several other markets has been mentioned in the trade press. In general, LRS is present in most of the markets for copper wire, and these constitute 60 percent of the demand for refined copper. More detailed information on LRS is provided in appendix 5-2.

Substitution for copper will occur only when the relative price of a substitute for copper becomes low enough to justify engineering and tooling costs required to alter the capital equipment of the using sector. The full substitution from copper to a competing commodity will occur only in the long run. In economic terms, the long-run own-price and cross-price elasticities will be greater than the short-run price elasticities.

Technological advances may contribute to LRS in two ways. On the one hand, fabricators and end-users are responsive to technical as well as economic considerations in choosing to use copper versus a substitute. Thus, LRS may be stimulated by changes in the technical and practical feasibility of substitution (i.e., mechanical and physical properties achieved in using a substitute material, safety, ease of handling and storing, size or weight limitations). Technological developments may also alter the relative price ratios at which substitutes for copper become economical. For example, developments in the past decade in the use of aluminum telephone cables and automobile radiators made aluminum a realistic substitute at prevailing relative prices.

During the past two decades, world market prices for refined copper have often experienced substantial and, at times, violent fluctuations. Producers in the industry have voiced fears that, regardless of the relative price of refined copper, the lack of stability in that price over time would by itself stimulate fabricators and end-users to substitute other materials for copper. It seems unlikely, however, that price fluctuations alone encourage LRS for copper. Most copper consumers base their purchasing plans, not on daily price fluctuations occurring on a free market, such as the London Metal Exchange, but rather on the monthly or quarterly average price. Short-term fluctuations leading to unusually favorable or unfavorable dates for buying may be expected to cancel each other out in the long run, regardless of the general buying practices of most firms. Thus, expectations of future long-term relative price trends are likely to be the most important determinant of LRS in the long-term investment planning of the user industries.

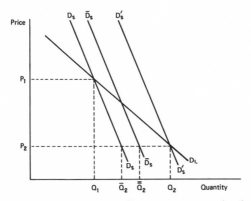

Figure 5-3.   Short-run and long-run adjustment process in demand for copper.

The fact that long-term substitution in demand requires a period of years during which changes in capital equipment take place implies that end-users of copper only "partially adjust" to a new copper price level each year. Their equipment will depreciate only so fast each year and because such equipment will not be replaced immediately, the derived demand for copper is less elastic in the short run than in the long run. In the long run, the end-use industries can fully adjust to new factor prices (price changes being assumed once-for-all) through structural and equipment alterations; hence, demand will be more elastic over the long run.

Short-Run and Long-Run Adjustments in Demand

The analytical framework for dealing with the short-run and long-run adjustment process in demand is provided by a class of models known as the "adaptive expectations" ("partial adjustment" or "distributed lag") models.[5] The dynamics of the adjustment process may be examined with the aid of figure 5-3. D_L in figure 5-3 is the long-run demand schedule of a group of copper-using industries and D_s is the short-run demand curve. Initial equilibrium is at (Q_1, P_1). If we assume there is a once-for-all price decrease from P_1 to P_2, the long-run desired quantity demanded would be Q_2. However, in the short run, equipment and

[5] The econometric specifications of such models are equivalent to those of a Koyck lagged model. However, the stochastic specifications will differ for different models. For a discussion of such models, see Henri Theil, *Principles of Econometrics* (New York, Wiley, 1971).

structural rigidities cannot be removed quickly enough. The copper-using industries would, therefore, end up operating on a new short-run demand curve $\bar{D}_s$, demanding $\bar{Q}_2$, which represents only partial adjustment to the new price situation. Eventually, as the copper-using industries continue to adjust by altering plant and equipment, their short-run schedule will move outward from $\bar{D}_s$ until it reaches a new short-run demand curve D'_s. Equilibrium is again achieved at (Q_2, P_2) by producers operating at the intersection of the short-run demand curve D'_s and the long-term demand curve D_L.

Equation (7) is similar to equation (5a) except that it relates the desired quantity demanded, Q_t^*, by semifabricators in a given year (rather than the actual quantity demanded Q_t) to prices and activity levels:

$$Q_t^* = \alpha_0 + \alpha_1 P_t + \alpha_2 P^s + \alpha_3 Y \tag{7}$$

Where the desired quantity demanded and the actual quantity demanded are the same, there is no problem. However, as discussed above, users of copper may not be able to consume Q_t^* (the desired quantity) because of technological constraints. Although in the long run they will move toward Q_t^*, they can adjust only partially to that level in the short run. We represent this latter substitution as follows:

$$Q_t - Q_{t-1} = \lambda(Q_t^* - Q_{t-1}) \qquad 0 \leq \lambda \leq 1 \tag{8}$$

which means that the users of the factor (i.e., copper) adjust the level of their actual demand from year $t - 1$ to year t (estimated as $Q_t - Q_{t-1}$) in some proportion λ of the difference between desired demand (Q_t^*) and actual demand during the preceding period (Q_{t-1}). If no technological constraints existed, $\lambda = 1$ and $Q_t = Q_t^*$. In that case, the short-run and long-run demand responses (and elasticities) would be equivalent.

Since "desired" quantities cannot be observed, we combine equations (7) and (8)

$$Q_t = \alpha_0 \lambda + \alpha_1 \lambda P_t + \alpha_2 \lambda P_t^s + \alpha_3 \lambda Y_t + (1 - \lambda)Q_{t-1} \tag{9}$$

which can be econometrically estimated because all the explanatory variables are observable.[6]

---

[6] It should be noted that this standard formulation of the adjustment model assumes that the adjustment coefficient is the same regardless of whether a change in the desired level of output is caused by a change in the price or a change in income (activity level).

The Relationship Between Short-Run
and Long-Run Elasticities

In equation (7), α_1 is a measure of the long-run own-price elasticity. If equation (7) were estimated in log-log form, α_1 would be that elasticity. In equation (9), $\alpha_1\lambda$ is a measure of the short-run elasticity, since the equation is specified with *actual price* and *actual quantity demanded*, rather than *desired quantity demanded*. If equation (9) were estimated in log-log form, the short-run elasticity would be $\lambda\alpha_1$. Hence, λ indicates the difference between the short-run own-elasticity[7] (e_{SR}) and the long-run own-price elasticity (e_{LR}) of demand; the two are related as follows:[8]

$$e_{LR}\lambda = e_{SR} \qquad 0 \leq \lambda \leq 1 \qquad (10)$$

Implicit in the short-run/long-run interrelationship is an outward movement in the short-run demand curves. As producers adjust to P_2, D_s moves out to $\bar{D}_s$, $\bar{\bar{D}}_s$, and so on[9] as Q_1 increases to $\bar{Q}_2$, $\bar{\bar{Q}}_2$, and so forth (where $\bar{Q}_2$, $\bar{\bar{Q}}_2$ etc. represent actual quantities demanded). Equilibrium is reached when the short-run demand curve reaches D'_s D'_s and equilibrium is again achieved at (Q_2, P_2) by the intersection of $D'_sD'_s$ and D_LD_L.

Stochastic Considerations

The above models represent simplified methods of dealing with the complexities of demand. Before such models can be utilized, they must be estimated. Econometric estimation of demand functions poses some potentially difficult problems. One possible difficulty is the identification problem, the technical aspects of which are not developed here.[10] Suffice it to say that in models of the size used for the nonferrous metals industries, underidentification is usually not the problem; overidentification is usually the case. Overidentification is a problem of riches; there exist more than enough restrictions on the parameters to yield several different estimates (in small samples) of the parameter.[11]

A second problem involves the presence of lagged endogenous variables. In single equation estimation under conditions of serial cor-

---

[7] The difference between short-run and long-run elasticity also applies to cross-price elasticities and the differential impact of Y in equation (9).

[8] See appendix 5-1, note 1.

[9] See appendix 5-1, note 2.

[10] See Franklin M. Fisher, *The Identification Problem in Econometrics* (New York, McGraw-Hill, 1966).

[11] Two-stage least squares may be employed to yield consistent estimates. See Henri Theil, *Principles of Econometrics*, chapter 10; and E. Malinvaud, *Statistical Methods of Econometrics* (Amsterdam, North-Holland, 1971) chapters 16–20.

relation,[12] the presence of lagged endogenous variables may yield inconsistent parameter estimates. Lagged endogenous variables in a simultaneous system lead to similar difficulties. However, there exist techniques to deal with the problems.

Finally, there is a potential "errors in variables" problem. In the typical nonferrous metals markets, demand specification may pose problems, depending on the availability of data on prices (e.g., actual transactions prices, or list prices) especially in the presence of "rationing" during periods of demand-crunch. It is obvious that in order to estimate the relationship between the prices actually paid (transactions prices) by users and the quantities demanded at such prices, the analyst must observe the actual quantities and prices. However, in some cases the only price series available are list prices, which may differ considerably from transactions prices, depending upon market conditions. In times of a supply glut, for example, sellers shave their actual transactions prices from list prices through various rebates, absorption of transportation margins, and various inventory financing schemes. It is the transaction price that is relevant for the analysis of demand for a given commodity. Furthermore, if a commodity is rationed in periods of excess demand, the actual quantity demanded at the observed price can be ascertained only by knowing who is rationed and by how much.

Results of Econometric Analyses of Demand for Copper

There have been a number of econometric studies of the copper industry in recent years. We consider here the results on short-run and long-run demand elasticities found by Fisher, Cootner and Baily (FCB),[13] Charles River Associates, Inc. (CRA),[14] and McNicol,[15] along with our own findings. Table 5-7 summarizes the short-run and long-run elas-

[12] Serial correlation will be particularly likely in time-series analysis. Further, it is well known that the use of some lag form induces serial correlation even if it were not present in the unlagged specification. For a discussion of the serial correlation induced by the Koyck lag, see Henri Theil, *Principles of Econometrics*, pp. 258–261.

[13] F. M. Fisher, P. H. Cootner, and M. N. Baily, "An Econometric Model of the World Copper Industry," *Bell Journal of Economics and Management Science* vol. 3, no. 2 (Autumn 1972) pp. 568–609.

[14] See *Economic Analysis of the Copper Industry* (March 1970); *An Econometric Model of the Copper Industry* (September 1970); *Forecasts and Analysis of the Copper Market* (May 1973); and *Policy Implications of Producer Country Supply Restrictions: The World Copper Market* (August 1976)—all by Charles River Associates, Inc., Cambridge, Mass.

[15] David L. McNicol, "The Two Price Systems in the Copper Industry" (Ph.D. thesis, Massachusetts Institute of Technology, February 1973). See also "Two Price Systems in the Copper Industry," *The Bell Journal of Economics and Management Science* vol. 6, no. 1 (Spring 1975) pp. 50–73.

Table 5-7. Price and Activity Elasticity Estimates from Various Studies

	Elasticities (at the mean)		Source	Period of analysis
	Short run	Long run		
Own-price (EMJ price)	−0.47	−0.64	ADL (Model)[a]	1950–73
Cross-price (aluminum)	0.61	0.84		
Activity variable (FRB index of durable manufacturers)	1.30	1.78		
Own-price (EMJ price)	−0.21	−0.90	Fisher–Cootner–Baily[b]	1950–58; 1962–66
Cross-price (aluminum)	0.24	1.01		
Activity variable (FRB index of industrial production)	0.33	1.40		
Own-price (EMJ price)	−0.17	−0.82	Fisher–Cootner–Baily[b]	1957–58; 1962–66
Cross-price (aluminum)	0.20	0.98		
Activity variable (U.S. index of construction materials)	0.15	0.73		
Own-price (EMJ price)	−0.21	−2.88	Charles River Associates (CRA)[c]	1950–67
Cross-price (aluminum)	0.46	6.30		
Activity variable (FRB index of durable manufacturers)	0.26	3.56		
Own-price (EMJ price)	−0.33	−0.77	D. McNicol[d]	1949–66
Cross-price (aluminum)	0.66	1.57		
Activity variable (FRB index of durable manufacturers)	0.44	1.06		
Own-price (EMJ price)	−0.12	−0.39	D. McNicol[d]	1949–66
Cross-price (aluminum)	0.35	1.13		
Activity variable (FRB index of durable manufacturers)	0.32	1.05		

Notes and Sources:

[a] Refer to Arthur D. Little, Inc., *Econometric Simulation and Impact Analysis Model of the U.S. Copper Industry, Technical Appendix* to *Economic Impact of Environmental Regulations on the U.S. Copper Industry,* draft report submitted to U.S. Environmental Protection Agency under Contract No. 68-01-2842 (October 1976).

[b] F. Fisher, P. Cootner, M. Baily, "An Economic Analysis of the World Copper Industry," *The Bell Journal of Economics and Management Science,* vol. 3, no. 2 (Autumn 1972) pp. 568–609.

[c] Charles River Associates, Inc. (CRA), *Economic Analysis of the Copper Industry* (March 1970) pp. 278–315.

[d] D. McNicol, "The Two Price Systems in the Copper Industry," unpublished Ph.D. dissertation, Massachusetts Institute of Technology (February 1973), pp. 68–69, from equations 2.15 and 2.16, respectively. (*Note:* Because of a typographical error, McNicol refers to these equations on pp. 68–69 as equations 2.14 and 2.15.) The results given here reflect the use of the domestic producers' price (eq. 2.15) and the domestic price of scrap (eq. 2.16) as noted by McNicol on p. 67.

ticities that have been estimated. These findings confirm some of the insights introduced earlier in this chapter. For example, seventeen out of eighteen short-run elasticity estimates indicate substantial inelasticity (or insensitivity) with respect to price and activity. The long-run elasticity estimates are all greater than the short-run estimates, indicating that the response of demand to relative prices and activity is, indeed, more sensitive to the long run. However, about half of the long-run estimates are in the inelastic range (i.e., less than 1.0). The long-run elasticity estimates of Charles River Associates are quite high. There are numerous reasons why the results differ. For example, each of the studies used slightly different estimation techniques. The activity variables and the aluminum prices utilized in the four studies also differ. The long-run elasticity estimates depend crucially upon the estimate of λ; the major reason for the difference in the long-run elasticity estimates is alternative estimates of λ.

An aggregate demand series of domestic semifabricators was presented in table 5-6. Equation (9) states that the amount of refined copper equivalent demanded by semifabricators is affected by the price of refined copper (P_t), the price of competing substitutes (P_t^s), and the production levels of the consuming industries (Y_t). The price series used for P_t is the deflated *EMJ* price of copper (i.e., U.S. producer refinery wirebar, f.o.b.).

We have focused our analysis of copper substitutes on aluminum because of its overriding importance as a potential competitor to copper. The price series used for P_t^s is therefore the monthly average New York dealers' buying price of new aluminum clippings. Production levels of consuming industries have been represented by the Federal Reserve Board (FRB) index of industrial production (durable manufacturers' production). Some analysts have utilized production levels (or indexes) for the semifabricating and fabricating industries.[16]

Estimates derived from our own study indicated that a 1.0 percent increase in the price of copper will lower demand (consumption) of refined copper equivalent by 0.47 percent in the short run and 0.64 percent in the long run. Furthermore, a 1.0 percent decrease in the market price of aluminum will stimulate substitution by aluminum (i.e., a decrease in demand for refined copper equivalent of 0.61 percent in the short run and 0.84 percent in the long run). Also, the income (activity) elasticities are both greater than unity, indicating that a 1.0 percent increase in the production of durable goods would generate a

---

[16] For example, an index of construction activity was examined by Fisher, Cootner, and Baily in "An Econometric Model."

1.3 percent increase in the demand for refined copper in the short run and 1.79 percent in the long run.[17]

Demand analysis is essential for projecting commodity prices, consumption, and production, but such projections require an analysis of short-run and long-run supply for the formulation of a complete econometric commodity model. The analysis of supply together with a brief review of several econometric copper models is given in chapter 6.

[17] The historical presence of a two-tier price system for copper described in chapter 4 has prompted the hypothesis of a rationing behavior on the part of the domestic primary producers. To account for the possible effects of such hypothesized rationing behavior, we performed alternative estimates of demand elasticities for differing sample periods which did not include rationing years. This yielded similar estimates for the *short-run* elasticities. However, the long-run elasticities differ since the estimate of λ did change. Information on rationing is quite inadequate to introduce it effectively into the analysis. None of the analyses summarized in table 5-7 appear to have accounted for the effects of rationing.

Appendix 5-1
Technical Notes on the Analysis of the Relationship Between Short-Run and Long-Run Elasticities

1. The equality between $e_{LR}\lambda$ and e_{SR} can be demonstrated by referring again to figure 5-3. Let D_L be the long-run demand curve of any group of producers demanding a given factor input and D_s be the short-run curve. Assume the curves are in equilibrium at $(Q_1\ P_1)$. Assume further that there is a once-for-all price decrease to P_2. By equation (7), the long-run desired quantity demanded is Q_2. However, in the short run, equipment and structural requirements cannot be expanded quickly enough and the producers only demand $\bar{Q}_2$ (i.e., demand is more inelastic in the short run, as $D_2 D_2$ is the relevant demand curve), where by equation (8)

$$\bar{Q}_2 - Q_1 = \lambda(Q_2 - Q_1) \tag{9a}$$

(*Note:* it should be remembered that Q_2 is desired while $\bar{Q}_2$ is actual.) Here we see that the short-run elasticity is λ times the long-run elasticity since:

$$e_{LR} = \frac{\Delta Q/Q}{\Delta P/P} = \frac{(Q_2 - Q_1)/Q_1}{(P_2 - P_1)/P_1}$$

$$e_{SR} = \frac{\Delta Q/Q}{\Delta P/P} + \frac{(\bar{Q}_2 - Q_1)/Q_1}{(P_2 - P_1)/P_1} = \frac{\lambda(Q_2 - Q_1)/Q_1}{(P_2 - P_1)/P_1} = \lambda e_{LR}$$

Hence,

$$\frac{e_{SR}}{e_{LR}} = \lambda$$

and

$$\frac{e_{LR}}{e_{SR}} = \frac{1}{\lambda}$$

2. In the second period, $\bar{\bar{Q}}_2$ can be solved as follows:

$$\bar{\bar{Q}}_2 - \bar{Q}_2 = \lambda(Q_2 - \bar{Q}_2)$$
$$= \lambda\{Q_2 - [Q_2 + \lambda(Q_2 - Q_1)]\}$$
$$= \lambda(1 - \lambda)(Q_2 - Q_1)$$

Likewise,

$$\bar{\bar{\bar{Q}}}_2 - \bar{\bar{Q}}_2 = \lambda(Q_2 - \bar{\bar{Q}}_2)$$
$$= \lambda\{Q_2 - [\bar{Q}_2 + \lambda(Q_2 - \bar{Q}_2)]\}$$
$$= \lambda\langle Q_2 - \{Q_1 + \lambda(Q_2 - Q_1) + \lambda[Q_2 - (Q_1 + \lambda Q_2 - \lambda Q_1)]\}\rangle$$
$$= \lambda\langle Q_2 - Q_1 - \lambda Q_2 + \lambda Q_1 - \lambda Q_2 + \lambda Q_1 + \lambda^2 Q_2 - \lambda^2 Q_1\rangle$$
$$= \lambda Q_2 - \lambda Q_1 - \lambda^2 Q_2 + \lambda^2 Q_1 - \lambda^2 Q_2 + \lambda^2 Q_1 + \lambda^3 Q_2 - \lambda^3 Q_1$$
$$= \lambda(Q_2 - Q_1) - 2\lambda^2 Q_2 + 2\lambda^2 Q_1 + \lambda^3(Q_2 - Q_1)$$
$$= \lambda(Q_2 - Q_1) - 2\lambda^2(Q_2 - Q_1) + \lambda^3(Q_2 - Q_1)$$

Since,

$$AB - 2A^2B + A^3B = AB(1 - 2A + A^2)$$

and since

$$(1 - 2A + A^2) = (1 - A)^2$$

then

$$AB - 2A^2B + A^3B = AB(1 - A)^2 = A(1 - A)^2B$$

Hence, setting $\lambda = A$ and $(Q_2 - Q_1) = B$, we have

$$\bar{\bar{\bar{Q}}}_2 - \bar{\bar{Q}}_2 = \lambda(1 - \lambda)^2(Q_2 - Q_1)$$

Appendix 5-2
Long-Run Substitution for Copper

This appendix presents detailed information on trends in long-run substitution for copper in markets.[18]

Conductor Applications

Aluminum has made significant inroads into copper markets in certain electrical conductor applications, specifically in busbar and switchgear, building wire, communication cable, and power cable. To a lesser degree, aluminum has been substituted for copper in motor and motor control parts and in automotive electrical apparatus and consumer electronics goods.

In the building wire industry, substitution of aluminum for copper has been increasing rapidly since 1964. The amount of substitution is directly related to the conductor size: the larger the conductor, the greater the percentage of aluminum building wire.

Substitution of aluminum for copper in the small building wire sizes is minor because little monetary savings per unit length can be realized in these sizes. In addition, mechanical connectors of aluminum to aluminum or aluminum to copper are a problem, particularly in the smaller wire sizes. Electricians frequently do not know how to make proper connections when installing aluminum building wires, and the resultant troubles have caused some building contractors to abstain from the use of aluminum conductor building wire.

The use of aluminum conductors in the communications industry is minimal at present. However, there is considerable research activity in this field by both manufacturers and end-users since large savings are indicated by the employment of aluminum conductors.

[18] The material in this appendix draws heavily on National Materials Advisory Board, *Mutual Substitutability of Aluminum and Copper,* Report of The Panel on Mutual Substitutability of Aluminum and Copper of the Committee on the Technical Aspects of Critical and Strategic Materials (prepared for the General Services Administration, Washington, D.C., April, 1972).

The substitution of aluminum for copper in the power-cable field has been rapid, and, in recent years, approximately 40 percent of insulated power cables and almost 100 percent of bare conductors have been aluminum. Aluminum has such a weight advantage over copper that aluminum-conductor, steel-reinforced cable has been used for most long transmission lines for more than a decade. Aluminum alloys are also being used as conductors on overhead transmission lines.

Copper remains the first choice for automotive wiring at current prices. In areas where space in an existing design is not a problem, the use of the larger sizes of aluminum wire will increase. Examples of such applications are battery cables, air conditioners, clutch coils, alternators, antiskid devices, horn coils, and some accessory motors.

Copper and aluminum are used widely as electronic consumer items (TV receivers, radios, record players, tape recorders, etc.). For many years the normal electrical conductor in consumer items was an insulated copper wire. However, with the advent of solid-state electronics, a large increase in aluminum usage occurred because of its excellent heat-sink capabilities. With the increasing usage of printed circuits or wiring boards, nickel, gold, silver, tantalum, and rhodium have also begun competing with copper for this application.

Heat-Exchanger Applications

All but a small proportion of the motor vehicles currently in service use radiators constructed of copper and copper alloys. Copper has been traditional for this application because of its heat transfer properties, corrosion resistance, ease of fabrication, and ease of joining the various components by conventional "soft" soldering techniques.

Substitution of aluminum for copper in radiators is possible given the fabrication techniques and the available supply of metal in the required sheet and strip forms. Automotive radiators have been built of aluminum in limited quantities and are similar to copper radiators in appearance and heat-transfer characteristics. However, experience has shown that copper radiators are quickly and economically repairable with minimal additional copper. Present repair techniques for aluminum radiators are either unreliable or available only at great expense at a limited number of shops. Most aluminum radiators today are replaced when leaks occur.

The major deterrent to volume production of aluminum radiators seems to be high capital equipment costs plus the unamortized cost of equipment presently used for production of copper radiators. Total cost of industry conversion has been estimated to be more than $200 million.

Currently, more than 90 percent of the primary surfaces in automotive air-conditioner evaporators and condensers are aluminum, and domestic refrigerators and freezers have used all-aluminum evaporators and steel condensers for years. Copper and aluminum are completely substitutable in this area.

Copper tubing is still the predominant primary surface in heat exchangers for commercial refrigerators and freezers, and room, central residential, and commercial air conditioners. Aluminum tubing is used in less than 10 percent of these products. Extensive manufacturing development is necessary before aluminum could be considered completely substitutable for copper in these applications. Aluminum-alloy tubing in air conditioners may have twice the wall thickness of copper, but still maintain a weight and cost advantage.

Production processes for most aluminum tube for commercial and residential air conditioners and commercial refrigerator and freezer heat exchangers are similar to those for copper-tube heat exchangers, with the exception of joining or assembly methods. The cost of converting an assembly line for copper-tube heat exchangers to aluminum is relatively low because most of the production equipment could be used with either metal, but not simultaneously.

Additional field experience is required before aluminum will be substituted widely for copper in room air conditioner condensers and commercial heat exchangers using water as a secondary refrigerant or as a heating medium. These products account for approximately 25 percent of the total tubing requirements and pose specific corrosion problems for aluminum. Codes now limit the use of aluminum-tube heat exchangers mounted in ducts. However, these codes are being reevaluated and soldered aluminum-tube heat exchangers may be accepted in the near future.

Aluminum has been tried in five different U.S. power plants. In two cases, failure occurred in about a year; in another instance, failure occurred in five years; and in the other two, condenser tubes lasted ten years. Fresh water was used for cooling in all cases.

Electroplating and Coatings

Copper has been, and will continue to be, widely used in coatings applied by electroplating and in forms made by electrodeposition. Electroplated aluminum coatings are not easily applied and currently are in negligible use. In coating applications, copper and aluminum are not interchangeable because the electrodeposition of aluminum requires highly special procedures. In recent years, electrodeposited aluminum coatings would have cost 6 to 10 times those of copper, and technical difficulties would require major changes in equipment. Recent developments in the thermal decomposition of liquid and vapor phase aluminum organometallic compounds may, however, permit the use of aluminum in coatings for steel and in protective paints in the future.

Alloying Applications and Coatings

Copper is essential in all U.S. coins because of the requirements of the large automatic vending machine industry. These machines are designed to accept coins with the properties of coin silver. To match these properties, silver-free coins must contain a high percentage of copper.

Aluminum is not used in any U.S. coins. It is too light in weight to operate coin-operated machines and has less wear resistance than currently used metals in coins. Thus, aluminum is an unlikely candidate for use in this field in the foreseeable future.

Ordnance and Accessories

Although other materials have been employed for certain fuse components, copper alloys continue to be the major ingredient. Periods of critical shortage in copper supplies have prompted efforts to substitute other materials in fuses for several years. Efforts to replace copper with aluminum also have been related to reducing weight.

In recent years, more than thirty different fuses have been used by the U.S. Army. Among standard models, the number of copper and/or aluminum components varies from practically none to a significant proportion. In some, the original functioning requirements were such that other materials (such as steel) were satisfactory for almost all components. In others, aluminum alloys have gradually replaced copper alloys. In still others, especially the recent models developed for new projectiles, aluminum alloys comprise a comparatively large proportion of the materials used.

6

Quantitative Analysis of Supply

Introduction

IN THIS chapter we are concerned with the quantitative analysis of the supply of copper, or of estimating copper supply from such variables as prices, production costs, inventories, and scrap arisings, among others. This discussion includes a brief introduction to econometric modeling of copper supply. There follows a review of the characteristics of a few econometric copper models designed to increase our understanding of the operation of the copper industry and to forecast future developments.

The sources of supply include primary refined copper originating from mines, secondary refined copper originating mainly from scrap, and unrefined scrap used directly by semifabricators such as brass mills. Producers' inventories may also be a source of supply, and imports of refined and unrefined copper (concentrates and blister) augment supplies in national markets. Each stage of production in primary copper supply—mining/milling, smelting and refining—has unique features that determine output and its responsiveness to changes in prices. However, the existence of a fairly high degree of integration of the copper industry in the United States, and to a lesser extent in the rest of the world, makes it difficult to analyze the supply and demand factors for each product stage separately. Some studies have modeled smelter/refinery supply while treating mine/mill supply as exogenous.[1] Yet the

[1] This is the method employed in the Arthur D. Little (ADL) copper model referred to in chapter 5. [See *Economic Impact of Environmental Regulations on the United States Copper Industry* (submitted to the Environmental Protection Agency) chapter 7.] An important reason for the approach taken in the ADL study was to highlight the effects of pollution abatement costs on U.S. smelter capacity. However, it is likely that reduced investment in smelter capacity as a consequence of increased pollution abatement costs would adversely affect decisions to expand or maintain U.S. mine capacity as well.

164

more basic factors affecting the supply of primary copper have their impact at the mine/mill stage.

Most studies seeking to relate world primary copper output to copper prices and other variables divide the world into major producing countries or regions since the response of output has been found to differ markedly from country to country. The United States, Canada, and the four principal CIPEC countries are frequently analyzed separately. Short-run price elasticities of supply are affected by the character of the market in which the copper is sold and by the nature of the variable cost functions. Under the producers' price system that exists in the United States, demand at the producers' price determines sales, but, depending upon interest rates and storage costs and upon the outlook for future demand, producers often produce for inventory in the face of cutbacks in demand. Where output is sold on the basis of open market prices, it is sometimes affected in the short run by a change in the LME copper price, but, since much of the output is contracted for sale before it is produced, a decline in the LME price need not have a significant effect on production in the short run. Because start-up costs are very high, a *temporary* shutdown of a mine rarely occurs (at least with the intention of reopening the mine in a year or two). However, cutbacks in mine production in the face of depressed prices are fairly common in the United States.

Mines differ in the degree to which variable costs can be reduced by reducing output. For example, in some countries labor is virtually a fixed cost because of high severance pay. Even in the United States, mines located in remote areas do not have a trained pool of labor to draw on outside of the existing mining community, so that cutbacks in employment may cause workers to leave for all time, thereby increasing costs of hiring and training when the work force is expanded. On the other hand, the ability of a mine and mill to expand output in the short run beyond their rated capacity is exceedingly limited. In the normal course of operations, the output of a given mine does change from time to time as a consequence of strikes, floods, technical breakdowns, and the depletion of economical grade ore in certain areas of the mine. In the latter case, time is required to develop other areas and to adjust the mill to variations in the ore grade. Such changes, since they affect large mines in different countries, make it difficult to identify changes in output resulting from price movements alone.

Even greater difficulties are encountered in relating changes in output or copper producing capacity over the long run to changes in prices. Investments in new mining capacity require a number of years before commercial production begins and such investments are made on the basis of *expected* price trends rather than simply on the basis of present or past prices. Investment decisions are also determined by the discovery of new ore bodies, the availability of capital, and, in the case of foreign investment, the investment climate in the host country, including the ability to negotiate a satisfactory mining agreement. In the United States, environmental policies and a variety of legal constraints with respect to both mining and smelting affect the rate of capacity expansion, or the scrapping of existing capacity. In countries where mining is under the control of a government enterprise, national policies with respect to the rate at which the country's copper reserves are to be developed may prove more important than current copper prices in investment decisions, subject to the ability of the government mining enterprises to obtain external capital and other inputs required for capacity expansion.

As discussed in chapter 12, copper prices determine the volume of copper reserves that are recoverable in various countries and for the world as a whole. However, there is no close relationship between the volume of recoverable reserves in various countries and the actual development of the reserves, including the exploration activity that would be required to determine the feasibility of specific projects. Nevertheless, higher copper prices (and mining company profits) usually tend to increase exploration activity for expanding measured reserves, at least in those countries where the investment climate is favorable.

The analysis of the supply of copper is also complicated by the fact that specific categories of copper demand purchase of output from different sources of copper supply. As was discussed in chapter 2, copper for wire mills comes almost entirely from primary copper, but primary copper may also be used to supply other semifabricators such as brass mills and foundries. Secondary refined copper goes mostly to other semifabricating industries, while unrefined copper scrap may be used by brass mills, ingot makers, foundries, and other industries. The supply of primary copper is determined ultimately by mine output and smelter and refining capacity, while the supply of secondary refined copper is determined by the supply of high-grade scrap and secondary refining capacity and to some extent by smelting capacity for low-grade scrap. Each type of scrap has its own special supply characteristics which differ considerably from the factors determining the supply of primary copper. The economics of scrap supply are discussed in chapter 13.

Many of the factors complicating the analysis of copper supply have been dealt with by econometric models, but no model has dealt satisfactorily with all of the important determinants of supply. In part, the problem arises from the absence of data on a number of variables, e.g., invisible stocks and, in part, from a lack of knowledge of the behavioral patterns of producers under various circumstances. For example, the entry of government mining enterprises into the copper industry in some of the major producing countries has resulted in a set of short-run and long-run responses to price changes different from those generally associated with private international mining companies in the past. Nevertheless, it is instructive to examine the approaches to supply employed in typical econometric copper models.

Econometric Modeling of Copper Supply

In this discussion we present elements of an illustrative copper supply model based on existing econometric models. Our purpose is to illustrate the methodology employed by copper models in analyzing the complex factors that determine copper supply. Copper models formulate and estimate equations that best explain the relation between copper supplies and prices and other relevant variables over an historical period.

The Partial Adjustment Approach to the Supply of Copper

The basic supply equation for primary copper may be written as

$$S_t = \alpha_0 + \alpha_1 P_t, \tag{1}$$

where S_t and P_t are supply and price respectively during the period t.

Some studies employ a partial adjustment hypothesis of copper supply analogous to that employed in the demand modeling described in chapter 5. It is assumed that suppliers can make only a partial adjustment in each period to a change in the current price, and that the change in the actual quantity supplied is equal to some fraction, λ, of the difference between the *desired* quantity in the given period, t, and the *actual* quantity in the previous period, $t - 1$. We may, therefore, express the partial adjustment hypothesis with respect to the supply of copper as follows:

$$S_t - S_{t-1} = \lambda(S_t^* - S_{t-1}) \qquad \text{where} \qquad 0 < \lambda < 1 \tag{2}$$

$$S_t^* = a + bP_t \tag{3}$$

Substituting (3) into (2) we derive

$$S_t = \lambda a + \lambda b P_t + (1 - \lambda)S_{t-1} \tag{4}$$

These equations state that the actual quantity offered at time t is not the desired quantity, S_t^*, corresponding to the price at time t, but that the adjustment from the quantity in the previous period, S_{t-1}, is some proportion, λ, of the difference between the desired quantity, S_t^*, and the actual quantity in the previous period, S_{t-1}. Likewise, in the previous period, S_{t-1} is not the desired quantity at P_{t-1}, but reflects a partial adjustment from the period $t-2$. Repeated substitution of S for previous periods in equation (4) would lead to a geometrically distributed lag. Under this hypothesis S_t becomes a function of all past prices, where the effect of each is less the further back we go in time. We may express this process mathematically by the following equation:

$$S_t = a + \lambda b \sum_{i=0}^{\infty} (1 - \lambda)^i P_{t-1} \tag{5}$$

We may, therefore, rewrite our basic supply equation for primary copper as follows:

$$S_t = \alpha_0 + \alpha_1 P_t + \alpha_2 S_{t-1} \tag{6}$$

The partial adjustment approach to estimating long-run supply provides a basis for estimating long-run elasticity of supply with respect to changes in prices. Short-run elasticity measures the response of supply to a change in price during a short period, t, say, a year. However, long-run elasticity is the response of the quantity supplied to a change in price after adjustments in capacity permit a shift from actual quantity supplied, S_t, to the *desired* quantity supplied, S_t^*. In the copper industry it will require a number of years to achieve the desired quantity corresponding to a change in the price of copper in a particular year. Now in a manner analogous to the estimation of long-run elasticity of demand in log-log form given in chapter 5, the relationship between long-run and short-run elasticity of supply is determined by the coefficient, λ, which measures the proportion of the difference between the desired quantity, S_t^*, and the actual quantity supplied in the preceding period, S_{t-1}. If there were no technical constraints in adjusting supply from year to year toward the desired supply, λ would equal 1 and the long- and short-run elasticities of supply would be the same. Actually, however, supply adjustments will be relatively small each year and full adjustment to the desired supply will take many years.

The relationship between short-run elasticity of supply, e_{SR}, and the long-run elasticity of supply, e_{LR}, may be expressed as

$$e_{LR}\lambda = e_{SR} \tag{7}$$

Since λ will usually be substantially less than 1, e_{LR} should be some multiple of e_{SR}, or the long-run elasticity of supply of copper should be substantially higher than the short-run elasticity.

Disaggregation of Copper Supply

As has been noted in earlier chapters, the sources of copper supply for a particular market, say, the U.S. market, include domestic mine copper (primary copper), scrap used to produce secondary refined copper, scrap that is used directly without refining, and net imports of concentrates, blister, refined copper, and copper scrap. The supply of mine copper in any given year is usually estimated as a function of the price of copper—in the United States, the producers' price—and the amount of mine production in the previous year.[2] However, some models take into account changes in the level of mine capacity, reflecting both increases in capacity and mine exhaustion. Obviously, the responsiveness of supply to changes in price in a given year depends upon the degree of capacity utilization and in subsequent years on the rate at which capacity can be expanded, once full capacity is reached.

Separate equations are used for new scrap and old scrap. New scrap production is mainly a function of total copper usage and tends to be rather inelastic with respect to price. However, the price of scrap, which usually tends to follow the LME or Comex price of copper, is often used as a secondary variable. Old scrap arisings depend upon the cumulative stock of products containing recoverable copper, the difficulty or cost of collection, and the price of scrap. Some scrap models use the estimated stock of (recoverable) copper-containing products, the amount of stock collected in the previous year, and the open market price of copper, e.g., the LME price, for estimating the supply of old scrap. The amount collected in the previous year is used as a measure of the difficulty of collection in the given year. For illustrative purposes, the U.S. domestic supply of copper may be given by the following three equations:

$$S_t^{usmp} = \alpha_0^{us} + \alpha_1^{us} P_t^{PRO} + \alpha_2^{us} S_{t-1}^{usmp} \tag{8}$$

$$S_t^{usos} = \beta_0^{us} + \beta_1^{us} P_t^{LME} + \beta_2^{us} S_{t-1}^{usos} + \beta_3 R_t^{us} \tag{9}$$

$$S_t^{usns} = \gamma_0^{us} + \gamma_1 P_t^{LME} + \gamma_2^{us} D_t^{us} \tag{10}$$

S_t^{usmp} = U.S. mine production
S_t^{usos} = U.S. old scrap production
S_t^{usns} = U.S. new scrap production
R_t^{us} = cumulative amount of copper-containing products.

Most copper models estimate supply functions for both the United States and one or more other major copper producing countries or

---

[2] A dummy variable is usually employed to reflect the effect of strikes.

regions. Since the United States is a net importer of copper, a complete analysis of supply to the U.S. market must include imports from the rest of the world. These are determined by U.S. demand and supply functions for copper and by the composite supply and demand functions for the rest of the world. Since prices in the United States and the rest of the world are not equal, trade does not result in a condition of world-wide equilibrium. Nevertheless, price differentials between the United States and the rest of the world provide an explanatory variable for the interregional trade flows.

In our illustrative model we use only two regions, the United States, denoted by superscript US, and the rest of the world, denoted by superscript RW. The symbol for the U.S. producers' price will be P^{PRO}; the symbol for the London Metal Exchange price will be P^{LME}. X^{RWUS} defines the exports of copper from the rest of the world to the United States. The new version of the model is now:

$$S_t^{us} = \alpha_0^{us} + \alpha_1^{us}P_t^{PRO} + \alpha_2^{us}S_{t-1}^{us} \tag{11}$$

$$S_t^{RW} = \alpha_0^{RW} + \alpha_1^{RW}P_t^{LME} + \alpha_2^{RW}S_{t-1}^{RW} \tag{12}$$

$$D_t^{us} = \delta_0^{us} + \delta_1^{us}P_{t-1}^{PRO} + \delta_2^{us}D_{t-1}^{us} \tag{13}$$

$$D_t^{RW} = \delta_0^{RW} + \delta_1^{RW}P_{t-1}^{LME} + \delta_2^{RW}D_{t-1}^{RW} \tag{14}$$

$$X_t^{RWUS} = \epsilon_0 + \epsilon_1(P_t^{PRO} - P_t^{LME}) \tag{15}$$

$$S_t^{us} = D_t^{us} - X_t^{RWUS} \tag{16}$$

$$S_t^{RW} = D_t^{RW} + X_t^{RWUS} \tag{17}$$

If the world market for copper were perfectly competitive and there was a uniform work price for standard grades of copper, modeling world supply would be simplified. However, U.S. and Canadian supply functions for primary copper are probably quite different from those in the developing countries because of differences in the behavioral characteristics of those responsible for production decisions among enterprises in different countries. For example, there is a tendency for mining industries in the developing countries to produce at full capacity regardless of price (unless constrained by other factors), while in the United States and Canada producers would be more likely to reduce output when price falls below marginal variable costs, even in the absence of a producers' price system. Long-run supply functions also differ substantially among countries. Some government-controlled copper industries are inclined to increase productive capacity as rapidly as their reserves permit, but they may be constrained by the availability of capital for mine development. Foreign investment is also determined by a number of factors other than expected long-run copper prices. On the other hand, investment in the United States is less constrained by the availability of capital and other inputs, but more by the outlook for the long-run rate of return on investment in copper mining.

*Criticism of Partial Adjustment Approach
to Long-Run Supply of Copper*

The partial adjustment approach to the long-run supply of copper summarized above provides an econometric tool for modeling supply under conditions of lagged adjustment of the desired quantity corresponding to the market price. However, it has serious weaknesses as a theory of supply. An adequate long-run supply theory must explain the relationship between long-run price expectations and the cost and profitability conditions determining investment decisions, given a wide variety of incentives, opportunities, and constraints. The current or expected price is only one of the many variables in the decision to expand (or shut down) capacity, and expected prices are in part a function of what each producer perceives that others are doing or believes they are likely to do. It might also be said that, even if all the factors determining long-run supply adjustment were known at a particular time, the existence of a particular market price, or of some average expected price, will not set in motion an invariable chain of adjustment period-by-period toward the desired level of supply. Long-run plans are subject to change as events unfold. As is discussed in chapters 8 and 9, each stage in the process by which copper mining capacity is created, from additional exploration to the construction of a mine, involves investment decisions that take into account a host of variables, among which long-run price projections are only one factor. A change in price or price expectation does not set in motion a series of adjustments that lead inexorably to a change in capacity coming on-stream eight or ten years hence. New ore bodies are continually being discovered or proved to be commercially feasible; technology, capital, and operating costs, and sources of financing are continually changing and plans can be altered or investments delayed at every stage in the process as new information becomes available. New environmental regulations affecting copper smelters have had important effects on smelting capacity in the United States and abroad, and have influenced not only the expansion of new capacity, but have led to the retirement of old capacity. They have also encouraged the development and employment of new technology for copper recovery.

Some copper studies have simply used planned mine and mill or planned mine/mill/smelter capacity[3] as an exogenous variable in projecting long-run copper supply. Although this approach is undoubtedly superior to forecasting on the basis of a calculated relationship between historical prices and capacity expansion, announced plans are frequently based on aspirations or goals rather than reflecting projects for which feasibility studies have been made, financing mobilized, and contracts negotiated. This is particularly true of plans announced by governments of developing countries. Even when construction is underway, there may be delays or postponements for various reasons.

Given measured reserves in various countries, information on capital and operating costs per pound of copper, and rates of return required in the mining industry (including allowance for risk), it is possible to calculate potential supply at various prices (assumed equal to long-run marginal cost of production) for different countries.[4] This method of estimating the elasticity of supply of world copper production has severe limitations, however. Only by examining particular projects can we determine the price at which it would be economical to construct a mine. This is especially true because of the large differences in infrastructure costs. For example, the rich Tenke-Fungurume mine in Zaire with an ore grade of 4–6 percent had to be abandoned in 1976 partly because of unacceptably high infrastructure costs. Also, metallurgical costs can only be determined after a feasibility study which may involve a pilot plant. Finally, a potentially profitable mine in certain countries at certain prices may not be developed because of obstacles to foreign private investment or constraints on the ability of the government to obtain the capital and other inputs required for exploration and development.

Econometric Copper Models

An econometric copper model constitutes an integrated quantitative analysis of the demand for and supply of copper, usually disaggregated by types of copper and geographical sources of demand and supply, and

---

[3] Data on planned additions to capacity are published by mining journals on the basis of public announcements or other sources of information.

[4] This method is employed by Kenji Takeuchi in "CIPEC and the Copper Export Earnings of Member Countries," *Developing Economies* vol. 10, no. 1 (March 1972) pp. 25–27; see also F. E. Banks, *The World Copper Market: An Economic Analysis* (Cambridge, Mass., Ballinger, 1974) pp. 121–123.

the interactions of the model's components in the determination of copper prices, production, consumption, and inventories. Econometric commodity models provide a mathematical framework for analyzing the complex interdependencies operating in an industry. These inter-relationships cannot be comprehended by ordinary two- or three-dimensional economic analysis. Even if the purpose of the analyst is to investigate some special aspect of the industry, such as oligopoly price setting in the U.S. market, he cannot realistically formulate and test his microeconomic model apart from the broader industry framework which includes the scrap market, international trade flows, changes in inventories, and so on. A short-run market-clearing model is essential for investigating market behavior for any of the individual sectors of the market. The purpose, however, may be to simulate the operation of the entire market by formulating a set of simultaneous equations to which actual data for the exogenous variables may be fitted over a period of time and to which the usual statistical tests may be applied. The resulting values of the endogenous variables may then be compared with the actual values of these variables over the period. Equations may be estimated on the basis of historical data ranging from ten to twenty years. If the set of estimating equations does a poor job of simulating the actual course of events, the usual practice is to change the assumptions or to add variables which take into account extraordinary influences such as strikes, war, or periods of extraordinary speculation.

The purpose of an econometric model may be to forecast the world price of copper, given a projection of industrial demand for copper based on a projection of industrial production or GNP. By testing the model for an historical period, the relationships between the independent or exogenous variables, such as the industrial demand for copper, and the dependent variable price, can be applied to projected exogenous variables to forecast copper prices.

Econometric copper models are also used to simulate a buffer stock operation over an historical period to determine the size and monetary-commodity composition of a buffer stock that would have been required to maintain market prices within a given percentage above and below the long-run trend or equilibrium price. Simulations of historical periods, while useful as guidelines for planning a buffer stock, provide no guarantee that the parameters of the past will hold true for future periods. This subject is discussed in chapter 7.

The 1976 CRA copper model was used to investigate the impact of foreign cartel activities or of an arbitrary cutoff of U.S. copper supplies from abroad, and the most efficient policy alternatives for dealing with such contingencies.[5] Such models provide a means of estimating the elasticity of demand for the output of a cartel by using the elasticity of world demand and the supply elasticities of alternative sources (see chapter 7).

Comments on Some Econometric Copper Models

The Fisher–Cootner–Baily (FCB) and Charles River Associates, Inc. (CRA) Models

Perhaps the best-known econometric copper models are the Fisher–Cootner–Baily (FCB)[6] and the Charles River Associates, Inc. (CRA)[7] models. The FCB study represents the development of a complete model of world copper markets. Demand equations are estimated for the United States, Europe, Japan, and the rest of the world, and supply equations for primary copper are estimated for four major producing countries—the United States, Canada, Chile, and Zambia—and the rest of the world. The 1970 CRA model is an econometric model of the U.S. copper industry. In 1976 CRA published a summary of an econometric model of the world copper market, but the entire study has not been available to the author.[8]

The regional disaggregation of supply in the FCB model raises some important issues. During the periods for which the supply estimates were formulated for Chile (1948–68) and for Zambia (1955–65), production was under the control of multinational corporations, but for most of the period since 1969 the copper industries of these countries

[5] Policy Implications of Producer Country Supply Restrictions: The World Copper Market (prepared for the National Bureau of Standards, U.S. Department of Commerce, by Charles River Associates, Cambridge, Mass., August 1976).

[6] F. N. Fisher, P. H. Cootner, and M. N. Baily, "An Econometric Model of the World Copper Industry," Bell Journal of Economics and Management Science vol. 3, no. 2 (Autumn 1972) pp. 568–664.

[7] Economic Analysis of the Copper Industry (March 1970) and An Econometric Model of the Copper Industry (September 1970) (both prepared for the U.S. General Services Administration, Washington, D.C., by Charles River Associates).

[8] Policy Implications of Producer Country Supply Restrictions: The World Copper Market (prepared for the National Bureau of Standards, U.S. Department of Commerce, Washington, D.C., by Charles River Associates, August 1976) pp. 106–111. The 1976 CRA copper model was also summarized in an unpublished paper by James C. Burrows and Marc J. Lonoff entitled "Charles River Associates Models of Metal Markets" (presented at the Ford Foundation Conference on Stabilizing World Commodity Markets: Analysis, Practices and Policies, held at Airlie, Virginia, March 17, 1977).

have been under the control of national mining enterprises. What factors other than the quantity and quality of ore reserves identify a unique supply function for an individual country? Would not a shift from multinational to national government ownership and control alter the parameters for the supply function of a national copper industry? Such questions appear not to be addressed in econometric quantity models.

The 1976 CRA model contains primary supply equations for mine production in the United States, Canada, Zambia, Zaire, Chile, and the rest of the world; and two regional demand equations, one of the United States and another for the rest of the world. The U.S. demand equations correspond to the five major end uses—electrical machinery, nonelectrical machinery, building and construction, transportation equipment, and consumer demand in general. An outline of the 1976 CRA world copper model is shown in figure 6-1. A modified version of this model was used by CRA to simulate the operations of a copper price stabilization program using a buffer stock and supply restriction over the period 1953–76 in accordance with a number of alternative assumptions and objectives.[9] The results of this series of simulations will be summarized briefly in chapter 7.

The structure of the demand equations is similar to that outlined in chapter 5 in all three studies, but the two CRA models undertake a disaggregation of the demand for copper by end use and their vulnerability to substitution by aluminum or other materials. The FCB model assumes that copper inventories are closely and consistently related to the overall durable goods inventory position, while the CRA models analyze both producers' and fabricators' inventories. However, the most important differences in the models are found in their treatment of supply.

In the FCB equations for estimating U.S. mine production (for the years 1949–58 and 1962–66), mine production is a function of the *EMJ* copper price deflated by the U.S. wholesale price index, and U.S. mine production in the previous year $(t-1)$. The authors found U.S. supply elasticities at the means to be 0.45 (short run) and 1.67 (long run). One can question the basis for such a supply function on several grounds. First, the U.S. primary copper industry is a price setter rather than a price taker so that the microeconomic meaning of such a supply function is questionable. Second, marginal or variable costs seem to have no

[9] See *The Feasibility of Copper Price Stabilization Using a Buffer Stock and Supply Restrictions from 1953 to 1976* (prepared for the United Nations Conference on Trade and Development, by Charles River Associates, November 1977).

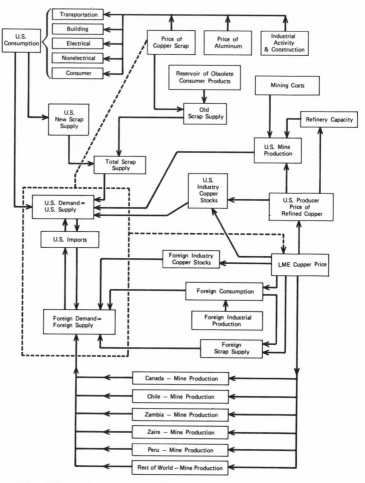

Figure 6-1. Schematic representation of the CRA copper model. (From Charles River Associates, *Policy Implications of Producer Country Supply Restrictions: The World Copper Market,* Cambridge, Mass., 1976, p. 107.)

relationship to the short-run supply function. Third, the partial adjustment hypothesis is both an inadequate and an unrealistic means of explaining expansion or contraction of mine capacity. The whole process of exploration and development over a period of ten years or more cannot be explained simply by reference to past prices and the lag structure that is assumed in the FCB model.

The 1970 CRA model treatment of primary copper supply is similar to that of the FCB model and suffers from some of the same difficulties.

However, certain exogenous explanatory variables are introduced, such as a capacity index and an index of factor prices in the U.S. primary supply equation. In the (1970) CRA model the short-run elasticity of copper supply with respect to price for the United States was calculated at 0.34 and the long-run elasticity at 0.85.

The FCB model was used in a number of simulation runs for the years 1969 to 1975. To run a simulation one needs two sets of data: (1) the values of lagged variables in the base year (1968) and (2) the values assumed for the exogenous variables for all years of the run (1969–75). For the 1969–71 period, predicted values could be compared with actual values. The one-year projections were reasonably good, but for later years predictions deteriorated rather rapidly.

The explanation given by the authors of the FCB model for the failure of their price forecasts beyond a one-year projection for 1969 represents a good summary of the inherent weaknesses of all econometric commodity models. The explanations are in part as follows:[10]

> 1. Since the model is dynamic, predictions several years in the future use predictions one or two years into the future as inputs. Thus errors tend to lead to further errors and the model tends to wander. Put more simply, in forecasting 1969, we were able to use actual values of the endogenous variables for 1968 for the lagged endogenous variables in the equations; in forecasting 1970 and later years, on the other hand, we could only so use the forecasted values of those variables for 1969 and later years.
>
> 2. For 1969 (and in nearly all cases for 1970) actual values of exogenous variables were used in the forecasts. For 1971 and thereafter, only values which were themselves forecasts could be used. As events catch up with such forecasts of exogenous values, their effect on our own forecasts for the copper market becomes increasingly severe.
>
> 3. Large new discoveries and the expectation of further ones may have depressed the price in a way not captured by the model. Our supply equations do include new discoveries, but only in a general and systematic way. Sudden success, particularly in new areas, will not be captured in our short-run forecasts.
>
> 4. It is possible that the model correctly predicts underlying tendencies but misses short-run deviations. If one believes this, then one must also believe that the fall in the LME price in 1970–71 was in some sense an aberration, which is far from clear. Certainly the model suggests that the general trend is up.

As regards the general trend, the FCB model did forecast rising prices in 1973 to the second quarter of 1974, but projected a continual rise through 1975. The projected rise in prices was not nearly as sharp

[10] Fisher, Cootner, and Baily, "An Econometric Model of the World Copper Industry," p. 600.

as actually occurred and, of course, the FCB forecast missed entirely the sharp decline in the second half of 1974 and the continued low level of prices in 1975.[11]

The ADL Copper Model

In 1976 Arthur D. Little, Inc. (ADL) prepared a model of the U.S. copper industry which is designed to assist in analyzing the impact of U.S. government pollution abatement regulations on the U.S. copper smelting industry.[12] The model simulates the U.S. copper industry's growth and evolution annually through 1985 under alternative macro-economic growth assumptions and environmental policy scenarios. The model considers, within an interdependent framework, such variables as demand (including substitution from aluminum), costs of production facing the primary producers, the relationship between primary and secondary producers, supply functions of secondary producers (refined and scrap), prices, inventories, investment, and international trade. Costs of production are directly factored into the model through engineering costs functions so that technological developments affecting mining, milling, smelting, and refining operations can be assessed.

The model has two basic components: the market-clearing module and the investment module. The market-clearing module, which consists of thirteen simultaneous equations, simulates every year the production and pricing behavior of the major producing groups in the industry, the inventory behavior of the major participants in the industry, the demand behavior of the users of copper, and the trade balance. The market is cleared in each year through materials balancing and price equilibrium equations. The investment module serves as the year-to-year "transit" connecting the solutions of the market-clearing module for successive years by simulating how smelting/refining capacity changes over time. The dynamic investment module simulates the evolving short run by taking into account the early solutions from the market-clearing module, plus certain exogenous as well as current and lagged endogenous factors. Smelting/refining capacity changes are estimated, translated into total fixed costs (along with increases in total fixed costs due to mining and milling investment, pollution abatement

[11] Ibid. The FCB model forecasted a U.S. producer average price of 54.6 cents per pound in 1972; 56.7 cents per pound in 1973; 61.2 cents per pound in 1974; and 65.3 cents per pound in 1975. See table 4-1 for actual prices.

[12] *Economic Impact of Environmental Regulations on the U.S. Copper Industry* (prepared for the U.S. Environmental Protection Agency, Washington, D.C., by Arthur D. Little, Inc. January 1978).

investment, and so on), which are then built into the cost functions of the primary producers. Since mining and milling investment decisions typically require profitability considerations extending over a long time horizon (typically twenty-five to thirty years), the model treats such investment as exogenous. However, capacity expansion and replacement investment at the smelting and refining level is made endogenous. Pollution abatement investment as well as pollution abatement increases in variable costs enter the model exogenously.

The model results include demand for and consumption of copper; refined copper production by primary and secondary producers; copper prices (domestic primary refined prices, secondary refined prices, and scrap prices); capital investment, capacity growth and capacity utilization; inventory changes (primary producers, fabricators/semifabricators, scrap); and international trade. The model also contains a financial model which computes a detailed set of financial variables: cash flow; flow of funds (sources versus uses); and changes in debt and equity in capitalization.

The ADL modeling effort differs from the FCB and (1970) CRA models of the copper industry in three important respects:

First, an effort is made to develop a dynamic model of the industry by explicitly imbedding into the model the industry's investment behavior. Accordingly, smelting-refining capacity expansion is made endogenous in the present model, but mining/milling capacity expansion was treated exogenously.

Second, an attempt was made to develop a nonlinear model of the U.S. copper industry. Static linear models fail to capture the dynamics of the behavior of producers operating with respect to their cost functions in either competitive or oligopolistic markets. The introduction of these behavioral relationships inevitably involves nonlinearities in the equations. Moreover, behavioral patterns differ for different stages of production—mining, smelting, and refining—and for suppliers of various grades of scrap.

Third, an explicit attempt was made to deal with the U.S. primary copper industry supply function under (current) conditions where the behavior of the firms in the industry is not characterized by perfect competition. This approach included estimation of engineering cost functions and building a link between capacity expansion and shifts in these cost functions.

An important shortcoming of the ADL model is that it fails to bring the rest of the world explicitly into the analysis. LME prices are treated as exogenous variables. However, the model was designed to deal specifically with the impact of EPA pollution abatement regulations on

the U.S. copper industry and not as a world copper model. The study's
findings are summarized in chapter 13.

The World Bank Models

The Commodities Division of the World Bank has used the following
two-equation model as an aid to forecasting copper prices and as a
supplement to expert opinion and extrapolation of price trends. In the
price equation, price (P) is assumed to depend on excess demand measured by the ratio between production lagged one year (Q_{t-1}), and consumption (C_t); lagged price (P_{t-1}), and output lost through strikes (OL).
Dummy variables are introduced for periods of extraordinary influences
such as the Vietnam war (1965–66) and extraordinary speculation (1973–
74). Consumption (C) depends on lagged price and industrial demand
for copper, measured by an index of industrial production (X) fitted to
annual data for 1955 to 1975. The regression equations are:[13]

$$\ln P_t = -0.428 - 2.250 \ln \frac{Q_{t-1}}{C_t} + 0.078 \ln OL +$$
$$\quad\quad (0.58) \quad (5.72) \quad\quad\quad (1.73)$$

$$1.013 \ln P_{t-1} - 0.269 \; Dum \; A + 0.276 \; Dum \; B$$
$$(10.38) \quad\quad\quad (2.01) \quad\quad\quad (2.60) \quad 1955\text{--}75$$

$$R^2 = 0.90 \quad\quad\quad DW = 1.83 \quad\quad\quad SE = 126.5$$

$$\ln C = 4.692 + 0.720 \ln X + 0.162 \; C_{t-1} - 0.147 \ln P_{t-1}$$
$$(3.47) \quad\quad\quad (0.56) \quad\quad\quad (2.94) \quad 1955\text{--}75$$

$$R^2 = 0.954 \quad\quad\quad DW = 1.16 \quad\quad\quad SE = 4.9$$

where

P = copper price (LME spot price of wire bars), annual average
in US$ per metric ton

Q = world production of refined copper (000 metric tons)

C = world consumption of refined copper (000 metric tons)

OL = output lost through strikes (000 metric tons)

X = index of industrial production (UN, manufacturing production, market economies, 1963 = 100)

Dum A = dummy variable = 1 in 1965 and 1966
= 0 for all other years

Dum B = dummy variable = 1 for 1973 and 1974
= 0 for all other years

---

[13] See Wouter Tims and Shamsher Singh, "A System of Linked Models for Commodity Market Analysis," (a paper presented at the Ford Foundation conference on
Stabilizing World Commodity Markets, held at Airlie, Virginia, March 17–20, 1977)
pp. 24–25. Issued as World Bank Commodity Note No. 8.

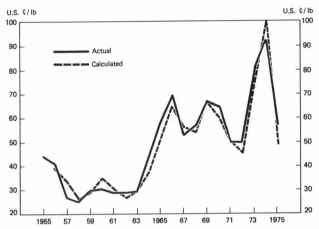

Figure 6-2. Copper price and consumption, actual and predicted, 1955–75. (From W. Tims and S. Singh, "A System of Linked Models for Commodity Market Analysis," World Bank Commodity Note No. 8.)

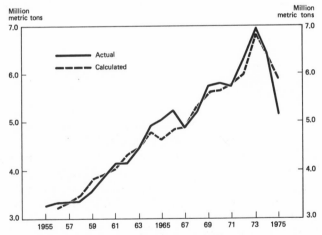

Figure 6-3. Refined copper consumption, actual and predicted, 1955–75. (From W. Tims and S. Singh, "A System of Linked Models for Commodity Market Analysis," World Bank Commodity Note No. 8.)

Figures 6-2 and 6-3 show the actual values for consumption and prices and those estimated from the equations.

Although the model described above does a fairly good job of predicting the LME copper price and world refined copper consumption over the 1955–75 period, there is no assurance that it will predict consumption and price for, say, the year 1980. For one thing, production of refined copper is an exogenous variable and production is a function of mine capacity and the supply of scrap. Projecting mine capacity requires an investment function, although over a five-year period knowledge of planned increases in capacity can provide a reasonably good basis for projecting mine capacity. However, mine production as a percentage of capacity may vary considerably with price. Old scrap supply is also a function of price, while new scrap supply is a function of consumption. Data on refinery production include production for producers' inventories, while consumption data include inventory accumulation by consumers and governments. Actual consumption by fabricators may be supplied in part by drawing down stocks so that there may be a wide divergence between production and actual use of refined copper in fabrication. Changes in inventories have important effects on price which are not reflected in the above model. This tends to make the assumed relationship between prices and the ratio of production lagged one year to current consumption somewhat suspect. The model also assumes that price in the current year is a function of price in the previous year, and that consumption in the current year is a function of both consumption in the previous year and of price in the previous year.[14]

Recycling, Inventory Behavior, and Short-Run Copper Price Movements

If the supply of copper were determined solely by primary copper production and the demand solely by the derived demand from the consumption of copper-containing products, plus inventory adjustments that followed the normal cyclical pattern for material inputs, modeling the copper industry with a view to explaining short-term price movements would be much easier. But primary copper output represents only 60 percent of the current supply of copper, with the remainder coming from old and new scrap, a portion of which is refined and another portion used directly without refining. Because of inadequate information, the modeling of scrap supply has not been very successful. We also lack full knowledge of inventories of both copper metal and of semifabricated and fabricated products, and of the behavior of the various categories

---

[14] The World Bank has developed more complex models, one of which divides the world into two major segments: (a) the United States using the producers' price; and (b) the rest of the world using the LME copper price. Tims and Singh, "A System of Linked Models," pp. 18–22.

of inventory holders, including both copper producers and users. Inventory behavior is not a constant function of known variables, but of
perceptions based on the outlook for copper prices and the availabilities
of a variety of copper-containing inputs in the production process.
Because producers' prices do not move directly with open market prices
on the commodity exchanges, hedging facilities are limited, and, in
addition, primary copper is subject to rationing as well as to minimum
purchase quotas which buyers are required to accept. Orders for semi-
fabricates and fabricates require varying lengths of time to fill, and
consumers are subject to "quantity risk" in times of heavy demand
which cannot be hedged in the futures market for copper metal.

Inventories play an important role in short- and intermediate-term
price fluctuations, but their role is obscured by inadequate data on
stocks. The level of stocks of different categories of holders—producers,
the LME and Comex exchanges, merchants and fabricators—is in part
a function of price or expected price changes, but holdings of the
different categories of holders do not necessarily move together. Prices
in turn are affected by the volume of reported inventories. In periods
of rising prices, stocks held by commodity exchanges and producers
have tended to decline and to rise in periods of declining and low prices.
Refined copper stocks held by producers and exchanges rose with the
sharp decline in prices in 1971, but declined drastically with the increase in prices in 1973 (see table 6-1). These stocks rose steadily during
1975 and the first half of 1976 despite the sharp increase in copper
prices in the second quarter of 1976 when they might have been expected to fall.[15]

Changes in fabricators' stocks from normal working levels reflect
shifts in the demand for their products, price expectations, and expectations of strikes or other supply interruptions. U.S. fabricators buy
from producers at producers' prices, but they also buy varying amounts
of primary copper and scrap from dealers or commodity exchanges, and
adjust their inventory positions in relation to their sales contracts
through the futures market. Hence, changes in reported stocks of fabricators may at times be difficult to interpret and, in addition, data on
world stocks of refined copper held by fabricators are incomplete, as
are data on stocks held by U.S. merchants and by foreign dealers.

In his dissertation[16] Steve Staloff seeks to improve on the explanation
of short-term fluctuations in copper prices presented by the FCB, CRA,

---

[15] Copper stocks were affected by the threat of a strike in U.S. copper mines and by
political disturbances in Zaire in 1976–77.

[16] "Stock-Flow Analysis of Copper Markets" (Ph.D. dissertation, University of Oregon, Department of Economics, 1977).

Table 6-1.   Refined Copper Stocks Held by Producers, Exchanges, and Merchants, and Average Annual LME Cash Prices, 1971–77
(*000 metric tons*)

Year	Stocks (end of period)	Average LME prices (cents)
1970	534	64
1971	647	49
1972	762	49
1973	384	81
1974	730	93
1975	1,369	56
1976 (Sept.)	1,591[a]	64 (1976 average)
1976	1,443	64
1977	1,507	60

Source: Copper Studies, November 12, 1976, p. 3; and *CIPEC Quarterly Review*, January–March 1978, p. 60.

Note: Stocks include holdings by LME, Comex, U.S. refiners, Japanese refiners, Japanese stockpile, Japanese dealers, and non-U.S. producers.

[a] Includes estimate of holdings by U.S. merchants of 200,000 mt. This figure not included for other years.

and other copper models by means of a more comprehensive analysis of both recycling and inventories. His concept of recycling goes beyond the use of scrap for the production of secondary refined copper and the direct use of scrap in semifabrication to include the recycling of the products themselves, e.g., auto parts, electric motors, nuts and bolts, and spare parts of all kinds. Recycling of copper-bearing products is believed to be price elastic. His concept of inventories is also extended from refined copper to stocks of copper-containing goods of all kinds. He divides inventories into *visible* inventories of refined copper and *invisible* inventories which include not only unreported refined copper held by consumers and dealers (which is the usual concept), but a large variety of fabricated products that are used as inputs in the production of finished manufactures.[17] Because of the time required to produce these copper-bearing inputs and the existence of capacity constraints, manufacturers are subject to "quantity risk" which cannot be avoided by purchasing copper futures on the commodity exchanges. They must

[17] A recent World Bank study develops a methodology for identifying invisible copper stock movements and analyzes the role of these movements in the determination of copper prices. *Fluctuations in Invisible Stocks: A Problem for Copper Market Forecasting,* World Bank Commodity Paper No. 27 (Washington, D.C., October 1977).

have copper-bearing inputs in forms not traded on the commodity exchanges.

Staloff develops a scenario for both the copper crunch and the glut that often follows. As the demand for copper metal and copper-bearing products increases, *visible* inventories of refined copper held by producers and exchanges decline, but producers of copper-bearing products increase their inventories of semifabricated and fabricated products all along the line. Moreover, Staloff finds evidence that they try to conceal their inventories from the merchants who supply them. Eventually the demand for products declines and, in addition, manufacturers become aware that total inventories, visible and invisible, have risen rapidly. At this point they reduce their orders from suppliers and draw down their inventories. Meanwhile, after a lag, higher prices have increased recycling, both in the form of scrap arisings and the recycling of copper-bearing products, and recycling adds to the total supply of copper. These events are self-reinforcing and may bring about a sudden fall in copper prices. At lower prices, producers either cut back on production or produce for inventory. Staloff's hypotheses seem plausible although he must substitute inference for much of the data required for a satisfactory proof. However, he has formulated a simultaneous copper market model incorporating his hypotheses, which generates satisfactory statistical results.

Econometric Copper Models and the Explanation of Copper Price Movements: Some Conclusions

In chapter 5 and here we have presented a disaggregated picture of both the demand for and the supply of copper, and examined briefly some econometric models designed to analyze historical relationships among copper demand, supply, and prices; to determine short-run and long-run elasticities of demand for copper; to determine the relationships among different sources of copper supplies and their relationships to copper prices; and to forecast future copper prices. This review of approaches to a quantitative analysis of the copper industry demonstrates the complexity of the factors behind short-run and long-run price movements in the copper markets described in chapters 3 and 4. The copper models help to increase our understanding of the relationships between changes in copper prices and those factors influencing market demand and supply by formulating hypotheses regarding complex interrelations among the variables and by testing these hypotheses with historical data.

Neither the state of the art of copper modeling nor the availability of data and information on behavioral patterns of consumers and producers are adequate for a fully satisfactory explanation of all historical price movements. Moreover, models have not been able to project future copper prices satisfactorily. This is due in part to the fact that parameters established on the basis of historical relationships, however valid, are themselves subject to change for a variety of reasons in a dynamic world. Nevertheless, as will be noted in subsequent chapters, copper models have provided guidance in dealing with important policy issues such as the international stabilization of copper prices and the impact of pollution abatement regulations on the U.S. copper industry.

7

International Copper Price Stabilization and Cartels

Introduction

THE EMERGENCE of CIPEC and the recent activities of UNCTAD and of the Raw Materials Commission of the Paris Conference on International Economic Cooperation (initiated in December 1975) have focused world attention on "stabilization" of the copper industry. Stabilization is a loosely employed term and is often confused with maintaining prices at some desired level or adjusting them in relation to other prices, that is, maintaining a "real" price by applying a general price index to a nominal base price. Stabilization is sometimes used to describe a system of floor prices or indexed floor prices with no ceilings.

It is important to distinguish between measures designed to reduce the amplitude of price fluctuations above and below the long-term equilibrium price, which we shall call pure price stabilization, and measures designed to fix prices at a certain level or prevent their falling below a given level without regard for the long-run equilibrium price. As a rule the mechanism employed for pure price stabilization operations is the buffer stock operation, which does not involve quantitative production or sales limitations. The fixing of prices generally involves some form of production or sales control. Recent discussions on the establishment of international commodity stabilization arrangements for copper and other commodities have been concerned with both buffer stock operations and production or export control measures.

Measures of Price Instability

There are several statistical measures of the degree of price instability which may be used to measure the results of a stabilization program or as a guide to operations, e.g., the activities of the buffer stock manager, or a system of adjusting export quotas. The degree of fluctuation encompasses both the amplitude of fluctuation and the frequency over a given time period. Stabilization objectives are usually concerned with quarterly or annual averages rather than with day-to-day or week-to-week movements. The degree of instability may be measured by the average percentage change in prices from quarter to quarter or year to year, or by the average percentage deviation of quarterly or annual prices from a trend. Measures of the degree of instability over periods of ten or twenty years during which prices are trending upward by means of the average change in prices from period to period would give an upward bias since the long-term upward movements would be included in the stability measure. Trends may be calculated by using, say, a three- or five-year moving average, or by fitting a trend line over the entire period during which instability is measured.[1]

Different statistical methods for calculating an index of price fluctuations for a given period give quite different results. For example, the index of annual fluctuations of the LME price of copper in constant 1974 dollars over the period 1955–75 was 8.4 percent based on the average deviation from a three-year moving average, but was 14.8 percent when calculated on the basis of a five-year moving average.[2] As was mentioned in chapter 4, fluctuations in the price of copper in terms of dollars or sterling might occur as a consequence of changes in the exchange value of the currency in which copper is priced, so that, ideally, changes in copper prices ought to be corrected for changes in the effective rate of exchange of the currency employed.

---

[1] The method used by a joint IMF–IBRD staff study for constructing an index of fluctuations in prices of a particular commodity was as follows: The trend for a given commodity price was estimated by fitting a linear relation between time and the logarithm of the annual price observations. The fluctuation index was calculated as the average over the period of annual percentage differences between observations and the calculated trend, disregarding the signs of the differences and expressing them as percentages of the trend. For some commodities there was no observable trend. See *The Problem of Stabilization of Prices of Primary Products*, A Joint Staff Study, Part I (Washington, D.C., International Monetary Fund and International Bank for Reconstruction and Development, 1969) p. 37.

[2] Taken from an internal IBRD report. The formula used was

$$\Sigma \left(\frac{(P_t - P_t')}{P_t'} \right) \times \frac{1}{n} \times 100$$

where P_t = price in year t, P_t' = the moving average centered on the year t, n = the number of observations of the relevant moving average. LME prices were deflated by the IBRD index of international inflation.

The UNCTAD Integrated Program for Commodities

The adoption of the resolution on an "Integrated Program for Commodities" at UNCTAD IV held in Nairobi in May 1976 was followed by a series of negotiations for the establishment of international commodity price stabilization agreements. The integrated program (IP) sets forth several objectives for international commodity arrangements, which for some commodities at least would not be mutually compatible. The objectives include "the avoidance of excessive price fluctuations;" improved terms of trade of the developing countries; and the promotion of "equilibrium between supply and demand within expanding world commodity trade."[3] The IP calls for the establishment of international commodity stocking arrangements for ten "core" commodities, including cocoa, coffee, copper, sugar, cotton, jute, rubber, sisal, tea, and tin, plus seven other commodities (bananas, bauxite, beef and veal, iron ore, rice, wheat, and wool) for which measures other than buffer stocks may be employed. In addition, the UNCTAD IV resolution provides for the negotiation of a "common fund" for financing the stabilization arrangements. An Intergovernmental Group of Experts on Copper began meeting at the UNCTAD headquarters in Geneva in November 1976 to lay the groundwork for the actual negotiation of an international buffer stock agreement on copper. During the course of the initial discussion it was clear that the LDC copper exporting countries would insist on some form of supply management in the international copper industry and would not be satisfied with the establishment of a buffer stock operation alone.[4] On the other hand, the representatives from the developed countries pointed to the legal difficulties in supply management involving copper producers in developed countries and to the possible incompatibility between supply restrictions and the reduction of the price fluctuations above and below a long-run equilibrium price.

The Benefits and Costs of Pure Price Stabilization Operations

Before considering the mechanisms for achieving price stabilization, I want to consider the arguments for pure price stabilization in the sense

[3] Resolution 93 adopted by the Conference, "Integrated Programme for Commodities" (mimeo, United Nations Conference on Trade and Development, 4th session, Nairobi, May 5, 1976) p. 3. Although the U.S. delegation voted for Resolution 93, the U.S. administration did not necessarily support all of the provisions.

[4] "Text Designed to Reflect the Main Points Made in the Discussion at the Second Session of the Intergovernmental Group of Experts on Copper" (mimeo, Trade and Development Board, UNCTAD, Geneva, March 14, 1977) pp. 11–14.

of reducing the amplitude of price fluctuations above and below the long-run equilibrium price. There are three sources of gains or losses arising from pure price stabilization operations: (1) the net discounted gains or losses to the stock itself (which must be borne by either the producers or the consumers or both); (2) the gains to risk-averse producers and consumers from price stability; and (3) gains or losses from resources transferred to or from producers and consumers as a consequence of changes in prices resulting from the stabilization operations.

It is widely believed that only a buffer stock type of stabilization operation would be potentially capable of reducing the amplitude of price fluctuations while maintaining relative neutrality with respect to the long-run equilibrium price.[5] Let us assume that the buffer stock is initiated with a certain composition of money and commodities and ends up at some point in the future with the same composition of assets. In the course of the buffer stock operations there will be storage, interest, and transactions costs on the one hand, and possible profits from the buffer stock operations on the other. Assuming that storage, interest, and transactions costs are not too high, it would appear that the buffer stock manager should be able to offset these costs from profits by buying low and selling high. However, the net profitability of the operation is by no means assured. For example, in one simulation of an international buffer stock operation over the 1961–75 period, the buffer stock manager earns positive profits but there is a negative net present value using the London Eurodollar rate of interest.[6] Moreover, the profitability of the operation may turn on the liquidation value of the stocks held at the end of the period. It should also be pointed out that buffer stock operations rarely start with a balanced portfolio of money and commodities. In fact, they frequently start with money and no commodities, and never return to the initial position until the whole operation is terminated.

Most students of commodity price stabilization agree that successful price stabilization operations will result in gains to both producers and consumers by reducing risk. Risk-averse consumers can plan their activities more efficiently and maintain smaller inventories, while producers and government fiscal authorities dependent upon revenues from commodity sales can make their decisions more confidently. It might be pointed out, however, that reducing short-run price fluctuations may

[5] It seems quite likely that short-term price stabilization itself would affect long-run supply and, hence, the long-run equilibrium price.

[6] R. A. Perlman (Commodities Research Unit, London), "Copper Stockpile Modeling," paper presented at the Ford Foundation Conference on Stabilizing World Commodity Markets, Airlie, Virginia, March 1977 (mimeo) p. 7.

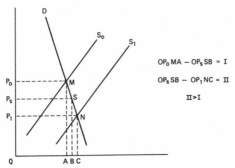

Figure 7-1.   Random shifts in supply. Stabilization favors producers.

not be of much help to investment decisions in minerals since the more important thing in such decisions is the long-run price trend.

Considerable theoretical work has been done on the question of resource transfers to and from producers and consumers arising from short-run price stabilization. B. F. Massell showed that under certain conditions producers gain from price stabilization if the source of the price instability is random shifts in supply, while consumers gain if the source of instability is random shifts in demand.[7] Where both demand and supply are random, the gains to each group are indeterminate and depend upon the relative sizes of the variances and upon the slopes of the demand and supply curves.[8]

Figures 7-1 and 7-2 illustrate the producer revenue or consumer expenditure effects of price stabilization operations given random shifts in supply and random shifts in demand, respectively. According to figure 7-1 the revenue that producers lose when stabilization reduces the price from OP_0 to OP_s (the target price) is more than offset by the revenue producers' gain from raising the price from OP_1 to OP_s assuming OP_0 and OP_1 are equidistant from the target price, OP_s. Figure 7-2 shows

[7] B. F. Massell, "Welfare Implications of International Price Stabilization," *Journal of Political Economy* vol. 78 (1970) pp. 404–417; see also Massell, "Price Stabilization and Welfare," *Quarterly Journal of Economics* vol. 83 (1969) pp. 284–298; and W. Y. Oi, "The Consumer Does Benefit from Feasible Price Stability: Comment," *Quarterly Journal of Economics* vol. 86 (1972) pp. 494–498.

[8] S. J. Turnovsky has pointed out that the distribution of the gains from stabilization between producers and consumers is highly sensitive to the precise specification of the model employed in the simulation. Turnovsky states that Massell's results depend upon the existence of linear demand and supply functions. See "The Distribution of Welfare Gains from Price Stabilization: A Survey of Some Theoretical Issues," in F. Gerard Adams and Sonia A. Klein, eds., *Stabilizing World Commodity Markets* (Lexington, Mass., Lexington Books, 1978) pp. 119–121.

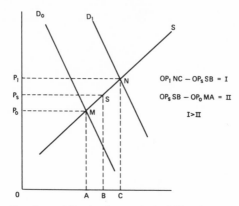

Figure 7-2.   Random shifts in demand. Stabilization favors consumers.

how price stabilization favors consumers under conditions of random shifts in demand: consumers' payments at the price OP_1 are reduced with a reduction in price to the target price, OP_s, by more than they are increased with an increase in the price from OP_0 to the target price, assuming OP_0 and OP_1 are equidistant from the stabilization price, OP_s. It should be emphasized that these diagrams are designed only to illustrate the propositions given in the previous paragraph and do not constitute proofs of these propositions. The proofs require mathematical analysis and certain additional assumptions. Moreover, the whole analysis is static and does not take into account such factors as the effects of stabilization on long-run supply and demand. Nevertheless, these propositions are frequently employed as a basis for quantitative analysis of the distribution of the gains or losses from price stabilization.

In the case of minerals such as copper and tin, instability usually arises from the demand side. Jere Behrman found that stabilization within a 15 percent band over the 1963–72 period on the basis of a secular trend for the 1950–74 period resulted in a revenue loss to copper and tin producers aggregating $2 billion compared with nonstabilization. On the other hand, Behrman found that stabilization over the same period resulted in revenue gains for the producers of coffee, cocoa, and rubber of over $6 billion, since instability for these commodities generally arises from the supply side.[9]

In considering the potential gains from stabilization of the price of a particular commodity for developing countries as a group, it must be

[9] Jere R. Behrman, "International Commodity Agreements: An Evaluation of the UNCTAD Integrated Programme for Commodities," in Adams and Klein, *Stabilizing World Commodity Markets*, p. 310.

kept in mind that most developing countries are importers of a commodity which may be exported by a few developing countries and perhaps by several developed countries as well. This is true in the case of copper, which is exported by a handful of developing countries, but developed countries such as Australia, Canada, and South Africa are also important exporters to both developed and developing countries. However, developed countries import more than three-fourths of the copper exported by world producers. Thus on the basis of the above hypothesis relating to the resource transfers arising from pure stabilization operations in copper, the developing country copper producers would appear to be net losers. On the other hand, Behrman argues that the gains to risk-averse copper producers in the LDCs offset the losses arising from the resource transfers, but this would be difficult to verify in quantitative terms. Important also is whether the buffer stock operations are profitable or incur losses, and how these profits and losses are divided between producing and consuming countries.

Stability of Export Earnings

It is frequently argued that what is most important to developing countries is not stability of prices for their exports, but stability of their total export earnings. Depending upon the relevant demand and supply elasticities, price stabilization will not necessarily achieve greater stability of export earnings. Given the inelasticities of demand and supply for copper, price stability would probably result in a greater degree of revenue stability. But even admitting this, it is argued that direct means of promoting stability of export receipts through compensatory arrangements would be cheaper and more effective than attempting to stabilize export prices. Finally, the assertion that instability of export receipts is a significant obstacle to economic development has been challenged by A. MacBean and by O. Knudsen and A. Parnes.[10]

Perhaps the most serious challenge to price stabilization operations in copper and other commodities comes from those who question the feasibility of pure stabilization operations and the ability of buffer stock operations to avoid contributing to long-run disequilibrium in

---

[10] See A. MacBean, *Export Instability and Economic Development* (Cambridge, Harvard University Press, 1966) chapter 2; and O. Knudsen and A. Parnes, *Trade Instability and Economic Development* (Lexington, Mass., Lexington Books, 1975) chapter 9. For a discussion of this literature, see David L. McNicol, *Commodity Agreements and the New International Economic Order*, Social Science Working Paper (California Institute of Technology, November 1976) chapter 2.

demand and supply. This subject will be taken up in the following section of this chapter.

Price Stabilization and Production Efficiency

It has been suggested that a strong argument can be made for market stabilization measures on grounds of productive efficiency.[11] Capital-intensive industries, such as the copper industry, which operate at 70 percent of capacity or less during temporary periods of low product prices, are probably wasting resources. Nevertheless, there is a question of whether short-term price stability in the sense of reducing fluctuations above and below a realistically determined long-run equilibrium price would in fact avoid investments leading to overcapacity. It is possible that the very existence of a price stabilization mechanism would induce a rate of capacity expansion that would not be justified by future demand. Moreover, cutbacks in production or the shutdown of high-cost operations constitute a stabilizing influence on world market prices. A more effective means of avoiding overcapacity might be better long-run demand forecasting and more complete information on plans for new capacity expansion. It should also be noted that mining firms differ in their responsiveness of output to changes in price, and that, in general, mining enterprises in the developed countries have been more willing to cut back production in the face of low prices than have government-owned enterprises in the developing countries. Stabilization measures that call for world-wide cutbacks in production or sales would tend to distribute the burden of production adjustments more equitably, but such arrangements have drawbacks from the standpoint of resource allocation since they would probably not distinguish between high and low cost producers.

International Buffer Stock Operations in Copper

Recently a number of simulations of the world copper industry have been undertaken in order to determine such variables as the size of the buffer stock that would have been required for stabilizing the price of copper within a given margin of the target price, say, 5 to 15 percent, and the cost of such operations for a historical period. The simulation of a buffer stock operation over a historical period can provide impor-

[11] This argument has been suggested to the author by Dr. John E. Tilton, professor of mineral economics, The Pennsylvania State University.

tant information and guidelines for establishing an actual buffer stock in the commodity, but simulation cannot provide a blueprint for the future. Speculation, inventory behavior, and factors governing long-run demand and supply such as the development of substitutes or the discovery of new ore bodies may alter substantially the requirements for an actual buffer stock operation in the future. A major problem for both simulations of buffer stock operations during an historical period and for the actual operation of a buffer stock lies in the method of determining the target price around which the actual price is to be stabilized. The methods employed in simulations include a three-year lagged moving average; fitting a trend line for prices in a past period; periodic adjustments in the target price in response to shifts in the composition of the buffer stock, that is, the ratio of financial to commodity assets; allowing the buffer stock manager to use his judgment regarding the long-run equilibrium price; and estimating long-run average production costs. Simulations usually employ some automatic method such as a three- or five-year lagged moving average, or fitting a trend line for prices over past periods. The method that seems to work well in a simulation may not constitute a proper means of determining a target or equilibrium price for an actual buffer stock operation. In fact, there may be no substitute for providing the buffer stock manager with a certain amount of discretion in adjusting the target price on the basis of extrapolating the effects of changes in long-run demand and supply conditions.

David McNicol suggests that the best criterion for establishing a target price is the long-run average cost of production.[12] However, in the copper industry, which is characterized by long gestation periods and substantial differences between the average cost of expanding existing mines and the creation of new ones in different regions of the world, long-run marginal cost might be a better criterion. But cost criteria are difficult to apply. For example, in countries where the copper industry is dominated by a government enterprise, social opportunity costs rather than monetary costs guide decisions for expansion. In the case of a government enterprise, not only are taxes on the enterprise a part of the revenues from the standpoint of the government, but the social opportunity cost of labor is substantially less than its monetary cost to a private international mining firm.

It has been suggested that if the target price is based on a calculated trend, deflated prices should be used so that the target price can be

[12] McNicol, *Commodity Agreements and the New International Economic Order*, pp. 65–72.

adjusted for the current rate of inflation. This approach assumes implicitly that all prices move together by the same percentage, an assumption not in accordance with the facts. Nevertheless, any calculated trend based on historical data which is used as a basis for determining a target price will be affected by varying rates of inflation. In the course of the UNCTAD discussions in 1977, representatives from some Third World countries put forward the idea of indexation of the target price in terms of a world index of the prices of manufactures, or of some other index, in order to keep the nominal price range constant in real terms. However, in a world of fluctuating exchange rates and of markedly varying rates of inflation in all developed countries, the choice of a price index for use in indexation becomes exceedingly complex, as does also the problem of determining the influence of inflation on the long-run equilibrium (nominal) price.

In practice, the target price employed by a buffer stock authority is likely to be a negotiated one between consumer and producer members of the international buffer stock agreement. Hence, adjusting the target price for changes in a world price index simply adds another arbitrary element to this determination, which may move the target price away from or toward the appropriate long-run equilibrium price.

If the buffer stock authority had a competent research staff, it would seem desirable to give the buffer stock manager freedom to adjust the target price from year to year in accordance with his perception of changes in the long-run equilibrium price. Such adjustments could also take into account changes in the asset composition of the buffer stock with a view to avoiding a depletion of either money or commodities. The target price would be adjusted downward when the financial assets declined below a certain level and upward when the supply of the commodity declined below a certain level.

Another issue in buffer stock management is whether the manager could operate by buying or selling the commodity within the permitted range above and below the target price or only at the extremes. Giving the buffer stock manager freedom to operate within the range would have the advantage of creating uncertainty for speculators, who could never be sure when the buffer stock purchases or sales would take place. In a period of market weakness or strength for the commodity, speculators would not have the advantage of knowing that the buffer stock support operations would not take place until the price had reached the floor or the ceiling, respectively.

Still another question that arises with respect to a pure price stabilization operation is whether the existence of the stabilization arrangement itself will affect the long-run equilibrium price. For example, will the existence of a stabilization operation encourage investment in new capacity because of a perceived reduction in the risk of having the new capacity come on-stream in a period of exceptionally low copper prices? Or are decisions relating to investment in new capacity made largely on the expectation of long-run price trends? The existence of a stabilization operation could also affect the demand for copper by consumers, who would avoid the risk of having to pay very high prices for copper at some time in the future. Inventory behavior might also be affected by the existence of a stabilization operation, which in turn would affect the equilibrium price trends. Finally, short-term instability in the copper industry generates certain stabilizing forces that operate at least in the intermediate term. In periods of high copper prices, more scrap is collected and marginal mines and other facilities come on-stream, while in periods of low prices suppliers may produce for inventory. Stabilization operations would reduce the impact of these forces.

Inventory behavior of copper consumers constitutes a major destabilizing force. As prices are rising and shortages are feared, not only are inventories of copper accumulated, but inventories of semifabricated products and even copper manufactures may be accumulated. As soon as it is believed that the peak has been reached and the trend of copper prices is downward, inventories are unloaded either on the market or are drawn down for use in place of orders from suppliers. An effective strategy for a stabilization program would be to counteract these inventory movements while at the same time allowing sufficient price movements to generate intermediate-term stabilizing forces. This strategy suggests the possibility of a stabilization operation with either no target prices or a very wide range within which prices might be permitted to fluctuate. Under this approach only extreme price movements generated by inventory behavior would be prevented, but price movements in response to fundamental demand and supply conditions would be permitted.

Estimating the Assets Required for a Copper Buffer Stock

Estimates of the assets required for a buffer stock to be employed for maintaining market prices within a given range of the target price (however defined) are generally made on the basis of a simulation of a buffer stock operation over some historical period covering two or more price cycles. Since the amplitude of fluctuations in copper prices occurring over the 1972–75 period was the largest in recent history, simulations have generally included this period. The required composition of the initial assets depends upon the point at which the simulation begins. Unless the simulation is initiated at a very low point in the price cycle relative to the maximum price over the period, a buffer stock with little or no commodities and only financial assets is likely to be unable to defend the ceiling, no matter how large the financial assets available for defending the floor. This will obviously be a problem for any future copper buffer stock unless it can acquire some of the large existing private buffer stocks. (By March 1977 the U.S. copper stockpile was drawn down to zero.)

The success of a simulation in determining the required size and composition of a buffer stock will depend upon (1) the degree to which the buffer stock target price approximates the long-run equilibrium price (or is adjusted from time to time to correct departures from the long-run equilibrium price), and (2) the degree to which the maximum amplitude of price fluctuations during the period of actual buffer stock operations corresponds to that during the simulation period. The amount of assets required for a buffer stock to defend successfully both the ceiling and the floor prices will also depend upon the selected range within which prices are to be maintained by the buffer stock operations. As a rule, the wider the range, the larger the required volume of assets.

Actual estimates of the size of a copper buffer stock differ considerably depending upon the methodology employed in the simulation, the long-run target price, and the width of the range. In a study released in January 1977, the UNCTAD Secretariat estimated the appropriate volume of a copper buffer stock for the period 1979–83 on the assumption that the agreed target price would be based on the five-year annual average price of copper wirebar on the London Metal Exchange (LME) either for 1971–75 or for 1974–78. It was further assumed that the width of the range would be 10 percent above and 10 percent below the target price. On the basis of these assumptions, the UNCTAD Secretariat estimated that a buffer stock of 855,000–1,029,000 metric tons would be required to maintain the price of copper within the 10 percent range for an assumed target price of $2,094 per metric ton or the average annual price of copper on the LME for the period 1971–75 expressed in 1976 dollars. For the highest volume, the estimated cost would be $1,939 million.[13] I rather suspect that the UNCTAD Secretariat's estimate is biased in the direction of determining the financial assets required to defend the price floor since no mention is made in the report of the initial composition of the assets. Unless the maximum volume of commodities was purchased prior to the time that they were

[13] "Consideration of the Matters Remitted by the Preparatory Meeting on Copper," report by the UNCTAD Secretariat (TD/B/IPC/COPPER/AC/L.4, January 21, 1977) pp. 3–4.

required to defend the ceiling price, the buffer stock manager might not have sufficient commodities to defend the ceiling.

Other studies have shown the UNCTAD Secretariat's estimates of the required size of a copper buffer stock to be quite inadequate. For example, simulation studies undertaken by the Commodities Research Unit, Ltd. (New York) suggest that for a stabilization scheme operating over the period 1961–75, a buffer stock of 2.5 million mt would have been needed at an acquisition cost of $4 billion.[14] However, if the range of permitted price fluctuation were 15 percent on either side of the equilibrium price, the largest stock required could be reduced to 2.0–2.25 million mt. Jere Behrman found on the basis of his simulation study that a maximum buffer stock of about 5.6 million mt would be required, and concluded that access to financial resources of $6 billion suggested by the UNCTAD Secretariat for financing buffer stocks for the ten core commodities is not likely to be sufficient and that a fund of over $10 billion would be required.[15] David McNicol estimates the capital cost of a buffer stock required to maintain copper prices within 10 percent on either side of the target level to be $5 billion.[16]

The 1977 CRA Copper Price Stabilization Study

In 1977 Charles River Associates, Inc. (CRA) prepared for UNCTAD a report entitled *The Feasibility of Copper Price Stabilization Using a Buffer Stock and Supply Restrictions from 1953 to 1976* (November 1977). The study was designed to answer the following questions: (1) "Would procedures to stabilize price using a buffer stock and supply restrictions have worked in the 1953–76 period?" and (2) "What would the buffer stock or supply restrictions cost, and how large would the stocks or supply restrictions have to be?" CRA undertook a number of simulations covering the 1953–76 period designed to analyze the results of alternative stabilization methods, including a pure buffer stock, pure production controls, and a mix of buffer stock action and production controls. A modified version of CRA's 1976 econometric model of the world copper market (discussed briefly in chapter 6) was employed for the simulations. The following buffer stock decision rules were assumed

---

[14] *Coordinated National Stockpiles as a Market Stabilizing Mechanism: Copper* (New York, Commodities Research Unit, 1976) chapter 13.3.

[15] Behrman assumed a 15 percent range and a price trend 2 percent greater than the actual secular trend for a decade. See Jere R. Behrman, "International Commodity Agreements: An Evaluation of the UNCTAD Integrated Programme for Commodities," in Adams and Klein, *Stabilizing World Commodity Markets*, pp. 312–313.

[16] McNicol, *Commodity Agreements and the New International Economic Order*, p. 95.

in the analysis: (1) the reference price was based on three- or five-year moving averages of past prices, and (2) alternative bands of fluctuation allowed around the reference price were set at 10 and 15 percent.

Results of the CRA study were scarcely encouraging to those who advocate the use of a pure buffer stock for maintaining price fluctuations within reasonable margins. The general conclusion of the CRA report was as follows: "Under these rules there was only a slight decrease in price instability during the period. In virtually every simulation the LME copper wirebar price broke through the price ceiling in the mid-1960s. It is the principal contention of this report that rigid *a priori* rules in general would have been unsuccessful. However, a complex set of rules developed after the fact might have improved price stability from 1965 to 1974."[17]

The CRA study found that a buffer stock with financing of $2 to 2.5 billion could have maintained a floor price within 10 percent of the reference price over the 1953–76 period. Any stock of reasonable size, whether accumulated by buffer stock operations or otherwise acquired, would have been exhausted without being able to maintain the price ceilings during specific years. The CRA study found that a stock with unlimited resources of money and copper would have sold some 22 million tons of copper (about $24 billion worth at 50 cents per pound) over the 1964–76 period in order to maintain the ceiling price on a slowly rising trend. Since only a fraction of this amount would have been accumulated by the buffer stock manager prior to 1964, it is obvious that a buffer stock operation capable of maintaining the ceiling price under the decision rules would not have been feasible. Moreover, since the principal problem was in maintaining the ceilings, the use of supply restriction would not have improved stabilization capabilities.

In its report, CRA cites a number of limitations on the inferences that can be drawn from their results. One important limitation is that changes in investment and in private copper stock behavior arising from the existence of the buffer stock operation itself could not be estimated. The most important limitation on inferences regarding the feasibility of any buffer stock operation arises from the assumption that the rules of the buffer stock operation are fixed. Moreover, it is unlikely that any set of fixed rules, unless they provided for very wide bands of fluctuations, would have worked. The CRA report, therefore, recommends that further research should concentrate on flexible decision rules which might be allowed to the buffer stock manager. For example, the buffer

---

[17] *The Feasibility of Copper Price Stabilization Using a Buffer Stock and Supply Restrictions from 1953 to 1976* (prepared for the United Nations Conference on Trade and Development, by Charles River Associates, November 1977) pp. 1-1 to 1-6.

stock manager might be given discretion to change the reference price on the basis of his perception of the long-run equilibrium price, or of trends in that price. This would be in line with traditional stabilization policy as it was developed by central banks for moderating short-run fluctuations in exchange rates while permitting average rates over time to follow perceived longer term trends.

The difficulty with a recommendation for giving a buffer stock manager broad flexibility in determining the reference price is that the determination of the reference price is regarded as a policy decision to be negotiated among the parties to the stabilization agreement rather than as a decision to be left to the experts. This is, of course, not to say that the experts will always make the right decision, but they should be in a position to correct their mistakes, it is to be hoped, before the buffer stock runs out of either money or commodities. The recommendation of the CRA report suggesting flexible decision rules for the buffer stock manager is a sound one, but whether country members of an international buffer stock agreement could reach an accord on such rules is a question on which I do not wish to speculate.

National Stockpiles

National stockpiles may be used in place of international buffer stocks for achieving international price stability. If each national stockpile manager operated under the same rules and with the same objectives and if the aggregate volume of financial and commodity assets allocated among the countries operating in the program were sufficient for achieving the stabilization objectives, the results could be much the same as they would be under an international buffer stock program.[18]

A national stockpile may also be employed to stabilize the volume of demand and supply in the national market and thereby indirectly contribute to price stabilization. For example, national stockpiling operations might be employed to stabilize producers' stocks. On the other hand, national stockpiles might be used for nonstabilization purposes such as the maintenance of strategic reserves; this is the purpose of the GSA stockpile of minerals and metals, created to ensure supplies of critical materials in the event of war. National stockpiles have been accumulated to support the domestic producing industry or to maintain a specific degree of national self-sufficiency. Finally, they might be held to combat possible foreign cartel activities designed to force up prices.

[18] For a discussion of the mechanism of stabilizing the international copper market by means of national stockpiling programs, see *Coordinated National Stockpiles as a Market Stabilizing Mechanism,* chapter 12.

Price Stabilization Programs Involving Supply Management

Since the UNCTAD integrated program is designed not only to reduce the amplitude of price fluctuations but also to raise the real incomes of the producing countries by improving their terms of trade, the Intergovernmental Group of Experts on Copper has discussed supply management measures, perhaps supplemented by import quotas imposed by the consuming countries.[19] Export restrictions might also be used to defend the floor price of copper if the financial resources of the buffer stock proved to be inadequate. However, in such an event the buffer stock would very likely not have a sufficient volume of commodities to defend the ceiling. Hence, the arrangement would prove unacceptable to the consuming countries.

In the case of copper, the use of export quotas for maintaining floor prices would give rise to difficulties not encountered in the International Coffee Agreement, which is based entirely on quantitative export and import controls. The reason is that countries such as the United States, which are both large producers and consumers of copper, might be required to impose output or sales limitations on their own producers for the domestic market since otherwise the supply reductions in the exporting countries would be offset in whole or in part by increased production in the consuming countries. It is most unlikely that the U.S. government would agree to the imposition of supply restrictions on its own products. There is also the problem of controlling the supply of scrap in national and international markets. Increased scrap arisings might well limit the ability of producers to raise prices by primary supply curtailment. Finally, export quotas would impair the validity of long-term supply contracts which are employed extensively by copper exporting countries, and thereby reduce the willingness of consumers to negotiate such contracts. This in turn might affect the ability of copper exporting countries to market their copper on world markets or their ability to borrow for new copper producing projects.

Even if all of the above problems could somehow be overcome, there remains the problem of reaching an agreement on price targets that are in excess of the long-run equilibrium price. It is one thing to ask U.S. consumers to pay more than the long-run equilibrium price for coffee as a means of transferring resources to the LDC coffee producers, but asking U.S. consumers to pay a monopoly price to U.S. copper producers

---

[19] See "Text Designed to Reflect the Main Points Made in the Discussion at the Second Session of the Intergovernmental Group of Experts on Copper" (mimeo, TD/B/IPC/copper/AC/CRP.3, Restricted, UNCTAD, Geneva, March 8, 1977).

or to Canadian copper producers is quite a different matter. The attempt to maintain a target price in excess of the long-run equilibrium price of copper appears to require rather complete government control of the U.S. copper industry.

*Impact on Investment in
New Copper Producing Capacity*

Any attempt to establish a target price in excess of the long-run equilibrium price would obviously affect investment in new copper producing capacity. Whatever their ability to agree on measures for controlling copper prices in the short run, the principal copper exporting countries are in long-run competition with one another for expanding or maintaining their shares of the world copper market. It is unlikely that any of the CIPEC countries would be willing to retard the development of their copper industry in accordance with some long-run market-sharing agreement. Given the large differences in the ratios of copper producing capacity to measured and inferred reserves among the major copper producing countries, it is unlikely that those with low ratios would be willing to accept a freezing of market shares. Moreover, any restriction in the development of the capacity of LDC copper producers would encourage a more rapid expansion of the capacity of other countries not party to the agreement.

Criticisms of Commodity Price Stabilization and Alternative Measures of Promoting LDC Objectives

Critics of commodity price stabilization schemes have not only pointed to the difficulties in achieving both pure commodity stabilization and an improvement in the terms of trade of the producing countries, but have also argued that there are more efficient and equitable means of achieving the basic objectives of price stabilization for the developing countries. The major objective for these countries is the stabilization of their export earnings.[20] It is argued, however, that this can be achieved more efficiently through a compensatory financing arrangement such as is already being provided by the International Monetary Fund. The IMF's compensatory facility could be expanded and the loan terms and

---

[20] Some economists have found no positive relationship between the stability of export earnings and economic growth or development. See, for example, MacBean, *Export Instability and Economic Development*, chapter 2; and Knudsen and Parnes, *Trade Instability and Economic Development*, chapter 9.

borrowing costs reduced so as to provide all developing countries with an adequate facility for stabilizing their export earnings. It is also pointed out that under some circumstances commodity price stabilization may not achieve stability of export earnings. Moreover, as has been noted, a pure stabilization operation in a commodity such as copper might tend to transfer resources from the producing countries to the consuming countries.

As regards the objective of increasing the real incomes of producing developing countries, increasing the target price above the long-term equilibrium price is both an inefficient and an inequitable method of promoting resource transfers. Not only will some developing countries receive no benefits (or negative resource transfers if they happen to be large importers of the commodities whose prices are raised), but much of the benefits from the higher prices will go to developed country exporters of the primary products affected. It is true, of course, that taking the UNCTAD list of ten core commodities as a group, developing countries export more of these commodities than they import, but the benefits will not be equitably shared and some of the large countries with very low per capita incomes, such as India and Pakistan, may be net losers. Direct transfers of resources through loan and grant programs would be a cheaper and more equitable means of transferring resources to the developing countries.

Jere Behrman, who is in general agreement with the UNCTAD integrated program, counters the above arguments as follows. First, he argues that commodity price stabilization benefits both producers and consumers by reducing risks, and that this advantage would be lost by concentrating wholly on stabilization of export earnings. Second, he believes that the transfers of resources from developed consuming countries to LDC producing countries as a result of the operation of commodity agreements are likely to be in addition to and not in place of other forms of direct aid transfers.[21] Nevertheless, the feasibility and the costs of the integrated program must be weighed against the alleged benefits.

A Producers' Copper Cartel

Concerted actions for controlling prices by producing countries alone, as distinguished from activities undertaken by a group representing both producing and consuming countries, are generally characterized as

[21] Behrman, "International Commodity Agreements: Evaluation of the UNCTAD Integrated Programme for Commodities," in Adams and Klein, *Stabilizing World Commodity Markets*, pp. 313–316.

cartel activities. However, there are several types of cartel activities, ranging from informal agreements to adopt similar policies with respect to export taxation or marketing and pricing practices, to formal agreements on uniform prices and limiting production or allocating markets for implementing the price objectives. Intergovernmental associations among producing countries have been formed for several minerals, including bauxite, copper, and iron ore, but only in petroleum has there been established an effective control of the world price. The International Bauxite Association under the leadership of Jamaica has been instrumental in establishing more or less common production levies by most of its members,[22] but since there is no free market for bauxite (and there are a variety of bauxite ores), no uniform world market price is currently envisaged. The Intergovernmental Council of Copper Exporting Countries (CIPEC) has achieved a certain amount of coordination among its members, including a 15 percent reduction in exports in 1974–75, but recently its activities have been directed toward the establishment of an international commodity agreement in copper to operate as a part of the UNCTAD Integrated Commodity Program. Should the effort to establish a satisfactory commodity agreement in copper fail, CIPEC will undoubtedly attempt some form of producer cartel arrangement in copper. In the following paragraphs I discuss two possible approaches by CIPEC: (1) the establishment of a world producers' price; and (2) control of the international price of copper by means of production or export quotas. Although the full members of CIPEC—Chile, Indonesia, Peru, Zaire, and Zambia[23]—control a sufficient portion of the total world copper exports to determine, for a time at least, the free market world price for copper, the economic feasibility of such control would depend upon CIPEC's ability to increase the revenues of its members over a given period of time by raising the world price.

A World Producers' Price for Copper

The simplest technique for controlling prices is an agreement among the major exporting countries not to sell below or above an agreed price. As was noted in chapter 4, there have been periods in the history of the copper industry during which the major world producers were able to maintain an agreed minimum price. Given the existence of CIPEC, would it be possible to have a world producers' price which would operate much like the U.S. producers' prices and which would

---

[22] C. Fred Bergsten, "A New OPEC in Bauxite," *Challenge* (July/August 1976) pp. 12–20.

[23] Australia, Mauritania, Papua New Guinea, and Yugoslavia are associate members of CIPEC, but are not obligated to abide by the decisions of the organization.

substitute for the LME price as a basis for transactions in the primary copper sector? As is the case with U.S. producers' prices, a world producers' price could not remain for long intervals substantially above or below outside market prices, including those on the commodity exchanges, prices charged by secondary refiners, and prices in the dealers' markets throughout the world. However, a decision by CIPEC to change the producers' price used by their members or, say, to follow U.S. producers' prices would involve a formal decision by an intergovernmental body. Decisions by CIPEC to change the producers' price would entail difficult time-consuming negotiations and agreement might not be possible at all (except in the unlikely event that such decisions could be made by the CIPEC Secretariat). Judging from the experience of its members in adhering to CIPEC decisions to cut back on exports, it seems doubtful whether CIPEC members have sufficient discipline for maintaining a common producers' price after they had agreed on one. Finally, a world producers' price system, even if successful, could do little more than reduce the frequency of price movements and moderate to a limited degree the amplitude of the price fluctuations. Since the costs of achieving even a modest reduction in the degree of price fluctuation would be borne unevenly among a group of relatively poor countries, the cost of maintaining a world producers' price might well exceed the benefits.

The Combined Pricing System Proposal

Members of the CIPEC Secretariat have suggested the adoption of a "combined pricing system" (CPS) as the basis for determining contract prices. Under the CPS, a reference price (presumably an estimated long-run equilibrium price) would be determined, together with an upper price limit and a lower price limit above and below the reference price. Within the "middle range," that is, one-third of the entire range above and one-third of the entire range below the reference price, the price at which sales are contracted would be the same as the market price. However, within the upper range in relation to the reference price, the contract price would increase by only half as much as any increase in the market price while within the lower range the contract price would be decreased by only half as much as any decrease in the market price.[24]

   It is conceivable that the proposed CPS could introduce a measure of short-term price stability in the international copper market, especially if the reference price used by the CIPEC countries were the same as U.S. producers' prices. However, success in reducing the amplitude of short-

[24] For a description see "The Combined Pricing System," *CIPEC Quarterly Review*, Paris (July-September 1976) pp. 26–29.

term copper price fluctuations would depend on the willingness of all producers to sell in accordance with the CPS formula and on the wisdom with which the reference price was adjusted from time to time. One danger with the introduction of such a system, however, is that the reference price might become a matter of political determination, or that those responsible for setting the reference price might be overly optimistic regarding the correct long-run equilibrium price.

The Ability of a Producers' Cartel to Control Copper Prices

The effectiveness of a producers' cartel for a commodity such as copper involves a number of questions, including: (1) whether it can successfully control prices and over what period; (2) whether it can raise export earnings and for how long; (3) what the long-run impact on demand will be, given the existence of substitutes; (4) how the costs will be distributed among the members of the producers' cartel; (5) how the cartel will affect the relative market shares of its members; and (6) how any gains and losses will be distributed among low income and high income countries in the world at large. These questions will be discussed in the following paragraphs.

As has already been noted, a regional or even a world producers' price might be maintained for a short time at a level higher than the free market price, but in the longer run all prices will move together, so that any attempt to control prices of the output of one group of producers must be achieved by controlling world prices. An increase in the world price over the competitive world market level can only be engineered by a reduction in supply on the part of the group seeking to influence the world price. The ability of any group to influence the world price will depend upon the group's share of total world supply and the willingness of members of the group to cut back on production or sales. We will assume for purposes of illustration in this discussion that the producers' cartel seeking to raise world copper prices above the competitive equilibrium level consists of the five regular members of CIPEC, and that CIPEC is able to exercise control over the exports of its regular members, but not over the exports of its associate members, Australia, Mauritania, Papua New Guinea, and Yugoslavia.[25] Since the

---

[25] It is, of course, quite conceivable that CIPEC's regular members could be expanded to include not only Australia, Papua New Guinea, and Yugoslavia, but most of the Third World copper producing countries not currently in CIPEC. This would give the CIPEC members controls over about 54 percent of the non-Communist world's mine copper production as of 1974.

CIPEC countries (as defined above) account for about 50 percent of the world's exports of mine copper (including refined, blister, and concentrate), it is sometimes argued that this is the proper figure to use in determining CIPEC's share of the world market. However, since national and international markets are linked together, and, in addition, most of the secondary refined copper produced in the United States, Europe, and Japan does not enter into international trade but represents an important part of the total world supply of copper, the share of exports would not constitute a proper measure of CIPEC's control of the non-Communist world market for copper. The CIPEC countries supplied about 38 percent of the non-Communist world's mine production in 1974, but mine production represented only 60 percent of the total world's supply of copper, with the remainder represented by old and new scrap output. Hence, the CIPEC countries supplied only 23 percent of the total supply of copper in the non-Communist world in 1974. If we consider refined copper alone, 83 percent of the Western world's refined copper was derived from primary or mine production, so that the CIPEC countries supplied only about 32 percent of the Western world's refined copper (including concentrates and blister that were actually refined outside the CIPEC countries).

Let us now consider the degree to which CIPEC countries would need to cut back their production or exports in order to influence the world price of copper in both the short and the long run. Let us assume for purposes of illustration that the elasticity of world demand for copper is −0.5, which means that a 5 percent decrease in world supply would raise the world price by 10 percent. Assuming the CIPEC countries control one-third of the world's supply, they would need to cut back their own output by 15 percent in order to achieve a 5 percent reduction in the world's supply and, hence, a 10 percent increase in world price *provided that the 10 percent increase in price did not bring forth an increase in supply from non-CIPEC sources.* However, if the 10 percent increase in price brought forth an increase of, say, 3 percent, in the output of non-CIPEC sources or 2 percent in the total world supply, this increase would have to be offset by a further cutback in CIPEC output or sales equal to 6 percent of the initial CIPEC output. In order to raise world prices by 10 percent, CIPEC would have to cut back its own output by 21 percent. Such a course would be disastrous for the CIPEC countries since their foreign exchange proceeds would decline by 13 percent as a consequence of their efforts to raise the world price by 10 percent.

We may formalize the relationships in the above illustration by means of a formula for determining the elasticity of world demand for

CIPEC's output. This elasticity will be a function of three variables: (1) the elasticity of world demand for copper, E_{Dw}; (2) the portion of world output supplied by CIPEC, m; and (3) the elasticity of supply of non-CIPEC sources, E_{Sr}. We may express the formula for determining the elasticity of demand for CIPEC's output as follows: [26]

$$E_{Dc} = \frac{1}{m} \times E_{Dw} - \frac{1}{m} \times (1 - m) \times E_{Sr}$$

It will be observed that if we employ the assumptions given in the illustration above in this equation so that $E_{Dw} = -0.5$; $E_{Sr} = 0.3$; and $m = \frac{1}{3}$, E_{Dc} will be equal to -2.1. This means that in order to increase the world price by 1 percent, the CIPEC countries would need to reduce their output by 2.1 percent.

The Demand and Supply Elasticities for Copper

There is a wide variation in estimates of the relevant elasticities of the demand for and supply of copper. Fisher–Cootner–Baily (FCB) estimate the short-run elasticity of demand for refined copper in the United States at -0.21 and the long-run elasticity of demand at -0.90.[27] The Charles River Associates (CRA) study gives the corresponding estimates as -0.21 and -2.9.[28] In chapter 5 of this book the authors give estimates of short- and long-run elasticities found by Arthur D. Little, Inc., of -0.47 and

[26] This formula was given by Kenji Takeuchi in "CIPEC and the Copper Export Earnings of Member Countries," in *The Developing Economies* vol. X, no. 1 (March 1972) pp. 14–15. The formula is derived as follows:

$$D_c(p) = D_w(p) - S_r(p) \qquad (1)$$

where D_c = the world demand for CIPEC's output, D_w = the world demand for world output, S_r = the non-CIPEC world supply, and p = world price. Differentiating both sides of equation (1) by p, we get

$$\frac{dD_c}{dp} = \frac{dD_w}{dp} - \frac{dS_r}{dp} \qquad (2)$$

Multiplying both sides of (2) by p/D_c we obtain

$$\left(\frac{dD_c}{dp} \frac{p}{D_c}\right) = \left(\frac{pdD_w}{D_w dp}\right) \times \left(\frac{D_w}{D_c}\right) - \left(\frac{dS_r}{dp}\right) \times \left(\frac{p}{S_r} \frac{S_r}{D_c}\right)$$

or $E_{Dc} = (D_w/D_c)E_{Dw} - (S_r/D_c)E_{Sr}$. Let $m = D_c/D_w$ or the share of CIPEC output in the world market. $(1 - m) = (S_r/D_w)$ or the non-CIPEC share of the domestic markte. Then $E_{Dc} = (1/m)E_{Dw} - (1/m)(1 - m)E_{Sr}$.

[27] F. N. Fisher, P. H. Cootner, and M. N. Baily, "An Econometric Model of the World Copper Industry," *Bell Journal of Economics and Management Science* vol. 3, no. 2 (Autumn 1972) p. 587.

[28] *The Economic Analysis of the Copper Industry* (Cambridge, Mass., Charles River Associates, March 1970) p. 294.

−0.64 respectively, again for the United States. The FCB and CRA studies show short-term elasticities of demand for refined copper for Europe to be less than that for the United States, although no rationale is provided for the difference. Inventory behavior in the short run makes it difficult to estimate short-run demand elasticity. The elasticities given above are "own" price elasticities, but the short-run elasticity of substitution between copper and aluminum is also estimated to be quite low. Econometric studies of the copper industry have also estimated short-run supply elasticities for copper, but there are no overall estimates for non-CIPEC supply elasticities. The FCB study estimates U.S. short-run elasticity of supply for primary copper to be 0.45 and the long-run elasticity to be 1.67.[29] Short-run supply elasticities for other countries are estimated to be substantially lower, but this may reflect differences in average capacity utilization. The elasticity undoubtedly changes with the price of copper and with the capacity at which mines are operating. For example, if mines are operating at or near capacity, the short-run response to higher prices will tend to be quite small. On the other hand, a sharp drop in the price of copper to a level below variable costs for a number of mines may result in a cutback in output as a consequence of the closing of mines.

An important factor in the elasticity of supply of refined copper (including both primary and secondary copper) is the elasticity of supply of scrap. FCB estimates the short-run supply of old scrap to be about 0.3,[30] while GRA estimates the short-run supply elasticity of old scrap at 0.47.[31] Takeuchi suggests a range for the short-run elasticity of supply of non-CIPEC refined copper (including secondary) of 0.2 to 0.4.[32]

For purposes of determining the short-run elasticity of demand for CIPEC's output, we shall use a range of −0.2 to −0.5 for the elasticity of total world demand, excluding Communist countries, and a range of 0.2 to 0.4 for the short-term elasticity of copper supply from non-CIPEC countries. We shall also assume that the CIPEC countries account for about one-third of the total supply of refined copper (including mine copper refined elsewhere). In the most favorable case for the CIPEC countries, assuming a world elasticity of demand for copper of −0.2 and a short-run elasticity of supply for non-CIPEC copper of 0.1, the elasticity of demand for CIPEC copper would be −0.8 or, in other words, the CIPEC countries could achieve an increase of 10 percent in the world price of copper by reducing their output by 8 percent. On the

29 Fisher, Cootner, and Baily, "An Econometric Model," p. 577.
30 Ibid., p. 582.
31 Charles River Associates, *Economic Analysis of the Copper Industry*, p. 310.
32 Takeuchi, "CIPEC and the Copper Export Earnings of Member Countries," p. 22.

other hand, assuming the least favorable case in which the short-run elasticity of world demand for copper is −0.5 and a short-run elasticity of supply of non-CIPEC copper of 0.4, the short-run elasticity of demand for CIPEC copper would be −2.3, or, in other words, the CIPEC countries would have to reduce output by 23 percent in order to increase the world price by 10 percent. The least favorable condition seems somewhat unrealistic except in periods of considerable excess mine capacity. It appears very likely that the short-run elasticity of demand for CIPEC copper is in the neighborhood of unity, which means in effect that they could not increase their export proceeds significantly, if at all, by cutting back on supply. However, much depends on market reaction, particularly on inventory accumulation. For example, if an announced cutback of exports by the CIPEC countries of 15 or 20 percent had the effect of stimulating inventory accumulation on the part of consumers in the expectation of a substantial increase in prices, prices might rise by a percentage considerably larger than the cutback in CIPEC's output. On the other hand, in 1975 when prices were depressed and there was plenty of excess world copper producing capacity, the announcement of a 15 percent decrease in CIPEC-country exports had virtually no effect on prices.

Turning to the longer run, virtually all estimates of world elasticities of demand and of the supply of non-CIPEC producers are near or well above unity. Assuming that the elasticities of both long-run world demand and of long-run supply of non-CIPEC sources are unity, the CIPEC countries would have to reduce output by 34 percent in order to increase world prices by 10 percent. If the long-run elasticity of world demand were only −0.6 and the long-run elasticity of non-CIPEC world supply were only 0.2, the CIPEC countries would have to reduce their output by 22 percent in order to achieve a 10 percent increase in world prices. Even if all of the developing country copper producers plus Australia joined in a producers' cartel and if the long-run elasticity of the supply of copper from the world outside the producers' cartel were zero, the elasticity of demand for the output of the producers' cartel would be only −1.1. This means that in order to raise the world price by 10 percent they would have to cut back their production by 11 percent so that the export proceeds of the members of the producers' cartel would actually be reduced.[33] There would be some saving of foreign exchange as a consequence of reduced foreign purchases of inputs for the copper industry, but these savings would probably not be large unless there was a reduction of capital goods imports.

33 The United States, Canada, Japan, Western Europe, and South Africa produced 46 percent of the world mine copper in 1974, leaving 54 percent for the rest of the non-Communist world.

In a more recent study, CRA estimated the elasticity of demand facing CIPEC for three time periods: after one year, -1.00; after five years, -2.98; and after thirty years, -5.31.[34] Hence, after one year CIPEC would not be able to increase its revenues by raising its price by withholding production, and after five years its revenue loss would be substantial. The CRA study also examines the market power of CIPEC if Canada were to join and concludes that, although the inclusion of Canada would lead to a substantial increase in short-run market power, the additional market power is substantially dissipated in the long run. They find that the price for CIPEC and Canada together, which would maximize their long-run revenue, is only 8 percent higher than the price for CIPEC alone. They conclude that it is unlikely that Canada would join CIPEC.[35]

We may conclude that under no conceivable circumstances could the CIPEC countries increase their export proceeds over the long run by cutting back on exports or production. An increase in the proportion of total mine copper supplied by CIPEC countries as a result of an increase in CIPEC membership would, of course, improve their short-term market power. However, even if all the non-Communist copper producing countries other than the United States, Canada, Western Europe, Japan, and South Africa joined CIPEC, it would not enable the CIPEC countries to increase their export proceeds by cutting back exports in the long run. Moreover, all of the CIPEC countries are in competition with one another in terms of expanding capacity, and, given the long-run national mine capacity objectives of these countries, it is most unlikely that they could reach any agreement on limiting investment in new capacity. If they did so, it would simply spur investment in mine capacity in the United States, Canada, South Africa, and other countries that are not likely to join a producers' cartel.

Substitution

The long-run elasticity of demand for copper is undoubtedly affected by long-run substitution for copper by aluminum and plastics for certain uses (see appendix 5-2). However, estimates of the long-run elasticity of substitution vary considerably and none has been particularly successful in terms of the econometric results achieved. Most of the substitution in the past has probably occurred as a consequence of technological developments that have more to do with the relative efficiency of sub-

---

[34] *Policy Implications of Producer Country Supply Restrictions: The World Market for Copper* (prepared for the National Bureau of Standards, U.S. Department of Commerce by Charles River Associates, August 1976) p. 59.

[35] Ibid., p. 60.

stitute materials for particular uses than estimates of long-run relative prices. Moreover, some of the factors that have increased the cost of producing copper also affect the cost of producing substitutes, such as aluminum and plastics. Both aluminum and plastics have been affected by the increase in prices of petroleum, and pollution abatement costs are of some significance, at least in the case of aluminum, although they are not as important as in copper smelting. Nevertheless, both CIPEC members and primary copper producers in the industrialized countries appear to be quite concerned about long-run substitution, and this concern could have a moderating influence on any cartel activities. Perhaps more important for the primary copper industry is the possibility of increased secondary output as a consequence of a rise in old scrap collections in response to higher scrap prices. As is discussed in chapter 11, recycled materials may well constitute an increasing proportion of total copper supply.

Sharing the Cost of Production Cutbacks
Among the CIPEC Countries

Collusive agreements for cutting back production in order to maintain or raise prices give rise to a number of problems. One has to do with determination of the base for a uniform cutback of production since any base year that is chosen is likely to be unique for particular countries as a consequence of strikes, transportation difficulties, and other factors affecting the capacity utilization for that year. A country whose output has been restricted by 20 percent as a consequence of special circumstances in the base year is likely to object to a 20 percent cutback on the basis of output during that year. It will prefer instead a cut in output in relation to its normal copper producing capacity. However, capacity is continually changing as new mines come on-stream or others are shut down. A country whose capacity is increased by 20 percent as a consequence of a new mine which has been completed in the year during which cutbacks are enforced will object to an arrangement which bases the cutbacks on its capacity in the base year. If the members of a producers' cartel simply agree to cut back on exports but not on production, there will be an accumulation of inventories that will overhang the market in future years, and their ability to finance inventory accumulation is very limited.[36]

[36] One advantage of cutting back on exports rather than on production would be that the production and sale of important by-products such as gold and molybdenum might continue, thereby providing some revenue from the mining operation. In some cases the revenue from the by-products would be sufficient to cover the interest and other costs of holding the copper inventories.

Effects on World Distribution of Income

Producers' cartels as well as international commodity agreements directed toward raising prices above long-term equilibrium levels are often justified in terms of a redistribution of income between industrialized and developing countries. In the case of copper, the relative distribution effects will not necessarily benefit the developing countries. Its production is fairly evenly distributed between industrialized and developing countries and in the developing world it is limited to a handful of countries. Although the vast bulk of the copper exports of the developing countries go to the developed countries for fabrication and manufacturing, a substantial portion of copper-bearing products go to the countries of the developing world that produce no copper. Hence, we have a situation similar to the case of petroleum price increases, in which the heaviest burden in relative terms and in terms of capacity to pay has been on the non-OPEC developing countries.

The 1977 Proposal for a U.S. National Copper Stockpile

Mining company officials have generally been cool toward the efforts in UNCTAD to create an international commodity agreement in copper or, for that matter, in any other mineral. The reasons for their opposition include most of the criticisms discussed above, plus the U.S. mining industry's concern that an international commodity agreement might go beyond a pure buffer stock arrangement to include restrictions on trade and production. U.S. mining officials have not been uniform in their attitude toward a national stockpile in copper, although historically they have tended to support the U.S. strategic stockpile initiated in the early 1950s.

Simon D. Strauss, currently vice chairman of ASARCO, has criticized the record of past U.S. administrations in the handling of strategic stockpiles. According to Strauss, the U.S. stockpile has been at times employed for holding down prices of certain domestically produced commodities while at other times it has been used to support prices. He believes that not only are such actions likely to have long-run harmful effects on both producers and consumers, but they defeat the original purpose of a strategic reserve. Strauss has suggested that a U.S. strategic stockpile should be governed by fixed rules established by the Congress whereby the amount of any commodity accumulated would be equal to, say, two years' supply of U.S. imports, and the stockpile would be available only for use in periods of national emergency such as might be created by a cutoff of foreign supplies. In the case of a commodity in which the United States is virtually self-sufficient, for example, copper, there appears to be little need for inclusion in the strategic stockpile.[37]

In 1977 several officials of large U.S. mining companies strongly supported the creation of a U.S. copper stockpile as a means of providing support for the price of copper. In September 1977 legislation was proposed by Senator Pete Domenici of New Mexico and supported by Congressman Morris K. Udall of Arizona whereby tin (the price of which has been soaring) would be sold from the U.S. stockpile and the funds used to acquire copper.[38] It is anticipated that some 250,000 mt of copper would be acquired in this manner.

But if the U.S. government initiates purchases of copper in order to raise prices to U.S. producers, what level of purchases would be required to have a significant effect on world prices? In 1977 U.S. copper imports were substantial, especially prior to the reduction in the U.S. producers' price in October 1977 to bring it in closer alignment with the LME price. In 1977–78, U.S. government representatives were negotiating in UNCTAD on an international commodity agreement for copper and it does not seem appropriate to establish a U.S. copper stockpile while these negotiations are proceeding. Given the large foreign output and visible copper inventories of nearly 1.5 million mt, 250,000 mt of copper would have a minimal impact on the world's market price. Furthermore, the Domenici bill as it stands provides no guidelines for future U.S. government policies with respect to the copper industry.[39]

[37] See Simon D. Strauss, "The Shifting Stockpiles," *New York Times,* February 6, 1977, p. 12; see also Simon D. Strauss, "Statement on Behalf of the American Mining Congress in Regard to Stockpile Goals Announced by the Administration, October 1, 1976," before the Joint Congressional Committee on Defense Production, November 24, 1976, American Mining Congress Press Release, Washington, D.C., November 24, 1976; and "Governments and Mineral Markets," Statement by Simon D. Strauss before the American Metal Market, London Metal Forum, London, England, October 27, 1976 (mimeo).

[38] "Stockpile Tin Release Hangs on Domenici Bill," *American Metal Market* (October 17, 1977) p. 36; see also "U.S. Copper Producers, with Big Inventories, Urge Federal Stockpile," *Wall Street Journal* (September 29, 1977) p. 24.

[39] Senator Domenici's proposal, which was an amendment to the Wilderness Bill, was defeated by a narrow margin in the U.S. Senate on October 20, 1977.

8

Investment in the Copper Industry: Practices and Approaches

HISTORICALLY the development of large mining companies grew out of important "discoveries" and the ability of the miners who discovered and explored valuable ore bodies to mobilize the capital for exploiting them. Successful mining firms tended to acquire other mineral deposits from prospectors who were unable to develop them. In the nineteenth century small U.S. prospectors were often able to sell stock in their ventures, and literally thousands of corporations were created, most of which failed or were absorbed by larger firms. After most of the obvious surface exposures of ore deposits had been located, exploration became more expensive. Techniques were developed that required large-scale operations to locate subsurface deposits and much of the exploration came to be concentrated in a few large mining firms. These firms also integrated forward into smelting and refining, processes which also required large amounts of capital with the development of new technology. Exploration, which is the foundation of the copper mining industry, is no longer dependent on prospectors who gamble their fortunes on finding a single commercial deposit, but has become systematic and subject to the same cost-return principles as any other investment.[1] In this chapter we examine the investment decision-making process as it applies to exploration, mining, and processing in the copper industry; the method of project appraisal; and capital costs and methods of financing.

[1] This is not to say that small prospectors no longer operate in the United States and elsewhere. In fact, in Australia and South Africa they continue to play a rather important role in the initial phases of exploration.

The Investment Decision-Making Process

Orris Herfindahl raised the basic question of whether aggregate investment in the copper industry responds systematically to expected returns
or whether investment is haphazard because of accidental finds and the
inability to predict the relationship between investment and returns.
He concluded that investment in the copper industry did respond
systematically to expected profit signals and that, therefore, it is possible
to develop a long-run supply function relating output or capacity to
cost of production and to copper prices.[2] Although Herfindahl did not
formulate a complete theory of investment in the copper industry, he
did outline a number of important elements in the decision-making
process.

A key problem in the analysis of nonfuel mineral markets lies in the
treatment of investment decisions for capacity expansion. As was noted
in chapter 6, some econometric metal models treat productive capacity
endogenously; that is, they explain changes in capacity by historical
prices, costs, and capacity utilization, with a long lag to these variables.
Although some commodity models have been able to simulate historical
capacity change fairly accurately in a statistical sense, their ability to
predict in a world of rapid structural change, including the emergence
of government decision makers in the developing countries, is extremely
doubtful. Investment decisions for mines and milling facilities require
profitability expectations over a long time horizon—twenty-five to
thirty years or more—and the gestation period from intensive exploration to production may be ten years or more. Decisions are made on the
basis of long-run price and cost expectations that are affected by a number of variables peculiar to each country and by expectations regarding
the current and future investment decisions of other world producers.
Moreover, large resource firms are influenced by such factors as the
desire to maintain or increase their market shares in particular products,
to integrate several stages of production, or to diversify among several
categories of resources. Such factors do provide an important explanation for the expansion of investment in copper and other resource
industries, but they reflect overall firm strategy rather than criteria for
evaluating specific projects.

I shall not attempt to formulate a comprehensive theory of investment in the mining industry, but rather review some of the factors that

[2] Orris C. Herfindahl, *Copper Costs and Prices: 1870–1957* (Baltimore, Johns Hopkins University Press for Resources for the Future, 1959) chapter 3.

influence investment decisions.[3] It is perhaps useful to distinguish between the aggregate investment policy of a mining firm and investment
criteria for individual projects. The overall capital budget, including
exploration outlays, of a large integrated mining firm is determined
in part by the occurrence of investment opportunities which may arise
from exploration activities or from acquisition opportunities, and in
part from broad company strategies such as long-run growth, balance
among stages of production in vertical integration, maintenance of the
firm's world market share, and company policies toward foreign investment. The ability of a company to carry out its objectives and to take
advantage of opportunities will depend in considerable measure on
internal sources of financing and the ability to raise new equity and
debt capital. It should be noted, however, that a major asset of a mining company consists of the ability and experience of its management
and professional personnel, and in most large mining companies a
substantial portion of the top management group has grown up with
the industry, starting as young mining engineers. In my own experience I have found that mining executives like to mine and are enthusi-
astic about creating new mining ventures. There is a desire for
optimum utilization of the human resources of the firm, the supply of
which is continually expanding as a firm grows. In recent years, when
nationalization of foreign mining investments has released experienced
managerial and professional people, there is a desire on the part of the
company to retain these people and to find opportunities for utilizing
them within the firm. This can best be done by developing new mining
properties.

Apart from the factors determining the total volume of investment
available for employment, capital budgeting policies differ greatly
among firms, and undoubtedly some of the decisions on the allocation
of funds are more a reflection of the internal politics of the firm than
a rational allocation procedure. Most large mining firms produce more
than one mineral as well as operate different stages of the production
and processing of minerals. There may be an exploration division, a
copper division, a lead and zinc division, a uranium division, a coal
division, and possibly a petroleum division, as well as a mineral refining

---

[3] There are several theories of corporate investment behavior, each of which empha-
sizes certain key explanatory factors or combinations of factors. Among these factors
are (1) the ratio of capital to output; (2) internal funds available for investment; (3)
expected profits; (4) the market value of the firm's securities; (5) the cost of capital;
and (6) the tax structure. See, for example, D. W. Jorgenson and C. D. Siebert, "A
Comparison of Alternative Theories of Corporate Investment Behavior," *American
Economic Review* (September 1968) pp. 682–712.

Table 8-1.   Unweighted Average Rate of Return on Stockholders' Equity
(*percent*)

	1946–66	1946–56	1957–66
Anaconda	6.5	7.2	5.8
Kennecott	12.7	15.9	9.5
Phelps Dodge	13.4	17.1	11.2

Source: *Economic Analysis of the Copper Industry*, Charles River Associates, Inc., March 1970, p. 191.

division. Each division will present its case to the management committee and the board of directors for a portion of the available capital budget. There are special aspects in foreign investment decisions, often involving joint ventures with governments and borrowing from international sources on the part of subsidiaries, that complicate the problem of the availability and overall allocation of capital funds.

In recent years diversification among the resource industries, as well as forward integration into fabrication, has played a role in the overall investment decision-making process. Not only are many of the large petroleum firms, such as Standard Oil Company of Indiana (AMOCO) and EXXON, becoming large investors in nonfuel minerals, but some of the firms that initially were exclusively in nonfuel minerals have diversified into coal and petroleum. Kennecott's large investment in Peabody Coal (now divested) is well known; and St. Joe Minerals Corporation, originally confined to lead and zinc mining, now receives half of its income from coal and is also engaged in petroleum exploration. In 1976 Anaconda was merged with Atlantic Richfield, a large petroleum company.

Profits not only guide investment, but profitability should determine the capacity of the company to expand. However, our limited investigation failed to show a close relationship between returns on equity over time and changes in investment. Comparison of average rates of return on stockholders' equity for three leading U.S. copper producers —Anaconda, Kennecott, and Phelps Dodge—provides no explanation for the relative changes in their U.S. productive capacities over time. This is indicated by tables 8-1 and 8-2. Despite the fact that the rates of return on stockholders' equity for both Anaconda and Kennecott were substantially less than that for Phelps Dodge for the 1946–66 period, the percentage increases in U.S. mine production between 1956 and 1970 for both Anaconda and Kennecott were substantially larger

Table 8-2.   U.S. Primary Copper Production of Three Leading
Copper Producers
(*000 metric tons*)

	1956	1960	1966	1970
Anaconda (own mines)	116	122	147	220
Kennecott	366	349	413	472
Phelps Dodge	246	213	253	286

Source: *American Bureau of Metal Statistics Yearbook*, 1964, 1970, and 1975.

than that for Phelps Dodge.[4] However, these companies are diversified
into other industries and into foreign investment so that rates of return
on stockholders' equity are only partly a reflection of primary copper
production.

Overall Investment Strategy in the Mining Industry

An integrated mining firm must carry on investment activities in several stages of production if it is to remain in reasonable balance. In
order to maintain their long-run position in the industry, large companies must continue to explore on a systematic basis domestically and
abroad, although foreign exploration is becoming increasingly risky
and less rewarding. Large firms also acquire reserves by buying or
merging with smaller companies that have substantial undeveloped ore
bodies. Small prospecting firms may acquire claims and do a certain
amount of exploration on them with the expectation of selling them to
large companies. This takes place in the United States, although not
to the extent of a half century ago. In developed countries such as
Australia and South Africa, where the laws favor private ownership of
claims, there are a large number of small firms or individual prospectors that operate in this way.

Even when large firms acquire ore bodies from prospectors, it is
necessary to undertake a substantial amount of exploration and engineering studies to ascertain whether they have an ore body that can be
profitably mined, and to determine the optimum size of the mine and
mill. Moreover, a mine is not a static entity. Continued sampling and
analysis are necessary as a guide to the mining process in revealing pos-

[4] In addition, Anaconda and Kennecott increased their foreign investments substantially during the 1956–1970 period, while Phelps Dodge did not.

sibilities for a major expansion in response to changes in copper prices or to new technological developments. Complete balance, even for an integrated firm, is not always necessary or desirable. Integrated firms may acquire a portion of their ore or concentrates from other firms for their smelters and/or refineries, or they may ship a portion of their concentrates to unaffiliated custom smelters and refineries. In fact, economies of scale and transportation costs may dictate that the output of a mine in a region far from the company's principal mine-smelter complex be shipped to nearby smelters of other firms, or shipped abroad. Nevertheless, there are both economies and strategic advantages in vertical integration, so that a large, vertically integrated firm is usually unwilling to increase its mine output by a substantial percentage without expanding its downstream processing facilities accordingly. Unless it has long-term contracts with a nonintegrated smelter, it cannot be sure of available smelter capacity or that a rise in custom or refining charges might not render its mining operation unprofitable. An integrated firm will need to consider the implications of an investment at each stage of production for its investment requirements at other stages.

In many ways the most interesting category of investment is exploration. (I use the term investment for exploration even though exploration activities are usually regarded as current expenditures for tax purposes.) Companies follow different policies in allocating funds for exploration. They may allocate a certain percentage of net sales or a certain percentage of their capital budget to exploration. However, exploration expenditures may be influenced by the requirements for achieving long-run capacity and output objectives for the mining sector. A company like Anaconda, which lost over half of its copper ore reserves and productive capacity with the nationalization of its Chilean mines in 1971, would undoubtedly be inclined to expand its exploration activity, with particular emphasis on exploration in the United States, Canada, Australia, and other relatively "safe" areas. A well-organized capital budget program should also be sufficiently flexible to react to opportunities for particular high-yielding investments. These might take the form of opportunities for acquiring existing productive facilities and ore reserves, or for increasing exploration expenditures on newly discovered mineral areas that were especially promising.

Large exploration programs not only spread the risk over a number of investigations, but the expenditures can be programmed with a view to achieving a target rate of return on the expenditures with a reasonably high probability of success. Firms with very large exploration budgets can afford to select a number of low probability-high potential return projects, while firms with smaller budgets would tend to favor high probability projects while sacrificing those with potentially high returns but a lower probability of success. This does not mean that a larger amount of money expended on exploration or a larger number of exploration projects will in itself assure an adequate return on the investment. The knowledge and experience of the geologists and engineers are crucial factors in the success of any exploration program, large or small. Moreover, it is conceivable that a few large firms exploring prudently with capital allocated on the basis of probabilities at each stage might not find as large a total value of additional reserves as thousands of small firms operating on the lottery principle—gambling for high stakes with little concern for probabilities.[5] Although it is possible to calculate the marginal returns from additional exploration outlays as a means of determining the total exploration budget, I suspect that such budgets are mainly determined by some combination of calculated returns from specific exploration projects or programs, and the need to generate reserves to sustain or expand the level of mine production. Individual projects at any stage, including exploration, may be justified by some kind of rate of return calculation, but overall outlays for exploration and development of capacity are also influenced by company policies with respect to growth, the desire for balance in overall operations, and, in some cases, by long-run market strategy.

Investment Criteria for Individual Projects

Mining companies employ several investment criteria singly or in combination in evaluating individual investment projects. These criteria include (1) the payback period; (2) the accounting rate of return; (3) net present value; and (4) discounted cash flow (DCF).

The Payback Period

The number of years required for after-tax earnings, including depreciation and depletion, to pay back the original investment is one of the most widely used criteria in the mining industry, and is almost universally used in foreign investments subject to a considerable degree

---

[5] For a discussion of the lottery principle, see Lee E. Preston, *Exploration for Nonferrous Metals: An Economic Analysis* (Baltimore, Johns Hopkins University Press for Resources for the Future, 1960) pp. 73–75.

of political risk. It is actually a temporal measure of risk exposure rather than a measure of return on capital. Since normally it does not provide for the capitalization of investment outlays prior to initiation of production (from which date the payback period is measured), it does not even provide a full measure of investment payback. More seriously, it ignores the positive return on capital which must include the period after the investment has been returned. Although consideration of the period of risk exposure or of the maximum period during which investors can be reasonably confident that their investment may not be expropriated or fall victim to other hazards is an important aspect of investment criteria, this evaluation should be combined with measures which take proper account of the return on capital in relation to the flow of capital investment.

The Accounting Rate of Return

Despite its obvious weaknesses, the accounting rate of return—the ratio of after-tax earnings to book value or stockholders' equity—is still employed by mining firms as a criterion for investment. There are several variants of the accounting rate of return, some of which approximate discounting methods.[6] Variants of the accounting rate of return are frequently used in negotiations with foreign governments as the basis for determining tax and other arrangements affecting the returns to the foreign investor. Therefore it is important that the foreign investor be able to translate his own investment criteria into a rate of return concept that is readily understandable by officials of foreign governments. It may also be noted that the accounting rate of return is an important determinant of the market value of a company's stock. Hence, the management of the firm might select, on the basis of a high accounting rate of return, an investment that would not be acceptable in terms of another criterion.

Net Present Value (NPV)

NPV is the discounted value of the net cash flow (after taxes) of an investment over its life or over a particular period plus a liquidation

---

[6] For a mathematical analysis of the relationship between the internal rate of return and the accounting rate of return, see Ezra Solomon, "Alternative Rates of Return Concepts and their Implications for Utility Regulations," *Bell Journal of Economics and Management Science* (Spring 1970) pp. 65–81; see also Thomas R. Stauffer, "The Measurement of Corporate Rates of Return: A Generalized Formulation," *Bell Journal of Economics and Management Science* (Autumn 1971) pp. 434–469.

value.[7] The rate of discount may be the cost of capital plus an allowance for risk, or some arbitrarily chosen rate. If the initial investment is not included as a part of the cash flow, the firm could then compare the net present value of the cash inflow with the present value of the initial investment, using the same discount rate for both. Alternatively, if net cash flow were discounted over the entire period beginning with the initial investment outlays, this method would determine when, if ever, the cumulative net present value became positive. Sometimes the net present value method is used without capitalizing the investment outlay prior to beginning production. This is improper since it ignores the element of time during the investment period. However, when the selected discount rate is applied fully to cash outflow before the beginning of production, the method determines whether the rate of return on the investment is less than or exceeds the rate representing the cost of capital. The method of determining the cost of capital will be discussed below.

Discounted Cash Flow (DCF)

The DCF rate (or the internal rate of return) together with net present value for a particular rate of discount (14 percent) which we may regard as the minimum acceptable rate is illustrated in tables 8-3a and 8-3b. The DCF rate is that rate of return which equalizes the present values of the streams of cash outflow and cash inflow. Alternatively, it is that rate of discount for which cumulative net present value is zero. Unlike the calculation of net present value, it is not necessary to select a rate of discount; the DCF rate is calculated from the timing and pattern of the cash outflows and inflows. It will be observed from table 8-3b that since cumulative net present value discounted at 14 percent over the twenty-year period is a positive number, the actual rate of return is higher than the minimum acceptable rate. It is, in fact, 16.6 percent, or the internal rate of return (DCF) over the twenty-year period. At the end of fifteen years the cumulative net present value is zero or the DCF rate at that point in time is 14 percent.[8]

DCF is generally recognized as the most satisfactory measure of the rate of return on an investment, but it is not an exclusive criterion that

[7] For an analysis of cash flow and rates of return in the mining industry, see R. F. Mikesell, *Foreign Investment in Copper Mining: Case Studies of Mines in Peru and Papua New Guinea* (Baltimore, Johns Hopkins University Press for Resources for the Future, 1975) chapter 1.

[8] Normally one would add a liquidation value at the end of the last year, which would raise the DCF slightly.

takes into account all investment objectives. Let us assume there are three alternative investments, A, B, and C, and that A has the highest DCF rate, followed by B and C. This information alone would not necessarily determine the optimum choice. For example, in order to achieve a maximum DCF for A, it might be necessary to continue operations for fifteen years, while a somewhat lower maximum DCF on an investment in B might be achieved in eight years. Alternatively, investment C might involve a much larger cash flow than A or B, and if C constituted a unique opportunity for expanding the firm's production, C might be preferred. Another factor to be taken into account is the possible relationship of an investment to complementary investment opportunities. For example, investment C might be large enough to justify the building of a smelter, which might not be true for A and B. This might be taken into account even though investment in a smelter was not contemplated in the initial investment program for C, but might be considered some time in the future.

The Cost of Capital

Whether a firm uses the net present value or the DCF criterion for evaluating a prospective investment, it must choose an appropriate rate of discount: it will require a rate of discount for a present value calculation and it must determine whether the calculated DCF rate is above or below its minimum acceptable standard. If a firm is concerned solely with the rate of return on equity, interest and principal payments on that portion of its investment covered by borrowing will constitute a charge against gross cash inflow in the calculation of net present value or DCF. However, many firms are concerned with the rate of return on total investment at risk even though the parent firm may not be legally responsible for the debts of the subsidiary which is actually making the investment. In the latter case, companies often argue that a default by a subsidiary would impair the credit standing of the parent, or the parent firm may regard itself as morally responsible for the debts of its subsidiaries.

Firms may determine the minimum acceptable discount rate by adding a more-or-less arbitrary risk premium to the cost of borrowing, or to the average rate of return on invested capital in the industry. Alternatively, they may employ a calculation of the equity cost of capital and of the cost of debt capital, averaged in proportion to the source of funds employed in the company or employed in the proposed investment. The cost of equity capital, k_e, may be determined as the ratio of the expected long-run average net profits per share, E, to the market price

Table 8-3a. Cash Flow for Hypothetical Mine[a]

(*millions of dollars*)

Year	Gross revenue (R)	Operating costs (C)	Equity outflow (E)	Loans & principal repayments (L)	Interest payments on debt (I)	Post construction capital expenditures (CE)
1	—	—	10	10	—	—
2	—	—	10	10	—	—
3	—	—	10	10	—	—
4	—	—	10	10	—	—
5	—	—	10	10	—	—
6	50	(20)	—	(5)	(13.4)	(2)
7	50	(20)	—	(5)	(3.6)	(2)
8	50	(20)	—	(5)	(3.2)	(2)
9	50	(20)	—	(5)	(2.8)	(2)
10	50	(20)	—	(5)	(2.4)	(2)
11	50	(20)	—	(5)	(2.0)	(2)
12	50	(20)	—	(5)	(1.6)	(2)
13	50	(20)	—	(5)	(1.2)	(2)
14	50	(20)	—	(5)	(0.8)	(2)
15	50	(20)	—	(5)	(0.4)	(2)
16	50	(20)	—	—	—	(2)
17	50	(20)	—	—	—	(2)
18	50	(20)	—	—	—	(2)
19	50	(20)	—	—	—	(2)
20	50	(20)	—	—	—	(2)

[a] Assumes an investment of $100 million over a five-year construction period and a fifteen-year operating life. Parentheses indicate cash outflow.

of a share of stock, P, or $k_e = E/P$. However, given the erratic performance of the market for shares, and the tendency of the market either to undervalue or overvalue shares in relation to expected earnings (for a given level of long-term interest rates), this might not be the most reliable method of determining the cost of equity capital. Also, financing an investment by issuing more equity shares is likely to reduce the market price of the shares and, hence, increase k_e. Moreover, net profits are not a reliable source of economic returns in mining, given the importance of depletion allowances and the existence of depreciation schedules which may undervalue or overvalue actual depreciation in constant dollars.

Table 8-3b. Net Cash Flow to Equity, Accounting Rate of Return to Initial Equity, Net Present Value at 14 Percent, and Internal Rate of Return, Assuming Accelerated Depreciation

(millions of dollars)

Year	Depre-ciation (D)	Taxable income (TI)	Tax payments (T)	Earnings after taxes[a] (Y)	Net cash flow to equity[b] (NCF)	Account-ing rate of return to initial equity (percent)	Net present value at 14 percent
1	—	—	—	—	(10)	—	−8.8
2	—	—	—	—	(10)	—	−7.7
3	—	—	—	—	(10)	—	−6.8
4	—	—	—	—	(10)	—	−5.9
5	—	—	—	—	(10)	—	−5.2
6	(16.6)	—	—	—	9.6	0.0	4.4
7	(26.4)	—	—	—	19.4	0.0	7.8
8	(26.8)	—	—	—	19.8	0.0	6.9
9	(27.2)	—	—	—	20.2	0.0	6.2
10	(3.0)	24.6	12.3	12.3	8.3	24.6	2.2
11	—	28.0	14.0	14.0	7.0	28.0	1.7
12	—	28.4	14.2	14.2	7.2	28.4	1.5
13	—	28.8	14.4	14.4	7.4	28.8	1.4
14	—	29.2	14.6	14.6	7.6	29.2	1.2
15	—	29.6	14.8	14.8	7.8	29.5	1.1
16	—	30.0	15.0	15.0	13.0	30.0	1.6
17	—	30.0	15.0	15.0	13.0	30.0	1.4
18	—	30.0	15.0	15.0	13.0	30.0	1.2
19	—	30.0	15.0	15.0	13.0	30.0	1.1
20	—	30.0	15.0	15.0	13.0	30.0	1.0

Mean accounting rate of return to initial equity—21.2 percent.

Cumulative net present value—6.3 million dollars. Becomes zero at end of fifteenth year.

Internal rate of return on initial equity—16.6 per cent.

[a] Assumes 50 percent tax on taxable income (TI)

TI = R-C-I-D

Y − TI-T, where T = tax payments.

[b] NCF = R-C-I-T-L-CE. During first five years NCF represents equity outflow.

The cost of borrowed funds for financing a potential investment involves more than the rate of interest paid by the investor since increased corporate debt may reduce the firm's borrowing capacity, or increase the cost of additional borrowing in the future. Funds may be borrowed at a variable rate of interest, as in the case of loans from the Eurocurrency market, so that the actual cost of borrowing may not be known.

Probably the best approach is to measure the cost of capital in terms of the expected return on alternative uses of capital, including both internal funds and borrowed funds, with the cost of borrowing setting the lower limit. Since new investments, wherever they are made, are usually more risky than those already in operation, as a consequence of cost overruns, errors in evaluating returns, and so forth, a certain number of percentage points are generally added for risk. Allowance for risk arising from political, economic, and technical uncertainties is usually quite arbitrary since for most risks sufficient historical information does not exist for estimating probabilities. Nevertheless, I suspect that a better job of evaluating relative risks associated with alternative investment projects could be done by means of a systematic probability analysis of each category of risk for each investment.

Exploration

Despite its treatment as a cost item for tax purposes, exploration is a form of high-risk investment that is essential for growth and continued existence over time of all mining firms and, of course, for the mining industry of every country. Exploration costs are high and rising and currently represent nearly 10 percent of the current price of copper.[9] I have found no recent aggregate data on U.S. or world exploration expenditures in mining, but a 1969 study found that 21 U.S. and Canadian mining firms spent on the average about 3.5 percent of their gross revenues for exploration.[10] There is some evidence that this percentage has declined since the late 1960s. For example, a study of surface diamond drilling in Canada showed that the number of drillings in 1965 were only two-thirds of the number in 1955, and by 1971 this proportion had

[9] According to a recent estimate, the average cost of exploration leading to a *successful* copper mining venture is $125 per metric ton.

[10] J. G. Wargo, "Corporate Mineral Exploration Expenditures in 1968," *Mining Congress Journal* vol. 55, no. 12 (December 1969) pp. 45–58; see also Peter G. Donald, "Investment Decisions in Nonferrous Metals: Exploration in Mexico" (Ph.D. dissertation in mineral economics, Pennsylvania State University, August 1974) p. 26.

declined to 54 percent, and the average number of drillings during the 1974–75 period was only about half of the 1955 level.[11] Kennecott Copper Corporation reduced research and exploration expenditures from $34.0 million, or 3.1 percent of net sales in 1970, to $22.8 million, or 1.4 percent of net sales in 1974.[12] Quite possibly the nationalization of Kennecott's Chilean properties, which Kennecott was in the process of expanding during the period 1966–70, had something to do with the decline in Kennecott's research and exploration expenditures. During the period 1972–74 Kennecott's research and exploration expenditures were fairly constant in 1972 dollars, but they declined as a percentage of net sales. On the other hand, St. Joe Minerals Corporation maintained exploration and research expenditures equal to approximately 1 percent of net sales for the period 1971–75, during which period net sales rose by about 160 percent while research and exploration outlays rose by 170 percent.[13]

Anaconda experienced a net loss of $1.80 per share in 1975 as contrasted with net income of $11.19 per share in 1974 and $3.93 per share in 1973. Nevertheless, it spent $5.8 million for mineral exploration in the first half of 1975 (or an annual rate of 4.2 percent of sales of its mining divisions), as contrasted with $7.1 million for all of 1974 (or 1.8 percent of mine sales), and $5.4 million for 1973 (or 1.6 percent of mine sales). According to the company's official statement, "Anaconda's exploration program has two specific goals: discovery of new mineral deposits and expansion of new mineral reserves at existing properties. In its search for new mineral deposits Anaconda is conducting geological work in the United States and in Canada, Mexico and Australia."[14]

The Hecla Mining Company, a much smaller firm, had exploration expenditures equal to 3.2 percent of product sales in both 1974 and 1975.[15]

In reviewing annual reports of mining companies, I have not been able to find any consistent pattern of exploration expenditures either over time for individual companies or among companies. It is likely that some pattern does exist for exploration on mines in operation and perhaps for initial investigations, but the bulk of the variation in expenditures probably arises from the emergence of opportunities for

[11] See Thomas N. Walthier (St. Joe Minerals Corporation), "The Shrinking World of Exploration," *Mining Engineering* (April/May 1976).

[12] Kennecott Copper Corp., *Annual Report*, 1971–1974.

[13] St. Joe Minerals Corp., *Annual Report*, 1975, p. 20.

[14] The Anaconda Company, *Prospectus Statement*, November 1975, p. 82, and Anaconda *Annual Report*, 1975, p. 5.

[15] Hecla Mining Company, *Annual Report*, 1975, p. 18.

intensive exploration, at which stage the expenditures tend to be relatively large. Also, once a company has developed a competent exploration team, there is an incentive to maintain activity at constant levels regardless of cyclical fluctuations in profits.

Types of Exploration Activities

There are different types of exploration from the standpoint of the probability of finding a potentially profitable ore body. Probably the lowest risk is associated with the reappraisal or further exploration of a known mining camp (operating or not), or of a prospect that has been previously explored but abandoned as uneconomical at the price of copper at that time. This type of exploration is generally characterized by low expenditure, perhaps under $100,000, by a relatively high success ratio, perhaps 1 in 20, and by a potentially rapid payback on exploration expenditures.[16] A second type of exploration involves a fairly intensive examination of a small area—10 to 100 square miles—selected on the basis of considerable knowledge of the geology of the area. The cost of this type of exploration might range from $100 thousand up to $1.5 million per project, and the success ratio would be lower than the first type, perhaps 1 in 50. However, there would be a much greater possibility of finding a major metal deposit than in the first type of exploration.[17] A third type of exploration involves a regional or large area program covering 600 to 2,000 square miles. Here the purpose would be the discovery of new mineral districts or regions, or the development of major new deposits in old districts. Expenditures for such undertakings would include airborne geophysics, photogeology, helicopter reconnaissance, and regional drainage surveys as well as drilling. The cost might run from a half million to several million dollars and require three to six years to complete. Only large integrated mining firms or joint ventures are likely to undertake this type of exploration. The success of an exploration program, including the choice of the areas for intensive work, will depend very heavily on the existence of geological surveys which are often undertaken by governments or international agencies such as the United Nations Development Program (UNDP). Areas of mineralization that have been prospected for many decades will have been the subject of a number of published studies and

16 The types of exploration described in this paragraph are based on Peter G. Donald, *Investment Decisions in Nonferrous Metals: Exploration in Mexico,* pp. 44–46.

17 Exploration costs for this type cover an amount sufficient to outline general tonnage and grade for a preliminary feasibility study, but not sufficient to cover drilling and sampling required for a production decision.

there will be official records of claims which can be researched to great advantage before any physical work is done. In the case of most of the large ore bodies that have been discovered during the past couple of decades, the existence of mineralization in the area has been known for decades, or even centuries. Very often further exploration was not undertaken because the ore grade was too low for profitable mining at the time or, in some cases, the size of the ore body was not suspected and could not be determined without considerable exploration.

Although exploration is high risk, large systematic, diversified, and carefully planned exploration programs covering a period of years need not be a lottery game. The probability of discovery of ore bodies of a minimum size and grade for particular areas by means of exploration programs carried on over several years can be estimated on the basis of past experience, but each aspect of an exploration program has its own probability pattern and cutoff point to minimize risk. Given an exploration program of several million dollars per year covering a number of examinations, it is possible to estimate both the present value of a discovery and the probability of a discovery over a six- to eight-year period. From this information it is possible to estimate the exploration profit ratio adjusted for the probability of discovery.[18]

This is not to suggest that there is not a large margin for luck, skill, and experience in exploration for all companies, regardless of the size of the exploration budget. Moreover, returns must be very high on exploration outlays that are successful to cover the many that are not. Even exploration which does not yield a potentially viable mine may be regarded as an investment in information which may have important uses in the future. The most obvious case is finding an ore body that would not be profitable to mine within the present decade, but might become so a decade or two hence. Provided the company can hold the claim at a cost which is not too high, the ore body constitutes an addition to the company's reserves.[19] Also, exploration may provide information useful for other exploration projects in the same or adjacent areas. Finally, exploration provides information regarding particular types of deposits and their spatial characteristics which can be applied to

[18] Peter G. Donald presents a model for the calculation of the exploration profit ratio adjusted for the possibility of discovery. He then tests his model for an area in Sonora, Mexico on the basis of a questionnaire and interviews with several geologists and mining engineers working in the area (Donald, *Investment Decisions in Nonferrous Metals*).

[19] The inability of mining firms to retain claims to ore bodies that they have explored in developing countries has undoubtedly reduced the volume of exploration in these countries.

other projects involving similar deposits and configurations in the future.[20]

Exploration programs are organized into several stages, with specific activities or operations associated with each stage. The first stage would include a literature survey, a study of existing geological maps, a rapid field survey, and an initial evaluation of potential targets, costs, and risks. If warranted by the data, the second stage would involve detailed mapping—geologic, geochemical, and geophysical delineation of the targets; testing of the ore body by means of drilling, trenching, or underground openings; and another evaluation for determining whether to go on to a third stage. The third stage might include detailed drilling and underground exploration for estimating grade, tonnage, and configuration of the ore body, and a preliminary mine feasibility study, including metallurgy of core samples and determination of mining methods and costs. The final stage, if warranted, would involve close pattern drilling and underground sampling to determine the pattern of the ore body and a full economic evaluation, including the estimated rate of return on investment and possibly the construction of a pilot plant. This final phase would provide the basis for determining whether the investment should go forward and at what level or capacity, assuming more than one would be economically feasible.[21] As a rule, each stage will involve a substantially larger outlay than the one before, and the decision regarding whether to move on to another stage, as well as the nature and cost of the stage itself, will be determined by the probability of finding a profitable mine. Moreover, on the basis of information available at the end of each stage, a projected rate of return on a potential mine investment may be made. In most cases exploration will not go beyond the first stage and will involve a cost of $100,000 to $500,000, or even less. A mining company or consortium is unlikely to undertake a feasibility study for a large ore body, which is likely to cost several million dollars, unless the odds are reasonably good, say 1 to 3, that an economically feasible mine will be determined. However, even a favorable feasibility report will not guarantee that a mine will be built since the economical size of the mine may prove to be too large for the

[20] Some practicing geologists with whom I have spoken have doubts about the possibility of estimating returns from an exploration outlay, however large and diversified. They are inclined to doubt the ability of assigning probabilities to exploration over time, at least from grass roots exploration, but assign a heavy weight to just plain "luck." The story is told of an exploration manager who said he would rather hire a lucky geologist than a good (well trained) one!

[21] For a discussion of activities encompassed by progressive stages of exploration, see Donald, *Investment Decisions in Nonferrous Metals*, pp. 50–57.

firm to finance and it may be unable to attract partners. Alternatively, the firm may not be able to make a satisfactory agreement with the government of the country in which the mineral is found.

Mine Feasibility Study

A mine feasibility study involves much more than geology and engineering. The economic evaluation must take into account a forecast of product prices and input costs as well as capital costs, taxes, and other factors determining the rate of return on the investment. A large number of variables determine the expected rate of return on a mining investment. (For purposes of illustration, a simulated cash flow analysis for a hypothetical copper mine is presented as an appendix to this chapter.) The input variables include the grade, size, and configuration of the ore body, wages, materials, and other elements of production costs, the capital expenditures, and the price of the product. For each of these variables it is possible to estimate the probability of its deviation above and below an expected value. Monte Carlo sampling procedures are employed to determine probability functions for each of the variables. Rates of return can then be computed for a large number of sets of values which are the inputs for cash flow analysis. By means of a large number of computer iterations, it is possible to calculate the internal rate of return within certain percentage upper- and lower-confidence limits.[22] This procedure may be supplemented with sensitivity analysis which involves setting each variable in turn to a value which differs by some percentage from the best estimate and then measuring the effect on the internal rate of return. For example, a 10 percent decline in the expected price for mine output for the first five years of the production period might be found to reduce the DCF rate by 25 percent, or a 10 percent increase in the expected capital cost of a mine and mill may be found to reduce the DCF rate by 35 percent. Thus sensitivity analysis can be used to evaluate the change in financial outcome of the project for a wide range of uncertainties in the input variables. Since assumptions regarding rates of taxation, depreciation allowances, royalties, and even interest on borrowed capital (if borrowed funds are subject to variable interest rates) must be built into a model for calculating expected

---

[22] See Brian W. Mackenzie, "Evaluating the Economics of Mine Development," Parts I and II, *Canadian Mining Journal* (December 1970) pp. 40–47, and (March 1971) pp. 46–54. See also David B. Hertz, "Risk Analysis and Capital Investment," *Harvard Business Review* (January/February 1964) pp. 95–106.

DCF rates, sensitivity analysis can be used to estimate the effects of changes in any of these parameters. If a mine development agreement must be negotiated with the host government after the completion of the feasibility study, it is possible to employ the feasibility study to determine the effects of various provisions of the agreement on the DCF rate. Likewise, changes in U.S. tax laws, including a change in the depletion allowance, could be evaluated from the standpoint of their effects on the DCF rate.[23]

Price Projections

Aside from estimating political risks involved in foreign investments, perhaps the major uncertainty facing a potential investor in a copper mine is the price of copper over the productive life of the mine. A confident expectation regarding the *average* price of copper over the period from the initiation of production to the year 2000 will not assure an adequate rate of return since it is the price during the first five years of operations that will have the greatest impact in determining the rate of return on the investment. Moreover, if a high proportion of the capital required to construct the mine is derived from debt financing, a low price for the mineral during the period of debt repayment may mean that cash flow will not be sufficient to cover debt service. Since most large mines require three to five years to construct (including the time for mobilizing the financing and, in some cases, for negotiating an agreement with the government of the host country), short-term price forecasting—with which commodity models have had some success—is of little value. Moreover, in the intermediate and long term, the relevant variable is the price of the mineral in constant dollars, since few decision makers want to project the general trend of world prices. Even if forecasts in constant dollars are reasonably accurate, operating costs may rise more rapidly than the general level of prices, thereby squeezing net profits. However, if the real costs of finding and producing the mineral are believed to be rising over time, mines that are constructed today will likely have a cost advantage over future mines and, unless prices rise in the future, new mine capacity will not be generated in line with the long-run growth in demand. For many companies an important consideration is the relative cost of production of the mine under consideration compared with production costs of other major mines.

---

[23] The growing importance of pollution abatement requirements, together with uncertainties regarding future requirements, have added a new element to the estimation of both capital and operating costs.

Capital Costs and Financing

Capital costs of mining, smelting, and refining capacity vary greatly from country to country and according to the conditions within the mining region. Costs in a remote region may be greatly influenced by the necessity of providing large amounts of infrastructure in the form of railroads, highways, and mining communities. Mining communities are no longer crude camps, even in developing countries, but rather the mining firm or the government must provide a modern town with comfortable living quarters and facilities for power, water, and essential services of all kinds. Capital costs in the mining industry appear to be rising more rapidly than the international price index, and in recent years nearly every cost estimate that has been made for a mine or processing facility has turned out to be substantially lower than the final cost. Current capital costs are reviewed in chapters 4 and 12.

Generally speaking, capital costs for mine and processing facilities tend to be higher in the developing countries than in the developed countries. This is true because of the higher transportation costs for equipment, the high cost of non-national engineers and other skilled personnel, and larger capital expenditures for power, water, and highway or rail and port facilities. These costs are not offset to any significant degree by the lower wages of local unskilled workers. In fact, capital costs for worker communities which must be borne by the companies may be higher than in developed countries where many of the workers live in existing communities.

Sources of Financing

Traditionally, U.S. mining firms have financed the bulk of their capital expansion programs out of reinvested earnings plus equipment credits and a certain amount of short-term bank borrowing. A review of the annual reports of several large U.S. copper mining firms during the 1960s showed that their long-term funded debt tended to be 10 percent or less of debt plus stockholders' equity. However, this ratio has risen rapidly in recent years. Kennecott's ratio of long-term debt to debt plus equity rose from 14 percent in 1973 to 28 percent in 1976. The corresponding ratio for Phelps Dodge was 38 percent at the end of 1976, while Anaconda's was somewhat lower. Recently, some of the mining firms with smelters have been taking advantage of the availability of low-cost loans for installation of pollution abatement equipment.

On the other hand, the bulk of the financing of new mines in the developing countries in recent years has taken the form of debt financing. Given the uncertainties for private foreign investment in the developing countries, foreign investors have sought to limit their equity participation as much as possible and, in some cases, to no more than the capitalized value of the preconstruction expenditures. Equity-debt ratios of 1 to 3 have become common. Debt financing has been derived from long-term suppliers' credits, Eurocurrency loans, credits made available by consumers with whom long-term contracts have been negotiated, and long-term loans from the World Bank and its affiliates. Mine processing facilities constructed by government enterprises in the developing countries also tend to be financed in large part by debt capital, including suppliers' credits and borrowing in the international money markets, since the governments lack the resources to provide a substantial amount of equity capital. A further discussion of methods of financing mine development is found in chapter 12.

Investment Decisions by Government Mining Enterprises in Developing Countries

In early 1977 the vice president of a large U.S. mining firm told me that he was very concerned about the future of the U.S. copper industry because foreign government enterprises, which control about half of the copper produced in the LDCs, make decisions to invest in new copper mining capacity on the basis of earnings criteria that differ substantially from those employed by private international mining firms. I suspect that government mining enterprises rarely employ a DCF calculation and, when they do, they are likely to accept a much lower rate of return than a private international firm. Moreover, a government would probably calculate a *social rate of return* which would include as income the taxes paid by the government enterprise, and would employ the social opportunity cost of domestic labor and other domestic inputs rather than their monetary costs. Since the social opportunity cost of native mine workers is probably low compared with the actual money wages paid, social costs would be less than monetary costs. In addition, a portion of the external capital might be obtained from the World Bank or other development financing institutions on terms much more favorable than those available in the private international financial markets.

If a government enterprise were making a decision with respect to a mining investment in a fully rational manner, it would be guided by the expected social rate of return on capital invested in the mining venture in relation to the social rate of return on alternative uses of capital, or the social opportunity cost of capital. Although it would need to take into account commercial risk, it would not need to take account of political risk, as is the case with private investors.

Actually, governments tend to use less sophisticated criteria in their investment decisions. If the mineral is to be used mainly in a domestic industry, as in the case of iron ore for the national steel industry, mining investment might be made in the interest of national self-sufficiency, even if the actual cost of producing the mineral in the country was higher than the price of the commodity in world markets. In the case of countries producing a substantial share of the world's output of a mineral, there is often a desire to maintain or increase the country's world market share or to increase the ratio of national output to measured reserves. Such objectives have been expressed regarding the copper industry by officials in Chile and Peru.

There are constraints on investment decisions by government enterprises even when they are very anxious to expand their mining capacity. For one thing, potential external creditors, including both private loan sources and development agencies such as the World Bank, will normally require feasibility studies for the projects to be financed which show a reasonable financial rate of return on the investment, including an allowance for risk. Also, since many large mining projects take the form of joint ventures with foreign enterprises, the criteria for investment decisions for such ventures will be similar to those employed in wholly or majority-owned private mining enterprises.

Where capital funds are not a constraint, as in the case of the Iranian government's Sar Cheshmeh project being developed under a management contract with Anaconda, the profitability calculations employed by private firms may play a very small role in the investment decision. In the case of Sar Cheshmeh, the government took over a project that private firms had found not to be financially feasible under the terms proposed by the Iranian authorities. An unofficial estimate of the capital cost per metric ton of refined copper for the Sar Cheshmeh mine is over $10,000—well in excess of any private copper mine project currently under construction.

Appendix 8-1
Simulated Cash Flow Analysis
of a Hypothetical Copper Mine

This appendix simulates the results of a feasibility study for a hypothetical mining project with a view to illustrating the estimation of the cash flow and internal rate of return (DCF) to equity of a potential copper mine. An attempt has been made to employ data and parameters that appear to be realistic as of mid-1974 on the basis of information contained in selected annual reports of existing open-pit copper mines in an (unnamed) Asian country. Nevertheless, the data employed should be regarded as illustrative.

It is assumed that this is a joint venture in which the majority (70 percent) equity holder (the investor) contributes both equity financing and advances (loans without interest) while the minority (30 percent) equity holder contributes only the ore body. (For example, the minority partner might be the host government.) The remainder of the capital is borrowed at interest from external sources, and repayment of the external loan has priority over the advances.

The accompanying tables provide an analysis of a hypothetical open-pit mine and concentrator producing 35,000 tons of ore per day and costing $200 million with no allowance for the cost of the ore body or of any preliminary work that may have been done in identifying the ore body. This represents an investment of $3,434 per annual short ton of copper metal. The average grade of the ore body is assumed to contain 0.56 percent copper and 0.02 ounces of gold per ton of ore.

The allocation of the capital expenditures shown in table 1 is somewhat arbitrary in the absence of knowledge regarding the conditions in the area, but the allocation of expenditure categories over time has been made on the basis of information on other mine projects and from U.S. Bureau of Mines data.[24] In the simulated "Operating Statistics" given in table 2 it is assumed that the ore grade declines from an initial 0.65 percent Cu to 0.55 percent Cu in the fifth year of production and continues

---

[24] See for example, "Cost Analysis of Open-Pit Mining Operations," in *An Economic Appraisal of the Supply of Copper from Primary Domestic Sources*, Bureau of Mines Circular 8598 (Washington, D.C., U.S. Department of the Interior, 1973) appendix A.

Table 1.   Schedule of Capital Outlays—Total $200 Million
(*millions of dollars*)

Facility	1975	1976	1977	1978	1979	1975–79
1. Exploration and evaluation	4	6	—	—	—	10
2. Mining	—	—	10	20	20	50
3. Concentrator	—	—	20	20	30	70
4. Roads, terminals, and port	4	6	20	10	—	40
5. Power and communications	2	2	2	4	6	16
6. Town	2	2	4	4	2	14
7. Total	12	16	56	58	58	200

at that rate thereafter. After allowance for mill recovery and shipping losses, contained copper output of the mine is 134 million pounds, plus 24,120 ounces of gold in the first year, declining to 113 million pounds of copper and 20,412 ounces of gold in the sixth year and thereafter (table 2). In table 2 operating costs, including depreciation and depletion,[25] average 47.6 cents per pound (total operating cost divided by pounds of copper sold), but the initial cost per pound is 39 cents, rising to nearly 50 cents per pound in the sixth year, mainly as a consequence of the assumed decline in ore grade. *Assuming 65-cent copper,* operating income (table 2) is $84.8 million (after the 6 percent export tax) in the first year, declining to $71.8 million in the fifth year and continuing at that level thereafter. Earnings after payment of the 35 percent income tax average $12.5 million per year during the first two years of operations and decline thereafter to a low of $7.5 million in the sixth year; earnings rise to $10.0 million in the eighth year and remain at that level thereafter. Table 3 gives earnings after taxes over the 1980–99 period for 70-cent, 75-cent, 80-cent, 85-cent, and 90-cent copper.

Table 4 provides an analysis of cash outflow and inflow for the mining investment over the investment and operating period assuming 65-cent copper and given the after-tax earnings data from table 3. Depletion and depreciation are added to after-tax earnings to arrive at gross cash flow from which external debt repayments must be subtracted to arrive at net cash flow. The investor's cash contribution is made partly in the

[25] I have assumed $10 million a year for depreciation and depletion beginning with 1980. This is a conservative figure so that if depreciation should be higher, net cash flow will be higher by 35 percent of the increase in depreciation allowance.

Table 2. Operating Statistics, Costs, Revenues, and Earnings—65-cent Copper

(millions of dollars)

	1980	1981	1982	1983	1984	1985	1986	1987	1988	1989
A. Operating statistics										
1. Tons ore (000)	12,250	12,250	12,250	12,250	12,250	12,250	12,250	12,250	12,250	12,250
2. Ore grade (%)	0.65	0.65	0.60	0.60	0.55	0.55	0.55	0.55	0.55	0.55
3. Mill recovery (%)	85	85	85	85	85	85	85	85	85	85
4. Tons of copper produced	67,680	67,680	62,475	62,475	57,270	57,270	57,270	57,270	57,270	57,270
5. Tons of contained copper sold	67,000	67,000	61,850	61,850	56,700	56,700	56,700	56,700	56,700	56,700
6. Lbs. of copper sold (millions)	134.0	134.0	123.7	123.7	113.4	113.4	113.4	113.4	113.4	113.4
7. Ounces of gold sold	24,120	24,120	22,267	22,267	20,412	20,412	20,412	20,412	20,412	20,412
B. Operating costs[a]										
1. Capital replacement	—	—	—	1.0	1.4	1.4	1.4	1.4	1.4	1.4
2. Mining	15.0	15.0	15.0	15.0	15.0	15.0	15.0	15.0	15.0	15.0
3. Crushing	2.5	2.5	2.5	2.5	2.5	2.5	2.5	2.5	2.5	2.5
4. Concentrating	14.4	14.4	14.4	14.4	14.4	14.4	14.4	14.4	14.4	14.4
5. Marketing	3.1	3.1	3.1	3.1	3.1	3.1	3.1	3.1	3.1	3.1
6. Smelting	6.0	6.0	6.0	6.0	6.0	6.0	6.0	6.0	6.0	6.0
7. General overhead	1.2	1.2	1.2	1.2	1.2	1.2	1.2	1.2	1.2	1.2
8. Depletion and depreciation	10.0	10.0	10.0	10.0	10.0	10.0	10.0	10.0	10.0	10.0
9. Mine production tax	—	—	—	—	—	2.3	2.3	2.3	2.3	2.3
10. Royalty	—	—	—	—	—	0.5	0.5	0.5	0.5	0.5
11. Total operating cost	52.2	52.2	52.2	53.2	53.6	56.4	56.4	56.4	56.4	56.4
C. Operating income										
1. Copper sales 65¢ per lb.	87.1	87.1	80.4	80.4	73.7	73.7	73.7	73.7	73.7	73.7
2. Gold sales $120 per oz.	2.9	2.9	2.7	2.7	2.5	2.5	2.5	2.5	2.5	2.5
3. Gross revenue	90.0	90.0	83.1	83.1	76.2	76.2	76.2	76.2	76.2	76.2
4. Export tax (6%)	5.2	5.2	4.8	4.8	4.4	4.4	4.4	4.4	4.4	4.4
5. Operating income	84.8	84.8	78.3	78.3	71.8	71.8	71.8	71.8	71.8	71.8
D. Interest (from table 4)	14.6	12.2	9.8	7.8	5.8	3.8	1.8	—	—	—
E. Earnings										
1. Earnings before tax	18.0	20.4	16.3	17.3	12.4	11.6	13.6	15.4	15.4	15.4
2. Income tax (35%)	6.3	7.1	5.7	6.1	4.3	4.1	4.8	5.4	5.4	5.4
3. Earnings after tax	11.7	13.3	10.6	11.2	8.1	7.5	8.8	10.0	10.0	10.0

	1990	1991	1992	1993	1994	1995	1996	1997	1998	1999
A. Operating statistics										
1. Tons ore (000)	12,250	12,250	12,250	12,250	12,250	12,250	12,250	12,250	12,250	12,250
2. Ore grade (%)	0.55	0.55	0.55	0.55	0.55	0.55	0.55	0.55	0.55	0.55
3. Mill recovery (%)	85	85	85	85	85	85	85	85	85	85
4. Tons of copper produced	57,270	57,270	57,270	57,270	57,270	57,270	57,270	57,270	57,270	57,270
5. Tons of contained copper sold	56,700	56,700	56,700	56,700	56,700	56,700	56,700	56,700	56,700	56,700
6. Lbs. of copper sold (millions)	113.4	113.4	113.4	113.4	113.4	113.4	113.4	113.4	113.4	113.4
7. Ounces of gold sold	20,412	20,412	20,412	20,412	20,412	20,412	20,412	20,412	20,412	20,412
B. Operating costs[a]										
1. Capital replacement	1.4	1.4	1.4	1.4	1.4	1.4	1.4	1.4	1.4	1.4
2. Mining	15.0	15.0	15.0	15.0	15.0	15.0	15.0	15.0	15.0	15.0
3. Crushing	2.5	2.5	2.5	2.5	2.5	2.5	2.5	2.5	2.5	2.5
4. Concentrating	14.4	14.4	14.4	14.4	14.4	14.4	14.4	14.4	14.4	14.4
5. Marketing	3.1	3.1	3.1	3.1	3.1	3.1	3.1	3.1	3.1	3.1
6. Smelting	6.0	6.0	6.0	6.0	6.0	6.0	6.0	6.0	6.0	6.0
7. General overhead	1.2	1.2	1.2	1.2	1.2	1.2	1.2	1.2	1.2	1.2
8. Depletion and depreciation	10.0	10.0	10.0	10.0	10.0	10.0	10.0	10.0	10.0	10.0
9. Mine production tax	2.3	2.3	2.3	2.3	2.3	2.3	2.3	2.3	2.3	2.3
10. Royalty	0.5	0.5	0.5	0.5	0.5	0.5	0.5	0.5	0.5	0.5
11. Total operating cost	56.4	56.4	56.4	56.4	56.4	56.4	56.4	56.4	56.4	56.4
C. Operating income										
1. Copper sales 65¢ per lb.	73.7	73.7	73.7	73.7	73.7	73.7	73.7	73.7	73.7	73.7
2. Gold sales $120 per oz.	2.5	2.5	2.5	2.5	2.5	2.5	2.5	2.5	2.5	2.5
3. Gross revenue	76.2	76.2	76.2	76.2	76.2	76.2	76.2	76.2	76.2	76.2
4. Export tax (6%)	4.4	4.4	4.4	4.4	4.4	4.4	4.4	4.4	4.4	4.4
5. Operating income	71.8	71.8	71.8	71.8	71.8	71.8	71.8	71.8	71.8	71.8
D. Interest (from table 4)	—	—	—	—	—	—	—	—	—	—
E. Earnings										
1. Earnings before tax	15.4	15.4	15.4	15.4	15.4	15.4	15.4	15.4	15.4	15.4
2. Income tax (35%)	5.4	5.4	5.4	5.4	5.4	5.4	5.4	5.4	5.4	5.4
3. Earnings after tax	10.0	10.0	10.0	10.0	10.0	10.0	10.0	10.0	10.0	10.0

[a] Average operating cost of 47.6 cents per pound over the 1980–99 period. Average grade mined is 0.56 percent over period.

241

Table 3.   Earnings After Taxes for Hypothetical Copper Mine at
Various Copper Prices[a]
(*millions of dollars*)

Year	65-cent Cu	70-cent Cu	75-cent Cu	80-cent Cu	85-cent Cu	90-cent Cu
1980	11.7	16.1	19.8	23.9	27.9	32.0
1981	13.3	17.6	21.3	25.4	29.5	33.6
1982	10.6	14.6	18.1	21.8	25.5	29.4
1983	11.2	15.3	18.7	22.5	26.2	30.1
1984	8.1	11.8	14.8	18.3	21.8	25.3
1985	7.5	11.2	14.3	17.8	21.4	24.8
1986	8.8	12.5	15.6	19.1	22.6	26.1
1987	10.0	13.7	16.8	20.3	23.8	27.2
1988	10.0	13.7	16.8	20.3	23.8	27.2
1989	10.0	13.7	16.8	20.3	23.8	27.2
1990	10.0	13.7	16.8	20.3	23.8	27.2
1991	10.0	13.7	16.8	20.3	23.8	27.2
1992	10.0	13.7	16.8	20.3	23.8	27.2
1993	10.0	13.7	16.8	20.3	23.8	27.2
1994	10.0	13.7	16.8	20.3	23.8	27.2
1995	10.0	13.7	16.8	20.3	23.8	27.2
1996	10.0	13.7	16.8	20.3	23.8	27.2
1997	10.0	13.7	16.8	20.3	23.8	27.2
1998	10.0	13.7	16.8	20.3	23.8	27.2
1999	10.0	13.7	16.8	20.3	23.8	27.2

[a] Based on the same assumptions employed in the preparation of table 2.

form of equity ($19.2 million assumed to represent 70 percent of total equity) and the remainder in advances ($44.8 million) for a total of $64 million. The remaining $136 million in project capital requirements is supplied by external loans repayable during the first seven years of operations at an interest rate of 10 percent. The advances made by the investor are assumed to have first claim on net cash flow after external debt repayment. In addition, the investor receives 70 percent of the amount available for dividends, with the remaining 30 percent going to the minority partner. Total cash flow to the investor is the sum of the repayment of the advances and 70 percent of the dividends.

Table 5 shows the internal rates of return (DCF) on the investor's capital outlay assuming various prices of copper based on the earnings after taxes data shown in table 3 and the cash flow analysis shown in table 4. For 65-cent copper, the investor's internal rate of return for the period 1975–94 is less than 5 percent, and for the period 1975–99 it is

Table 4. Cash Flow Analysis—65-cent Copper

(millions of dollars)

	1975	1976	1977	1978	1979	1980[a]	1981	1982	1983	1984	1985	1986	1987
1. Project capital requirements[b]	12	16	56	58	58	—	—	—	—	—	—	—	—
2. Equity contribution	3.6	4.8	10.8	—	—	—	—	—	—	—	—	—	—
3. Advances	8.4	11.2	25.2	—	—	—	—	—	—	—	—	—	—
4. External debt financing	—	—	20	58	58	(24)	(24)	(20)	(20)	(20)	(20)	(18)	—
5. Interest at 10%	—	—	—	2	8	14.6	12.2	9.8	7.8	5.8	3.8	1.8	—
6. Loan status	—	—	20	80	146	122	98	78	58	38	18	—	—
7. Earnings after taxes	—	—	—	—	—	11.7	13.3	10.6	11.2	8.1	7.5	8.8	10.0
8. Depreciation and depletion	—	—	—	—	—	10.0	10.0	10.0	10.0	10.0	10.0	10.0	10.0
9. Gross cash flow	—	—	—	—	—	21.7	23.3	20.6	21.2	18.1	17.5	18.8	20.0
10. Net cash flow (after debt repayment)	—	—	—	—	—	-2.3	-0.7	0.6	1.2	-1.9	-2.5	0.8	20.0
11. Repayment of advances	—	—	—	—	—	—	—	—	—	—	—	—	—
12. Available for dividends	—	—	—	—	—	—	—	—	—	—	—	—	—
13. 70% of (12)	—	—	—	—	—	—	—	—	—	—	—	—	15.2
14. (11) + (13)	—	—	—	—	—	—	—	—	—	—	—	—	15.2

	1988	1989	1990	1991	1992	1993	1994	1995	1996	1997	1998	1999
1. Project capital requirements[b]	—	—	—	—	—	—	—	—	—	—	—	—
2. Equity contribution	—	—	—	—	—	—	—	—	—	—	—	—
3. Advances	—	—	—	—	—	—	—	—	—	—	—	—
4. External debt financing	—	—	—	—	—	—	—	—	—	—	—	—
5. Interest at 10%	—	—	—	—	—	—	—	—	—	—	—	—
6. Loan status	—	—	—	—	—	—	—	—	—	—	—	—
7. Earnings after taxes	10.0	10.0	10.0	10.0	10.0	10.0	10.0	10.0	10.0	10.0	10.0	10.0
8. Depreciation and depletion	10.0	10.0	10.0	10.0	10.0	10.0	10.0	10.0	10.0	10.0	10.0	10.0
9. Gross cash flow	20.0	20.0	20.0	20.0	20.0	20.0	20.0	20.0	20.0	20.0	20.0	20.0
10. Net cash flow (after debt repayment)	20.0	20.0	20.0	20.0	20.0	20.0	20.0	20.0	20.0	20.0	20.0	20.0
11. Repayment of advances	20.0	9.6	—	—	—	—	—	—	—	—	—	—
12. Available for dividends	—	10.4	20.0	20.0	20.0	20.0	20.0	20.0	20.0	20.0	20.0	20.0
13. 70% of (12)	—	7.3	14.0	14.0	14.0	14.0	14.0	14.0	14.0	14.0	14.0	14.0
14. (11) + (13)	20.0	16.9	14.0	14.0	14.0	14.0	14.0	14.0	14.0	14.0	14.0	14.0

[a] Parentheses indicate cash outflow.

[b] No allowance made for working capital or for purchase of ore body.

243

Table 5. Net Cash Flow and Internal Rate of Return to the Investor[a]
(*millions of dollars*)

Year	65-cent Cu[b]	70-cent Cu	75-cent Cu	80-cent Cu	85-cent Cu	90-cent Cu
1975	(12)	(12)	(12)	(12)	(12)	(12)
1976	(16)	(16)	(16)	(16)	(16)	(16)
1977	(36)	(36)	(36)	(36)	(36)	(36)
1978	—	—	—	—	—	—
1979	—	—	—	—	—	—
1980	—	2.1	5.8	9.9	13.9	18.0
1981	—	3.6	7.3	11.4	15.5	19.6
1982	—	4.6	8.1	11.8	15.5	15.7
1983	—	5.3	8.7	12.3	11.3	14.1
1984	—	1.8	4.8	5.8	8.3	10.7
1985	—	1.2	4.3	5.5	8.0	10.4
1986	—	4.5	7.1	7.8	10.2	12.7
1987	15.2	23.1	18.8	21.2	23.7	26.0
1988	20.0	16.6	18.8	21.2	23.7	26.0
1989	16.9	16.6	18.8	21.2	23.7	26.0
1990	14.0	16.6	18.8	21.2	23.7	26.0
1991	14.0	16.6	18.8	21.2	23.7	26.0
1992	14.0	16.6	18.8	21.2	23.7	26.0
1993	14.0	16.6	18.8	21.2	23.7	26.0
1994	14.0	16.6	18.8	21.2	23.7	26.0
1995	14.0	16.6	18.8	21.2	23.7	26.0
1996	14.0	16.6	18.8	21.2	23.7	26.0
1997	14.0	16.6	18.8	21.2	23.7	26.0
1998	14.0	16.6	18.8	21.2	23.7	26.0
1999	14.0	16.6	18.8	21.2	23.7	26.0
IRR[c]						
1975–94	0.0478	0.0775	0.1018	0.1263	0.1485	0.1690
1975–99	0.0716	0.0971	0.1184	0.1401	0.1602	0.1788

[a] See text for assumptions.

[b] Parentheses indicate cash outflow.

[c] No liquidation value is assumed, but this would not greatly affect the *IRR*.

only 7.2 percent. Moreover, as is shown in table 4, line 10, net cash flow (after debt repayment) is actually *negative* during the early years in the sense that gross cash flow does not fully cover external debt repayment. Only for 85-cent copper does the internal rate of return rise to 15 percent and for a 20 percent internal rate of return it would be necessary for the price to exceed 95 cents per pound.

9

Foreign Investment in Copper Mining

Introduction

THIS CHAPTER is concerned with the role of foreign investment in the future world supply of copper and the sources of conflict between foreign investors and host countries.* Chapter 10 deals with conflict resolution and the negotiation of mine development agreements, while chapter 11 treats more specifically certain problems of developing countries in exploiting their mineral resources. Much of the discussion in these three chapters will apply generally to investment in nonfuel minerals rather than to copper alone. This is because the problems with which we are concerned are more or less common to all nonfuel minerals and much of the relevant data are not disaggregated by individual minerals, for example, copper, bauxite, iron ore, lead, nickel, tin, and zinc. However, most of our specific examples of investment relate to the copper mining industry.

Despite widespread nationalization of foreign-owned mining properties in the developing countries over the past decade, there remains a substantial foreign equity in mining, especially in copper, bauxite, iron ore, and nickel. Over half the copper output of the developing countries is produced by companies in which there is foreign ownership, and companies in which foreigners own a majority of the equity produce about one-fourth of the copper output of the developing countries. U.S. and British ownership play an important role in the Australian and South African copper mining industries, and although the bulk of the Canadian copper output is produced by Canadian companies, several U.S. companies, including Newmont Mining, Utah International, and Texas-

* For a further discussion of some of the topics dealt with in this and the following chapter, see Raymond F. Mikesell, *New Patterns of World Mineral Development* (British-North American Committee, 1979).

gulf, either have majority-owned Canadian subsidiaries or a substantial
equity interest in Canadian companies. The principal U.S. company
investments in the mining industries in the developing countries are
listed in chapter 1. Canadian, Australian, and South African companies
are also important investors in copper mining enterprises in the developing countries, and the problems arising from these investments are
similar to those of American companies.

Foreign investment is likely to continue to play an important role in
the development of copper, but most of the new mines in the Third
World countries are likely to take the form of joint ventures involving
foreign and domestic partners, and, in a large proportion of the joint
ventures, the foreign investor is likely to be a minority partner either
because of legal restrictions or because the foreign investors themselves
believe that the security of their investment is better served by a minority
interest. Majority foreign equity ownership in mining is prohibited in
Mexico (by severe tax penalties), the Philippines, and Zambia; while
Brazil, Chile, Indonesia, Papua New Guinea, Peru, and Zaire permit
majority ownership. A minority position creates problems for foreign
investors, the nature of which will be discussed later in this chapter.
Even where majority foreign ownership is permitted, the traditional prerequisites of control over marketing, purchasing, employment, and
various aspects of production and management are constrained in various ways by many host governments. New patterns of host country-
foreign investor relationships are emerging, and in many countries the
traditional mining concession agreement has disappeared.

The Meaning of Foreign Investment

Because of the wide variety of legal forms and contractual arrangements
employed by foreign companies in host countries for resource development, it is important to set forth exactly what is meant by a foreign
investment. Regardless of what the contract is called, a foreign investment involves some risk and uncertainty with respect to compensation
for the resources transferred. If a government mining enterprise hires a
foreign engineering firm for a fixed fee to explore and construct a mine,
and the fee, together with all attendant expenditures, is paid periodically
without any conditions other than those related to performance under
the contract, it is not a foreign investment but simply a straightforward
sale of a service. There is always a risk of nonpayment as there is a risk
of nonpayment for commodities acquired under a credit contract, but
such risks can generally be insured by government agencies in the home
country of the firm providing the services. However, if the foreign firm

contracts to construct a mine and agrees to be paid a certain percentage of the product and perhaps, in addition, be subject to an income tax, such an arrangement is a foreign investment. This is true even though they are frequently called "service contracts" or "works contracts" in petroleum and certain mining industries. In contracts of this nature costs are sometimes shared by the government, but in most cases they are borne entirely by the foreign investor. Thus the foreign investor is subject to both economic and political risks on the investment and an uncertain rate of return. Product-sharing arrangements are one of the ways of determining payment for the resources provided by the foreign investor, and the host government frequently levies a tax on the earnings and may also control the price and conditions of marketing the foreign investor's share.

Most developing countries prefer an arrangement whereby the supplier of foreign resources bears all or a portion of the risk of a mining venture rather than acquiring the foreign inputs by outright purchase. In addition to reducing or even eliminating entirely the government's own risk exposure, a foreign investor is likely to perform more efficiently than a contractor supplying services without risk. Moreover, if the host government expects to finance a substantial portion of the cost of the venture by external borrowing, its ability to obtain debt financing will be greatly enhanced if all or a portion of the equity or risk capital is supplied by a reputable international mining firm. In fact, the ability to obtain external financing on reasonable terms may be enhanced if the foreign investor has a majority or a 100 percent equity interest in the venture. This is true even though effective control may be determined more by the conditions set forth in the mine development contract than by the nominal degree of control indicated by the portion of the total equity shares held by the foreign investor. Actually, the potential creditors, including public international institutions such as the World Bank, may be more interested in the competence and independence of the management of the operation than in actual shareholdings. Hence, a long-term management contract which is an integral part of the mine development agreement may be necessary to assure potential creditors of competent management in cases of minority foreign ownership.

Depackaging Foreign Investment

The developing producer countries have increasingly sought to acquire as separate inputs the elements that make up the package associated with traditional foreign investment. This disaggregation is desired for two reasons. First, certain traditional prerequisites of foreign investment, such as policy determination and ownership status, are desired by the government of the host country. And second, it is believed that the necessary inputs can be acquired at an international competitive price without having to pay a rent to the foreign investor. There are three general difficulties with this approach. First, the integrated investment package provided by an experienced international mining firm with its own risk capital and reputation at stake is far more valuable than the sum of the identifiable inputs. Second, rents in the form of a surplus above cost accrue to every input that is scarce, whether it be a manager with twenty-five years' experience in the mining business, or a process, or the technical personnel to operate it. Third, the host country must bear the risk if it hires all the inputs at their international market price. However, it is sometimes possible to contract with foreign investors to assume the risk related to the development of an ore field that has been fully explored and evaluated in exchange for a fixed portion of the output. High-risk exploration, however, is another matter. Any arrangement acceptable to the foreign investor will need to provide a rate of return consistent with the risk, regardless of the structural form of the investment.

Declining Foreign Investment Expenditures in Developing Countries

Despite the fact that the developing countries hold well over half the world's measured reserves of copper and that the average grade of ore tends to be higher than in the developed countries,[1] exploration and development expenditures by international mining firms are currently higher in the developed countries. Moreover, there is considerable evidence that expenditures by international mining firms for exploration and development in the developing countries have been declining. Data on exploration expenditures are scarce and global figures are nonexistent. However, articles and speeches by U.S. mining officials, company annual reports, and personal interviews by the author provide strong evidence that U.S. mining firms are concentrating their exploration expenditures in the United States and other developed countries, especially Canada and Australia, and that they have reduced exploration

---

[1] The average grade of copper mined in the United States (1972) was 0.55 Cu while in most copper exporting countries in the Third World the average grade exceeds 1 percent.

Table 9-1.   Mining and Smelting: Value of U.S. Foreign Direct
Investment, 1960, 1965, 1970, 1975, and 1976
(*millions of current dollars; end of period*)

	Developing countries	Developed countries	Total
1960	1,600	1,411	3,011
1965	1,814	1,971	3,785
1970	2,522	3,646	6,168
1975	2,150	4,398	6,548
1976	2,309	4,749	7,058

Source: "U.S. Investment Abroad in 1976," *Survey of Current Business,* Washington, D.C.: U.S. Department of Commerce, August 1977 and earlier issues.

expenditures in the developing countries.[2] According to a survey of eighteen U.S. and Canadian mining companies, over 90 percent of these companies' exploration expenditures in recent years have been in the developed countries.[3] A study of the investment experience of fourteen European mining firms revealed that between 1961 and 1975 the share of these companies' exploration expenditures in the less developed countries declined from 57 to 15 percent.[4]

A direct indication of the decline in U.S. investment in the mining industries of the developing countries in recent years is provided by the data shown in table 9-1. Between the end of 1965 and 1970, the book value of U.S. direct investment in mining and smelting in the developing countries rose from $1,814 million to $2,522 million, but by the end of 1976 the book value of this investment had declined to $2,309 million in current dollars. This decrease reflected the nationalization of U.S.

[2] See, for example, Thomas N. Walthier, "The Shrinking World of Exploration," *Engineering Mining Journal* (April and May 1976); see also J. S. Carman, "A Case for Greater Investment of the United Nations in Third World Mineral Developments," paper presented at the 1977 annual meetings of the American Institute of Mining and Metallurgical Engineers, Atlanta, Georgia, March 1977 (mimeo); and *Mineral Development in the 80's: Prospects and Problems,* a report prepared by a group of members of the British–North American Committee (published by the British–North American Committee, November 1976) pp. 14–16.

[3] E. A. Scholz and A. G. Spat, "The Economics of Foreign versus Domestic Mineral Exploration," *Mining Engineering* (June 1977); and M. Chender, "Copper Exploration Restrained by Resource Nationalism and Low Prices," *Engineering and Mining Journal* (August 1976).

[4] European Group of Mining Companies, "Raw Materials and Political Risk" (a report submitted to the President of the Commission of the European Communities, 1976).

Table 9-2.   Mining and Smelting: Capital Expenditures by
Majority-Owned Foreign Affiliates of U.S. Companies, 1967–77
(*millions of 1967 dollars*)[a]

	Developing countries	Developed countries	Total
1967	285	444	729
1968	413	453	866
1969	460	511	971
1970	492	621	1,113
1971	287	998	1,285
1972	239	811	1,050
1973	169	587	756
1974	197	477	674
1975	198	473	671
1976	123	363	486
1977	54	292	346

Source: "Capital Expenditures by Majority-Owned Foreign Affiliates of U.S.
Companies," *Survey of Current Business*, Washington, D.C.: U.S. Department of
Commerce, March 1978, March 1976, March 1975, March 1974, and December
1973.
[a] Deflated by U.S. wholesale price index 1967 = 100.

mining investments in Chile and elsewhere, and the decrease would have
been much greater except for the $650 million investment in the Cuajone
mine in Peru by Southern Peru Copper Corp. during this period. However, between 1970 and 1976 U.S. direct investments in mining and
smelting in the developed countries rose from $3,646 million to $4,749
million in current dollars. It is also worth noting that in 1960 U.S. foreign investment in the mining industry was larger (in current dollars) in
the developing countries than in the developed countries.[5]

A further indicator of the decline in U.S. activity in mining in the
developing countries is shown in table 9-2 which provides data on the
capital expenditures of majority-owned foreign affiliates of U.S. companies in the mining and smelting industries over the 1967–77 period.
Over 1967–72, average annual capital expenditures of majority-owned
affiliates of U.S. companies in the developing countries were $363 mil-
lion (in 1967 dollars) while from 1973 to 1977 average annual expenditures were only $148 million (in 1967 dollars). Except for the large

[5] Deflating these book value figures would not be appropriate since replacement
value in current dollars would be substantially higher in later years than in the earlier
years.

expenditures on the Cuajone mine from 1973 to 1976, capital expenditures by U.S. majority-owned affiliates in the mining industries in the developing countries would have been less than half of the amounts indicated in table 9-2. It will also be noted that during the 1973–77 period capital expenditures of U.S. majority-owned affiliates in the developed countries declined from an annual average of $640 million from 1967 to 1972 to an annual average of $438 million in the 1973–77 period. Much of this decline reflected a decrease in U.S. investments in the Canadian mining industry, largely as a consequence of deteriorating tax and other investment conditions in certain Canadian provinces. This decline has also been influenced by the low prices of minerals since mid-1974.

By contrast, domestic expenditures of U.S. firms for new plant and equipment in the mining industry have risen from an annual average of $1.8 billion over the 1967–72 period to $2.3 billion (in 1967 dollars) over the 1973–77 period.[6] These figures suggest that U.S. mining firms have been shifting their investment activities from foreign countries to the United States. Some of the U.S. investment expenditures have reflected those mandated by U.S. environmental regulations.

The reasons for the decline in exploration and investment activity by international mining firms in the developing countries are detailed later on in this chapter. It seems doubtful whether this trend can be reversed significantly in the near future.

How Important Is Foreign Direct Investment?

It is difficult to provide a satisfactory answer to the question of how essential foreign investment is to the development of the world's mineral resources. Officials of international mining firms usually regard foreign investment as virtually indispensable to the growth and efficient operation of mineral industries in developing countries. Many government officials, including trained and experienced mine managers, regard this allegation of the international mining firms as chauvinistic, and point to their own accomplishments. Moreover, many are convinced that foreign investment can be "depackaged" so that the pieces can be purchased at international market prices without paying rents to the international mining firms. Empirical support for both positions tends to be weak

---

[6] *Economic Report of the President,* Washington, D.C., Council of Economic Advisers (January 1977) p. 247; and *Survey of Current Business* (Washington, D.C., U.S. Department of Commerce, March 1977) p. 31.

and slanted. Considerable evidence has been put forward to show that international mining firms can bring a new ore body into production more quickly and efficiently than can a government mining enterprise, and that reduced production and operational efficiency usually follow nationalization of a mining industry. For example, the Cerro Verde project was initiated by the Peruvian government enterprise, Minero-peru, at about the same time the Cuajone project was initiated by SPCC. Cuajone came on-stream at its full capacity of 155,000 mt in 1976, but Cerro Verde is not expected to come on-stream at full capacity until late in 1978, if then. Nevertheless, "best-worst" case comparisons do not provide an adequate basis for generalization, especially since some private foreign ventures have been disasters. More detailed case studies are needed to determine exactly which government mining enterprises have been relatively efficient and which have been inefficient, and what are the reasons. If certain inputs are lacking or of poor quality, it is important to determine what if any of the specific elements in a foreign investment package cannot be transferred to the developing countries without a foreign equity commitment.

Without taking an extreme position on either side of the issue discussed above, I would like to suggest several reasons why foreign investment is important in both developed and developing countries. First, and perhaps foremost, the larger the number of experienced international mining firms engaged in exploration and development in a country, whether it be Canada, Mexico, Peru, or the United States, the larger the mineral output of the country is likely to be. If a government mining enterprise is operating in a country, it should have competition from private domestic and foreign mining enterprises that can provide a yardstick for measuring government performance. Those that take the position that all mineral development, or the development of certain minerals, should be planned and implemented by the government must answer the charge that government-planned and controlled economies have had a far poorer performance record than free enterprise economies, and that a government monopoly in the minerals area is not likely to perform any better than a government monopoly in industry or agriculture.

Second, foreign direct investment is more capable of providing politically independent management, whether the managers be nationals or foreigners. Top management and boards of directors of government enterprises not only tend to be political appointees, but are under constant pressure to put certain national economic and political objectives above the objective of running the mining enterprise with a view to maximizing efficiency. This is, of course, a major argument that is given for government operation of a mining industry: to make sure that the industry is operated in the national welfare. This is the same issue raised in the previous paragraph: is it better to have a number of competitive enterprises each seeking to maximize net revenue within the framework of a general set of laws designed to protect the national welfare, or is it better to have a government-planned economy?

Third, foreign investment provides a continuing association with an experienced international mining firm for problem solving and for the introduction of new technology. Rarely do operations in mining and milling go as planned and without difficulties. No two ore deposits are exactly alike and problems in the treatment of the ores are very common in new mines. Following the expropriation of the large Chilean mines by the Allende government, technical consultants from all over the world were brought in both by Allende and later by the military junta to help solve the production problems, but production by the new installations, which had been introduced prior to the Allende regime by Anaconda and Kennecott, continued to be low and inefficient for several years. One of the new Chilean mines, Exotica, was operated for only a limited time because of metallurgical problems which rendered the mine unprofitable.

Fourth, international mining companies are better able than governments to undertake the high risks of exploration, both because of their size relative to the budgets of many governments, and because of their ability to pool risks involved in many projects for producing a variety of minerals in countries and regions throughout the world. Their ability to pool a large number of risks and to determine probabilities of success for each one reduces the cost of risk-taking as contrasted with that for most government mining enterprises. But cannot high-risk exploration be undertaken by international agencies such as the UNDP or the UN Revolving Fund for Natural Resources Exploration which was established by the UN General Assembly in June 1974? The UNDP has rendered an important service to the developing countries in undertaking mineral exploration and geological surveys in cooperation with national geological and exploration institutes. UNDP geologists have played an important role in the discovery of large copper ore bodies such as La Caridad in Mexico, Los Pelambres in Chile, Sar Cheshmeh in Iran, and Mamut in Malaysia. However, UNDP officials are the first to admit that their past and potential future operations constitute only a fraction of the geological survey and exploration requirements in the developing countries.[7] Moreover, UNDP does not have the financial and

---

[7] During the period May 1959–June 1976 expenditures and commitments of the UNDP Mineral Survey Program totaled $139 million, with host government counterpart contributions of $124 million. See John S. Carman, "A Case for Greater Involvement of the United Nations in Third World Mineral Development," table 2.

other resources to make the large exploration outlays required for feasibility studies of large mining projects. The UN Revolving Fund does provide a means whereby developing countries can pool exploration risks by requiring that a share of the proceeds resulting from the production of successful projects be paid into the fund. However, the fund must for a number of years rely on voluntary contributions by member governments before it can become self-sustaining, and as of January 1978 the fund had received contributions and pledges of less than $10 million, including $1 million from the U.S. government.

Fifth, international mining companies are better able to mobilize the necessary technical and managerial inputs, together with the international loan capital required for a large mining project than are government enterprises. This is true even though government enterprises can hire the services of geologists, engineers, construction firms, and managers from a variety of sources throughout the world. Sometimes a government can hire an international mining firm to provide all the inputs for each phase of the development of a mine, and then manage it under a management contract. This was the route taken by the government of Iran in the development of Sar Cheshmeh. But such arrangements are costly and expose the government to all of the risks. Moreover, they are not generally available since most international mining firms prefer to use their technical and managerial resources for their own projects.

Sixth, in the case of minerals such as bauxite, iron ore, and manganese for which organized international markets and commodity exchanges do not exist, vertically integrated international mining firms can provide a market for the minerals produced. Even in the case of commodities such as copper, much of which is traded on a world-wide competitive basis, the marketing organizations and affiliate relationships of international mining firms are generally more efficient than the marketing staffs of government mining enterprises in the developing countries. The negotiation of long-term contracts for the bulk of the output of a new mine during the debt repayment period is frequently a condition for obtaining the necessary international loan capital for the construction of a mine. International mining firms are generally in a better position to negotiate such contracts.

Finally, equity participation by an international mining firm is frequently indispensable for raising the large amount of private international debt capital required for a modern mine. Many large mines are now costing a half billion to a billion dollars or more,[8] and most of

[8] The Sar Cheshmeh mine in Iran has an estimated capital cost of $1.4 billion, and the proposed Cerro Colorado mine in Panama will cost at least that amount if it is built.

this capital must be raised by borrowing from international banking consortia and by credits from foreign suppliers of equipment. Governments of developing countries usually prefer to have such borrowing done by the mining enterprise rather than obtaining the funds directly in the form of a public external debt transaction, since the latter would reduce the government's own borrowing capacity. International creditors usually look to future mineral exports of the mining project to service the debt. This means that the creditors will probably insist on the construction and management of the mine by experienced mining firm which has an equity stake in the venture. Unless the government enterprise has an exceptionally good reputation, even public international development institutions such as the World Bank will require participation by an experienced international mining firm as a condition for financing the enterprise.

An indication of the importance of foreign investment in the minerals industry is the growing desire on the part of experienced national mining enterprises, such as Codelco in Chile, Mineroperu in Peru, CVRD in Brazil, and Mindeco in Zambia, to have international mining companies as partners in their mining ventures. Moreover, a number of countries that have nationalized large foreign mining enterprises in the past are welcoming majority-owned foreign companies to explore and develop mines for extracting the same minerals produced by the nationalized mines. This is true, for example, in Chile and Zaire. If the nationalized mining companies mentioned above believed that they could acquire all of the inputs supplied by foreign investors without accepting foreign equity investment, why would they be willing to share the rents from mineral exploitation with foreign firms? If the governments of many developing countries with government enterprises operating in minerals believe that their national welfare is maximized only by government or private national exploitation of minerals, why do they welcome majority-owned foreign enterprise to share in the development of their mineral resources? The reasons given by government officials of developing countries are the same as those outlined in the paragraphs above: the need for high-risk capital, foreign technology and management, marketing outlets, and the mobilization of international loan capital.

Although it cannot be argued that foreign investment is indispensable to the growth of the mineral industries in developing countries, there is reason to believe that the creation of the amount of mineral producing capacity warranted by the resource potential of these countries will require a large volume of foreign direct investment. This conclusion does not suggest that foreign direct investment must be of the traditional 100 percent or majority foreign-owned type. However, foreign investment must involve equity investment as the principal vehicle for the transfer of technology, skills, and management.

Economic Issues in the Negotiation and Implementation of Mine Development Contracts

Because in most developing nations the minerals in the subsoil belong to the state and because of the strong national interest of governments in the exploitation of their natural resources, foreign investments in minerals generally require the negotiation of a contract between the foreign investor and the government of the host country. If it were not for the high-risk nature of mine exploration and development and for the relative scarcity of the special skills involved in finding and evaluating ore bodies, the government of a developing country might simply set forth the provisions of a foreign investment contract and put the contract up for international competitive bidding. If there were no takers, the government could make the contract more attractive and resubmit it for bidding. Except for service contracts for petroleum production in areas of proved reserves, this approach has rarely been tried. The nature of exploration in nonfuel minerals does not ordinarily make this approach feasible. Mine exploration and evaluation cannot be a well-specified service or product. Even if the developing country has done a certain amount of exploration on an ore body, it requires years of intensive exploration and analysis before a feasibility study can be completed indicating the size and the grade distribution of the ore, the economical size of the mine and mill, and the metallurgical processes that must be employed. Before a mining firm can bid on a contract or agree to accept certain financial terms, it must make a fairly extensive examination with its own geologists and engineers. This procedure does not lend itself to international competitive bidding. Moreover, there are a large number of detailed conditions in the mining contract that differ with the nature of the operation and with the policies of the various prospective investors. Hence, the process tends to involve investigation and negotiation on an individual company basis.

The Content of Mine Development Agreements

The content of a typical mine development agreement and the process of negotiation have been well described by other studies, including a recent book by David N. Smith and Louis J. Wells, Jr. entitled *Negotiating Third World Mineral Agreements: Promises as Prologue.*[9] I do

9 Cambridge, Mass., Ballinger, 1975.

not propose to deal comprehensively with all aspects of the negotiation of mine agreements, but rather with the economic implications of these agreements. Most contracts are negotiated within the context of a country's foreign investment law and mining laws or codes. In recent years, many countries have revised and brought together into a single statute the regulations applying to foreign investment and have established foreign investment committees or boards, together with procedures for applying for authorization to bring capital into the country and for negotiating special contracts. Foreign investment committees are generally composed of representatives from several ministries, including the ministry of finance, the ministry of development, the ministry of foreign affairs, and, where applicable, the ministry of mines. In some cases approval by the foreign investment committee is necessary only where special incentives are requested and where the foreign investor desires to register his investment with the ministry of finance or the central bank, a procedure that usually facilitates obtaining exchange for remitting profits and amortization, or the proceeds from the liquidation of the investment. There has also been a tendency to bring together the mining statutes into a single mining code which usually applies to both domestic and foreign investors in the mining industry.

Areas subject to negotiation with the foreign investment committee are usually set forth in the law or decree establishing the negotiating and approving body. The subjects for negotiation may include special tax incentives, a reduction of duties on capital goods imports, the capital structure of the investment, the term of the investment contract, exchange regulations, including the right to hold abroad a portion of the export proceeds, acquisition of surface rights, and guarantees regarding the stability of tax and other conditions applicable to the foreign investor. Where the foreign investment takes the form of a joint venture with a government agency, a special contract with that agency is required, together with approval by the foreign investment committee. In some cases, the negotiation of an agreement by a foreign investor is not required, but is in fact necessary in order to obtain certain tax exemptions and the right to transfer dividends and profits or to transfer the proceeds of the liquidation of the investment.

In the following paragraphs I will deal with four major aspects of mine development agreements, with special emphasis on the economic considerations of importance to both the host country and to the foreign investor. They are as follows: (1) ownership and financial structure; (2) taxation, including both direct and indirect taxes; (3) marketing and export proceeds; and (4) renegotiation and revision of the contract. Some of the requirements governing foreign investments in mining in the major copper producing countries are outlined in table 9-3.

Table 9-3.   Outline of Requirements for Foreign Investment in Copper

	Chile	Indonesia	Mexico
1. Maximum percent permitted foreign equity ownership	100	Gradual shift to 51% Indonesian ownership	49% for private lands; 34% for govt. reserve areas
2. Approval of investment by foreign investment committee	Yes	Yes	No
3. Rate of taxation	Negotiable	Negotiable Previous tax holidays terminated	Negotiable for production and export taxes
4. Accelerated depreciation and amortization	Negotiable	Fixed by law at 12½% per year	Fixed by law
5. Debt-equity ratio	Negotiable	No provision in law	No provision in law
6. Control of marketing	Mining company	Mining company	Domestic buyers have priority
7. Control of export receipts	Negotiable	Surrender to central bank with negotiated provision for portion paid to external creditors	No govt. control
8. Ownership preference in new investment	Private and joint venture for govt.-owned ore bodies	Joint ventures with Indonesians	Govt. participation and private domestic

n.a. = not available.

Ownership and Financial Structure

Large 100 percent foreign-owned copper mines in developing countries are becoming rare.[10] A notable exception is the Cuajone mine which in 1976 (the year production was initiated) was owned 88.5 percent by Southern Peru Copper Corporation, and 11.5 percent by the Dutch firm

[10] By large I mean mines with an annual capacity of 50,000 mt or more.

Mining in Selected Copper Producing Countries

Peru	Philippines	Zaire	Zambia
100	30–40	100	49
Yes	Yes	Yes	Yes
Fixed by law with graduated tax	Fixed by law	Provision for five-year tax holiday	Fixed by law at 73%
Negotiable	Fixed by law	Provides for carry forward of losses before and after commercial production	Annual write-off of capital expenditure and carry forward
n.a.	Determined by central bank	No provision in law	n.a.
Govt. agency	Mining company	Mining company	Govt. agency
Surrender to central bank with negotiated provision for portion paid to external creditors	Surrender to central bank	Surrender to central bank but with negotiable arguments for external credits	Full surrender to central bank
Government majority ownership	Private domestic	Foreign investment with govt. participation	Govt. with minority foreign participation

Billiton, N.V. However, as soon as the Cuajone begins to make a profit, 6 percent of the annual profit will accrue to the Mining Communities, a system of worker-ownership participation, and Cuajone will join her sister mine, Toquepala (formerly owned 100 percent by SPCC), in being partially owned by the Mining Communities. To my knowledge, all large copper mines currently being planned in the developing countries will have at least some host government participation, and in many cases the mines will either have no foreign participation or only a minority foreign equity participation. The latter include the Sar Chesmeh mine in Iran (100 percent government owned); La Caridad in Mexico; Cerro Colorado in Panama; and several large government-owned ore bodies in Peru which the government hopes to develop on the basis of joint ventures with foreign companies which would have a minority equity interest. There are some notable exceptions, however. Several new large copper mines with majority foreign ownership are expected to be constructed in Chile. When construction is resumed on the Tenke-Fungurume mine in Zaire, very likely it will continue to be owned 80 percent by foreign interests. The Kinsenda mine currently being constructed in Zaire by Japanese interests will also be a majority foreign-owned mine. The Ok Tedi mine in PNG is also expected to be developed on the basis of majority foreign equity ownership. Finally, the Pachon copper deposit in Argentina will probably be developed under majority foreign equity ownership.

Domestic equity participation may arise from several sources. First, the government as owner of the minerals in the subsoil or a domestic owner of a mine or claim to an ore body which is acquired by a foreign company may be given a certain percentage of the equity shares as compensation for the ore body, or the right to mine it. The Zairian government was given 20 percent of the equity shares in the company which initiated construction of Tenke-Fungurume, while the Japanese consortium gave the Zairian government 15 percent of the shares in Sodimiza. In other cases, the government has been given an option to acquire up to a certain percentage of the shares, which it may exercise at any time before the initiation of commercial production. Since the option usually provides for the purchase of the shares at book value, the government can acquire a valuable property with little risk and at a price well below the actual cost, which should include the capitalization of the preproduction expenditures.

Government ownership in most mines in developing countries today has been acquired by partial or complete nationalization, in which case the government has simply forced the foreign investor to sell, usually at book value, either all or a majority of the shares of the mining company operating in the country. In 1969 the Zambian government forced the foreign investors in the large Zambian copper mines to sell 51 percent of their interests and in that same year the Chilean government under President Frei forced Anaconda to sell 51 percent of the shares in its large mines—Chuquicamata and El Salvador.[11] However, in 1966 the

[11] In addition to the sale of 51 percent majority ownership, The Anaconda Company requested that the Chilean government acquire 100 percent of the shares over a period of several years.

Kennecott Corporation voluntarily offered to sell to the Chilean government 51 percent ownership in the El Teniente mine in exchange for a reduction in taxes and certain guarantees. Again, nearly all of such sales have been made at book value, which means that the government has received an equity interest in a property whose replacement value was substantially higher than the book value.

In some countries, foreign owners of mines have been required, or induced by tax penalties, to reduce their equity holdings to that of minority shareholders. The foreign investors have usually sold all or a portion of their equity to private domestic groups or to a combination of domestic private interests and government enterprise. Several years after the initiation of the Mexicanization program, Anaconda reduced its equity shares in the Cananea mine in Sonora to 49 percent, with the remainder of the equity being held by two government enterprises and private interests. ASARCO reduced its interest in ASARCO Mexicana (now Industrial Minera Mexico, SA) to 49 percent and later to 34 percent. ASARCO Mexicana had held controlling interest in the La Caridad ore body, one of the largest copper deposits in the world. Because the Mexican government also held a substantial interest in the La Caridad deposit, ASARCO agreed with its Mexican partners in Industrial Minera Mexico to have the property transferred to a new company, Mexicana de Cobre, in which ASARCO holds no interest, but which its Mexican partners now control. Foreign companies entering the mining business in Mexico must now form joint ventures with Mexican interests, private or government, in which Mexicans not only have a majority equity interest but also effective policy and management control.[12]

The Philippine government currently requires that 60 percent of the voting shares of mining enterprises be held by Filipinos. However, it has been possible for foreign minority owners of Philippine mines to retain control through management contracts. Some of the large foreign-owned mining companies such as Atlas Consolidated were apparently successful in changing their structure to 60 percent Philippine ownership, while maintaining a substantial measure of foreign control. It is reported that new investments in the Philippine mining industry must be structured with no more than 30 percent foreign equity ownership.

A requirement limiting foreign investors to a minority equity position constitutes a serious barrier to new foreign investment in mining, whether the majority interest is held by the government or by private

---

[12] Until recently it was possible to establish a company in which nominal majority ownership would be in the hands of a law firm or an industrial company with the understanding that actual policy control and management would be in the hands of the foreign owner. However, new Mexican laws and regulations have made this virtually impossible.

domestic investors. Domestic high-risk capital for exploration is not available in most developing countries, so the foreign investor must finance all of the exploration outlays through the feasibility study, following which the domestic partner—whether government or private —will usually compensate the foreign investor for no more than the actual exploration outlays. Such an arrangement is generally unsatisfactory since the foreign investor must bear all of the risks of exploration while retaining less than half the equity. After the initiation of production, the position of the foreign investor becomes quite uncertain. He may be little more than a portfolio stockholder with no effective voice in policy or management. Moreover, he may realize little or no return on his investment if the majority partners decide to reinvest the bulk of the earnings, or if the enterprise is poorly managed, with managers chosen on the basis of political favoritism or family connections with the private domestic partners. I have investigated the opportunities for entering the mining business in Mexico on behalf of two U.S. firms in recent years, and found no satisfactory way for these firms to make a mining investment in that country. Few American firms have gone into Mexican mining since the Mexicanization program, and a substantial flow of foreign mining investment to this mineral-rich country appears most unlikely under present circumstances.

In some countries the minority equity holder can operate under a long-term management contract, but management contracts are frequently terminated prior to the agreed termination date, especially where the government is the majority partner. This is well illustrated by the experience of AMAX and the Anglo-American group which were awarded long-term management and sales contracts after the Zambian government forced them to relinquish 51 percent of their equity holdings in the large Zambian copper mines in 1969. In 1974 the Zambian government cancelled the management and sale contracts and the minority foreign investors were left with virtually no voice in the management and only a very small return on their investment. In a few cases governments have invited foreign companies to undertake exploration and development programs as minority shareholders, but with the government financing its share of the exploration outlays from the beginning. For example, the Zambian government enterprise, Mindeco, has negotiated joint venture arrangements with Noranda, a private Canadian company, and with Geomin, a Romanian corporation, with exploration expenditures shared by both Mindeco and the foreign investors. In the Noranda agreement exploration, expenditures may be capitalized, with the capitalized amounts representing the equity shares at the time of the construction of the mine, assuming a commercially viable mine is found. It is expected that the construction costs will be financed by external borrowing, and under Zambian law the capitalized expenditures may be written off against earnings as soon as they are available. If such an arrangement were combined with a management contract which would give the foreign investor a continuing control in the enterprise, a minority foreign equity position might prove to be attractive. However, in the case of Zambia, there are other requirements such as reinvestment of 50 percent of the dividends, plus exchange controls that greatly limit the remittance abroad of the remainder of the dividends. Such conditions have made foreign investment in Zambia generally unattractive.

Fade Out. In recent years some governments have adopted the policy known as "fade out" in which foreign investors are required to sell portions of their equity holdings to domestic investors until a majority of the equity shares is held domestically. This principle is embodied in Resolution No. 24 of the Cartegena Agreement Commission (the Andean Pact) which calls for the progressive sale of 51 percent of the equity in the foreign investment over a fifteen-year period; no less than 30 percent of the shares must be owned by domestic investors when one-third of the time since the initial investment has elapsed and no less than 45 percent after two-thirds of the period has elapsed.[13] Although some members of the Andean Pact have questioned whether this resolution applies to mining, the idea of "fade out" is quite popular in Latin America and elsewhere, and is, therefore, worth discussing at this point.

Such arrangements are especially inappropriate for mining enterprises which are faced with substantial uncertainties in developing countries under the best of conditions. Fade out usually means that the foreign investor must find a market for the shares of his company in countries where the equity market is not well developed and therefore he may be unable to obtain a price equivalent to the discounted value of future earnings. If the foreign investor cannot sell to private interests, he may be forced to sell to the government, which is unlikely to pay more than book value less depreciation for the shares. If the time period for the liquidation of 51 percent of the shares begins with the initial investment in exploration, or even with the initiation of construction of the mine, the foreign investor might have to liquidate half of his investment over a ten-year period, the first five to seven years of which may be required for paying off the indebtedness. International mining companies would

---

[13] A translation of Resolution No. 24 of the Cartegena Agreement Commission is printed in C. Vaitsos, "Foreign Investment in Latin America," *Journal of World Trade Law* vol. 7, no. 6 (November/December 1973) pp. 647–665.

clearly not be interested in an arrangement which would make it impossible for them to secure an adequate return on their investment. Moreover, the "fade out" principle is likely to induce the foreign investor to mine the richest ore in a deposit first and to take his funds out of the country as quickly as possible, rather than reinvest them for the growth of the mining industry. Large mining companies are interested in continuous exploration and development over several decades. It is the prospect of a long period of operation that makes it worthwhile to undertake the high risks of exploration. Long-term investment and gradual growth of a mining investment through continuous exploration also maximize the benefits to the host country.

The Debt-Equity Ratio.   The debt-equity ratio is frequently an important issue in the negotiation of mining agreements. The foreign investor is usually interested in minimizing the equity contribution since the smaller the equity, the smaller the amount of capital at risk and the larger the leverage for profit if the venture proves successful. On the other hand, the host government usually desires to minimize the fixed obligations of the foreign enterprise and maximize the equity portion of the investment, the earnings on which are subject to taxation. Debt financing may be provided by international banks and financial institutions, and by equipment suppliers not affiliated with the foreign investor, or they may be provided directly or indirectly by the foreign investor himself.[14] In recent years there has been a tendency for foreign investors in mining in developing countries to limit their equity contribution to the capitalized value of the exploration expenditures through the feasibility study, plus whatever the foreign investor must pay for the land or the claims on the ore body, and to finance the remainder in the form of debt. Nonaffiliated creditors will require a substantial contribution to the project by the foreign investor himself, but, as has been noted, a portion of this can be contributed in the form of advances by the foreign investor which would constitute junior capital while the senior capital (or that which has a prior claim on gross earnings) is represented by the nonaffiliated financing. By supplying a portion of his investment in the form of advances or loans, the foreign investor is assured of being able to recover his capital plus interest during the early part of the production period. Sometimes governments require that interest payments be subject to taxation but in the case of loans from nonaffiliated sources, the creditor would simply add the tax to the interest charged. In some cases the advances made by the foreign investor do not bear interest, but the

---

[14] The foreign investor might make advances to the foreign subsidiary repayable with or without interest, or he may channel such advances through a foreign bank so it appears that the creditor is the bank rather than the foreign investor.

investor still has the advantage of being able to withdraw his capital rapidly without the withdrawals being subject to taxation. This was the case in the financing of the Toquepala mine by the owners of Southern Peru Copper Corporation, who advanced $75 million in lieu of additional equity contributions.[15] The advances were repaid before any dividends were declared on the equity capital.

Taxation

Given a favorable outlook for before-tax earnings, the tax regime is perhaps the most important single factor in the investment decision. We may divide tax arrangements into *direct* taxes which fall on net revenues, or the difference between gross receipts and all items charged as costs, including operating costs, interest, depreciation, and other items allowed as deductions in the determination of taxable income; and *indirect* taxes such as royalties, import duties on capital goods and materials, and taxes on commodities and services required for current operations. Prior to World War II, there was a heavy reliance on indirect taxation, especially royalties and import duties. Since that time there has been a shift in emphasis from royalties and import duties[16] to income taxation for the following reasons. First, developing countries became aware that since the U.S. government, as well as certain other governments, allows the foreign investor to credit income taxes paid abroad against the foreign investor's income tax liability to the home country, income taxes can be paid to the host country without any burden on the foreign investor with respect to income transferred. Second, royalties and other taxes that fluctuate with output may lead investors to cut output in periods of low prices or concentrate on the high-grade ore, leaving the lower grade ore in the ground.[17] Of course, a high income tax rate, even if no higher than the rate paid by the foreign investor to his own government, does affect the incentive to reinvest profits. Hence, some countries have reduced the income tax rate on reinvested earnings. This is frequently achieved by a dividend withholding tax or a tax on earnings transferred abroad.

DCF calculations for determining the commercial viability of a mine are particularly sensitive to capital costs, and since import duties in

---

[15] Raymond F. Mikesell, *Foreign Investment in Copper Mining: Case Studies of Mines in Peru and Papua New Guinea* (Baltimore, Johns Hopkins University Press for Resources for the Future, 1975) pp. 47–48.

[16] Export taxes based on sales have been a major problem for investors in Mexico and currently in Peru.

[17] Lower grade ore not mined is usually lost forever since it would not pay to mine low-grade ore by itself.

most developing countries tend to be quite high—from 50 to 100 percent or more—exemption of capital goods imports from duties is often an essential condition for an investment to be made. However, many countries permit exemption from import duties on capital goods imports only on condition that the goods are not produced in the country in which the investment is made. Where this rule is enforced, the foreign investor may be required to pay an even higher price for the domestic articles than he would pay if the goods were imported subject to duty, plus being faced with slow delivery and inadequate service from the domestic suppliers. Since investment decisions are very sensitive to costs, foreign investors are likely to be more amenable to higher rates of taxation on income after they have recovered their capital than to taxes that raise their capital and current costs. On the other hand, governments of developing countries are usually very anxious to earn at least some tax revenue during the preproduction period and during the period of debt retirement and capital recovery when there is likely to be little or no taxable income and, hence, no income taxes are collected. This situation often presents a dilemma for the host country.

Another problem for the host government is its reluctance to provide foreign investors with tax exemptions that are not available to domestic investors. It is far easier politically to discriminate *against* foreign investors than to favor them. The answer to this problem would appear to lie in eliminating all duties on imported capital goods whether they be foreign or domestic investors. Such exemption is especially important in the case of commodities produced for export in competitive world markets. Recently the Chilean government, in response to demands of prospective foreign investors in the mining industry, inaugurated an arrangement whereby customs duties on imports of capital goods could be "postponed" for up to twelve years, following which the obligation could be credited against the value of exports from the project employing the capital goods. However, the government established the same rules for domestic as for foreign investors. Moreover, the new Chilean foreign investment law of March 1977 provides for virtually no discrimination in treatment between domestic and foreign investors in Chile.

Amortization and Depreciation. Foreign investors in developing countries seek a high rate of amortization on their invested capital or, alternatively, a tax holiday, or both,[18] but in recent years tax holidays have become unpopular and are rarely granted. However, the basic

---

[18] In the agreement for the establishment of the Bougainville mine in PNG in 1967, the investor was granted both a tax holiday and accelerated depreciation. See Mikesell, *Foreign Investment in Copper Mining*, pp. 113ff.

objectives of a tax holiday can be accomplished through accelerated depreciation. The reason why foreign investors desire accelerated depreciation is twofold. First, most foreign mining investments today are financed with a high proportion of debt capital, the bulk of which becomes due in the first five years of operations, and mining enterprises require a high cash flow in the early period of operations to meet the debt service. Second, investors in developing countries are concerned with the stability of the host government and its willingness to honor the agreement over the life of the contract. A high rate of amortization will enable the investor to recover his capital quickly without being subject to income taxation. Moreover, the larger the net cash flow during the early period of production, the higher will be the DCF rate. Amortization usually consists of a combination of depreciation on physical assets and an annual writeoff of other capital expenditures, including exploration expenditures. A few countries, including Zambia and the Philippines (for the export industries), permit full amortization one year after the investment is made to the extent that cash flow permits. However, most developing countries either fix by law the maximum rate of depreciation of specified physical assets as well as the maximum rate of amortization of other capital expenditures, or these rates are subject to negotiation with the foreign investment committee.

Because accelerated depreciation and amortization reduce taxable income in the early years of production, governments are reluctant to grant it, but there may be a tradeoff between rapid depreciation and amortization and the rate of tax on earnings. By giving the investor greater security through rapid recovery of his investment, he may be persuaded to accept a higher rate of taxable income—even one which exceeds the rate paid by the investor in his home country. Also, the foreign investor may be willing to accept a higher rate of income taxation if the contract with the government guarantees that there will be no change in the tax regime applicable to him, at least during the period of capital recovery.

A serious problem in negotiating rates of taxation and related matters, such as amortization and depreciation, lies in the uncertainty regarding the profitability of mines. In recent years most foreign investors want to reach an agreement regarding the tax regime and other conditions fairly early in the exploration phase, at which time it is very difficult to predict whether the return on the investment will be high or low or whether a commercially viable mine can be developed even with zero taxation. If the foreign investor bargains successfully for a low rate of taxation and the mine proves to be a bonanza, there will be general dissatisfaction on the part of the host country, leading to a demand for a renegotiation.

This would appear to argue for some form of graduated tax rate. However, given the fluctuations in the price of copper, the foreign investor is reluctant to accept a high tax rate when profits are high since this would not enable him to offset years of low after-tax earnings or losses in some years with high after-tax earnings in other years. An approach for dealing with this problem is outlined in chapter 10.

Marketing and Control of Exports

Government controls on marketing, especially where the output is sold abroad, may constitute an important issue in the negotiation of mine development agreements. The foreign investor usually requests complete freedom to sell his product and to make contracts for such sales without government interference and to hold the foreign exchange proceeds of exports abroad, except to the extent they are required to make domestic payments, including tax obligations. The host government will as a minimum require the foreign investor to sell his product on terms and conditions that correspond with those existing in the world market and will usually insist on surveillance of export transactions, including the inspection of the product being exported, such as concentrates, in order to ascertain its composition and value. Understandably, the host government wants to make sure that the company is recovering the full market value of its exports, which serves as the basis for taxation.

In recent years, governments have gone much further in controlling sales. For example, the Peruvian government has established a sales monopoly on all minerals and it charges a commission for its sales even when the product goes to a foreign affiliate of one of the foreign-owned mines operating in Peru. The author has been told by mining people in Peru that delays of six months or more have occurred in obtaining the proceeds of sales, thereby greatly increasing the working capital requirements of the mining enterprises in Peru.

Governments may want to control copper exports in order to implement bilateral agreements[19] with other countries, or, more important, to participate in export controls determined by CIPEC, or by some future intergovernmental commodity agreement.

A major issue arises when the government insists on the surrender of all foreign exchange from exports. Indonesia's insistence on full surrender of export proceeds in the so-called "third generation" contracts virtually precluded any new foreign mining investments in that country

---

[19]The Peruvian government has made bilateral barter agreements with China and Mexico involving the exchange of copper for imports from these countries.

for several years.[20] Control over foreign exchange proceeds assures the foreign investor that he will be able to meet external debt service obligations, make payments for foreign supplies and equipment, and remit earnings without having to seek authorization from the central bank or other host government authorities. External creditors usually demand the retention abroad of that portion of the export proceeds necessary to cover the debt service.

Revision and Renegotiation

Regardless of the importance of sanctity of contracts, it would be unrealistic to argue that foreign investment agreements should never be revised or renegotiated. The concession agreements negotiated in the early part of this century with a duration of forty to fifty years or more had clearly become outmoded in terms of the tax systems and other conditions affecting private investment, both foreign and domestic, after World War II. No government should bind itself rigidly to agreements relating to the exploitation of the country's resources over very long periods of time. Such arrangements establish in effect a discriminatory regime in favor of one group of investors. On the other hand, foreign investors must have confidence that contracts entered into with governments will be honored. The principle often advanced by representatives of developing countries, or by Third World groups, that a sovereign state has a right to revoke its covenants whenever it finds it convenient to do so, is political and legal nonsense. In effect, this principle means that a government cannot enter into meaningful contracts.

One approach to the problem of contract revision would be to shorten the duration of contracts to, say, six or seven years after the initiation of commercial production, or the period required for capital recovery, whichever is longer. However, a contract of this duration would not be satisfactory to most investors in the mining industry since it is too short for investors to earn the expected return on the investment. Moreover, once the investment has been made, the bargaining power of the foreign investor falls toward zero. Another approach is to provide for periodic review and possible revision of the contract, say, every five years, following the period of capital recovery. However, for such an arrangement to be acceptable it would be necessary to limit the provisions that were renegotiable and put some limit on the financial impact of any revisions demanded by the host country. Some developing country spokesmen

---

[20] Earlier contracts such as that with Freeport Minerals Company for the construction of the Ertsberg mine placed no restrictions on the holding of export proceeds abroad by the foreign investor.

have argued that a contract revision is justified whenever the government negotiates an agreement in the same industry with another foreign investor that is less favorable to the foreign investors operating under earlier contracts, or whenever agreements are negotiated among third parties that are less favorable to the foreign investors. This is likely to be unfair to the original investor. For example, if the original investor has undertaken high-risk exploration and found several ore bodies, one of which was selected for development, another investor could afford to negotiate a somewhat less favorable agreement based on the knowledge gained by the earlier explorations.

10

Conflict Resolution in Mine Development Contracts: Some Recent Examples

CONFLICTS BETWEEN host governments and foreign investors arise from: (1) opposing objectives in the negotiation of a mine development agreement; (2) the interpretation of the agreement after it is negotiated; (3) alleged violations of the agreement; and (4) demands for renegotiation of the agreement or its denunciation by one of the parties. In this chapter we are mainly concerned with the resolution of opposing objectives in the negotiation of agreements, not only as a means of promoting the consummation of the agreements themselves, but also for building conditions into the agreement that will minimize conflicts and facilitate the settlement of disputes during the tenure of the agreements.[1]

The negotiation of modern agreements is not simply an application of game theory in which the side with the most information and the best bargaining strategy wins. In the past both of these negotiating cards tended to be held by the foreign investor, but this is no longer the case. Modern negotiating techniques are highly sophisticated and governments usually obtain the services of foreign advisors who are well acquainted with the technical and financial characteristics of the industry in question. Since there is a great deal of knowledge and experience on both sides, the outcome of the negotiation, if it is successful, is determined less by negotiating strategies and more by the willingness of negotiators to find ways by which the minimum conditions of each side can be satisfactorily met. I do not believe that bargaining strategy or

[1] For an excellent discussion of dispute settlement and contract revision, see David N. Smith and Louis T. Wells, Jr., *Negotiating Third World Mineral Agreements: Promises as Prologue* (Cambridge, Mass., Ballinger, 1975) chapter 5.

the theory of conflict plays the role that it once did in contract negotiations. Rather, success depends in considerable measure on the ability
of technicians to find acceptable solutions to highly complex problems.

The Political and Economic Interests of Host Countries

In analyzing foreign investment policies of developing countries with
respect to the mineral industries, it is often difficult to distinguish
between national xenophobia and bona fide national economic interests.
Official policy statements are often a collection of slogans condemning
colonial governmental and foreign investor practices of fifty to one
hundred years ago which have little relevance for foreign investment
today. In most countries the motivation for national ownership or for
majority domestic control is not only political, as contrasted with
national economic advantage, but is frequently socialistic since it is the
government that wishes to extend its direct ownership and control over
a major resource. This latter has not been entirely the case in Mexico
and the Philippines, where provision was made for a gradual transition
to domestic private majority ownership. However, in Mexico government ownership of the mineral industries has been expanding. Socialism
was clearly the motivation for the nationalization of copper companies
in Chile and Peru in the early 1970s, while in Zaire and Zambia domestic
private interests were incapable of taking over the mining industries,
even if the governments had not desired public ownership.[2]

The reason national ownership or the elimination or reduction of
foreign equity ownership is mainly a political and not an economic issue
is that national ownership provides no necessary national economic
advantage over private ownership. (An economic analysis of national vs.
foreign ownership is given in chapter 11.) Given the fact that nearly all
developing countries require foreign capital, technology, and managerial resources to develop their mineral industries, the legal form by
which these resources are transferred may have little more than semantic
significance. Normally, it is the mine development agreement between
the host government and the foreign investor that sets forth the conditions under which foreign resources enter the country. The same kind

[2] In Chile, gradual private domestic ownership of the large copper mines would
have been possible, especially since Chilean copper mining has a long tradition going
back to the early part of the nineteenth century, and the managerial personnel were
largely Chileans. Even prior to the Allende administration, the Frei administration
was dedicated to public ownership of the large mines. See R. F. Mikesell, ed., *Foreign
Investment in the Petroleum and Mineral Industries* (Baltimore, Johns Hopkins University Press for Resources for the Future, 1971) chapter 15.

of an agreement may be called a "works contract" by the government in one country and a "concession agreement" in another. In only a few developing countries are foreigners afforded property rights in minerals which they are free to acquire by purchase to do with as they please, including the right to hold them for future exploitation. (In many countries domestic investors must also contract with the government to exploit mineral deposits under specified conditions.) In most developing countries the minerals in the subsoil are the property of the state, and mining is only permitted under the terms of a contract with the state. The vast bulk of the physical assets provided by the foreign mining company would have little or no value apart from the mine. Once the investment has been made, about the only thing in which the foreign firm has a significant proprietary interest is the agreement with the host government. In nearly all cases mine development contracts between the government and the foreign investor are of limited duration, ranging from twenty to thirty years. In most cases all of the assets of the mine revert to the government at the termination of the agreement unless both parties agree to renew the agreement on terms that are generally directed by the government.

The economic interests of the host government include (1) the net foreign exchange income, or exchange savings (if all or a portion of the resource product is used by domestic industries); (2) government receipts in the form of a variety of taxes and fees, including royalties, income taxes, import duties, and land taxes; (3) domestic employment at all levels; (4) the sale of domestic materials and equipment and the stimulation of domestic industry; (5) the creation or expansion of a domestic resource industry that will continue as a valuable asset long after the foreign investor's concession or contract has expired; and (6) a variety of external economies such as the acquisition of skills and technology that may be diffused throughout the domestic economy. National interests also involve certain perceived costs, such as damage to the environment, depletion of natural resources, heavy economic dependence on an export industry, and social difficulties created by foreign and domestic personnel who receive incomes substantially above the national average. Some of these perceived costs are reflected in foreign investment policies, including the conditions demanded in foreign investment agreements. For example, environmental protection clauses are becoming increasingly important in such contracts. Concern with the rate of depletion of natural resources sometimes limits foreign investment, either directly or by making the terms unattractive. (A discussion of the economics of resource depletion is given in chapter 11.)

The government of the host country seeks to acquire the inputs of the foreign investor on terms that will maximize the economic rewards indicated above while at the same time minimizing the economic and social cost to the host country. A part of the perceived social cost is relinquishing control to the foreign investor over the extraction and marketing of the natural resources. The contract negotiations are by no means a zero-sum game. Both parties want to maximize gross revenues from the production and sale of the resources; both want to minimize costs through efficient operations; and there is a mutual interest in maximizing the contribution of the resource industry to the economic and social development of the country. But conflicts inevitably arise in the sharing of the rents, in the allocation of managerial and policy decision making, and in tradeoffs among mutually desired objectives.

Conflicting Investment Conditions Demanded by Host Countries and by Foreign Investors

In the following paragraphs I have set forth investment conditions typically demanded by foreign investors in the mineral industries and those typically demanded by host governments which are likely to be in conflict. The next section describes some approaches to the resolutions of these conflicts, most of which have been embodied in one or more mine development agreements negotiated in recent years.

Conditions Desired by the Foreign Investor

Regardless of the ownership structure of an investment, the following conditions are generally believed by foreign investors to be vital to the efficient operation and profitability of a resource enterprise:

1. Full management control of operations, including the right to appoint managers and other top personnel and to determine conditions of employment of all workers subject to conditions negotiated with trade unions.

2. Policy determination in such areas as mine development programs, the distribution or reinvestment of earnings, external financing, and investment allocations, including exploration.

3. Tax provisions that will enable the investor to earn and repatriate the capitalized value of his investment, including the repayment of external indebtedness, within a reasonable period of time. Foreign investors generally demand a fixed rate of taxation on accounting profits no higher than the corporate tax rate in the country of the parent company, and no excess profits tax.

4. Foreign exchange arrangements that permit the foreign investor to withhold sufficient export proceeds to meet all external obligations plus dividend remittances and authorized capital repatriation.

5. Guarantees against the imposition of any new taxes and against other legislation or regulations that would affect the operation and profitability of the investment which did not exist at the time of the investment agreement or were not provided for in the agreement.

6. Guarantees against demands for contract renegotiation during the life of the contract and provision for international arbitration of disputes arising over the interpretation of the contract or contract violations.

7. Complete freedom to market the product and to acquire equipment and materials from any source, foreign or domestic.

Conditions Demanded by Host Governments

Although the contractual conditions demanded by host governments differ from country to country, they frequently include the following:

1. Majority government ownership or the option to acquire a majority of the equity at some time following the exploration period; and in some cases the option to acquire 100 percent of the equity after a certain number of years of operation with compensation to be made at book value and often in long-term bonds.

2. The gradual replacement of all nonnational personnel with nationals, and the establishment of training programs designed to achieve localization targets in accordance with rigid timetables.

3. The imposition of a high excess profits tax on accounting profits in any given year, with no carry forward and no accelerated depreciation.

4. The repatriation of all export earnings to the central bank and the application of existing foreign exchange regulations to the foreign investor.

5. Government control over marketing of the products.

6. Preference to be given by the foreign investor to domestic products in purchasing capital equipment and materials.

7. The right of the government to limit dividends and the transfer of earnings, depreciation, and amortization abroad.

Approaches to Reconciliation of Positions

The governmental policies and conditions set forth above are often incompatible with those required by foreign investors in resource industries in order to maintain managerial and policy control and to have an opportunity to earn an adequate return on their investment. Without some form of compromise, new investments are unlikely to be made. However, we are witnessing some new and imaginative contractual arrangements that go a considerable distance toward meeting certain of the policies of host governments while at the same time satisfying minimum requirements of the foreign investor. In the following paragraphs are listed certain features, one or more of which may be found in recent mine development agreements.

1. Management control delegated to a foreign investor with a minority equity participation by means of a long-term management contract and by the establishment of a management committee on which the minority investor has a majority vote. In addition, the minority investor may be given an equal vote on the board of directors of the company with respect to certain important policy issues, such as the distribution of earnings and investment and financing policies.

2. The government and the foreign investor share high-risk exploration outlays in proportion to their equity ownership in the mining enterprise, and the decision to construct a mine following the feasibility study is made by mutual agreement. The amount and nature of the equity contribution of each party may be determined in the initial contract, corresponding to each stage in the development of the mine. The government equity contribution may constitute in part the assessed value of the ore body and any previous work done on it. The government may also be given credit as an equity contribution for funds borrowed at relatively low interest from an international development institution, such as the World Bank.

3. The mine development contract covers all phases of the development of a mine, including exploration, feasibility study, mine construction, and mine operation, with the maturity of the contract, say, thirty years, beginning with the date of commercial operations. If at any time the foreign investor decides not to go ahead with mine construction, the results of the exploration work become the property of the government; but if the government proceeds with the construction of the mine, either on its own or under contract with a third party, the original foreign investor has the right to demand compensation equal to the capitalized value of his exploration expenditures.

4. A tax formula is built into the contract which assures capital repatriation before any corporate tax is levied. This may be accomplished through accelerated depreciation or by means of a tax holiday. In addition, the tax formula may provide for carry forward provisions

that assure no more than an average tax rate on earnings over a period of years. Finally, the tax formula may provide that no more than the normal tax would be levied until the investor has earned a minimum DCF rate on his investment, following which an excess profits tax would apply. In addition, the excess profits tax may be eliminated in years when the accumulated earnings reflect a DCF rate lower than the agreed minimum.

5. Foreign exchange earnings are deposited in a special account of the central bank with a foreign commercial bank under an arrangement whereby debt service and other obligations must be paid from this account before the funds could be used by the government for any other purpose.

6. The foreign investor is exempted from any new taxes, such as production taxes, export taxes, import duties, and so on, for a period of years following the initiation of commercial operations.

7. Provision is made for a review of the contract a certain number of years after the full repatriation of the investor's capital, together with safeguards against demands for contract revision that would significantly impair the profitability of the investment.

8. Provision is made for the arbitration of disputes over the interpretation or the implementation of the contract in ways satisfactory to both the foreign investor and the government.

9. The government is given the option to acquire all or a portion of the equity shares after a certain period of commercial operations, say, twenty years, with the terms of payment fully specified.

10. The investor is given the option of financing with a high debt-equity ratio, with all or a portion of the debt constituting parent company advances.

11. Provision is made for a joint committee with equal representation from the government and the foreign investor to establish feasible targets for the replacement of nonnational personnel with nationals and a training program designed to meet these targets.

12. Provision is made for a joint committee with equal representation from the host government and the foreign investor to implement environmental policies which have been established by the government and set forth in general terms in the mine agreement.

Some of these approaches to conflict resolution require further amplification which is given in the following paragraphs, followed by specific examples of their embodiment in recent agreements. Whether these arrangements will prove successful remains to be seen, but in any case they are not to be regarded as necessarily the most desirable pattern for future contracts. In fact, many of them have not found general acceptance with either foreign investors or host country governments.

Host Country Majority Ownership

The demand for majority equity ownership by governments of developing countries during the life of the project raises several problems. One has to do with payment for the 51 percent or more of the equity to be held by domestic investors. Private domestic capital is frequently not available, and governments often demand the option to buy the 51 percent equity at book value. The latter may be unacceptable to foreign investors since they are required to put up all the high-risk money and then sell half of the investment at cost. The second problem arises over the control of the enterprise in which the government demands a majority equity share. Management control includes the right to appoint managers and other top personnel. Competent and experienced management that is independent of political control by the host government is essential not only to safeguard the investment of the foreign enterprise, but also to raise the large amount of debt capital required for mines today. A third problem has to do with the control of the policies of the company other than those that are the direct operating responsibility of management. These include the distribution of earnings, investment policies, mine development plans, exploration, etc. As will be seen in the description of the Texasgulf-Panama agreement, means have been found in mine development agreements for dealing with each of these problems. Management rights can be protected with management contracts; the minority shareholders can be given a veto with respect to certain issues; and governments can agree to share the risk capital outlays in joint ventures in proportion to their equity holdings.

Although majority equity ownership continues to have considerable symbolic importance for host country governments, the substantive importance of whether a party has majority equity interest has declined for both the foreign investor and the host government. What is actually owned by the corporation (usually a subsidiary of the foreign investor, organized under the laws of the host government) that develops and operates a mine? The minerals in the subsoil usually belong to the state, and a substantial part of the actual investment is represented by exploration and development costs, e.g., sinking of mine shafts, removal of the overburden, building roads and other infrastructure that have absolutely no value apart from the minerals that are to be extracted. Even the buildings and the installed equipment are likely to have little liquidation value apart from the operating mine. Conceivably the mining corporation could be sold to another party, but such transferability is possible only if the agreement between the corporation and the government is transferable. Hence, the real value of the enterprise rests on the mining agreement.[3]

It is true that majority stock ownership usually carries with it the right to appoint managers for the enterprise and to make basic policy decisions. However, agreements often give certain powers, including veto powers, to the government which may or may not have any equity in the enterprise. On the other hand, agreements may give to the foreign investor the right to appoint managers plus a veto over major policy questions, even if the foreign investor has a minority equity position. Hence, the fundamental rights of the foreign investor are to be found more in the terms of the mine development agreement itself than in its percentage equity ownership in the operating company.

Contributions to National Objectives

In the past, a variety of conflicts have arisen over the insistence of the host country that exploitation of a resource must make a positive contribution to economic and social development, while the foreign investor has resented the imposition of regulations which he deemed an unwarranted interference and, in some cases, a violation of the agreement. As a consequence, new agreements contain a number of provisions such as those having to do with employment, employee training, environment, the processing of materials, and community facilities. Moreover, governments are playing a more direct role in providing infrastructure for resource investments, often with their own funds, which may be borrowed from the World Bank or some other external source, as their contribution to the resource investment. The creation of the mining community is not left solely to the foreign investor, but rather constitutes a joint effort or one in which the government has a major responsibility.

Negotiating Rates of Taxation

Governments are frequently reluctant to enter into an agreement with a foreign investor for the development of a mine at the beginning of the exploration stage until they have an idea of what the net revenues are likely to be and whether special taxes over and above those provided by existing tax legislation should be imposed. Governments are

[3] Once in operation, working capital is a substantial asset and may provide some protection to the foreign investor if it can be held abroad in the name of the investor.

fearful that the foreign investment will turn out to be a bonanza even though they will share in half the net revenues. On the other hand, foreign investors are reluctant to undertake expensive exploration without an agreement which covers conditions during the exploitation period. A good example is the refusal of the Papua New Guinea (PNG) government to enter into negotiations with Kennecott Copper Corporation until the company had undertaken additional drilling of the Ok Tedi ore body. However, after Kennecott had spent some $12 million on Ok Tedi, it refused to incur additional expenditures until it had an agreement.[4] Most new agreements are negotiated before the foreign investor undertakes substantial exploration expenditures and before there can be a determination of the likely profitability of the mine. However, this suggests the need for tax formulas that are sufficiently flexible to deal equitably with a broad range of possible before-tax earnings.

Most foreign investors prefer a flat rate of taxation on accounting profits, preferably no higher than the rate the parent company must pay to the home government since taxes paid by subsidiaries to foreign governments may usually be credited against the parent company's tax obligations. Host governments, on the other hand, have been inclined to establish excess profits taxes on earnings that exceed a certain accounting rate of profits, say, 15 percent, and frequently excess profits taxes are as high as 70 percent of earnings. Given the fact that earnings in the mining industry tend to fluctuate widely, the foreign investor is unable to offset low earnings in certain years against high earnings in others. Tax laws sometimes permit the carry forward (or backward) of losses to years in which there are net earnings, but this does not provide a full solution to the problem. Moreover, foreign investors seek to earn a minimum DCF rate of return on their investment, and as was indicated in chapter 8, no tax formula based on accounting rates of return is likely to provide a satisfactory means of relating taxation to the DCF rate of return. In the case of a few recent agreements, the DCF principle has been embodied in the formula for taxation.

One approach to taxation is to permit the investor to realize an agreed minimum DCF rate of return on his investment provided sufficient net revenue is earned. This principle is embodied in the proposal by Ross Garnaut and Anthony Clunies-Ross which applies the DCF principle to corporate taxation[5] with a carry forward provision. Essentially this proposal provides for the calculation each year of the present value of

---

[4] See appendix 10-1 for a review of the unsuccessful negotiations between the PNG government and Kennecott Copper Corporation for the development of Ok Tedi.

[5] "Uncertainty, Risk Aversion and the Taxing of Natural Resource Projects," *Economic Journal* (June 1975) pp. 272–287.

the investment at an agreed minimum rate of discount, say, 10 percent. During the period of exploration and construction the annual present values will be negative, becoming positive early in the production period. Eventually the *accumulated* net present value becomes a positive figure, at which time this amount is taxed at, say, 50 percent, and each year thereafter taxable income is taxed at the 50 percent rate. However, if there should be a loss in subsequent years, the accumulated net present value would be calculated to include the discounted amount of the loss and a new accumulated net present value would be used as the basis for the 50 percent tax on that amount. This assures the carry forward principle. The present value could also be calculated at a higher rate, say, 20 percent, and the annual present values accumulated until a positive figure is obtained. This amount might become the basis for an additional tax or surcharge which would be added to the amount of the 50 percent tax. Under this arrangement the investor would be subject to a normal income tax only when the earnings exceeded the amount corresponding to the minimum DCF rate; earnings above this amount would be subject to a graduated increase in the normal tax. An example is given in appendix 10-2.

An objection to the Clunies-Ross approach is that so long as accumulated earnings have not reached the level corresponding to the minimum DCF rate, the host government receives no income tax revenue. This might be remedied by the inclusion of a low rate of taxation on all net revenue in the tax formula.

Replacement of Nonnational Employees with Nationals

Provision for replacement of nonnational employees with nationals at all levels has become an important feature of recent agreements. Although such replacement was frequently mentioned in general terms in the older agreements, many of the new agreements provide for a specific timetable according to which nationals must occupy a certain percentage of the positions in each employment class—skilled, supervisory, professional, and managerial. In order to realize this requirement, the operating company must establish a training program designed specifically to meet the localization objectives. Such programs require not only on-the-job and formal class education at the mine, but sending nationals to technical and graduate professional schools for the training necessary to fill higher echelon positions.

It may be impossible for mining companies to adhere to rigid localization timetables without seriously impairing productivity. In such

cases, a dispute may arise over whether the foreign investor has undertaken in good faith to meet the targets, including the establishment of
an adequate training program. For this reason some agreements provide
for the establishment of a joint host government-foreign investor committee to approve the training program and the annual company program for replacing nonnationals. Such committees should have sufficient
flexibility to approve temporary deviations from any localization targets
that may be contained in the body of the agreement.

Limiting Risk Exposure

The central banks of some developing countries have fought hard to
maintain the principle of full repatriation of export proceeds, but they
have frequently been forced to permit the holding of export proceeds
abroad, at least for specified purposes. They have discovered that international credit institutions refuse to make loans to mining companies
unless a portion of the export proceeds is retained abroad for meeting
debt obligations.

In order to reduce risk exposure, foreign investors are also limiting
their equity investment in favor of debt financing, when available. In
some recent agreements, foreign investors are permitted to limit their
equity contribution to as low as 15 percent of the total investment. The
increased debt-equity ratio and the necessity of raising huge amounts of
debt capital for modern mines have increased the influence of the
potential creditors, and companies frequently bring banking firms into
the negotiations at an early stage.

The Guarantee of Investment Conditions

In the past, the profits of foreign investors have been curtailed by the
introduction of new taxes. Therefore, foreign investors are demanding
the freezing of existing taxes, including not only corporate profits taxes,
but production and export taxes, as a part of the contractual agreement.
Governments, on the other hand, are reluctant to tie their hands by
giving guarantees to foreign investors which might require discrimination in favor of foreign investors at some future date if the government
decided to change existing tax legislation. Nevertheless, governments
have agreed to special guarantees to foreign investors, especially in
matters relating to taxation and foreign exchange. In some cases, foreign
investors have been satisfied with an agreement whereby the government will not enact any legislation that discriminates in favor of domestic over foreign enterprises. However, if there is no private domestic

investment in a mining industry producing for exports, a guarantee against nondiscriminatory taxes on mineral exports provides no safeguard to the foreign investor.

Foreign investors are also demanding various safeguards against arbitrary violations of agreements, and governments have found that they must give up certain long-cherished positions if they want foreign investment. For example, for many decades Latin American countries have refused to accept any form of international arbitration of disputes over investment conditions with foreign investors; but in the agreement with Texasgulf for the development of the Cerro Colorado mine, Panama broke with the traditional adherence of Latin America to the "Calvo doctrine" by agreeing to a form of international arbitration. Most recent agreements outside of Latin America provide for some form of international arbitration of disputes. Moreover, it should be possible to formulate arbitration arrangements that are satisfactory to both the foreign investor and the host government.

Foreign investors want to be protected from demands by the host country for contract renegotiation. In some instances governments have demanded contract renegotiation shortly after a mine has gone into production. Such action would appear to indicate bad faith. However, conditions may change over a period of twenty or thirty years, which will lead a government to believe that it has a legitimate right to demand a renegotiation of a contract, and it is unrealistic to believe that it will be constrained from demanding contract renegotiation under conditions not foreseen when the original contract was negotiated. There is no wholly satisfactory way to deal with this problem from the standpoint of protecting the interest of the foreign investor. The amendments to the Bougainville Copper Agreement negotiated in 1974 provide for a review of the agreement every seventh year and contain some very broad guidelines with respect to negotiation of changes "to insure that this agreement will operate fairly to both of the parties."[6] Provisions for periodic revisions have the advantage of providing for a regular machinery for revision and should tend to avoid sudden demands for revision by the host country, particularly in periods of high earnings. On the other hand, such provisions might set up political expectations in the country that the government should amend the terms of the agreement in its favor at the scheduled times.

Perhaps the best approach is to build as much flexibility as possible into the agreement itself without specific periods for revision. My own

6 See "Heads of Agreement for Variation of the Agreement of 6 June 1967 Between the Government of Papua New Guinea and Bougainville Copper Ltd." (mimeo, Port Moresby, 1974) IV D.

approach to flexibility in contract provisions involves the following elements:

1. Contracts would provide for no change in terms relating to taxation or other matters unfavorable to the foreign investor until six years after the beginning of commercial production, or until after the period of capital recovery, whichever is longer.

2. Any change in the laws and regulations available to any other firms in the same industry, domestic or foreign, which are more favorable than those contained in the foreign investor's contract would be granted automatically to the foreign investor at any time during the life of the agreement.

3. After the period indicated in (1) above, there could be a change in taxation and other conditions applying to the foreign investor if that change were uniform in its application to all new investments in the same industry, both domestic and foreign, and if it did not result in a reduction in the rate of return on the investment below a stated amount.

4. A tax formula should be built into the agreement which would involve an increase in taxes whenever the internal rate of return on the investment exceeded a specific rate, with a carry forward provision for applying abnormal taxes paid in years of high earnings to tax obligations in periods of low earnings.

Specific Examples in Recent Agreements

I want now to turn to a few recent agreements in the mining industry that illustrate how some problems and issues are being dealt with.[7] It should be said that modern resource development agreements bear little relationship to traditional long-term concession contracts which often ran to fifty or seventy-five years, or more, and which provided for an initial lump sum to the sovereign plus a royalty rate. Modern agreements tend to have shorter maturities, twenty to thirty years, following the initiation of commercial production; they combine several phases of investment—exploration, feasibility study, construction, exploitation and, in some cases, processing; they establish taxation in relation to

[7] Not all agreements discussed in this section have been made public, but the author has obtained copies of the texts. In the analysis and interpretation of certain of these agreements, the author has benefited greatly from articles written by Stephen A. Zorn, "New Developments in Third World Mining Agreements," and Thomas W. Waelde, "Lifting the Veil from Transnational Mineral Contracts: A Review of Recent Literature," both in *Natural Resources Forum* vol. 1, no. 3 (April 1977).

profitability; there is usually some direct equity participation by the government in the venture; and they cover a variety of aspects of special interest to both parties in considerable detail.

The Broken Hill Pty. Agreement on Ok Tedi (1976)

The Broken Hill Pty. (BHP) agreement (1976) with the government of Papua New Guinea for the exploration and development of the Ok Tedi copper mine illustrates the introduction of the DCF principle in tax arrangements, although neither the term DCF nor any specific DCF rate is overtly stated in the agreement. The negotiation of this agreement followed a long, unsuccessful negotiation with Kennecott Copper Corp. for the development of the Ok Tedi mine and the successful renegotiation of the Bougainville agreement with Conzinc Riotinto of Australia, from which the Papua New Guinea government and its nonnational advisors learned a good deal. The BHP agreement was signed in March 1976 but did not become final until October 1976 when Amoco Minerals and a German consortium, made up of Metallgesellschaft, Siemens, Degussa, and Kabell und Metallwerke, joined the project. BHP and Amoco will each hold 30 percent of the equity; the German consortium will hold 20 percent; and the PNG government will hold 20 percent (as it does in Bougainville Copper Ltd.).

The companies can claim accelerated depreciation sufficient to give a total cash flow in each year of at least 25 percent of the initial investment so that, if earnings are adequate, the project should earn its original cost back within four years. After capital recovery, the normal corporate tax ($33\frac{1}{3}$ percent) plus a dividend withholding tax of 15 percent will apply until the mine has earned a "reasonable return" which is in effect defined as a 20 percent DCF return on total project funds (equity plus debt finance capital). For profits in excess of this rate of return, the corporate tax rate rises to an effective rate of about 58 percent. For example, for a debt-equity ratio of 3 to 2 and an average interest rate of 8 percent on debt financing, the foreign investor could earn a DCF return on equity of about 38 percent before the excess profits tax cuts in, assuming no reinvested profits.

In the BHP-PNG agreement, the equity share of the PNG government will be covered in part by the work that Kennecott had already done on the project, for which $17.5 million in bonds has been offered to Kennecott, subject to the actual construction of the Ok Tedi mine. Also, any infrastructure provided by the government, even if financed by agencies such as the World Bank or Asian Development Bank, will be credited to the government's equity interest.

The foreign companies which hold 80 percent of the equity must bear the entire risk of the project through the feasibility study, which is expected to be completed at the end of three years at a cost of $12 million. If the foreign companies decide not to go ahead with the project after the feasibility study has been completed, they have no further obligation.

According to the BHP-PNG agreement, the company must prepare proposals, to be approved by the government, for the progressive replacement of foreign technicians, operators, supervisors, clerical, professional, administrative, and managerial staff, and for a training program designed to achieve this objective. The agreement also provides for the preparation of an environmental impact study, the scope of which is set forth in some detail, and the company is required to comply with specified environmental protection standards.

Arbitration procedures are also set forth in considerable detail. Each side nominates one arbitrator and if they cannot agree on a third arbitrator he shall be appointed from a panel of five arbitrators to be nominated by the president and chairman of the board of directors of the Asian Development Bank.

The agreement recognizes the right of the company to retain foreign exchange proceeds of exports outside PNG to the extent necessary to enable the company to meet its foreign exchange obligations or to pay dividends to overseas shareholders.

The Texasgulf Agreement on Cerro Colorado (1976)

The Texasgulf-Panama agreement for development of the Cerro Colorado copper ore body was also preceded by lengthy negotiations on the part of the Panamanian government with two other firms, Canadian Javelin and Noranda. In this agreement Texasgulf holds only 20 percent of the equity, with the remainder being held by the Panamanian government enterprise, CODEMIN. Under the agreement, the Panamanian government shares in proportion to its equity interest the cost of the feasibility study.[8] The government has paid $20 million in bonds to Canadian Javelin for the work that it did on the project, and the government receives credit for this amount as a contribution to its equity interest in the mine if it is built. Texasgulf's earnings from its 20 percent equity participation are supplemented by a management fee (initially at a rate of 1.5 percent of gross sales, and declining to 0.75 percent) over the period of the management agreement (covering the first fifteen years of production), plus a sales and marketing fee. The joint venture will

---

[8] The feasibility study was completed in May 1978 at a cost of $18 million.

pay a 50 percent corporate tax to the Panamanian government, and there is, in addition, a 10 percent dividend withholding tax. I was told by one of the Panamanian negotiators that the management and sales and marketing fees, together with the expected after-tax income from the investment was calculated to yield a 23 percent DCF rate of return to Texasgulf on its equity investment. (This statement was not confirmed in an interview with a Texasgulf official.) In any case, the calculation was based on certain assumptions with respect to the price of copper, the estimated capital cost of the project (which now appears to be in the range of $800 million to $1 billion), and the operating costs.

Despite the fact that the company will have only 20 percent of the equity in the project, management control is guaranteed to Texasgulf for the first fifteen years of commercial production. After this period, management reverts to the Panamanian government and, in addition, the government has the option of acquiring Texasgulf's 20 percent equity at the end of the twenty-year period at a price based on average earnings during the last five years. It is interesting to note that during this five-year period, management will be fully in Panamanian hands so that Texasgulf would be encouraged to do a good job in training the new managerial team. The management agreement provides that in hiring personnel preference shall be given to Panamanians in all job classifications and that administrators shall submit to the board of directors of Cerro Colorado S.A. (the operating company) a program for training and instruction of personnel, which is designed to achieve for succeeding phases of the project the gradual transfer to the hands of Panamanian personnel all employment classifications in order that such transfers shall be virtually complete at the expiration of the management agreement. This program, together with subsequent modifications, requires the approval of the board of directors of Cerro Colorado S. A., on which Panama will have a majority vote.

Disputes arising in connection with the management agreement are to be settled by arbitration under the Rules of Procedure of the Inter-American Commercial Arbitration Commission. If the two arbitrators chosen by the parties to the dispute are unable to agree upon a third, the commission designates the third arbitrator and the decision of the arbitral tribunal is by simple majority. It is interesting to note, however, that "judgments of execution of the arbitral awards" are to be issued by "courts of justice of the Republic of Panama." Such arbitral awards "shall be considered as if they had been rendered by Panamanian arbitral tribunals in accordance with provisions of laws presently enforced." Presumably this language was used in order to preserve the principle that all matters of litigation shall be in accordance with Panamanian law. Whether this provision actually avoids compromising the "Calvo doctrine" on international arbitration is something on which I am not qualified to express an opinion. However, one of the Panamanian negotiators told me that if a dispute under the agreement ever goes to international arbitration "the agreement is dead."

The 1977 Chilean Agreements

The mining agreements negotiated between the government of Chile and St. Joe Minerals Corp., Noranda, Falconbridge, and Metallgesellschaft in 1977 recognize the right of the foreign investor to retain sufficient foreign exchange abroad to meet debt service and certain other obligations which become due within a stated period of time. The Chilean agreements also provide that the foreign investor shall have the right to retain abroad foreign exchange derived from export sales in an amount equal to profits that have been delayed in remittance for more than one year from the date of application for remittance in compliance with applicable laws and regulations.

Another interesting feature of the 1977 Chilean agreements is the fixing of the total income tax burden at 49.5 percent of profits (including the housing tax and dividend withholding tax). However, should the normal tax regime applicable to domestic firms in Chile be reduced during the life of the contract, the companies have the right to elect the normal tax, but in this case they lose the guarantee that the tax applicable to them will not be changed.

The 1977 Indonesian-RTZ Agreement

The unwillingness of the Indonesian government to grant foreigners the right to retain export proceeds abroad required for meeting foreign currency obligations was a major barrier to the negotiation of any mine development agreements in Indonesia for about four years prior to the agreement with Rio Tinto-Zinc in March 1977. The issue was settled in the agreement between PT Rio Tinto Indonesia and the Indonesian government by the adoption of an arrangement whereby export proceeds would be deposited in a foreign bank account held in the name of the Central Bank of Indonesia; these funds, or an appropriate portion of them, would be available solely for use by the company in discharging its obligations according to regulations set forth in the agreement. A similar arrangement was negotiated between Southern Peru Copper Company (SPCC) and the Central Bank of Peru for handling export proceeds of the Cuajone mine required for meeting SPCC's external debt obligations.

The 1974 PNG-Bougainville Copper Agreement

The 1974 agreement renegotiated between the PNG government and Bougainville Copper Ltd. provided for a normal rate of corporate tax (currently $33\frac{1}{3}$ percent) on corporate income up to 15 percent of the capitalized value of the investment (adjusted for future additions to capital investment) and a 70 percent corporate tax rate on taxable income above this amount.[9] But no provision was made for the carry forward of the excess profits taxes when earnings are lower than the amount subject to the normal tax rate. However, provision is made for an adjustment of the tax formula in favor of the company under conditions of "abnormal inflation" (defined as an annual increase in the U.S. consumer price index in any tax year that exceeds by 20 percent or more the average rate of increase in that index in the five years ending with the tax year). Another interesting feature of the 1974 agreement is the provision for its review and possible renegotiation every seven years. However, the language of this provision appears to assure that changes in the agreement will be made only on the basis of mutual consent. The arbitration arrangement which provides for the appointment of a third arbitrator from a panel of five arbitrators to be nominated by the president of the Asian Development Bank appears to safeguard the company against being forced to accept highly unfavorable conditions at the time of the periodic renegotiations.

Conclusions

Of the various approaches to facilitating the flow of foreign direct investment in the minerals industries of developing countries, more imaginative mine development agreements designed to anticipate future sources of conflict appear to me to offer the greatest promise. Of course, no agreement is likely to be successful in dealing with conflicts in the absence of willingness on the part of governments of developing countries to abide by their covenants. Governments that take the position that they have a sovereign right to violate contracts with foreign investors whenever such violations are perceived to be in the national interest may be denying themselves the opportunity of negotiating foreign investment contracts.

[9] For a discussion of the negotiation of the Bougainville Copper Ltd.–PNG agreement (initially negotiated in 1967), see Raymond F. Mikesell, *Foreign Investment in Copper Mining* (Baltimore, Johns Hopkins University Press for Resources for the Future, 1975) pp. 130–132.

Appendix 10-1
Kennecott's Experience with the Ok Tedi Prospect in Papua New Guinea: An Unsuccessful Negotiation of a Copper Investment

In the late 1960s the Kennecott Copper Corporation began exploring an ore body known as the Ok Tedi prospect, located high in the mountains of northwestern Papua, near the Indonesian territory of Irian Jaya. A preliminary evaluation of this ore body was completed in September 1971, followed by an engineering study prepared by McKee Pacific Pty. Ltd. and completed in May 1971. By the time Kennecott presented a preliminary evaluation of Ok Tedi and a proposal for a mine development agreement to the PNG government (which was still an Australian dependency) in mid-1972, the company had spent over $12 million and another $8 million would be required to complete the feasibility study. Kennecott had operated under the terms of the Australian Territorial Mining Law governing exploration and development in PNG, but had spent considerably more on exploration than had been spent by Conzinc Riotinto prior to the negotiation of the Bougainville mine agreement in 1967, an agreement which was approved by both the Australian government and the PNG House of Assembly.

The Ok Tedi ore body has an average grade of about 0.8 percent Cu plus less than 0.02 ounces of gold per ton of ore. The most economical mine and mill was believed to be one with a throughput of 30,000 tons per day, which would produce 95,000 tons of copper per year for the first few years, but declining later to 70,000 tons per year. The estimated cost (in 1971) of the mine and mill was nearly $300 million plus $50 million for infrastructure, including roads, communications, and communities for the workers. Kennecott presented cash flow and DCF analysis on several bases. The only one which was potentially attractive projected a DCF rate of 13 percent. The latter required that the government finance the infrastructure, which the company believed could be done through a loan from the World Bank or from the Australian government. Kennecott's financial plan for the remainder provided for a 1-to-1 debt-equity ratio.

Kennecott's proposal also called for a 30 percent income tax *without* accelerated depreciation and no tax holiday. It might be noted that this proposal was more favorable to the government than the original Bougainville mine agreement which provided for a three-year tax holiday followed by a period of accelerated depreciation, after which the tax rate would be 20 percent and gradually rise to 30 percent in the fifth year.[10] The Bougainville agreement provided that the payment of dividends to nonresidents of PNG was subject to a withholding tax of 15 percent, but the 30 percent income tax proposed by Kennecott included the withholding tax.

The PNG government delayed for over two years before it initiated formal negotiations with Kennecott on the Ok Tedi mine project. 1972 was an inconvenient time for the PNG government to enter negotiations for a large mining investment. It expected to become independent within a relatively short time and had not formulated a foreign investment policy. There was substantial criticism both within and outside the government of the terms of the Bougainville agreement and it was expected that that agreement would be renegotiated, even though production had only begun in 1972. The PNG government felt that it would be in a stronger position to negotiate with Kennecott after it had completed a renegotiation of the Bougainville agreement. Meanwhile, various criticisms of the Kennecott proposal were made which were reported in the press. (I do not know whether any of the criticisms were ever formally made.) One of the actions taken was to invite a delegation from Peru to visit PNG and evaluate the project, at least on the basis of Kennecott's data. According to press reports, the Peruvian delegation criticized Kennecott's estimates of the ore reserves at Ok Tedi on grounds that sufficient drilling had not been done and they suggested that the ore reserves might be considerably larger than were indicated. More important, they criticized Kennecott's tax proposal of an average rate of taxation of 30 percent during the first fifteen years of the mine's life and recommended that Kennecott be asked to pay 40 percent during the period of capital recovery and 55 percent thereafter.[11] Other proposals made by the Peruvians included provision for smelting, refining, and fabricating plants in PNG and a hydroelectric scheme on the Purari

10 For a description of the tax arrangements under the 1967 Bougainville mine agreement, see Mikesell, *Foreign Investment in Copper Mining*, pp. 112–117.

11 "PNG Takes Leaf from Peru's Copper Book," *Sydney Morning Herald*, May 18, 1973; see also, "PNG Turns to Peru," *Australian Financial Review*, March 20, 1973.

River in Northeastern Papua. Interestingly enough, the Peruvians also allegedly criticized Kennecott's financing plan for the mine and suggested a 2 to 1 debt-equity ratio instead of the 1 to 1 proposed by Kennecott. It should be said that most, if not all, of these positions were held by people in the PNG Ministry of Mines even before the Peruvians arrived and it is quite conceivable that these positions were leaked to the press as expressing the view of the Peruvians.[12]

Kennecott took the position that it would undertake no more drilling until it had an agreement and that it would not spend an additional $8 million, which it admitted was necessary before a proper evaluation could be made of the mine, unless it had an agreement on the terms of the development and operation of the mine. What had already been done was more than enough for purposes of negotiating a mine development agreement. Nevertheless, it was necessary for Kennecott to spend a certain amount of money just to maintain its installations at Ok Tedi.

Since the negotiations for the revision of the 1967 Bougainville mine agreement were not completed until the fall of 1974, and since the government wanted to embody the results of these negotiations in a new general mining law, the negotiations on the Ok Tedi prospect did not begin until late 1974 and continued to about February 1975. The PNG government representatives wanted to base the tax provisions in the agreement with Kennecott on the new formula negotiated for Bougainville which provided that earnings up to 15 percent of the total expenditure on the project would be taxed at the normal rate of 33⅓ percent and earnings in excess of this amount would be taxed at the rate of 70 percent. According to unofficial information obtained in Port Moresby (but not from Kennecott officials), Kennecott requested that the normal corporate tax should apply on earnings up to 25 percent of total capital expenditures on the project.

In contrast with most negotiations between foreign companies and economically and culturally backward countries, the PNG technical personnel in these negotiations were highly sophisticated, largely Australian and North American nationals. I was told by one member of the PNG delegation that his delegation had run over 75 cash-flow and DCF calculations in an effort to determine the DCF implications of various formulas that were proposed by one side or the other. On the assumption of a debt-equity ratio in excess of 2 to 1, the PNG representatives pointed out that a 25 percent return on total capital invested would give Kennecott an after-tax accounting rate of return on equity of 50 percent

[12] The author visited Port Moresby before the Peruvian delegation arrived and many of the above views were being expressed "off the record" by officials in the PNG government at that time.

before the excess profits tax would be applied.[13] Depending upon the pattern of the cash flow, this might give Kennecott a DCF rate on equity of 25 percent before the 70 percent excess profits tax would apply.

Another issue had to do with the escalation of the income subject to no more than the normal tax by an index of inflation so that in effect this critical income would mean *real* income. The renegotiated Bougain-ville agreement provides that in the event of "abnormal conditions of inflation" in any tax year (defined as a condition in which the rate of increase in the U.S. consumer price index in the tax year exceeds by 20 percent or more the average rate of increase in that index in the pre-ceding five years), the company may claim an increase in the amount of taxable income that is subject to no more than normal tax. The amount is to be determined by mutual agreement, but BCL does not have an enforceable claim to a specific remedy. It is reported that Kennecott wanted a specific formula according to which the amount of income subject to no more than normal tax would be adjusted by the U.S. con-sumer price index, or wholesale price index, and that this adjustment would be enforceable under the agreement. After considerable debate, the PNG delegation rejected Kennecott's proposal and the negotiators were unable to find a formula that was acceptable to both parties. This is particularly interesting since, so far as I am aware, no agreement involving graduated taxes has sought to use *real* income rather than nominal income as the tax base. Nevertheless, its importance is obvious since world-wide inflation could eventually mean that virtually all in-come would be taxed at the highest marginal rate.

Finally, it is reported that Kennecott's representatives objected to the arbitration provisions contained in the renegotiated BCL agreement which provide that if the parties cannot agree on a third arbitrator, one shall be appointed from a panel of five arbitrators nominated by the chairman of the board of directors of the Asian Development Bank. Kennecott wanted ICSID procedures or those provided by the Inter-national Chamber of Commerce.

Following the breakdown of the negotiations between Kennecott and the PNG government in February 1975, the government sought to interest other companies in the Ok Tedi mine. In 1976, an agreement was reached with the Broken Hill Company of Australia to explore and develop the ore body with minority government participation. Mean-while, Kennecott has stated that it expects to be compensated for the

[13] Since I have not heard Kennecott's side of the story on these negotiations I cannot vouch for the correctness of this analysis. However, a 25 percent DCF rate is in line with what most mining companies are currently seeking on investments in developing countries.

$17 million that it spent in exploring the mine, with the compensation to come from any mining firm or joint venture that negotiates an agreement to develop the mine. The PNG government recognized Kennecott's claim in the 1976 BHP-PNG agreement, but prefers to negotiate the claim directly with Kennecott. This is an interesting case since in all other similar situations that I know anything about, the company initially undertaking the exploration received nothing.

In concluding this brief case history, I should point out that, while the outcome was a financial loss and disappointment to Kennecott, it was a tragedy for a poor country like PNG. If, as seems likely, Ok Tedi is eventually constructed, it will operate under terms not too different from what could have been negotiated with Kennecott. But meanwhile, PNG has lost many millions of dollars at a critical point in its history. The ore is still there, but the capitalized value of income forgone is lost forever.

Appendix 10-2
An Example of the Operation of the Garnaut–Clunies-Ross Tax Formula

In the example given in appendix table 1, column 1 shows that deductible payments, including all investment expenditures, exceed receipts during each of the first three years, following which receipts exceed deductible payments every year except the eleventh year.[14] Column 2 shows the accumulated present value (at 10 percent) of the series of net annual incomes shown in column 1 for each year. Not until the eighth year does accumulated present value at 10 percent become a positive number, meaning that in that year the foreign investor has received 109 in excess of the amount which just equalizes the present value of past expenditures and receipts discounted at 10 percent, which, of course, is the DCF rate. This amount (109) is taxed at 50 percent and in each year thereafter the excess of receipts over deductible payments is taxed at the rate of 50 percent except in the eleventh year when deductible payments exceed receipts, when no tax is levied. In the twelfth year the accumulated present value at 10 percent is again calculated and the amount (95) is taxed at 50 percent. Assuming thereafter that receipts exceed deductible payments, the tax on the excess continues at 50 percent. The example in appendix table 1 is further complicated by calculating the accumulated present value of column 1 at 20 percent (column 4), and imposing an additional tax of, say, 25 percent on receipts in excess of amounts in each year required to equalize the present value of past receipts and expenditures. The accumulated present value at 20 percent becomes positive (19) in the twelfth year and this amount is taxed at 25 percent, so that the tax on this amount is 4.75 (column 5), and the total amount of tax in that year becomes 52.25 percent (column 6). The following year taxable income above the 10 percent present value threshold is taxed at 50 percent and the amount above the 20 percent present value threshold is taxed at 25 percent, or at 75 percent in all;

14 Receipts include all operating receipts, and deductible payments include all current and capital expenditures, but exclude interest or principal payments on indebtedness.

Table 1. Hypothetical Example of Taxation of Increase of Accumulated Present Value

Year	Receipts less deductible payments[a] (1)	Accumulated present value at 10 percent (2)	Tax on returns over 10 percent threshold 50 percent rate of tax (3)	Accumulated present value at 20 percent (4)	Tax on returns over 20 percent threshold at 25 percent rate (5)	Total tax (3) + (5) (6)
1	−100	−100		−100		
2	−300	−410		−420		
3	−50	−501		−554		
4	150	−401		−515		
5	150	−291		−468		
6	150	−170		−412		
7	150	−37		−344		
8	150	109	54.5	−263		54.5
9	150		75	−166		75
10	150		75	−49		75
11	−50	−50	—	−109		—
12	150	95	47.5	19	4.75	52.25
13	150		75		37.5	112.5
14	150		75		37.5	112.5
15	150		75		37.5	112.5

Source: Ross Garnaut and Anthony Clunies-Ross, "Uncertainty, Risk Aversion and the Taxing of Natural Resource Projects," *Economic Journal* (June 1975) p. 287.

[a] Deductible payments include all capital outlays.

this continues so long as the receipts less deductible payments (column 1) are positive.

The host government might object that the Garnaut–Ross proposal exempts the foreign investor from income taxation until all capital expenditures have been repatriated and the basic DCF rate has been realized.[15] However, since interest on borrowed capital is not deductible in the calculation of accumulated present value in the example given in appendix table 1, the use of a 10 percent discount—which is roughly equivalent to the interest charged on external debt—would give a result nearly equivalent to one in which current interest payments were deductible in calculating taxable income, and capitalized preproduction outlays were subject to rapid amortization. On the other hand, the foreign investor might object to the proposal unless the discount rate employed was equal to his expected DCF rate, say, 20 percent, over the life of the mine. In this case there would be no income tax collected until the twelfth year in the example given in appendix table 1, following which the host government would perhaps be justified in taxing all net earnings. However, this would reduce the incentive for the foreign investor to produce beyond the twelfth year. Given the principle involved in the proposal, bargaining could determine the rates of discount and the rates of taxation to be employed. It may be noted that the DCF rate for the tax agreement in the hypothetical example given in appendix table 1 is 16.8 percent over a fifteen-year period, and 17.9 percent if the earnings and tax conditions for the fifteenth year are extended to the twentieth year.[16] These rates might be regarded as unattractive by foreign investors planning to undertake exploration and mining in the developing countries today. On the other hand, the formula which embodies the carry-forward principle might be sufficiently attractive to make the tax arrangement acceptable.

[15] When the accumulated present value calculated at a given discount rate is equal to zero, the DCF rate is equal to the given discount rate.

[16] These DCF rates were calculated by determining that rate for which the after-tax accumulated present value returns to capital were equal to zero in the fifteenth and twentieth years, respectively.

11

Some Economic Issues in Nationalization, Exploration, and the Rate of Exploitation of National Mineral Resources

IN THE preceding chapters we touched on three issues of special concern to developing countries endowed with copper resources, namely, national versus foreign development of their copper industries, exploration, and the rate of exploitation of these resources. This chapter provides an economic analysis of these issues.

National versus Foreign Ownership: An Economic Analysis

Nearly all large copper industries outside the Soviet countries were initially developed by private international mining companies and few, if any, developing countries have been able to create a modern copper mining industry without equity investment by an experienced international mining firm or under a management contract, as in the case of Iran's Sar Cheshmeh project, which was developed by Anaconda.[1] Virtually all large government-owned copper mining enterprises in the developing countries were acquired through the expropriation and nationalization of foreign-owned properties. Nationalization usually

[1] RTZ and Charter Consolidated explored Sar Cheshmeh and preliminary work was done by the UNDP before the ore body was taken over by the Iranian government. Anaconda's contract with the Iranian government is officially known as a technical advisory agreement rather than a management contract. Anaconda does not have full management responsibility.

occurs either because of a strong ideological or political motivation that overshadows all calculations of economic benefits and costs, or because of the inability of the host government and the foreign investor to settle a dispute. In the latter case, I strongly suspect nationalization is almost always a nonoptimal solution in the sense that the economic welfare of both parties is less than it could have been had one or both sides made some additional concessions. In fact, I doubt if there has ever been a case of nationalization where both the host government and the foreign investor were coldly calculating the economic benefits and costs of alternative solutions with respect to a particular investment and were guided by no other principles. I say this with respect to the particular investment since there have been cases where a foreign investor has refused to make a concession to avoid nationalization in one country on grounds that it would jeopardize its position in another country, while conceivably a host country might refuse to make concessions to a foreign investor on the grounds that it might jeopardize its bargaining position with respect to other foreign investors in the country.

It can be argued that when a government nationalizes a mining enterprise and makes only a small compensation to the former owners in the form of long-term bonds that can readily be serviced with the income that would have been paid to the owners in the form of dividends, there is a once-for-all economic gain. In some cases virtually nothing was paid for the foreign properties. Nevertheless, there are economic costs involved in expropriation in terms of productive efficiency and the loss of potential capital imports, but these costs are difficult to identify.

Aside from any net once-for-all expropriation gains, I want to develop the basis for comparing the social value returns to a country from foreign development of a resource industry with the social gains from national development and ownership. In the following analysis I shall exclude all ideological and political factors and consider the question of national versus foreign investment operation solely from the standpoint of the economic benefits and costs relating to a particular investment.

A Benefit-Cost Analysis

The full analysis of all the factors in a benefit-cost equation relevant to nationalization versus foreign investment in an export resource industry would be extremely complicated, so I have provided a simplified model designed to compare the present value of a resource investment to the host country under foreign operation and ownership, PV_f, with the present value under national ownership and operation, PV_{nat}, following an expropriation. In the equation below it is assumed that the mining enterprise had no external debt prior to nationalization and that all capital replacement is treated as a current expense.

$$PV_f = \sum_{t=1}^{n} \frac{X_f + EE_f - (M_{if} + M_{df} + L_{df} + L_{ff} + T_f)}{(1 + r_h)^t}$$

$$PV_{\text{nat}} = \sum_{t=1}^{n} \frac{X_h + EE_h - (M_{ih} + M_{dh} + L_{dh} + L_{fh} + A + TM)}{(1 + r_h)^t}$$

X = annual value of output at world market prices
EE = annual social value of external economies less diseconomies
M_i = annual cost of imported materials at world market prices
n = expected life of project
M_d = annual social opportunity cost of domestic materials[2]
L_d = annual social opportunity cost of domestic labor
L_f = annual cost of foreign personnel
T_f = annual earnings transferred by foreign investor
A = annual compensation payments for nationalized enterprise over a long period
TM = annual cost of replacing technology and marketing services supplied by foreign investor
r_h = domestic social rate of return
f and h indicate the appropriate variable under conditions of foreign investor and nationalized operation, respectively.

First of all it is necessary to consider whether X_h is equal to or less than X_f and whether EE_h is equal to or less than EE_f.[3] The degree to which $X_f > X_h$ will be determined by the relative efficiency of domestic and foreign management, including marketing capacity. The external economies and diseconomies may also differ as a consequence of such factors as the impacts on other domestic industries, labor training programs, and so on. The utilization of domestic labor and material inputs as against foreign inputs may or may not differ after nationalization, provided the foreign investor has been maximizing the rate of replacement of nonnational personnel and the use of domestic materials in a manner consistent with efficiency. It must be noted, however, that we are concerned here with social opportunity costs of domestic labor and materials and not absolute costs. For example, under nationaliza-

[2] Social opportunity costs of domestic materials and labor refer to the marginal productivity of these inputs in the absence of the resource industry. If some of these inputs would otherwise be unemployed, their social opportunity cost would be zero.

[3] X and EE may not be the same in each year (t) depending, among other things, upon the replacements and additions to capital equipment financed out of depreciation and reinvested earnings.

tion, higher priced domestic materials might replace lower priced imported materials, but the social opportunity cost of the domestic materials and the labor employed to produce them might be low. Replacement of foreign labor with domestic labor otherwise unemployed would reduce social costs except for the cost of additional training. Many of these comparisons will be difficult to make *ex ante*. However, it should be easier to compare T_f with the sum of A and TM.

If compensation for the nationalized mining investment were based on the present value of future transferred earnings, T_f, averaged over good years and poor, nationalization would be unlikely to result in a gain for the host country. Even if compensation were considerably less than the present value of expected future transferred earnings, nationalization might still be costly if productive efficiency declined and if there were increased costs in replacing technical and managerial services provided by the foreign investor. Some of these services are often provided by the home office of the foreign investor with little or no charge to the subsidiary. Another factor which is not explicitly taken into account in the above formulation is reinvested earnings. If the social rate of discount for the host country is quite high, the cost of forgoing the use of a portion of current earnings for reinvestment would be substantial, while the foreign investor who is often more interested in growth than in maximizing current returns may be quite willing to reinvest a substantial proportion of his current earnings. Reinvested earnings by the foreign investor will increase the future returns to the host country at no additional cost (unless there is a withholding tax on transfers of profits). Since the host country will normally capture by taxation half the additional earnings on the reinvested profits of a foreign firm, the earnings on reinvested profits would need to be double the social opportunity cost of capital for the country to gain by reinvesting the profits of a nationalized industry.

No conclusions are to be drawn from the model presented above. Its purpose is simply to identify the elements that need to be taken into account by a government in deciding on nationalization or expropriation, and to provide a simplified model of the potential benefits and costs. Unfortunately, however, most decisions to expropriate foreign-owned properties are not made on the basis of rigorous social benefit-cost calculations.

A Note on Compensation for Expropriation

The laws of most countries recognize the right of foreign investors to compensation in the event of expropriation, and there are several U.S.

laws imposing sanctions on countries that expropriate the property of U.S. citizens without "adequate and prompt compensation."[4] The perception of what is adequate compensation differs substantially between the officials of an expropriating government and the foreigners whose investment has been expropriated. Some developing governments frequently regard adequate compensation as equivalent to book value (actual investment outlays) less capital repatriation or less depreciation, with compensation made in the form of long-term bonds at low or modest rates of interest. Most foreign investors would argue that such terms were confiscatory unless they were accompanied by other benefits, such as would be the case if partial expropriation were accompanied by more favorable tax treatment on the remaining investment. They would probably argue that a proper compensation would be an amount equal to the present value (calculated at the current rate of interest) of the stream of expected net returns over the life of the investment. In some cases the foreign investor has enjoyed a high rate of return or DCF rate on his investment over a twenty-five or thirty-year period, and has recovered his original capital several times. Some governments have been inclined to argue that in such cases foreign investors are not entitled to compensation in the event of expropriation. This is a fallacious argument since what is being expropriated is an asset which has value because it is capable of producing future income; what it has earned in the past is irrelevant. Actually, the original foreign investors may not be involved at all if they sold out to the present owners at the capitalized value of the investment.

In the United States and other developed countries, the standard for adequate compensation in cases of eminent domain is usually market value, or what the owner could have sold the property for prior to any change in the economic environment which the government itself had brought about and which was associated with the action of the government in acquiring the property. (The government's intended use might enhance or reduce the market value.) Market value of a large mine or manufacturing complex might be the market value of the equity shares, but the market value of the equity shares of a firm the government intends to expropriate is not a very useful criterion unless one could use the market value of the shares prior to the government's decision to expropriate. Moreover, unless the shares were traded on domestic or international stock exchanges, the market value would be impossible to determine.

---

[4] The best known of the U.S. laws is section 301(e) of the U.S. Foreign Assistance Act of 1961, usually referred to as the Hickenlooper amendment.

Replacement value is another approach which is sometimes employed as a basis for negotiating compensation, but replacement value would apply only to the physical capital assets and perhaps to the present-day cost of digging the shafts and otherwise preparing the mine. However, a mine is much more than its tangible assets since its capitalized value lies in years of exploration and evaluation prior to construction of the mine, the mobilization and training of the workforce, and all of the other intangible assets associated with a productive concern.[5]

Turning to the present value concept based on discounting expected financial returns, these returns depend in large measure upon a number of government policies relating to taxation and other matters that determine net income to the equity shareholders. If the government threatens to change these conditions, the present value of the mine is reduced. These conditions are usually embodied in the contract with the government and a change in these conditions that is adverse for the foreign investor would itself constitute a form of expropriation.

There is simply no set of internationally recognized guidelines for determining compensation in the event of expropriation. Unless the amount of compensation is determined by a decree from which there is no appeal through the courts, as was the case when Allende confiscated the properties of the large U.S. mining enterprises in Chile in 1971,[6] the usual method of determining compensation is by negotiation. Frequently, the foreign investor's government is a party to the negotiations, not only because governments have a policy of supporting their own citizens in such cases, but also because large losses resulting from expropriation without compensation can be credited against the income tax obligations of the parent company to its government. Hence, the government of the investor country has an important financial stake in the outcome. Also, in cases in which a government agency insures the foreign investment, as in the case of insurance contracts made by the U.S. Overseas Private Investment Corporation,[7] the insuring agency will

[5] For a discussion of various methods of valuation, see R. Lillich, ed., *The Valuation of Nationalized Property in International Law* (Charlottesville, University of Virginia Press, 1972).

[6] The Allende government, through a process of accounting that it was never willing to explain, charged that the foreign companies owed the Chilean government several hundred million dollars, rather than the other way around, and even denounced the credits owed to the foreign companies arising out of the sale of a portion of their assets under the partial nationalization which took place in the previous administration. One of the tricks used was to declare a high *ex post facto* excess profits tax which the Chilean government then claimed that the foreign companies owed it.

[7] OPIC has its counterpart in other developed countries with important foreign investments abroad. Investment insurance is discussed in chapter 12.

become a party to the negotiations. It should be noted, however, that the governments of the foreign investors are not always willing to use their bargaining power to promote adequate compensation. Frequently they are more interested in maintaining or in reestablishing normal commercial relations with the expropriating country. This is well illustrated in the negotiations undertaken by James Greene, a New York banker sent to Peru as former president Nixon's personal representative, to reach an agreement on compensation for the expropriation of the properties of Cerro Corporation, W. R. Grace, and a number of other U.S. firms, the assets of which totalled several hundred million dollars. Greene reached an agreement whereby Peru would pay only $76 million in compensation for the expropriation of these assets.[8] This agreement, which was regarded as outrageous by some of the U.S. companies affected, made it possible for the U.S. administration to make available Export-Import Bank loans and other forms of assistance to Peru. The James Greene agreement with Peru undoubtedly increased the confidence of other developing country governments that they could expropriate foreign-owned property without compensation while maintaining their international credit standing.

Restrictions on Exploration

As is discussed in chapters 8 and 12, continuous exploration is vital to the maintenance and growth of a national copper industry and for meeting future world requirements of copper. In the past, most of the exploration has been undertaken by international mining firms, but such activities are declining in the developing countries. There are special reasons for this decline in addition to the general deterioration of the investment climate. One reason is the placing of severe time limits on the exploration period and requiring certain minimum amounts to be spent each year as a condition for retaining an exploration license. A second reason is the tendency of governments to reserve certain mineralized areas for the state and to impose special restrictions which limit or constrain foreign investment in these areas. Both of these policies have the effect of limiting exploration and the development of a country's resources.

Large mining companies undertake a variety of types of surveying and exploration throughout the world, concentrating on those areas that

[8] "Peru Will Pay $76 Million for Seized U.S. Concerns," *New York Times,* February 20, 1974, p. 4.

they believe have the greatest promise from a geological viewpoint and in those countries with the greatest political stability and economic attractiveness. They cannot undertake exploration with the expectation that each activity will lead to the development of a mine. In a very real sense, grass roots exploration should be regarded principally as an investment in knowledge rather than as the first step in the development of a mine. This is true for several reasons. First, the ratio of exploration activities to the finding of a commercially viable mine is very large. Second, a deposit that may not qualify as a mining opportunity or one not judged good enough to warrant moving into the phase of intensive exploration that leads to a feasibility study during a particular year may nevertheless be regarded as a potential opportunity for further exploration or development five or ten years hence. Companies like to put such opportunities in their bank of reserves for possible exploitation in the future. Third, there are times when a company may not be in a financial position to develop any mine, or it may be limited to developing only one or two mines with the highest-grade ore, perhaps of medium size. The outlook for the price of the mineral or minerals produced by the potential mine may also determine the timing of development. For these and other reasons, if a mining firm is strictly limited in the duration of an exploration contract before it must undertake exploitation, and, in addition, must spend $100,000 or more on the project each year, it may have little interest in an exploration program. It will, therefore, only undertake exploration of a deposit on which sufficient work has been done in the past to enable the company to make a decision to move as rapidly as possible through the exploration and construction stages. Such conditions obviously limit the amount of private exploration that is likely to be undertaken. Of course, this type of exploration can be done by the host government or by an international agency, such as the UNDP or the UN Revolving Fund for Natural Resources Exploration, but thus far the financial resources of such agencies have not been sufficient for the grass roots exploration that ought to be undertaken in order to provide a continuous expansion of production in relation to demand.[9]

The position of some developing countries has been that international companies should not be permitted to hold large ore bodies for long periods of time, but they should be required either to develop them or relinquish any rights to exploit them and turn over the geological data

[9] In some countries a certain amount of prospecting is permitted without need for a contract, provided it does not go beyond surface reconnaissance and the collecting of small samples.

that have been gathered to the government. The host country would then be free to develop the ore body itself or, more likely, to negotiate an agreement with another mining firm. Agreements negotiated by Indonesia, Peru, and Zaire, among others, have these provisions. In the case of joint venture contracts with private holders of mines in Chile, Mexico, and other countries where private domestic claims are permitted, the contracts usually stipulate a maximum exploration period and minimum annual expenditures by the foreign investor. In virtually all cases involving contracts for exploration and development of government-held claims, such stipulations have been included.

Although it is appreciated that governments may have been disadvantaged in the past by permitting international mining companies to tie up their mineralized areas indefinitely, while paying only a small rental, some formula should be found to encourage grass roots exploration. One approach would be to negotiate mineral exploration contracts with firms whereby they could explore over wide areas for, say, ten years and report their findings periodically to a government commission. If the government commission and the private investor agree that a particular ore body is sufficiently promising to warrant intensive exploration or preparation of a feasibility study, the company would have the option either to undertake the work itself or to sell the claim to the government, or to a third party, at the capitalized value of the exploration expenditures. So long as neither the government nor a third party were willing to take over the claim at a price which covered the exploration costs plus interest, with the express intention of developing the ore body, the company initially exploring the ore body could hold it by payment of an agreed annual fee to the government. Such an arrangement would enable the finder to hold explored properties until such time as the price of the mineral or its own financial position warranted further exploration looking toward development of a mine. This would also protect the government from an unwarranted retardation of the exploitation of its resources.

A final suggestion is that prospecting permits be liberalized to include a number of activities, such as limited amounts of drilling and trenching, and aerial photography on both government and private lands, provided appropriate arrangements, including the payment of fees, are made with the owners. Such activity, of course, would need to be regulated so that activities of several companies would not conflict. Nevertheless, liberalization of prospecting without the prospectors having to negotiate exploration contracts at considerable cost would be an important factor in encouraging exploration.

The Economics of National Conservation
of Diminishing Copper Resources

Government policy makers are often faced with a dilemma regarding the rate of exploitation of their diminishing reserves of copper and other minerals.[10] Recently I had an interview with the minister of economy of a Latin American country, in the course of which I pointed out that certain of the government's tax policies were tending to discourage investment in all but the richest mineral deposits. His reply was that the government had to have a large tax take to meet its current requirements—thereby suggesting a high social rate of discount—and that, in addition, a level of taxes which reduced the rate of exploitation was desirable since it would conserve the nation's resources for future development. But, if the social rate of discount is high, it makes no sense to conserve resources unless the expected rate of increase in the price of the minerals, or in the government's share of the revenues from their production, is greater than the social rate of discount on future over current income. But the minister was mistaken for another reason. In a conversation with the head of that country's geological institute the day before, I was told that the nation had enormous copper reserves and that its ratio of current production to reserves was uneconomically low. The geologist apparently knew what the minister of economy did not, namely, that the *present* value of copper extracted 75 or 100 years from now is almost sure to be very low!

During the 1960s the Venezuelan government adopted a policy of slowing down the rate of development of its petroleum and iron ore reserves.[11] The Mexican government sought to reduce the rate of development of that country's sulfur deposits for export, partly on the grounds that the sulfur should be conserved for the future development of Mexico's chemical industry.[12]

[10] Portions of the material in this section were published in R. F. Mikesell, "Rate of Exploitation of Exhaustible Resources: The Case of an Export Economy," *Natural Resources Forum* vol. 1, no. 1 (October 1976) pp. 39–46.

[11] The chief architect of this policy was J. P. Perez Alfonza, Minister of Mines and Hydrocarbons in the Betancourt government. See Gertrud G. Edwards, "Foreign Petroleum Companies and the State of Venezuela," and Henry Gomez, "Venezuela's Iron Ore Industry," in Raymond F. Mikesell, ed., *Foreign Investment in the Petroleum and Mineral Industries* (Baltimore, Johns Hopkins University Press for Resources for the Future, 1971) chapters 5 and 12.

[12] See Miguel F. Wionczek, "Foreign-Owned Export-Oriented Enclaves in a Rapidly Industrializing Economy: Sulphur Mining in Mexico," in Mikesell, ed., *Foreign Investment in the Petroleum and Mineral Industries,* chapter 11.

The popular notion that developing countries which are heavily dependent on resource production should not exploit their resources at the maximum rate lest they exhaust them too fast is based on several questionable arguments. First, it is believed that if they exhaust their principal source of foreign exchange income over two or three decades, they will have insufficient income in the future. Second, they argue that since prices of depletable resources will always be higher in the future, it will pay to keep them in the ground. A third argument voiced by policy makers in some countries is that their raw materials should be conserved for the day when their entire output will be required by domestic industries. Conservation for domestic use would, of course, be unnecessary so long as the country could obtain its needs in a free world market. On the other hand, conservation for domestic use is understandable in the case of commodities such as petroleum, which may be subject to embargoes by foreign producers, or where foreign monopolists might increase prices severalfold at a time when the nation became heavily dependent upon imports. This is apparently the explanation for Canada's desire to limit her petroleum exports.

The Theory of Exhaustible Resources

Since the objectives of a resource exporting nation are analogous but by no means identical with those of a private firm, I shall begin with a brief review of the theory of exhaustible resources for a private entity that is assumed to possess an oil field or an ore body with known reserves. The basic theory of exhaustible resources from the standpoint of a private producer or cartel was formulated by Harold Hotelling,[13] with important additions made later on by Herfindahl,[14] Gordon,[15] and Solow,[16] among others. A pool of oil or an ore body is a capital asset which can either be left in the ground and allowed to appreciate with the rise in world prices as demand increases, or it can be produced and sold at a

[13] Harold Hotelling, "The Economics of Exhaustible Resources," Journal of Political Economy (April 1931) pp. 137–145.

[14] Orris C. Herfindahl, "Depletion and Economic Theory," in Resource Economics: Selected Works of Orris C. Herfindahl, David B. Brooks, ed. (Johns Hopkins University Press for Resources for the Future, Washington, D.C., 1974) pp. 64–89. (Originally published in Extractive Resources and Taxation, Mason Gaffney, ed., Madison, University of Wisconsin Press, 1967.)

[15] Richard L. Gordon, "A Reinterpretation of the Pure Theory of Exhaustion," Journal of Political Economy (June 1967) pp. 274–286.

[16] Robert M. Solow, "The Economics of Resources or the Resources of Economics," American Economic Review (May 1974) pp. 1–21.

"net price" equal to the world price less the marginal cost of extraction.[17] (In the case of a monopoly, e.g., a world cartel, "net price" is equal to marginal revenue minus marginal cost.) Now it would only pay to leave the resource in the ground if the capitalized value of the asset is increasing at a rate equal to or greater than the rate of interest appropriate to that particular class of asset, including allowance for risk. The capitalized value of the deposit is the present value of the net returns from exploiting it, which in turn is a function of the net price as just defined and the rate of interest. If the net price is increasing exponentially at a rate in excess of the rate of interest appropriate for the asset, there would be an advantage in leaving the asset in the ground. On the other hand, if the rate of increase in net price is less than the appropriate rate of interest, there would be an advantage in extracting the resource. This should tend to reduce prices now and raise them later. If the expected rate of rise in net price is higher than the rate of interest, prices will rise until it becomes profitable to produce more of the resource currently.

The above analysis may seem paradoxical because we generally regard an expected rise in the net price of a mineral as associated with an increase in world production, and an expected decline in net price as associated with a fall in production, or at least a delay in investment in new productive capacity. Clearly, the above analysis would have greater relevance if private individuals were holding known ore bodies containing 50 percent gold, or oil fields with known reserves where extractive costs are relatively low. In such cases the rate of extraction and sale of the gold or the oil should follow the pattern set forth in the previous paragraphs: the higher the expected rate of rise in the price of the resource in relation to the rate of interest, the lower would be the rate of production. However, a mining firm deciding whether to enter a mine development agreement with the government of a developing country for the exploitation of a 0.5 percent copper deposit will be encouraged to develop the mine if the management expects a rise in the net price

[17] Under constant cost conditions, the marginal cost of extraction would be equal to average cost, and over long periods of time in a competitive world market the relevant "net price" would be the world price minus average cost of extraction, processing, and marketing. The difference between the present value of the expected difference between future price and average factor cost, and the current net price (equal to marginal cost plus monopoly profits) has been given the name of "user cost." Alternatively, we may define user cost as the highest present value of marginal future profits given up by producing a unit of output currently rather than in the future. For a discussion of user cost, see P. Davison, L. Falk, and H. Lee, "Oil: Its Time Allocation and Project Independence," *Brookings Papers on Economic Activity*, No. 2 (Washington, D.C., Brookings Institution, 1974) pp. 411–448.

of copper relative to the rate of interest, and will be discouraged by an expectation that the net price may not rise or may even fall in the future.

This seemingly contradictory behavior in terms of the theory of exhaustible resources outlined above can be explained by two factors. First, as has already been noted, most governments in developing countries no longer permit private firms to hold mineral concessions indefinitely without developing them; and second, in the case of nonfuel minerals, capital costs and the cost of servicing the debt are so large relative to the value of the output that mining firms cannot afford to reduce output because they believe that the growth in the capitalized value of the minerals in the mine is higher than the rate of interest. The behavior of private holders of oil fields with known reserves is more in line with the theory of exhaustible resources. When petroleum prices are expected to rise rapidly in the future, existing wells may be capped and drilling in well-established fields may be retarded. For example, when the U.S. government introduced a dual price for domestic petroleum production in 1974—a high price for oil from newly developed sources and a low price for oil from existing wells—there was a decline in old oil output in the expectation that the higher price for new oil would in time become the legal price (or free price) for all oil.[18] At the same time the completion of new wells has been encouraged.

Application of the Theory of
Exhaustible Resources to a Nation

The theory of exhaustible resources that relates the exponential rise in net price of a resource to the rate of interest has considerable relevance for a resource exporting country where the government is formulating a policy for the rate of extraction and has the power to determine whether resources shall be held in the ground or produced. In this case, however, it is necessary to substitute net social returns for private net price and the social rate of discount for the market rate of interest. The social benefits from exploiting resources may include external economies and stimuli to other industries in addition to export revenues. The social costs of using unemployed or underemployed labor or domestic material inputs will tend to be less than private costs. Although social benefits and costs are more difficult to calculate than the private net price, it is, nevertheless, possible to estimate net social benefits derived from the

[18] *Is the Energy Crisis Contrived?* Report of a Roundtable Moderated by Paul W. McCracken (Washington, D.C., American Enterprise Institute for Public Policy Research, 1974) p. 7.

production and sale of a unit of resources as well as the expected rate of rise in net social benefits over time.

A more difficult conceptual problem is presented by the choice of the social rate of discount with which the rate of increase in net social benefits from the exploitation of a particular resource must be compared. Some economists have argued that under equilibrium conditions, the market rate of interest on relatively riskless securities should express society's preference for present over future consumption, or the social rate of time preference. However, this is denied by others who believe that the market rate of interest does not constitute a proper indicator of the true social rate of time preference, or at least what they believe it should be. Thus it has been argued that it is wrong to apply the time preference of the present generation to future generations and that the social rate of discount with respect to an exhaustible resource ought to be low enough to provide future generations with at least the same level of benefits as the present generation.[19] But if we apply the theory of exhaustible resources described above, a low social rate of discount might mean that the expected rate of growth in net social benefits from producing a resource (and hence the rate of increase in capitalized value) would always be greater than the social rate of discount; hence, the country would put off producing its exhaustible resources indefinitely. This would be nonsense, of course, since we cannot compare a nation with a private firm choosing between earning current income and reaping capital gains from the sale of assets in the future. Moreover, it is scarcely equitable for the present generation to sacrifice present consumption to enhance the income of a future generation that is likely to be richer in any case!

In the view of the author, it would be more appropriate to capitalize the annual net earnings (or net social benefits) from an exhaustible resource at the social rate of return on the nation's reproducible capital stock (after allowing for depreciation). Since the social rate of return on reproducible capital is likely to be fairly high for most developing countries—at least 10 percent—it is unlikely that the rate of increase in net social benefits from producing an exhaustible resource would exceed the social rate of return on reproducible capital except for short periods. Hence, a nation would normally want to develop its exhaustible resources rather than hold them for development in the future.

A nation may want to treat its exhaustible resources as a part of the national capital stock that produces a net social return for all time. If a

19 These issues are discussed in Raymond F. Mikesell, *The Rate of Discount for Evaluating Public Projects* (Washington, D.C., American Enterprise Institute, 1978).

nation desires to maintain the capitalized value of its exhaustible resources, it can save a sufficient proportion of the annual net return
from the exploitation of the resources so that the capitalized value of the
expected net social returns from the resources plus the additions to
reproducible capital accumulated from the annual returns will remain
the same.[20] After the resources are completely exhausted, the earnings
from the savings reinvested in reproducible capital should have the
same capitalized value as the initial value of the exhaustible resources
and would provide an annual return for all time. The proportion of
the annual net return from the production of the exhaustible resource
that would need to be saved in order to maintain its original capitalized
value is a function of the social rate of return on reproducible capital
assets and of the time required to exhaust the resource. Thus, for any
given annual net return from an exhaustible resource, the proportion
which must be saved to maintain the original capitalized value of the
asset will be higher the shorter the time required to exhaust the resource
and lower the lower the social rate of return on reproducible capital.

The proportion of the net earnings from the production of an exhaustible resource that must be saved for mineral deposits of varying
maturities and varying social rates of discount is shown in appendix
table 11-1. For a mineral deposit producing a constant net value output
for ten years and a social rate of discount of 10 percent, 39 percent of the
annual return must be saved in order to accumulate a stock of reproducible capital with a capitalized value identical to that of the exhaustible resource before it was produced. However, for a thirty-year mineral
deposit only 6 percent of the annual net return from the mine or oil
field would need to be saved. With higher social rates of return, the percentages that would need to be saved are proportionately lower. If the
government decided that it wanted to allow the capitalized value of its
exhaustible resources to increase over time as their asset value was converted into reproducible assets, it could save a higher proportion of the
annual net returns.[21] If a country wanted to double the capitalized value
of an exhaustible resource with a life of twenty years by the end of the
twenty-year period, it would need to save about 30 percent of the annual
net returns each year, assuming a social rate of return on reproducible
assets of 10 percent.

How does the approach outlined above affect the socially optimum
rate of exploitation of an exhaustible resource? For most developing

[20] The same principles would apply if the proceeds from the development of mineral resources were invested in human capital, such as education, in a form that would
enhance the country's productivity.

[21] This might well be the case if the perceived social rate of time preference were
lower than the social rate of return on reproducible assets.

countries today the social rate of return on reproducible capital assets is at least 10 percent in real terms. It would only pay them to restrict the development of their exhaustible resources if they confidently believed that the rate of increase in net social returns from exploitation of resources is higher than the social rate of return on capital. This would probably mean a rate of rise in the world price of an exhaustible resource in excess of 20 percent in money terms under present conditions of inflation, and no commodity, not even gold, may be confidently expected to increase in price at that rate over the longer run.

There are a number of other factors that mitigate against a country's keeping its exhaustible resources in the ground. Potential reserves are generally several times known reserves in a given area and there tends to be a relationship between the production of resources and the discovery of additional reserves. Moreover, the value of an ore body in terms of the capitalized value of net returns cannot be known with any degree of accuracy until it is developed. This is true even apart from uncertainties relating to the selling price of the product. Technological developments often make feasible the development of lower grade ores in other areas so that the scarcity value of high-grade ores, and hence the rents from their development, may be substantially reduced over time. This has happened in the case of copper as well as in other minerals. New techniques are being developed for the use of clays as a substitute for bauxite ores in the production of aluminum so that scarcity value of bauxite may decline over time. Finally, by hoarding its exhaustible resources, a country is denying its economy the benefits of the capital that can be accumulated from the production of these resources for broadly based economic development.

I want to make clear that I am not arguing that every country should undertake the maximum possible development of its mineral resources without regard for market conditions. Such a policy would be disastrous for copper as well as for other mineral industries, and, indeed, some countries have been too zealous in wanting to develop their mineral resources without regard for the expected social rate of return on the investments. This means in general that the highest grade reserves should be developed first, and then only if the investment is expected to yield a rate of return on the invested capital equal to or higher than that on alternative uses of the capital. This requires taking into account future prices of the product as determined by the growth of world demand in relation to current and planned additions to world productive capacities. Such judgments are not easy to make in a world of uncoordinated investment activity, but this is essentially the same kind of judgment faced by every industry producing for a competitive world market.

Appendix 11-1
The Conversion of a Short-Term
Income Stream from a Depleting Mine
to a Self-Maintaining Annuity

The problem is to determine how much needs to be saved to convert the income (R) from a mine with a life of n years to a reproducible capital stock with the same value at the nth year as the present value of the mine in year 0. We assume R is net of factor payments but is not net of depreciation or depletion. The social rate of discount (r) is both the discount rate used to evaluate the mine and the rate of return on new projects. R and r are both invariant over time. Savings are reinvested and earn compound interest at r. At the end of the period the accrued savings must equal the initial present value of the income stream. The mine and all its equipment are assumed to have no liquidation value. Given these assumptions we may write

$$\sum_{t=1}^{n} S(1 + r)^{n-t} = \sum_{t=1}^{n} R/(1 + r)^t$$

If S is constant, a single savings ratio will accrue the necessary capital stock at the end of n years.

$$S/R = \sum_{t=1}^{n} (1 + r)^{-t} \bigg/ \sum_{t=1}^{n} (1 + r)^{n-t} = \frac{1}{(1 + r)^n}$$

Appendix table 1 shows the savings rates required for the conversion of a million-dollar income stream from ten-, twenty- and thirty-year life mines to long-term investments at social rates of discount of 10 and 20 percent. Since savings are compounded at the assumed rate of discount, the longer the life of the mine and the higher the interest rate, the lower the savings ratio required to accumulate a stock of capital equivalent in value to the present value of the mine at the beginning

This appendix was prepared by Steve Staloff.

Table 1.   Savings Ratio Required for Converting a Mine with an
n-Year Life with an Annual Net Income of $1 Million to a Capital
Investment with a Value Equal to the Initial Present Value of the
Mine at the Social Rate of Discount (*r*)

r	*n*	Present value of mine (millions)	Savings ratio required
10	10	6.14	0.39
10	20	8.51	0.15
10	30	9.43	0.06
20	10	4.19	0.16
20	20	4.87	0.03
20	30	4.98	0.004

of commercial operations. The savings ratio varies in the examples from
39 percent of income at *r* = 10 percent and *n* = 10 to 0.4 percent at a
social rate of discount of 20 percent and a mine life of thirty years.

12

World Copper Resources, Mine Capacity, and Future Demand

OVER THE past few decades "informed" public expression has alternated between alarm over the depletion of the world supply of mineral resources and confidence that exploration and technology will inevitably provide either an adequate flow of specific minerals to meet demands or a means of substituting more abundant for less abundant materials. This cyclical behavior has been particularly evident in the case of copper. The pessimism of the early 1950s was followed by an expectation of unlimited abundance during the 1960s. This assessment shifted in the early 1970s when broad concern was expressed both for the depletion of world copper reserves and the ability of the developed countries to obtain essential supplies from developing countries at reasonable prices. We now appear to have returned to a world outlook for copper of long-term reserve abundance and short-term surplus of producing capacity. No doubt this will change, possibly before this manuscript goes to press.

Economists who have faith in both the price system and the advancement of technology have rejected the possibility of a neo-Malthusian depletion catastrophy at some predetermined date based on the life-years of existing reserves.[1] Even if we knew the absolute amount of reserves of a nonrenewable resource (which we do not), it is not correct to predict the year of reserve exhaustion on the basis of an assumed exponential rate of increase in world demand. According to the theory of exhaustible resources described in chapter 11, an ore body is a capital asset which can either be left in the ground and allowed to appreciate

[1] See for example, Edward S. Mason, "Resources in the Past and for the Future," in *Resources for an Uncertain Future*, Charles J. Hitch, ed. (Baltimore, Johns Hopkins University Press for Resources for the Future, 1978) pp. 1–24; and H. J. Barnett and C. Morse, *Scarcity and Growth: The Economics of Natural Resource Availability* (Baltimore, Johns Hopkins University Press for Resources for the Future, 1962).

with the rise in world prices as demand increases, or it can be produced and sold at a "net price" equal to the world price less the marginal cost of extraction. In practice, there would always be some extraction, but the rate of rise in the "net price" would adjust so as to maintain a rate of exploitation that would never fully deplete the resource.

Actually, the above model is much too simple: the "net price" is a function of the cost of extraction which may be rising or falling; potential reserves that can be extracted economically at various prices are not known; and the increase in net price will itself generate an increase in the volume of reserves that can be economically exploited. In addition, the supply of copper can be augmented by recycling and we do not know the full potential of this source.

The remainder of this chapter is divided into six sections, all of which are interrelated: (1) estimates of world copper reserves; (2) the outlook for productive capacity; (3) demand forecasts; (4) financing future copper producing capacity; (5) sources of financing of mineral producing capacity; and (6) international action for promoting nonfuel mineral investment.

Estimates of World Copper Reserves

The determination of world copper reserves poses a number of conceptual problems. Reserves constitute that portion of total copper resources that can be economically extracted at the time of determination.[2] A complete determination of reserves on the basis of this definition would require estimates of costs of extraction, given present technology, and the determination of economic feasibility at various prices in terms of some minimum DCF rate of return for private projects or other criterion of economic feasibility for government projects. The method used in a recent UN report[3] avoids these complications by including three categories of reserves as reported by private or government enterprises operating or constructing mines or holding the ore bodies: (a) reserves in producing mines; (b) reserves in mines presently under construction; and (c) reserves in deposits for which there is sufficient information to provide reasonable assurance that exploitation is economically

---

[2] See chapter 2 for the method of estimating copper reserves.

[3] "Future Demand and the Development of the Raw Materials Base of the Copper Industry," Report of the Secretary General (mimeo, UN Committee on Natural Resources, Geneva, March 1977, E/C.7/65) p. 25. See also "World Copper Reserves and Resources," a preliminary report proposed by the UN Centre for Natural Resources, Energy and Transport (mimeo, Copper study papers, no. 1, New York, November 1976).

feasible under present conditions. This approach to estimating reserves suffers from the fact that different methods of estimation are used by reporting companies as given in trade journals, company annual reports, and direct information from company officials.

On the basis of this approach, the UN survey estimates total world reserves (copper content) to be 451 million mt, of which 303 million mt (67 percent) are in category a; 58 million mt (13 percent) are in category b; and 90 million mt (20 percent) are in category c. Reserves will, of course, tend to expand with further exploration, including exploration of mines already in production or under construction. These estimates make no allowance for copper deposits in the seabed.

Table 12-1 shows the geographical distribution of world copper reserves covering 90 percent of the UN estimate of 451 million mt of total reserves in categories a, b, and c combined. It may be noted that developing countries hold nearly 59 percent of the world's reserves and that the vast bulk of these (49.4 percent) are held by Chile, Zaire, Peru, Zambia, Mexico, and the Philippines. The developed market economies accounted for 39.8 percent of world mine production (1973/75 average) while holding only 26.2 percent of world reserves, and the developing countries accounted for 38.7 percent of world mine production with 58.8 percent of world reserves.

One of the interesting findings emerging from the UN report is that the average grade of ore in operating mines and those likely to be developed between now and 1990 declines by only 5 percent—from 1.07 percent copper in 1975 to 1.02 percent in 1990. On the whole, there will not be a sharp reduction in average grade of porphyry-type deposits, although individual mines may operate with lower grades. The average grade of reserves in producing mines varies substantially from country to country, from 0.6 percent in Mexico and 0.7 percent in the United States and Canada to 3.9 percent in Zaire. Recent studies of grade-tonnage relationships indicate that the metal content of copper deposits does not necessarily increase substantially if a lower average grade is accepted.[4] This implies that in the longer run, beyond 1990, average recoverable copper content in future deposits may be lower, and that more deposits will have to be developed with smaller metal producing capacity and with increased infrastructure requirements due to the larger number of deposits.

Based on current rates of production, the static life of existing world copper reserves is estimated by the UN report (451 million mt) at 59

    [4] See D. B. Brooks, "Mineral Supply as a Stock," in W. A. Vogeley, ed., *Economics of the Minerals Industries,* 3rd ed. (New York, AIME, 1976); and E. Cook, "Limits to Exploitation of Non-Renewable Resources," *Science* (February 20, 1976) pp. 677–682.

Table 12-1.   Geographical Distribution of World Copper Reserves
(*million mt Cu content*)

Region or country	Volume	Share (%)
Asia and Oceania	39.9	9.5
Africa	72.6	17.2
North and Central America	126.9	30.1
South America	110.5	26.3
Europe[a]	71.1	16.9
Total, of which:	421.0	100.0
Developed market countries	110.2	26.2
Developing countries	247.8	58.8
Socialist countries	63.0	15.0
CIPEC (full members)	172.6	41.0
Chile	78.1	18.6
United States	69.9	16.6
Zaire	40.1	9.5
Peru	27.6	6.6
Zambia	26.4	6.3
Mexico	21.6	5.1
Canada	20.4	4.8
Philippines	13.7	3.3
Panama	12.2	2.9
Papua New Guinea	6.7	1.6
Australia	6.2	1.5

Source: "World Copper Reserves and Resources," a preliminary report proposed by the UN Centre for Natural Resources, Energy and Transport (mimeo, New York, November 1976) p. 26.

[a] Includes socialist countries.

years. However, assuming a production growth rate of 4 percent per annum, the dynamic life of these reserves is thirty-one years. Copper reserves have been growing at a rate in excess of current world production so that such calculations provide no indication of the rate at which the world is depleting its copper reserves. This is well illustrated by table 12-2, which shows estimates of world copper reserves for different years beginning in 1950 when they were estimated at 100 million mt. Between 1950 and 1974 cumulative world production of copper was estimated at 110 million mt, exceeding the estimate of world reserves for 1950.[5] Estimated copper reserves continue to expand every year and

[5] John E. Tilton, *The Future of Nonfuel Minerals* (Washington, D.C., Brookings Institution, 1977) table 2.2, p. 10.

Table 12-2.   Comparison of World Copper Reserve Estimates Since 1950
(*million mt of contained copper*)

Date and source	Million tons
1950: Tilton[a]	100
1960: U.S. Bureau of Mines[b]	154
1970: U.S. Bureau of Mines[c]	279
1975: U.S. Bureau of Mines[d]	408
1976: UN[e]	451
1977: U.S. Bureau of Mines[f]	458

Sources:

[a] John E. Tilton, *The Future of Nonfuel Minerals* (Washington, D.C., Brookings Institution, 1977) p. 10.

[b] *Mineral Facts and Problems: Copper*, Bureau of Mines Bulletin 585, (Washington, D.C., U.S. Department of Interior, 1960).

[c] *Mineral Facts and Problems: Copper*, Bureau of Mines Bulletin 650, (Washington, D.C., U.S. Department of Interior, 1970).

[d] *Mineral Facts and Problems: Copper*, Bureau of Mines Bulletin 667, (Washington, D.C., U.S. Department of Interior, 1975).

[e] "World Copper Reserves and Resources," p. 21.

[f] *Mineral Commodity Summaries 1978*, Bureau of Mines (Washington, D.C., U.S. Department of the Interior, 1978) p. 47.

eventually when more is known about the economic feasibility of mining manganese nodules from the seabed, a portion of the copper in these vast resources may be added to the estimates of copper reserves. Moreover, hypothetical copper resources, located near known deposits, probably contain as much or more copper than can be economically extracted as presently estimated reserves.[6] A vast amount of additional copper resources are presumed to exist from geologic knowledge (speculative resources) and there are also large *known* deposits that are subeconomic. Such deposits could become reserves if prices rose relative to costs of extraction. Advances in technology are continually reducing the real cost of extracting lower grade deposits. However, the cost of energy constitutes an important limitation on the economic feasibility of mining deposits with lower metal content and less accessible locations. It seems reasonable to conclude that, on the basis of the expected rate of growth in the demand for copper, resource depletion is unlikely to

[6] The Bureau of Mines estimates hypothetical copper resources located near known deposits to be some 436 million mt as contrasted with the estimate of 458 million mt in measured copper reserves. *Mineral Commodity Summaries, 1978* (Washington, D.C., Bureau of Mines, U.S. Department of Interior) p. 47.

constitute a constraint on world output or raise real prices of copper to a point where it would be uncompetitive with substitute materials for many decades in the future.

Outlook for Productive Capacity

The growth of copper production depends upon the creation of new mine capacity less closures and depletion of existing mines, the building of new smelting and refining capacity, and the future volume of scrap arisings. Since mine and mill construction has the longest gestation period, ranging from five to ten years even after sufficient exploration to identify the ore body, new mine construction constitutes the most important single variable in determining future copper producing capacity. Moreover, most of the large mine and mill projects are either accompanied by smelters, or by long-term contracts with existing smelting and refining companies negotiated before mine construction begins. It is for this reason that publicly announced additions to capacity to be completed in specified future years have played an important role in estimating future copper producing capacity. Such announcements are made by companies and governments and published in trade journals, such as the *Engineering and Mining Journal (EM/J).*[7] Projections of additional mine, smelter, and refining capacity are prepared annually by the International Wrought Copper Council, by the research departments of several major mining companies, and by CIPEC. These projections are based on public announcements of planned additions to capacity plus unofficial contacts with the mining enterprises concerned, and an evaluation by those preparing the projections of the likelihood of the projects being completed by the target dates. The public announcements tend to be overoptimistic and target dates for completion are often given before feasibility studies have been completed or the financing for the projects has been arranged. This is especially true for projects initiated by government enterprises in the developing countries. In addition to new mine capacity, there are additions to the capacity of existing mines. The latter require less time to complete, usually 18 to 36 months, are often not announced until they are underway, and can be readily adjusted to the intermediate outlook for copper prices. Periods of low copper prices may result in a slowing down of planned construction of new mines or a delay of announced additions to existing mines.

[7] The *EM/J* publishes an annual survey of mine and plant expansion for the principal nonfuel minerals, by project.

The capacity of older mines may be declining as a consequence of a reduction of the ore grade, and higher cost mines may close for an indefinite period when copper prices are low.[8] Although the rate of decline in output for certain mines is sometimes known,[9] closures are difficult to project except in cases where the size and grade of the ore body is known with reasonable accuracy. Hence, allowance for closures in capacity projections must usually be made by simple extrapolation of the rate of past closures. Even when metal output with existing mill capacity is expected to decline with a reduction in the grade of ore mined, capacity may be maintained by an expansion of the mill and increased hauling capacity.

Estimated copper mine capacity in the market economies at the end of 1976 was 6.9 million mt. On the basis of announced plans for the construction of new mines and the expansion of old ones, a number of agencies have made forecasts of mine capacity for 1980 and beyond. Five forecasts (for copper mine capacity in the market economies in 1980 made in 1977) are as follows: Kennecott Copper Corporation, 7,535,000 mt;[10] Commodities Research Unit Ltd., 8,542,000 mt;[11] Phelps Dodge Corporation, 8,000,000 mt;[12] CIPEC, 7,849,000 mt;[13] and United Nations, 8,221,000 mt.[14] Thus we see a range of a million metric tons between the highest and the lowest projections for these five sources. In part these differences arise from the degree to which the investigators have adjusted the announced additions to world mine capacity by a probability factor, and in part from differences in estimates of actual capacity in the base period.

[8] During 1975 some 180,000 mt capacity was closed, mainly in the developed countries, leaving less than 100,000 mt in net additions to capacity for the year. (*Mining Annual Review*, 1976, p. 37). Some of the mines will probably be reopened when market conditions improve.

[9] Output of Chile's CODELCO mines is projected to decline from 813,000 mt in 1976 to 794,000 mt in 1980 (*World Mining*, January 1977, p. 56). Also, output of some of the large Zambian mines is projected to decline over the next few years.

[10] Kennecott Copper Corp., *Annual Report*, March 1977.

[11] "The Impact on the U.S. Copper Industry of the Proposed Standard for Occupational Exposure to Sulfur Dioxide," OSHA Docket No. H-039 (mimeo, Commodities Research Unit, New York, April 1977) p. 23.

[12] Phelps Dodge Corporation Controller's Department Release, January 1978.

[13] *Outlook for Development in the World Copper Industry* (Paris, CIPEC, November 1977).

[14] *Future Demand and the Development of the Raw Materials Base for the Copper Industry*, Committee on Natural Resources, United Nations Economic and Social Council, Geneva (March 1977) p. 32.

A CIPEC study[15] includes in its forecasts of world copper mining capacity planned additions to producing capacity in the centrally planned economies. Copper mine producing capacity in these countries in 1978 is estimated at 1,825,000 mt and is projected to rise to 2,060,000 mt by the end of 1980 and to 2,245,000 mt by 1982. Although in the past the Soviet bloc countries and China have not exported significant amounts of copper to the Western world, the large increase in Poland's copper mine capacity from about 270,000 mt in 1976 to an estimated 450,000 mt in 1982 may mean that this country will become an important exporter of copper to the market economies.

CIPEC forecasts the copper mine producing capacity of the market economies at the end of 1982 at 8.0 million mt.[16] Assuming that at the end of 1976 this capacity was 6.9 million mt, copper producing capacity is, therefore, projected to rise by about 2.5 percent a year over the 1977–82 period. Total mine production in the market economies in 1976 was 6.2 million mt (see table 1-1). Assuming a 93 percent utilization rate in 1982, the projected capacity expansion would accommodate an annual rate of growth in the demand for primary copper of about 3 percent, excluding any allowance for inventory liquidation. Much of the projected capacity expansion is accounted for by Peru (mainly the Cuajone mine which came into production in 1977), Zaire, Mexico (mainly La Caridad), the Philippines, Iran (Sar Cheshmeh), Canada, and the United States; nearly all the projects have either been completed or are well underway.

CIPEC's estimate of copper mine producing capacity of the market economies at the end of 1982 assigns 52 percent of the capacity to the developing countries and 48 percent to the developed countries. This compares with 51 percent of total market economy capacity in the developing countries in 1976, and about 46 percent for 1970.[17] This increase in the share of copper producing capacity of the developing countries since 1970 is interesting since foreign investment in nonfuel minerals has declined rather sharply since 1970. Part of the explanation arises from the fact that some of the additions to capacity in the developing countries were initiated before 1970, for example, the Bougainville mine in Papua New Guinea and the large capacity expansions in Chile before the expropriations that took place during the Allende re-

15 See *Outlook for Development in the World Copper Industry* (Paris, CIPEC, November 1977) p. 18.
16 Ibid., p. 19.
17 The 1970 and 1976 capacity estimates were made by the Controller's Department, Phelps Dodge Corporation.

gime. Nevertheless, it does indicate that the decline in foreign investment has not prevented a substantial increase in copper producing capacity in the developing countries. Most of the exploration for the increased capacity in the developing countries had been done by foreign investors, even though government mining enterprises undertook the actual development of the ore body. Whether the developing countries will be able to maintain the present rate of expansion of copper mining capacity over the next two decades will depend on their ability to conduct the necessary exploration and to attract the large amounts of external capital required to develop their mining industries.

Demand Forecasts

The basic elements governing the demand for copper are discussed in chapter 5. Although the methodology employed in projecting demand differs among investigators, the principal differences in their actual projections are to be found mainly in the assumptions with respect to the rate and geographical pattern of industrial growth, the rates of growth for various copper-using industries and the perceptions of technological change involving substitution between copper and other minerals. Long-run demand projections also take into account future copper prices and the relative prices of substitutes for copper, such as aluminum.

Despite differences in demand projections, there is general agreement that world (excluding centrally planned economies) consumption of copper, which grew at a rate of 4.2 percent over the 1954–74 period, is likely to increase at a somewhat lower rate in the future. For 1977–80, the growth in world demand for primary copper is especially difficult to project because of the large accumulated stocks,[18] including inventories for which no reliable data exist. Projections of total world demand by market economies beyond 1980 have been made by the research staffs of a number of agencies, including the U.S. Bureau of Mines, the World Bank, the United Nations, and research departments of mining companies. Many projections are not comparable because they employ different concepts of consumption (e.g., refined versus total copper consumption), or because of differences in geographical coverage, or the use of different base years. However, even allowing for these differences,

[18] In June 1977 copper stocks held by producers and the exchanges totaled nearly 1.5 million mt. If merchants' stocks are added, the volume of inventories is over one-fourth Western world consumption in 1976 (see table 7-1).

the following table shows a fairly wide range of projections of annual growth rates of copper consumption between now and 1985 or to the year 2000:

	Annual rate of growth in percent	Remarks
U.S. Bureau of Mines[a]	4.5 over 1975–85 3.75 over 1985–2000	World demand for primary copper
World Bank[b]	3.6 over 1977–90	Refined copper consumption in market economies
Kennecott Copper Corp.[c]	3.25 over 1977–86	
United Nations[d]	4.3 for world, 1976–90 4.1 for market economies, 1976–90	Consumption of refined copper
Malenbaum[e]	2.8 for world, 1975–2000 2.6 for industrialized nations, 1975–2000 2.9 for world, 1975–85 2.8 for industrialized nations, 1975–85	Demand for refined copper

a H. J. Schroeder, *Copper*, Bureau of Mines (Washington, D.C., U.S. Department of the Interior, June 1977) p. 14.

b Internal staff report.

c Kennecott Copper Corporation, *Annual Report 1976*, p. 5.

d "Future Demand and the Development of the Raw Materials Base for the Copper Industry," UN Committee on Natural Resources, Geneva, March 1977.

e Wilfred Malenbaum, *World Demand for Raw Materials in 1985 and 2000* (Philadelphia, University of Pennsylvania, October 1977) p. 116.

Malenbaum's estimated annual rate of growth of world copper consumption, which is the lowest of the forecasts shown above, is based on the concept of the "intensity of use" (i.e., the amount of material consumed per unit of GDP). According to Malenbaum, the intensity of use first increases in a given economy and then levels off and declines as per capita GDP grows. The forces responsible for the declining intensity of use of copper include (1) a relative reduction in the goods with a high copper content demanded by consumers and investors; (2) technological developments that increase the efficiency with which copper is utilized in the production of final goods; and (3) substitution of copper inputs in response to relative price movements of copper and to technological developments.[19]

Financing Future Copper Producing Capacity

Although in 1978 the copper industry was generally depressed and faced with low prices in relation to costs and overcapacity in relation to demand, productive capacity must expand to meet future requirements. Regardless of which forecasts we choose, world demand for copper is likely to grow at an average annual rate of 3 to 4 percent over the next twenty years. Because of the long gestation period, investment for capacity growth must be initiated now or in the near future if supply shortages are not to be encountered during the 1980s. This means at a minimum that the ore body has been discovered and the reserves reasonably defined, and that for a number of deposits work toward the completion of the feasibility study is well under way or has been completed. In a large number of cases the capital that will be required has not been mobilized and the organizational structure and management have not been determined. The following analysis illustrates the determination of the capital requirements for meeting the growth in demand for the market economies, and is not intended as a forecast.

Table 12-3 gives projections of copper mine, smelter, and refining capacity requirements for the market economies for 1985 and 2000, assuming an annual growth rate of refined copper consumption of 3.5 percent over both the 1976–85 and 1985–2000 periods. Required capacities would approximately double between 1976 and 2000, but in order to project required additions to capacity it is necessary to allow for estimated closures of existing mines, smelters, and refineries over the periods. Hence, between 1976 and 2000, required additions to mine capacity ex-

---

[19] Malenbaum's October 1977 study, *World Demand for Raw Materials in 1985 and 2000*, is an updated version of his 1973 study entitled *Materials Requirements in the U.S. and Abroad in the Year 2000* (a report prepared for the National Commission on Materials Policy, Philadelphia, Wharton School, University of Pennsylvania, March 1973). Malenbaum's earlier study forecast the annual rate of growth of demand for refined copper over the 1975–2000 period at 3.4 percent as contrasted with 2.8 percent in the October 1977 study. Ibid., p. 116.

Table 12-3.   Required Copper Producing Capacity in Market
Economies, 1985 and 2000

(*000 metric tons per year*)

	1976	1985	2000
Refined copper consumption (average annual growth rate, 3.5%)	6,417[a]	8,746	14,650
Secondary refined consumption	986[b]	1,300[b]	1,818[b]
Primary refined production	5,431	7,446	12,832
Required mine capacity (allowing for 93% capacity utilization and 3% efficiency factor)	—	8,191	14,115
Required smelter capacity[c] (ratio smelting capacity to mine capacity, 1.11)	—	9,092	15,668
Required refining capacity[c] (ratio refining to mine capacity, 1.17)	—	9,583	16,515

[a] *Metal Statistics, 1966–76*, Metallgesellschaft, 1977.

[b] Joseph F. Shaw, "Investment in the Copper Industry," *Natural Resources Forum*, (January 1978) p. 106. Estimates were based on study by Commodity Research Unit, Ltd.

[c] Ratios taken from Shaw, "Investment in the Copper Industry," p. 107.

ceed 1976 capacity by 31 percent and required additions to smelter capacity exceed 1976 capacity by 48 percent (see table 12-4).[20]

The investment requirements for creating the additional capacity projected in table 12-5 are staggering. Over the 1977–85 period, average annual investment requirements are estimated at $1,762 million and for the 1977–2000 period this figure rises to $2,687 million for an aggregate of $64.5 billion. To these capital requirements must be added expenditures for pollution abatement, estimated by the UN at $300 million per year over the 1977–85 period, and for exploration estimated at $50 million annually.[21] If copper consumption were estimated to grow by 3

[20] In table 12-4 I have scaled down the UN estimates of smelter and refinery closures substantially, except for smelter closures over the 1977–85 period when they are likely to be fairly high in the developed countries as a consequence of pollution abatement regulations. For UN estimates, see Joseph F. Shaw, "Investment in the Copper Industry," *Natural Resources Forum* (January 1978) pp. 101–120. Shaw's article was based on a UN study in which he participated entitled *Future Demand and the Development of the Raw Materials Base for the Copper Industry*, Report of the Secretary General (mimeo, United Nations, New York, March 1977, E/C.7/65).

[21] Based on UN estimates. See Shaw, "Investment in the Copper Industry," p. 110. The exploration expenditure estimate applies only to successful exploration leading to the establishment of mines.

Table 12-4. Required Additions to Copper Capacity in Market Economies, 1977–2000
(000 metric tons per year)

	Actual capacity[a] end-1976	Total closures 1977–85	Required[a] capacity end-1985	Required additions 1977–85	Total closures 1977–2000	Required[a] capacity end-2000	Required additions 1977–2000
Mine	6,900	650[b]	8,191	1,941	1,800[b]	14,115	9,015
Smelter	7,830	2,250[c]	9,092	3,512	3,750[e]	15,668	11,588
Refining	8,320	900[d]	9,583	2,163	2,400[d]	16,515	10,595

[a] Joseph F. Shaw, "Investment in the Copper Industry," *Natural Resources Forum* (January 1978) p. 108 for 1976 capacity. See table 12-3 for 1985 and 2000 capacities.
[b] Assumes 75 thousand mt per year. Shaw, "Investment in the Copper Industry," p. 108.
[c] Assumes 250 thousand mt per year. Ibid.
[d] Assumes 100 thousand mt per year. My estimate.
[e] Assumes 250 thousand mt per year for 1977–85; and 100 thousand mt per year for 1985–2000. My estimates.

Table 12-5.   Investment Requirements for Copper Capacity Additions in Market Economies
(1977 dollars)

	Required[a] additions 1977–85 (000 mt per year)	Investment[b] cost per mt per year	Total required investment 1977–85 (millions of dollars)	Average required investment per year 1977–85 (millions of dollars)	Required[a] additions 1977–2000 (000 mt per year)	Total required investment 1977–2000 (millions of dollars)	Average required investment per year 1977–2000 (millions of dollars)
Mine	1,941	$4,040	$ 7,842	$ 871	9,015	$36,420	$1,518
Smelter	3,512	2,000	7,024	780	11,588	23,176	966
Refinery	2,163	460	995	111	10,595	4,874	203
Total	—	$6,500	$15,861	$1,762	—	$64,470	$2,687

[a] From table 12-4.
[b] See Joseph F. Shaw, "Investment in the Copper Industry," *Natural Resources Forum* (January 1978) p. 108. Assumes a ratio of new mines to expansions of existing mines of 3 to 2.

percent instead of 3.5 percent per year, total investment requirements would be reduced only by about 12 percent in 1977 dollars. No allowance was made for a rise in the real capital cost per ton of output, although such a rise seems likely over the next two decades.

On the basis of current production, reserve potential, and announced plans, it might be expected that over half of the projected additions to copper producing capacity during the remainder of this century would be located in the developing countries.[22] However, the actual allocation of investment expenditures for the developed countries will depend upon the ability of the developing countries to obtain the necessary financing and technology.

If we assume that half of the capital expenditures for additional mine and smelter capacity plus half the exploration expenditures are in the developing countries, we arrive at an average annual investment expenditure of about $1.3 billion per year for capital investment in the copper industry in the developing countries over the period 1977–2000. A study by three World Bank economists on investment requirements for nonfuel minerals industries estimates that three-fourths of the financing for these capital outlays will need to come from abroad. This would mean that developing countries would require about a billion dollars a year from foreign sources to finance capital expenditures in the copper industry warranted by their reserves and growth in world demand.

In another study,[23] I have estimated annual capital requirements (in 1977 dollars) from external sources for providing warranted additional capacity for six major nonfuel minerals—bauxite-alumina-aluminum, copper, nickel, iron ore, lead and zinc—in the developing countries at about $5 billion annually for the 1977–90 period.[24] The availability of financing for capacity expansion in the copper industry must be con-

[22] A study by three World Bank economists assumes that over 70 percent of the additions to market economy copper mine and smelter capacity will be located in the developing countries over the 1975–85 period. See K. Takeuchi, G. Thiebach, and J. Hilmy, "Investment Requirements in the Non-Fuel Minerals Sector in the Developing Countries," *Natural Resources Forum* vol. 1, no. 3 (April 1977) p. 273.

[23] Raymond F. Mikesell, "Financial Requirements and Sources of Financing for Expanding Free World Mine Producing Capacity Through 1990," *Mining Congress Journal* (July 1978) pp. 31–36.

[24] The estimate of foreign financing requirements given above is lower than the $7 billion annual average made by World Bank economists in a recent study. (See Takeuchi et al., "Investment Requirements," p. 270.) Another study suggested a figure on the order of $4 billion (in 1975 dollars) annually for financing mining and mineral processing facilities in the developing countries for the same six minerals. See Stephen A. Zorn, "The United Nations Panel on International Mining Financing," *Natural Resources Forum* (April 1978) pp. 292–293.

sidered in the context of total financial requirements for nonfuel minerals production in the developing countries.

Sources of Financing for Expanding Copper and Other Nonfuel Mineral Producing Capacity

Given a favorable outlook for metal prices, international mining companies are unlikely to have serious difficulty in mobilizing the capital required for new mine and processing capacity in the developed countries. Although many mining companies have experienced low earnings or losses in recent years, and, in addition, have been faced with large capital expenditures for pollution abatement, increasing activity of the international petroleum companies in nonfuel minerals production will probably assure ample equity and loan financing for capacity expansion. The major problem lies in the availability of high-risk capital for exploration and of equity and loan capital for the expansion of mine and smelting capacity in the developing countries. The following paragraphs will be concerned exclusively with the sources of financing for metal producing capacities in developing countries.

In the previous section it was estimated that an average annual investment of $5 billion (in 1977 prices) over the 1977–90 period would be required from foreign sources to expand metal producing capacity for six major metals in developing countries in line with the reserve potential of these countries and the growth of world demand for these metals. About $1 billion annually would be required for copper alone. Compared with the total annual flow of net financial resources to the non-oil developing countries from the developed countries, OPEC countries, and multinational agencies of $59 million[25] in 1976, this amount does not appear large. However, relative to recent performance and to the likely share of total external capital flow for the six major metals, the amount is very large. The vast bulk of the private and public external capital flow to the developing countries is used for financing public utilities, social programs, manufacturing, and the oil deficit. It may also be noted that foreign capital for metal producing capacity is concentrated in the important mineral exporting countries, which represent less than one-fourth of the developing countries of the world.

25 *Development Cooperation, 1977 Review*, Development Assistance Committee, Organisation for Economic Cooperation and Development, Paris (November 1977) p. 53.

Although there are no data known to the author on the annual volume of aggregate investment in the metals industries in the developing countries over the past few years, external capital flow to these industries during the 1970s has been only a fraction of the projected $5 billion for the 1977–90 period. Over the period 1973–76 net U.S. direct investment capital flow to *all* mining and smelting industries in the developing countries averaged less than $200 million per year. Over the five-year period ended June 1976, World Bank and IDA loans to the nonfuel minerals sector averaged only $50 million per year. In recent years most of the external capital to the mining industries of the developing countries has taken the form of intermediate and commercial bank loans, credits from mining equipment companies supplied or guaranteed in part by government credit institutions, and loans from copper consumers. Much of these credits have been associated with equity investment by international mining companies. On the basis of a very rough review of the financing of known projects, I conclude that external financing of mining projects in the developing countries has averaged less than $1 billion per year over the past five years. How can this level be increased fivefold over the next decade?

The outlook for sources of external financing differs considerably for each of the major metals and for the developing countries that are planning to expand their productive capacity. Most of the planned iron ore mining and aluminum smelting projects will be in the hands of government mining enterprises and much of the output will be used domestically. On the other hand, a number of the bauxite-alumina, nickel, and copper projects are expected to involve joint ventures with foreign firms or, in the case of bauxite-alumina, with governments of oil producing countries. Some governments have either ample revenues or borrowing capacity (and are willing to use external credits obtained or guaranteed by the government) to finance their resource industries. Other countries must depend on project loans without government guarantees. Where equity participation and management by experienced international mining companies are assured, there should be little difficulty in raising the loan capital. But state mining enterprises may have difficulty in raising loan capital for new mining projects from private international sources in the absence of a governmental guarantee. With the trend toward a lower percentage of foreign equity participation, the bulk of the external financing for new mining projects in the developing countries is likely to come from commercial bank project loans, and equipment credits guaranteed or financed by the Export-Import Bank or similar institutions in other countries.

International Action for Promoting Nonfuel Mineral Investments

The U.S. government and the secretariats of several international agencies have emphasized the need for promoting an adequate level of investment in the mineral industries of the developing countries. This issue was dramatized by Secretary of State Kissinger's proposal for an International Resources Bank (IRB) at the Ministerial meeting of UNCTAD in Nairobi, Kenya in May 1976.[26] Although the IRB proposal was largely rejected by the Third World members of UNCTAD, principally because of its emphasis on promoting private foreign investment in the resource industries, there is, nevertheless, widespread recognition of the problem. For example, the staff of the World Bank has prepared several internal studies on the technical, financial, and managerial requirements for expanding mineral producing capacity in the developing countries and the possible roles of the bank in facilitating these transfers.[27] In 1976, the General Assembly of the Organization of American States (OAS) passed a resolution calling for a study of an Inter-American Resources Financial Mechanism to be presented in 1977 to the Special OAS Assembly on Development Cooperation. A further indication of the interest in this problem is found in a proposal for an International Minerals Investment Trust (IMIT) which was presented in May 1977 to the United Nations Committee on Natural Resources.[28] Although the Carter administration does not support the Kissinger proposal for an IRB, the problem of promoting mineral investments in the developing world has been the subject of considerable discussion, especially within the departments of treasury and state.

We may distinguish between activities of governments or international agencies which promote or facilitate investment in the mineral industries of developing countries generally, and those activities, such as investment insurance, that are specifically designed to encourage foreign direct investment in these industries. However, the former type of activi-

---

[26] "UNCTAD IV: Expanding Cooperation for Economic Development," an address by Secretary Henry A. Kissinger, May 6, 1976, Nairobi, Kenya, Bureau of Public Affairs, U.S. Department of State, PR 224, May 1976.

[27] Some of these studies have been reflected in a World Bank research publication entitled *The Mining Industry in the Developing Countries*, by Rex Bosson and Bension Varon (Oxford University Press, 1977).

[28] See *Minerals: Salient Issues*, Report of the Secretary General of the UN, Committee on Natural Resources, Geneva (March 1977) annex II; see also Zorn, "The United Nations Panel," pp. 291–297.

ties may also serve to promote foreign direct investment. For example, increased loans or equity participation by the World Bank may facilitate both national investment and foreign direct investment in the mineral industries. The following paragraphs deal mainly with public activities for expanding foreign direct investment in minerals.

Public International Financial Assistance

Neither the World Bank nor the regional public development banks, e.g., the Inter-American Development Bank (IDB) or the Asian Development Bank (ADB), have made a significant proportion of their resources available to the mining sectors of their members. During the post-World War II period to mid-1977 the World Bank Group, which has been the most active in this area, has made some thirty-four commitments totaling about $850 million to the mining sectors of developing countries. According to new policies with respect to the extractive industries adopted by the World Bank in 1977, that institution plans to increase its lending for nonfuel mineral projects in developing countries to a total of $800 million, spread over 1977–80.[29]

Although it is unlikely that public international development institutions can be counted on to provide a large share of the financial requirements for expanding nonfuel mineral capacities in the developing countries, their participation in both loan and equity financing could be a powerful instrument for mobilizing private international loan financing and for giving confidence to foreign equity investors. Even a modest participation by a public international agency in the debt financing of a mining project will give greater confidence to potential private international lenders for two reasons. First, they can rely on the project investigation and evaluation undertaken by the international agency; and, second, there is a general belief that governments are less likely to default on loans in which international agencies have participated. This confidence might be increased by the use of cross-default obligations which provide that a default to one creditor constitutes a default to all creditors. It may be noted that the IFC recently made three loans of $15 million each in support of mining operations, one of which represented IFC's participation in a $404 million loan package for the Cuajone copper mine in Peru; another represented a share in the loan financing of a $100 million nickel mining and processing plant in Guatemala spon-

[29] *International Finance*, Annual Report of the National Advisory Council on International Monetary and Financial Policies for 1977 (Washington, D.C., GPO, April 1978) p. 62.

sored by the International Nickel Company of Canada, Ltd.; and the third was made to a Brazilian company, Mineracao Rio Do Norte, S.A., a joint venture involving Brazilian and foreign equity organized to mine and process bauxite.

Both loan and equity investments by the IFC have been a factor in attracting private investment in developing countries, but equity investment has rarely been used in support of foreign investment in mining. A notable exception was an IFC loan of $26 million plus an equity subscription of $4 million to CODEMIN, a Brazilian nickel mining and refining project sponsored by the Hochschild Group, an international mining and metal trading organization. International agency participation in project formulation and equity financing should give foreign equity investors considerable security against expropriation or other contract violations which would affect the earnings of the enterprise. In such cases, the initial amount of participation would not need to be large.

The degree to which public international development agencies should be involved in the actual negotiation of mine development agreements has been a matter of some concern to international mining officials. The head of a large U.S. mining firm expressed the view that a three-way negotiation would be cumbersome and that in any differences between the foreign investor and host government the international agency might well side with the host country. On the other hand, it might be argued that the international agency would be able to view objectively the conditions necessary to attract foreign direct investment, and that its participation in the negotiations would provide a measure of political support to host government officials who accepted politically unpopular provisions of the agreement.

UN Investment Code, Bilateral Treaties,
and International Arbitration

The outlook for a UN investment code that would provide much, if any, encouragement for foreign investors in developing countries is not promising. In fact, the kind of code advocated by a majority of the Third World countries appears likely to place additional obligations on foreign investors without according any protection to their investments. On the other hand, several European countries, including France, Germany, the Netherlands, and the United Kingdom, have negotiated bilateral treaties with a number of developing countries covering such important issues as nondiscriminatory or national treatment, expropriation, compensation, and arbitration.[30] The United States has not ratified an investment treaty with a developing country since June 1968 (Thailand).

An important component of any investment treaty should be the agreement to submit disputes arising out of operations under investment agreements to international arbitration—through the International Center for the Settlement of Investment Disputes (ICSID), the International Chamber of Commerce, or some other international tribunal. The unwillingness of most Latin American countries to submit investment disputes to arbitration procedures involving nonresident arbitrators is regarded by international mining firms as a serious barrier to investment. It has been suggested, however, that some form of OAS arbitration procedure in which all or most OAS members would participate might be acceptable.

Investment Insurance

In the past, the U.S. government's Overseas Private Investment Corporation (OPIC) has made important contributions to U.S. direct investment in the copper industries of the developing countries by insuring both equity investments and the debt obligations of U.S. mining subsidiaries against noncommercial risks. However, several disputes by U.S. companies over claims against OPIC arising out of the expropriation of insured investments have reduced OPIC's credibility among U.S. investors. Prominent among these disputes has been that with Anaconda over its claim for compensation for the expropriation of its copper mining properties in Chile by the Allende government. Aside from its claim history, U.S. mining firms have made two major criticisms of OPIC insurance covering equity investments. First, it has been argued that such insurance provides no protection against "creeping expropriation" involving contract violations that impair earnings. In order to deal with this criticism, OPIC has recently inaugurated a program under which OPIC insurance contracts define the insurable event to include not only full nationalization of an enterprise, or the expropriation of property, but also a variety of situations which have been described as "creeping expropriation." An action may be considered as expropriatory if it has a specified impact on the operations or financial returns of the insured

---

[30] For a description of these treaties, see "Bilateral Treaties for Encouragement of International Investment," International Chamber of Commerce (mimeo, Paris, November 1975).

investor. Violations of specific contract provisions may be insured against at the request of the investor.[31]

A second major criticism is that OPIC will guarantee no more than the book value of capital outlays, less earnings and capital repatriations. However, if an investor makes expenditures over a period of eight or ten years and is expropriated before receiving any return on the investment, the amount of compensation may be less than half the present or discounted value of the capital outlay. So far as the author is aware, OPIC has not undertaken to write insurance covering the capitalized value of past expenditures. Another limitation on OPIC insurance is that it will not insure more than $50 million of project costs for any one investment. With the equity investment on large mining projects running several hundred million dollars, this is a serious limitation on OPIC's ability to promote mining investments in developing countries.[32]

Since the governments of several developed countries currently operate systems that offer investment insurance against noncommercial risk, it has been suggested that there be established a foreign investment insurance scheme operated jointly by governments or by governmental insuring agencies of the individual countries. Such an arrangement would have the advantage of pooling a larger number of risks, and, in addition, insurance by a consortium of governments might serve to deter the expropriation of foreign investments without prompt and adequate compensation. A further advantage might be the establishment of international standards of compensation in cases of expropriation, creeping or otherwise.

An International Minerals Investment Trust

In May 1977 a proposal for an International Minerals Investment Trust (IMIT) was presented to the United Nations Committee on Natural Resources.[33] According to this proposal, the assets of the IMIT would consist of both debt and equity issues of companies established under the laws of developing countries and set up specifically to exploit ore

---

[31] See *Investment Insurance Handbook (New Program for Minerals and Energy)* (Washington, D.C., Overseas Private Investment Corporation, November 1977).

[32] A further limitation on OPIC's operations is the U.S. government's policy of not providing any form of assistance to countries deemed to be violating human rights. Currently this makes OPIC insurance unavailable for Argentina and Chile, countries in which U.S. mining companies are interested in making investments in copper mining.

[33] *Minerals: Salient Issues,* Report of the Secretary General, annex II.

bodies in those countries. Seed capital would be provided by the governments of the developed countries and possibly by the OPEC nations, while subsequent financing would be provided by sales of shares of the IMIT to both public and private agencies. Unlike the IRB, which was rather heavily oriented to the financing and guaranteeing of private international mining investments, IMIT would provide a mechanism for financing national mining enterprises in developing countries. The proposal suggests that international mining firms would play a role in the provision of technology and management and possibly of minority equity shares in new projects. Nevertheless, the IMIT does not appear to be a proposal that is likely to prove very interesting to the international mining community or able to deal with obstacles to foreign direct investment discussed in chapters 9 and 10 of this book.

Conclusions

Of the various approaches to facilitating the flow of foreign direct investment in the minerals industries of developing countries described above, participation by existing public international financial agencies such as the World Bank Group and the IDB in both debt and equity financing[34] appears to offer the greatest promise. The amount of the actual financial participation need not be large since the principal objective would be to provide foreign investors with the protection afforded by having an international public financial agency as a party to the creditor agreement in the case of loans and to the mine development agreement in the case of equity participation. In negotiating three-way agreements, the international financial agency should avoid trying to dictate the terms of mine development agreements or develop rigid standards of its own. Its role should be confined largely to technical advice and conciliation.

[34] Currently the IDB cannot make equity investments, but proposals have been made for an equity affiliate of the IDB.

13

Special Problems in the
Future Supply of Copper

THIS CHAPTER rounds out our study of the world copper industry by examining some of the factors that will affect the future supply of copper which we have not as yet considered in a systematic way. They include (1) the future contribution of recycling; (2) the potential supply of copper from the oceans; and (3) the impact of pollution abatement regulations and other environmental regulations affecting copper production and exploration. Each of these factors involves governmental policy issues, including those related to recycling, the law of the sea negotiations, and environmental standards. These policies and their implementation may affect in considerable measure the location pattern and cost of future world copper production.

The Future Contribution of Recycling to
Copper Production

The major problems in determining the future supply of and demand for scrap in the United States and other developed countries center on the availability and use of "old scrap," since there is a fairly close correlation between the generation of "new scrap" and total copper consumption.[1] As may be noted in table 13-1, the ratio of new scrap arisings to total copper consumption in the United States averaged about 0.25 over the period 1965–74. Although the volume of new scrap generated will bear a close relationship to the level of fabrication, the amount of new scrap that is recycled domestically will depend on price. A low

[1] See chapter 2 for technical discussions of the role of scrap in copper production.

Table 13-1. New Scrap Arisings and Copper Consumption in the
United States, 1964–74

(*000 metric tons*)

Year	New scrap arisings (1)	Total copper consumption (2)	Ratio (1) ÷ (2) (3)
1965	671	2,717	0.247
1966	725	3,056	0.237
1967	614	2,586	0.237
1968	633	2,552	0.248
1969	726	2,870	0.253
1970	675	2,657	0.254
1971	685	2,682	0.255
1972	764	2,963	0.258
1973	805	3,159	0.255
1974	761	2,818	0.270

Source: World Bureau of Metal Statistics and "End-Use Investigation of the World Copper Market with Emphasis on the Prospects for Recycling and Substitution," Commodities Research Unit, Ltd., New York (mimeo), prepared for the Centre for Natural Resources, Energy and Transport, United Nations, January 1976, table 2, p. 8.

price for scrap relative to foreign prices will lead to increased scrap exports.

Scrap is used both for the production of refined copper and directly (without refining) in copper fabrication. In the United States an average of 20.4 percent of refined copper output was produced from scrap by primary and secondary refiners together over the 1971–75 period. In Western Europe the ratio of secondary refined copper to total refined output over the same period was only 17.8 percent, while Japanese secondary production was only about 12 percent of total refined production during 1971–75.[2]

The total use of copper scrap is much more important in terms of volume than secondary production of refined copper. Over the 1971–74 period, the ratio of directly used scrap to total U.S. copper consumption averaged 0.31 (see table 13-2). In 1974, U.S. production of refined copper

[2] U.S. data from *American Bureau of Metal Statistics Yearbook 1975;* data for Japan and Europe from unpublished UN source. Although there are data on secondary and primary production of refined copper for European countries and Japan, it is not always clear how much of the primary refined output is based on scrap as contrasted with mined copper.

Table 13-2. U.S. Direct Use of Scrap and Total Copper Consumption, 1971–74

(*000 metric tons*)

Year	Direct use of scrap (1)	Total copper consumption (2)	Ratio (1) ÷ (2) (3)
1971	851	2,682	0.32
1972	934	2,963	0.32
1973	940	3,159	0.30
1974	860	2,818	0.31

Source: "Secondary Copper in the Developed Market-Economy Countries," preliminary unpublished paper prepared in the UN Centre for Natural Resources, Energy and Transport, New York, December 1976, table 1.

from scrap plus direct use of scrap was 46 percent of estimated U.S. total consumption. This estimate could involve some double counting, but it is in line with an estimate made by Bonczar and Tilton.[3] In 1974 Germany produced 202,000 mt of refined copper from scrap and 424,000 mt was recorded as primary copper, including scrap used by primary producers. These data suggest the possibility of higher ratios of secondary refined to total refined copper than exist in the United States. Germany also employed scrap in direct use in the amount of 144,000 mt in 1974, representing a somewhat lower ratio of direct use to total copper production than in the United States.[4] It appears that it is technically feasible to employ a larger ratio of scrap to total copper production, provided the scrap is available at a price competitive with primary copper.[5] For example, primary copper refineries may use more secondary feed on a routine basis.

[3] The authors found for an unspecified date (about 1970) that 42 percent of total copper metal consumption in the United States was derived from scrap, of which 57 percent was from new scrap and 43 percent from old scrap. E. S. Bonczar and J. E. Tilton, *An Economic Analysis of the Determinants of Metal Recycling in the United States: A Case Study of Secondary Copper*, prepared for the U.S. Bureau of Mines. Available from National Technical Information Service, Springfield, Va. PB 245832.) table 1, p. 2.

[4] "Secondary Copper in Developed Market-Economy Countries," preliminary unpublished paper prepared in the UN Centre for Natural Resources, Energy and Transport, New York, December 1976, table 4.

[5] It should be noted, however, that secondary production as a percentage of total refined copper production declined in Western Europe over the 1966–75 period. This probably reflects a shortage of scrap in the 1970s.

The future of scrap as a competitor with mine copper depends on: (1) the growth of the pool of old scrap; (2) the technology of smelting low-grade scrap; (3) the operating and capital costs of scrap processing relative to the cost of producing primary copper; (4) the cost of scrap collection; and (5) governmental policies designed to encourage recycling.

Growth of the Pool of Old Scrap

Information on fluctuations in arisings of scrap in Western Europe and the United States and on the volume and composition of the pool of old scrap is inadequate for a comprehensive analysis of the industry and for predicting future supply. A once-for-all U.S. source of old scrap appeared in the late 1950s and early 1960s when many overhead electrical transmission lines made of copper were being replaced by aluminum, at a time when the high price of copper scrap made such substitution commercially attractive.[6] Another factor accounting for the high levels of secondary production in the second half of the 1960s was the relatively high average price of copper, which drew out larger supplies of price-sensitive high-grade scrap. The large increase in exports from the United Kingdom to the rest of Western Europe in recent years and the fluctuations in U.S. exports of copper scrap (which declined in the 1970s) have complicated the problem of making a systematic analysis of long-term trends in the availability and utilization of scrap.

Recently there have been attempts in various studies to combine historical consumption statistics with estimates of the asset life of copper-containing products to generate predictions of scrap supply. One such study prepared in 1972 by the Battelle Memorial Institute[7] estimated the weighted average life of copper-bearing materials in the United States to be twenty years. The results of a study by the U.S. Bureau of Mines showing life cycles of various copper products in the United States and the proportion of copper recovered are given in table 13-3. However, average length of life estimates for total copper in use varies substantially and, in any case, scrap availability in any one year may not be identical to scrap supply since current and anticipated prices as well as other factors are important in determining the rate

[6] A similar phenomenon could take place if optic fiber transmission technology becomes widely adopted for intracity telephone communications.

[7] "A Study to Identify Opportunities for Increased Solid Waste Utilization," Battelle Memorial Institute, Columbus, Ohio Laboratories, 1972 (quoted by Bonczar and Tilton, *Economic Analysis of Determinants of Metal Recycling*, table 5, p. 37).

Table 13-3.   Life Cycles of Copper Products in the United States
and Proportion Recovered

End use	Life cycles (years)	Percent recovered
Brass mill products		
Sheet		
Building construction	29	28
Transportation	9	28
Consumer and general	4	20
Industrial machinery and equipment	18	40
Electrical	24	24
Rod		
Building construction	19	20
Transportation	9	20
Consumer and general	4	12
Industrial machinery and equipment	18	40
Electrical	24	24
Plumbing tube		
Building construction	24	36
Transportation	9	44
Consumer and general	9	12
Industrial machinery and equipment	18	40
Electrical	24	24
Commercial tube		
Building construction	24	36
Transportation	9	44
Consumer and general	9	20
Industrial machinery and equipment	18	40
Electrical	24	24
Other[a]		
Building construction	29	28
Transportation	9	36
Consumer and general	7	20
Industrial machinery and equipment	18	35
Electrical	19	42

Source: Recovery of Secondary Copper and Zinc in the United States, Bureau of Mines
Information Circular 8622 (Washington, D.C., U.S. Department of the Interior,
1974) p. 8.

[a] Includes all copper products other than brass mill products.

at which scrap availability becomes scrap supply, at least in the short run.[8] Since a large portion of copper in use is in the form of capital goods, the timing and rate of replacement will depend upon business conditions which affect the rate of investment.

Estimates of the pool of copper in use vary substantially. For example, an unpublished UN report estimates the pool of copper in use at the end of 1970 at approximately 38 million mt in the United States, 41 million mt in Western Europe, and 11 million mt in the rest of the world. A more recent study by Tilton and Bonczar estimates the U.S. old scrap pool accumulated since 1953 to be 27.4 million mt.[9]

Estimates of old scrap arisings and the future of secondary copper production have tended to be somewhat pessimistic regarding the growth of this source of copper. A 1976 CRA projection of secondary copper production indicates a modest growth rate: 3.7 percent per annum 1973/75–1980, and 2.7 percent for 1980–85.[10] An annual growth rate of less than 1 percent for secondary copper produced from scrap over the 1977–85 period was estimated for the United States in a 1978 study by Arthur D. Little, Inc. (ADL). However, the ADL study predicts an annual growth rate of 3.5 percent for scrap generated in the United States over the same period.[11]

A 1974 Bureau of Mines study[12] provides data on U.S. consumption of obsolete copper products (old scrap) for 1961–70 and projected consumption for 1971–2000, together with estimates of unrecovered copper for the two periods. The estimates and projections are based on the following assumptions: (1) all copper products become available for recovery when their life cycle is complete (see table 13-3); (2) the life cycles of copper products and the percentage of recovery for each end use at the time of obsolescence remain over the projected period 1971–2000 as in the period 1961–70; and (3) recovery techniques and scrap prices continue in the future as they were in 1961–70 period. The projections of consumption of each end use were made using straightline regressions based on individual consumption figures for 1961–70. Table

[8] The life-cycle estimates given in table 13-3 have been criticized as being too short. For example, the life cycle of plumbing tube is believed by some to be on the order of forty to fifty years rather than twenty-four years.

[9] Bonczar and Tilton, *Economic Analysis of Determinants of Metal Recycling*, p. 35.

[10] "Secondary Copper in Developed Market Economy Countries," p. 24.

[11] *Economic Impact of Environmental Regulations on the Copper Industry* (prepared for the U.S. Environmental Protection Agency, Washington, D.C., by Arthur D. Little, January 1978) p. xii–25.

[12] *Recovery of Secondary Copper and Zinc in the United States*, Bureau of Mines Information Circular 8622 (Washington, D.C., U.S. Department of Interior, 1974).

13-4 shows the actual and projected copper recovered from copper products and the unrecovered products for each year over the 1961–70 period, along with projections for 1971–2000. The annual amounts of unrecovered products were computed by subtracting the yearly amount of each copper product eventually recovered from the yearly amount of copper products becoming obsolete. The latter in turn were calculated by applying the average life year for each copper product to the yearly amounts of copper products entering the domestic market over 1932–70. Of the total copper materials becoming obsolete each year over the 1961–70 period, about 30 percent is recovered and 70 percent goes unrecovered.

Of the total amount of unrecovered copper over the period 1961–70, an estimated 1 percent is dissipated beyond recovery, so that the cumulative amount of potentially recoverable copper during this period totals about 11.8 million short tons.[13] However, it is estimated that 30 to 50 percent of the unrecovered products is presently entering solid waste disposal sites, while the remainder is "randomly distributed throughout the country and their whereabouts unaccountable."[14] This suggests, therefore, that of the total volume of obsolete copper products becoming available every year, 30 percent is recovered; 1 percent is dissipated; 21–35 percent finds its way into solid waste disposal sites and may be lost forever;[15] and 34–48 percent is unaccounted for. Just what proportion of the unaccounted-for obsolete copper products, which amounts to 5.9–8.3 million short tons over the 1961–70 period, constitutes a pool potentially available for use in the copper industry is unknown. It seems reasonable to believe that the amount is fairly substantial. Moreover, given the projected 51 million short tons of accumulated unrecovered copper products over 1971–2000, the accumulated increase in unaccounted-for obsolete copper products would amount to 25–35 million short tons. The Bureau of Mines report suggests that these unrecovered copper products may still be in the "consuming pipeline," and randomly distributed throughout the country, and that this amount may be recirculated at some future time, "depending upon improved collection methods or higher prices for the materials." It is also possible that some of the durable goods containing substantial amounts of copper which are now dumped in solid waste disposal sites will in time be collected, although the small particles of copper in household waste will continue to be unrecovered.

13 Ibid., p. 37.
14 Ibid., p. 29.
15 Some students of recycling believe that solid waste disposal sites will be important "mines" of the future, and that the minerals will eventually be recovered.

Table 13-4. Copper Recovered and Unrecovered from Obsolete
Copper Products, 1961–70 and Projected 1971–2000

(*000 short tons*)

Year	Copper recovered for domestic consumption	Unrecovered copper products
1961	381	1,176
1962	428	1,210
1963	457	1,198
1964	435	1,206
1965	503	1,177
1966	556	1,166
1967	489	1,048
1968	521	1,146
1969	574	1,272
1970	498	1,300
Projected		
1971	587	1,324
1972	587	1,356
1973	599	1,395
1974	646	1,486
1975	583	1,500
1980	590	1,541
1985	691	1,664
1990	772	1,867
1995	841	2,062
2000	900	2,231

Source: *Recovery of Secondary Copper and Zinc in the United States*, Bureau of Mines
Information Circular 8622 (Washington, D.C., U.S. Department of the Interior,
1974) pp. 11–12, 24, 26.

What the above figures suggest is that the roughly 30 percent of
obsolete copper products which is currently being recovered might well
be increased to 50 to 60 percent, with the result that obsolete material
(old scrap) might in time account for as much as one-third of U.S.
copper consumption as contrasted with 17 percent over the past decade
or so. This possibility is in sharp contrast with the pessimistic outlook
for increasing the portion of scrap in total copper consumption suggested by other studies.

It may be noted that in the Bureau of Mines projections shown in
table 13-4, the ratio of annual copper recovered for domestic consumption to the yearly accumulation of unrecovered copper products (and
by implication, the ratio of old scrap utilized to total domestic con-

sumption) remains fairly constant to the year 2000, regardless of the size of the pool of potentially recoverable scrap. Moreover, the ratio of old scrap arisings to the size of the pool declines indefinitely. If we assume that only half of the unaccounted-for accumulation of unrecovered obsolete copper products is potentially available for industrial use, the pool of usable scrap will increase by 13 to 18 million short tons over the 1971–2000 period. It seems reasonable to believe that this substantial increase in the size of the potentially usable pool would tend to increase the annual scrap arisings from the pool, in addition to the annual arisings calculated on the basis of yearly increases in the total volume of obsolete copper products becoming available. Admittedly, since we do not know the past or present size of the pool of old scrap recoverable at any price that is likely to prevail, we have little basis for determining the relationship between the size of the pool and scrap arisings from past experience. But if we assume that future cost-price relationships will tend to favor production from scrap over primary copper, a rise in the size of the pool should facilitate the use of scrap.

Processing Old Scrap

Although relatively high-grade industrial scrap can usually find its way to the market with a varying time lag, there are problems with the recovery of copper from low-grade scrap. There are few smelters capable of treating this scrap in the world today, and according to a recent CRU study, no new ones are currently being planned. However, there do not appear to be any especially difficult technical problems in extraction.[16] There is abundant capacity for converting low-grade scrap into alloy ingot for which there is a good market.

Estimates of the cost of converting low-grade scrap vary considerably. A study by the U.S. Environmental Protection Agency published in March 1975 gives a variable cost of 7.8 cents per pound, plus 2.5 cents per pound fixed cost.[17] However, an unpublished CRU study found that the total cost of smelting and refining low-grade scrap was considerably more than 10 cents per pound, perhaps over 16 cents per pound,

[16] The technology of smelting low-grade scrap closely parallels that for the primary recovery of concentrates. Scrap is charged into a blast furnace, the mix is heated, and the air is blown through. Oxidizable and volatile impurities are blown out or converted into slag and the "black" copper is then put into a converter and converted into rough copper equivalent to primary blister. It is then cast into anodes and electrolytically refined. Lead, zinc, tin, nickel, and precious metals may also be recovered.

[17] *Economic Impact of Proposed Water Pollution Controls on the Non-Ferrous Metals Manufacturing Industry* (Washington, D.C., U.S. Environmental Protection Agency, March 1975).

or at the lower range of custom smelting and refining charges for concentrates. The CRU study estimated the capital costs for a smelter and refinery for low-grade secondary materials as being similar to those for constructing new primary capacity. If the CRU estimates are correct, the cost advantage, if any, of low-grade scrap over concentrates must be found in the cost of collecting and handling low-grade scrap versus the cost of producing concentrates, in both cases in terms of metal content. But to the extent that low-grade scrap can find a market when made into alloy ingot, the high cost of smelting and refining is avoided.[18]

Scrap Collection

Little appears to be known about the cost of scrap collection. Scrap supply does respond to changes in price over a period when the supply of mine copper may be inelastic. According to one study, a sustained 10 percent rise in price will call forth a 2.6 percent increase in the supply of old scrap.[19] Unlike the content of copper ore, which on the average has been declining, the copper content of the pool of old scrap is unlikely to decline.

Technological developments may concentrate on scrap handling, with the maximizing of "mechanical refining," sorting, upgrading, and so on rather than on furnace refining. The aluminum industry has introduced innovations in secondary metal recovery which could be used in the copper industry. Refining techniques may become more sophisticated with the more widespread use of oxygen-blown furnaces. Moreover, there are undoubtedly opportunities for improving the efficiency of scrap collection, particularly if governments adopt policies, including subsidized programs, to encourage the recovery and recycling of waste materials.

In a paper prepared by the U.K. department of industry, it is stated that the highest copper losses from uncollected scrap, both new and old, occur in the semiindustrialized and developing countries where secondary refining facilities and markets for scrap for domestic use or export are either absent or deficient.[20] Moreover, the projected rate of

[18] The author is indebted to Simon Strauss for pointing out the importance of producing alloy ingot as an alternative to refining copper from low-grade scrap.
[19] Bonczar and Tilton, *Economic Analysis of Determinants of Metal Recycling*, p. 70.
[20] "Copper Scrap and the Implications of Its Role for the Effectiveness of Any International Copper Arrangement Incorporating a Buffer Stock," paper submitted by the UN Delegation to the Intergovernmental Group of Experts on Copper, UNCTAD, Geneva (January 1977).

growth in copper consumption in the developing countries is several times that for the developed countries. The U.K. report estimates that between 4.5 and 5.2 million mt of copper are available annually world-wide in old and new scrap, of which only about 3.6 million mt are used. Thus, it is concluded that the amount of copper-base scrap available to industry world-wide could be increased by some 1.0 to 1.5 million mt per year, given suitable governmental policies and economic incentives to encourage greater collection and use of scrap materials.

Copper Resources of the Oceans

Copper resources in the oceans are found in two broad mineral-bearing areas: seawater proper and the underlying ocean basins.[21] The ocean basins in turn can be divided into the continental margin consisting of the shelf, slope and rise, and the deep ocean floor. Although estimates of the concentration of dissolved copper in seawater reported by various investigators differ substantially, the actual figure is irrelevant for any estimate of potential copper resources since its recovery from seawater is unlikely to be economically feasible in the foreseeable future.

The consolidated rocks on the continental shelf include the same range of sedimentary, metamorphic, and igneous rock types found on the continents. It can, therefore, be expected that the types of copper deposits occurring on land can be found in the consolidated rocks of the shelf. Copper deposits in offshore consolidated rocks have been discovered in Hudson Bay, off the southern coast of Ireland, and off the southwestern coast of Britain.

The more recent unconsolidated sediments which blanket the basement rocks of the shelf contain two copper-bearing mineral provinces. First, there are the polymetallic nodules (manganese nodules) which tend to occur in larger quantities and richer concentrations in deeper waters, and second, there are offshore copper-bearing placers. The most notable nodule deposits of the shelf are on the Blake Plateau off the eastern coast of the United States, the west coast of Baja California, certain areas of the Baltic Sea, and near some of the islands in large ocean basins. However, nodule deposits of the shelf have a much lower metal content than deposits farther from land. Known offshore placers of copper include areas in Hudson Bay, off the southern coast of the Fiji Islands, and off the northern coast of Chile.

[21] This section has drawn heavily on a (draft) study entitled "Copper Resources of the Oceans," UN Centre for Natural Resources, Energy and Transport (November 1976).

The deep ocean floor contains three types of copper-bearing mineral provinces, namely, (1) the extensive copper-bearing polymetallic nodules; (2) the polymetallic incrustations which are found on exposed rocks in regions where earth movements have caused fractures in the seabed; and (3) the metalliferous sediments and brines, also associated with seafloor spreading. Current data and theory suggest that the encrustations may be the most extensive provinces on the ocean floor, with the copper-bearing polymetallic nodules representing the next most extensive. It is these latter whose exploitation prospects are more advanced and have been under active evaluation for a longer period. However, a potential source of marine copper is the metal-enriched mud deposits which form on the bottom of the continental shelf and the deep ocean. These deposits consist partly or predominantly of precipitates of metal oxides, sulfides and carbonates, with the principal metals being iron, manganese, copper, zinc, and lead, which occur as metallic sulfides disseminated throughout the sediments. Reports have been made for the Red Sea, the Banu Wuhu volcano, Indonesia, and the rift zone of the East Pacific rise. The only occurrence already subject to speculation with regard to exploitability is the Red Sea deposit of Atlantis II Deep. The copper content of the sediments of the Atlantis II Deep was found to be 1.3 percent and on the basis of sparse data it was estimated that the area contained 1.1 million tons of copper.

Copper in Polymetallic Nodules

The nodules are usually round, reniform, or spherical, and range in diameter from about 1 to 20 centimeters, with an average of about 5 centimeters. They commonly lie on the sea floor with little or no cover or sediments, and in places form an almost continuous layer. The nodules vary substantially in composition, the principal elements being iron, manganese, silica, and lime in varying proportions. Manganese is nearly 50 percent in some samples, while copper and nickel tend to vary in rough proportion to each other and may be as much as 2 percent each; cobalt also may be as much as 2 percent.

Knowledge of the regional distribution of the nodules is based on only a few hundred samples taken from the world's oceans. All publicly known information about nodules is based on about 600 samples, but a large number of samples have been collected and analyzed by private companies. The nodules occur in a number of areas in the Atlantic, Pacific, and Indian oceans. The most important "prime area" with respect to copper, both in terms of size and metal content, is the Clarion and Clipperton fracture zones of the northern Pacific ocean floor east of Hawaii. Concentration of nodule occurrences in this zone has been estimated to range from 5.0 to 20.0 kilograms per square meter. A recent study by the Ocean Mining Administration, U.S. Department of Interior, estimates that between 190 and 460 mine sites exist in the world's oceans which might permit economical exploitation. They are defined by the following parameters: (1) a minimum abundance of 10 kilograms per square meter; (2) a combined nickel-copper content of 2.25 to 2.4 percent; (3) a cutoff grade of not less than 2 percent of combined nickel, copper, and cobalt; and (4) dimensions for the production of 3 million tons per year for twenty-five years.[22] In order to estimate the magnitude of the copper resources of nodules it is necessary to determine: (1) the cutoff grade; (2) the average grade of deposit above the cutoff grade; (3) the concentration and extent of deposits above cutoff grade; and (4) the percentage of recoverable nodules in (3).

In a recent study undertaken by the Committee on Mineral Resources and the Environment, U.S. National Academy of Sciences, the maximum recoverable quantity of copper in nodules was estimated to be 10^9 tons.[23] However, with further exploration and increasing knowledge of nodule mining, this figure will undoubtedly change. Since the results of privately financed exploration are not available, little else regarding the total recoverable quantity of copper in nodules can be added.

Factors Affecting Commercial Exploitation

Aside from the legal framework for exploration and exploitation of nodule deposits (which is still under negotiation), the main considerations in determining feasibility of exploitation are: (1) the location and metal content of deposits; (2) the technological constraints on the exploitation and beneficiation of the nodules; and (3) the economic determinants of the venture.

Location and Metal Content of Deposits. Nodules of current commercial interest occur at depths of 4,500–6,000 meters. In order to locate a mine site with the minimum conditions for commercial production described above, at least 300 samples over a 10-kilometer area would need to be taken to provide a 90 percent confidence. The abundance and dispersion of nodules are determined by means of photographs cov-

---

[22] Alexander F. Hosler, *Manganese Nodule Resources and Mine Site Availability,* Professional Staff Study, Ocean Mining Administration (Washington, D.C., U.S. Department of Interior, August 1976).

[23] National Academy of Sciences, *Mineral Resources and the Environment* (Washington, D.C., 1975).

ering a measured area, or by television camera. It is also necessary to examine the character of the seabed since a relatively smooth surface is needed for collection. At the time of writing, no mine site meeting all the conditions required for commercial operations had been announced. It is possible that sufficient exploration for positive identification has not been completed. However, a claim to 60,000 square kilometers in the Northwest Pacific has been made by Deepsea Ventures, Inc.

Exploitation and Beneficiation. The four components of a nodule mining system are the collector, the lifting device, the mining vessel, and the transporter. Several types of collectors have been investigated, including rakes, buckets, scoops, and hydraulic equipment. Collectors may be powered or towed. For lifting the nodules up to the surface vessel, the devices could be a continuous line bucket system, a batch lift, or a hydraulic lift.[24] In the spring of 1978, Ocean Management, Inc. announced that it had successfully pumped a continuous stream of nodules aboard a pilot ocean mining ship from a depth of 3 miles, using a collector riding on the seabed that picked up the nodules and injected them into a 3-mile-long pipe for pumping to the surface.[25] The technology and lifting of the nodules appears to be well on the way to solution. A large surface vessel capable of handling lifting equipment of enormous weight (perhaps some 4,000 tons) would remain at sea and would be accompanied by a fleet of three or four transport vessels for shipping the nodules to a port. Several systems are the subject of continuing research and development by international deepsea mining consortia, a list of which is given at the end of this section.

The extractive metallurgy of nodules appears to be fairly well understood. The hydrometallurgical route in which reduction is followed by leaching with sulfuric acid, hydrocloric acid, or ammonia appears to be the most favorable, although the International Nickel Company consortium has continued developmental work on a possible roast-leach process. This is a technique of leaching metal nodules that permits the separation of nickel, copper, and cobalt without getting either manganese or iron ore into the solution. It thus permits nodule processing with rather low initial plant, capital, and operating costs. Recovery of about 90 percent of the copper and nickel is widely predicted. Ocean Mining Associates owns a process which may lead to recovery of as much as 96 percent of the nickel and 94 percent of the copper, as well

24 "Seabed Mining—Background and Current Outlook: Systems, Methods," *World Mining* (December 1977) pp. 54ff.

25 *Mining Activity Digest* (published by the *Engineering and Mining Journal*, May 5, 1978) p. 1.

as 93 percent of manganese and 96 percent of cobalt. A recent comprehensive review concludes that it is likely that one or more of these
processes is now ready for commercialization, requiring only limited
effort on scale-up equipment.[26]

The Economic Determinants. The major components of the cost of
nodule exploitation will be the mining operation, transportation to the
land-based plant, and metallurgical processing. The economic feasibility of a venture will depend on the expected market prices, which
cannot be considered as fixed parameters since they will be influenced
in some degree by the actual supplies from the enterprises.

Given the metal content of nodules, the limitations of the mining
systems, the capital investment required for a nodule venture, the
projected operating costs, and the expected prices of the metals, it has
been tentatively agreed that: (1) nickel will account for over 50 percent
of the total revenues, with copper, manganese,[27] and cobalt accounting
for the remainder; (2) economies of scale will require a typical operation to recover between 1 and 3 million tons (dry weight) of nodules
per year over at least a twenty-year operating life.

The economic feasibility of seabed mining depends ultimately upon
the long-run competitive cost of producing nickel and copper from
nodules in relation to their extraction from land mines. Although there
is general agreement that seabed production will eventually provide an
important supplement to land mine production, there are differences
of opinion regarding the profitability of nodule mining, taking into
account the very large capital outlays for each venture—over a half
billion dollars in 1977 prices for each operation—and the high risks
involved. The Ocean Mining Administration of the U.S. Department
of the Interior concluded that nodule mining would return an annual
profit of 12 to 22 percent.[28] At the lower range, returns would scarcely
justify the risk. Alfred P. Stathan, Vice President of International
Nickel Company, Ltd., stated recently that in his view the cost of
producing nickel from seabed nodules would be higher than the cost
of producing nickel from existing land mines in the foreseeable future.[29] However, according to a study conducted at the Massachusetts

[26] J. C. Agarwal, N. Beecher, D. S. Davies, G. L. Hubred, V. K. Kakaria, and R. N.
Kust in a paper presented at the 104th Annual Meeting of the American Institute of
Mining and Metallurgical Engineers, New York, February 17, 1975.

[27] There is some question whether manganese will be recovered. See C. R. Tinsley,
"Economics of Deep Ocean Resources—A Question of Manganese or No Manganese,"
Mining Engineering (April 1975).

[28] William Wertenbaker, "Mining the Wealth of the Ocean Deep," *New York Times
Magazine,* July 17, 1977, pp. 14ff.

[29] "Seabed Mining," *World Mining* (December 1977) p. 58.

Institute of Technology and released in the spring of 1978, a seabed mining venture might produce a return on investment of 15 to 22 percent. The basic model for the MIT study involves a mine site in about 18,000 feet of water, 2,640 miles from the nearest port, with about 2 pounds of nodules per square foot of ocean floor. It also assumed nodules containing 1.5 percent nickel, 1.3 percent copper, 0.24 percent cobalt, and 26.9 percent manganese. Such a mining venture would require an investment of $560 million with annual revenues of $250 million after operating expenses of $100 million per year beginning in the sixth year and lasting through thirty years.[30]

Impact on Metal Markets. Of the four metals concerned, the production of copper from nodules is likely to have the least immediate impact on metal markets. This is true for two reasons: (1) the demand for copper is about 10 times larger than that for nickel; and (2) the composition of copper production from nodules will range from a high of 4 tons of copper for each 5 tons of nickel to a low of 1 ton of copper for each 2 tons of nickel.

Taking the metal content of nodules in prime areas as being representative of mineable ore and assuming 94 percent recovery of metals after processing, the average recovery from each million tons of dry nodules would be: 15,000 tons of nickel; 13,000 tons of copper; 2,000 tons of cobalt; and 230,000 tons of manganese (if recovered).[31] Table 13-5 presents a hypothetical quantity of each metal that might be produced from nodules at a 5 million ton per year level and at a 10 million ton per year level by 1985. For a level of 5 million tons per year, copper production would be 65,000 mt and double that for a 10 million mt per year production of nodules. Assuming Western world demand for primary copper of 8,500,000 mt in 1986, nodules would represent a range of 0.8 percent to 1.6 percent of the projected world demand for mine copper.[32] By 1990 these percentages could double, but the percentages are still small compared with all of the other uncertainties regarding the long-run supply and demand for copper metal. If, as now seems likely, production at the levels indicated in table 13-5 is delayed

[30] *Mining Activity Digest* (May 5, 1976) p. 1.

[31] UNCTAD, "The Effects of Possible Exploitation of the Seabed on the Earnings of Developing Countries from Copper Exports" (United Nations, Geneva, TD/B/484/28, May 1974); see also H. Drechsler, "The Potential Impact of Seabed Nodule Mining on the World Copper Industry," paper presented at the 1974 World Mining Congress, Lima, Peru.

[32] The percentage contribution of seabed nodules to world demand for nickel and cobalt would be quite significant.

Table 13-5. Hypothetical Mineral Production from Nodules by 1985
(*000 metric tons*)

	Nickel	Manganese	Cobalt	Copper
At 5-million-ton per year level	75	1,150	10	65
At 10-million-ton per year level	150	2,300	20	130

Source: "Copper Resources of the Ocean," Centre for Natural Resources, Energy and Transport, United Nations, New York, November 1976, p. 18 (mimeo, copper study paper no. 2).

for several years, the percentage that seabed nodules contribute to world demand for copper will be even lower.

Activities of International Mining Consortia

Several interested groups are continuing with their surveys and developmental work for mining and metallurgical systems.

Ocean Mining Associates. This consortium consists of United States Steel Company and Union Miniere, S.A. The group controls Deepsea Ventures, Inc. The consortium reports having found several mine sites in the Pacific, and has been collecting nodules on a test basis from a site in the northwest Pacific.

Kennecott Consortium. With Kennecott Copper as the project manager and biggest shareholder, this consortium consists of Kennecott Copper Corporation, Rio Tinto-Zinc, British Petroleum, Consolidated Gold Fields, Mitsubishi, and Noranda Mines. The consortium reports that their hydrometallurgical process is well developed and it is entering the prototype equipment phase for at-sea mining tests.

Ocean Management, Inc. This consortium consists of four groups, each with a 25 percent equity. The four groups are International Nickel (INCO), AMR (Metallgesellschaft, Preussage, Rheinische Braunkohlenwerke and Salzgitter), Deep Ocean Mining Company (consisting of Sumitomo, Nippon Mining, Dowa Mining, and other Japanese companies), and Sedco. This consortium successfully pumped a continuous stream of nodules aboard its pilot ocean mining ship in the spring of 1978. However, it announced that, because of the uncertain outlook in the copper and nickel markets as well as the unresolved international political questions concerning deepsea mining, no further work on the project is planned beyond metallurgical analysis of the nodules.

Ocean Minerals Company. The companies participating in this joint venture, either directly or through an affiliate, are Lockheed Corporation, Amoco Minerals Company, Billiton BV (a member of the Royal Dutch Shell Group), and BKW Ocean Minerals BV.

The Law of the Sea Conference

At the time of writing, uncertainty exists over who will be permitted to engage in seabed mining and under what conditions, pending the outcome of the Law of the Sea Conference, which has been going on for a number of years.[33] The negotiations relating to seabed mining concern the character of the proposed International Seabed Authority (ISA). Several models have been proposed, ranging from an international enterprise that would have a monopoly of all seabed mining activity, to an ISA that would serve merely as a claims registry. Third World countries are demanding a monopoly enterprise while the United States has offered a compromise which would permit both production by an international authority and development by private firms which would pay a royalty to the ISA.[34] It is difficult to believe that an international enterprise lacking the technology and management of the experienced mining firms would be able to extract significant amounts of minerals, if any, from the sea for many years to come. Because of the stalemate in the international negotiations, the U.S. Congress has been considering legislation for licensing U.S. firms for deepsea mining. Although it seems likely that some form of legislation will pass, there is a dispute over whether Congress should provide insurance against losses which U.S. mining firms might incur as a consequence of any future international treaty on seabed mining that the United States might sign. The Carter administration has strongly opposed an insurance plan while the mining companies claim that without such protection they cannot take the risks of seabed mining and that banks won't lend them the large sums required for such operations while there is a chance that the U.S. government will sign a treaty setting up an international authority to regulate ocean mining.[35]

---

[33] For a discussion of the issues in the Law of the Sea Conference relating to seabed mining, see Dennis E. Logue and Richard J. Sweeney, *Economics and the Law of the Sea Negotiations* (International Institute for Economic Research, March 1977) pp. 25–31; see also "Outlook is Dim for Pact on Use of Oceans," *Wall Street Journal* January 24, 1978.

[34] "UN Conference Will Attempt to Break Deadlock on Seabed Mining," *New York Times* May 21, 1977.

[35] "Seabed Mining Bill Receives a Go-Ahead from Carter, But Without Insurance Plan," *Wall Street Journal* October 5, 1977.

Environmental Problems in Copper Production

The U.S. copper industry is subject to controls administered by the Environmental Protection Agency (EPA) under the Federal Water Pollution Control Act Amendments of 1972 and the Clean Air Act Amendments of 1970. There are also controls by the state and local governments. There are in general two types of standards: (1) emission and effluent standards for existing plants to be achieved by certain dates; and (2) new source standards which apply to new plants or the expansion of existing plants. Most other industrialized countries also have pollution abatement standards, which in some cases are more restrictive than those in the United States. Much less has been done or is contemplated in the copper producing countries of the LDCs.

The major environmental problems in the copper industry occur at the smelting stage. There are some water effluent problems at all stages—mining, concentrating, smelting, and refining—but costs per pound of copper for meeting present federal standards are less than those for meeting the air standards. The domestic copper industry is also affected by land restoration standards,[36] especially in the case of open-pit mines. Finally, legislation requiring zero deterioration of environmental conditions in certain areas could affect the expansion of some stages of the copper industry.

Smelter Emissions

In 1975 there were eighteen smelters in the United States, most of which used reverberatory furnaces to form matte (mixture of copper and iron sulfide plus slag) which is then fed into a Pierce–Smith converter to produce blister copper. About half of the U.S. copper smelters roast the concentrates before feeding them into the reverberatory furnace, while the other half feed concentrates directly into the furnace. In addition to the traditional U.S. smelters, Phelps Dodge has constructed an Outokumpu smelter, and Anaconda has built a hydro-metallurgical plant using the Arbiter process (now closed down), both of which have substantial advantages in dealing with SO_2 emissions. The new Hecla-El

36 See *Analysis of Economic Impact of Proposed Effluent Guidelines for the Metallic Ore Mining and Dressing Industries for U.S. Environmental Protection Agency,* Arthur D. Little, Inc. (Cambridge, Mass., August 30, 1976); and *Development Document for Interim Final Effluent Limitations Guidelines and Proposed New Source Performance Standards for the Primary Copper Smelting Subcategory and the Primary Copper Refining Subcategory of the Copper Segment of Nonferrous Metals Manufacturing* (Washington, D.C., U.S. Environmental Protection Agency, February 1975).

Paso Natural Gas plant uses a roast-leach-electrowin technology (see chapter 2).

In order to comply with state, local, and EPA standards, firms with existing reverberatory-converter systems are employing or constructing various devices for controlling SO_2 emissions. These include hoods on converters and chemical processes to increase SO_2 concentration, together with a single or double contact sulfuric acid plant; 1,000 foot stacks; and, in some cases, the replacement of existing smelters with electrical furnaces.[37] It is not entirely clear whether the devices introduced for controlling SO_2 emissions in some of the existing smelters will meet the governmental standards.

There are two issues which are as yet unresolved relating to existing U.S. smelters. The first is the tradeoff between permanent and intermittent controls for meeting ambient air quality standards. The copper industry has argued that meeting EPA standards with control equipment that would reduce emissions to levels that would meet the standards at all times, regardless of ambient air conditions, would involve a very high marginal cost for eliminating small amounts of additional SO_2 emissions. In other words, it is argued that marginal costs would exceed marginal benefits by this method. The industry proposes controls to capture, say, 80 percent of the sulfur emission with permanent controls, leaving the additional 10 percent for meeting a 90 percent objective to intermittent output, cutting back or shutting down plants during those times during the year when the elimination of the additional 10 percent is necessary to achieve EPA ambient air quality standards.[38]

The second unresolved problem for existing smelters is whether the industry shall be required to establish double acid absorption plants as opposed to single acid absorption plants in plant alterations to meet the standards. Double acid absorption plants absorb marginal amounts of SO_2 but at substantial additional cost.

In many ways the conflict between the industry on the one hand, and state and federal legislations and governmental administrative authorities on the other, arises over the question of whether there shall be

[37] For a discussion of the various devices used in existing plants, see *Background Information for New Source Performance Standards: Primary Copper, Zinc and Lead Smelters, Volume I: Proposed Standards* (mimeo, Research Triangle Park, N.C., U.S. Environmental Protection Agency, October 1974) pp. 5–10, 5–16.

[38] For a statement of the industry's position, see Testimony by David Swan, Vice President for Technology, Kennecott Copper Corporation, before the Subcommittee on Environmental Pollution of the Senate Committee on Public Works, April 29, 1975.

fixed standards with no attention being paid to the relationship between marginal cost and marginal benefit, or whether benefit-cost relationships should enter into environmental control regulations. To take an example which is not too extreme in some cases, it may be shown that to get rid of 99 percent of the polluting emissions would cost a half billion dollars, but to get rid of an additional 1 percent would cost another half billion dollars. Are the benefits from getting rid of 1 percent of the emissions worth a half billion dollars (which ultimately must be borne by the consumer)? Alternatively, might there be some compromise in adjusting emissions to ambient air conditions on particular days which would achieve much the same purpose but would involve a much lower cost?[39]

New source standards which are applied to new smelters are more strict and require control of 90 percent or more of the SO_2 emissions. Hence, it appears unlikely that any new reverberatory-converter smelters will be constructed in the United States in the future. The new source standards might be met with two general types of processes: pyrometallurgical processes using techniques such as Outokumpu flash smelting which achieves a high concentration of SO_2 suitable for the manufacture of sulfuric acid;[40] and the hydrometallurgical processes, only two of which have been placed in commercial operation in the United States. The Arbiter process, like most hydrometallurgical processes, causes little direct air pollution, but it is generally believed that the Arbiter process can be economical only for treating certain types of concentrates such as the chalcocite concentrates being utilized by Anaconda (see chapter 2). The recent shutdown suggests that the Arbiter process may not be competitive in periods of low prices. To a considerable degree the feasibility of the pyrometallurgical processes depends upon the ability to sell sulfuric acid. It should also be mentioned that the newer smelting processes are energy efficient compared with the conventional smelters.[41]

The copper industries in Europe and Japan and other countries have been using techniques that provide a high concentration of SO_2 in mak-

[39] For a good discussion of application of cost–benefit principles to environmental controls, see Allen V. Kneese and Charles L. Schultze, *Pollution, Prices and Public Policy* (Washington, D.C., Brookings Institution, 1975) chapter 6.

[40] Other pyro processes include the Noranda process which combines in a single reactor the three operations of roasting, smelting, and converting copper concentrates; and the Mitsubishi process.

[41] For a technical discussion of the various new smelting processes and the problems that they pose, see *Assessment of the Adequacy of Pollution Control Technology for Energy Conserving Manufacturing Process Options: Industry Assessment Report on the Primary Copper Industry*, Arthur D. Little (Cambridge, Mass., December 1, 1975).

ing sulfuric acid for years since the plants tend to be located near industrial markets for sulfuric acid. This gives them an advantage over the U.S. copper industry since most of the mine production and smelting is in the Southwest, far from the markets for acid. If sulfuric acid can be sold for a good price, the proceeds may offset all or a good part of the cost of concentrating the SO_2 and of producing the acid. It has been suggested that new smelters should be located near the markets for sulfuric acid and the concentrates shipped from the mines in the southwestern part of the United States and Montana to the industrialized areas of the mid-West and East Coast.

Effects on U.S. Copper Production

Some students of the U.S. copper industry are fearful that a rise in both operating and capital costs associated with meeting pollution abatement standards will reduce the competitiveness of the U.S. copper industry and, hence, reduce investment and output at all stages from mining through refining. An increase in cost ranging from 5 to as high as 15 cents per pound for pollution abatement has been estimated, although there are fuel and other economies associated with the new techniques. An important deterrent to new investment is the uncertainties regarding future U.S. government standards, both for existing and for new smelters. A Bureau of Mines study[42] reflects some of the uncertainties mentioned above (despite its apparent contradictions):

> New mine projects and expansion plans are in approximate balance with the forecast consumption and should maintain the present high degree of self-sufficiency. Concern over emission of sulphur compounds to the atmosphere during smelting is a pressing problem facing the domestic copper industry. Uncertainties surrounding air quality standards has delayed construction of new smelter facilities and could create a problem if older facilities were forced into earlier closure. New technology and large capital investments will be required to either modify existing pyrometallurgical practices or adopt new hydrometallurgical processes as a solution to the problem if the United States is to maintain a viable copper industry. The domestic copper industry also faces potentially critical conflicts on land restoration standards, waste disposal, water supply, and aesthetic value.

In January 1978 Arthur D. Little, Inc. published a comprehensive study under contract for the U.S. Environmental Protection Agency en-

[42] *Commodity Data Summary 1974,* appendix I to Mining and Mineral Policy, Third Annual Report of the Secretary of the Interior under the Mining and Minerals Policy Act of 1970 (Washington, D.C., U.S. Bureau of Mines, 1974) p. 5.

titled *Economic Impact of Environmental Regulations on the United States Copper Industry*. The impacts on the domestic copper industry were determined on the basis of two alternative scenarios which are possible within the bounds of the current EPA regulations: (1) *Constrained capacity* under which none of the existing smelters will be shut down and all smelters currently employing reverberatory furnaces will make progress toward compliance with EPA regulations by January 1, 1988; no new smelter capacity will be coming on-stream during this period; and only marginal electrowinning capacity will be introduced over the five-year period 1983–87. (2) *Reduced capacity* according to which three smelters with a combined capacity of 268,000 annual short tons of refined copper equivalent will close down in 1983 and no new smelter capacity will be coming on-stream during this period; and only marginal electrowinning capacity will be introduced during the five-year period 1983–87. Cumulative spending by the industry for pollution control over the period 1974–87, including both capital and direct operating costs, is estimated to range between $2.8 and $3.0 billion (in 1974 dollars) under either scenario.

Price impacts of present environmental regulations reflect the combined influence of compliance costs and constraints on capacity growth. Under constrained capacity, prices are estimated to be 23.3 percent higher in 1985 and 29.4 percent higher in 1987 than those prevailing under baseline conditions. (The baseline forecasts assume the existence of national ambient air quality standards, but the absence of additional restrictions on how such standards might be achieved.) Under reduced capacity, prices are higher than baseline prices by 32.8 percent in 1985 and 38.7 percent in 1987. Under constrained capacity, domestic production is estimated to fall 24.9 percent below the baseline forecast and 32.9 percent under reduced capacity. The full force of the production impact is felt in 1987.

These price and production forecasts reflect price levels that would be expected to result from environmental regulations in the absence of a massive infusion of imports into the United States. Imports would, of course, be much higher if LME copper prices stay lower than levels assumed under baseline conditions which themselves reflect a significant increase in the level of imports. Under constrained capacity, net imports in the 1980s are estimated to be 13–15 percent above baseline levels, while under reduced capacity net imports are estimated to be 20.7 percent higher than the baseline level by 1987. However, imports could be much higher, depending on the level of LME copper prices. Presumably substantially larger imports would mean a further reduction in domestic production. Finally, total copper consumption is projected to decline by 8 percent under constrained capacity and by 10.7 percent under reduced capacity by 1987. The decline in total consumption is not as large as the decrease in domestic refined copper production since a larger portion of the demand would be met from secondary output from scrap and from imports. The ADL study did not attempt to quantify the incremental national economic benefits and costs associated with present EPA regulations.[43]

The ADL study assumed that the reduction in domestic smelter capacity will have a corresponding effect on domestic mining output. In other words, it is not assumed that U.S. concentrates will be shipped abroad for smelting and refining. On the other hand, it is possible that a substantial proportion of U.S. copper imports would take the form of blister copper which could be refined in the United States.

International Implications

The effects of pollution abatement regulations on the competitive position of the domestic industry will depend upon the growth of primary copper producing capacity abroad. If foreign copper producing capacity does not expand in line with world demand, including the demand created by increased U.S. imports, world prices will tend to rise. Assuming that smelter capacity will not be constrained in Canada and Australia, slower growth in U.S. output will encourage expansion of primary copper capacity in these countries. The ADL report suggests that constrained or reduced capacity in the United States will stimulate development of new capacity in the LDCs and will encourage foreign investment in these countries. However, as noted in previous chapters, capacity expansion in developing countries will depend on the investment climate in these countries and the ability to raise the billions of dollars required to develop their mineral reserves.

Land Withdrawals for Mineral Exploration and Development

The removal of land from the public domain for the preservation of recreational and environmental amenities has undoubtedly been responsible for a substantial reduction in copper and other mineral producing potential in the United States, and in some cases important known copper deposits have been withdrawn. It has been established that between 1968 and 1974 more than two thirds of the federal lands originally subject to the Mining Law of 1878 and the Mineral Leasing

[43] Arthur D. Little, *Economic Impact*, chapter 1, 8–9.

Act of 1920 were withdrawn from mineral development or their utilization severely restricted. Much of the area withdrawn is in Alaska.[44] It has been argued that these withdrawals, totaling over 600 million acres, cannot be regarded simply as a tradeoff between the preservation of the lands for recreational use and environmental enjoyment on the one hand, and the social value of their mineral potential on the other, since no more than a small fraction of 1 percent of the lands withdrawn are likely to have mineral potential.[45] On the other hand, mineral exploitation requires roads and other facilities that tend to open up an area and reduce its wilderness value.

Without prejudice to the importance of preserving the environment, proper social accounting requires social benefit-cost comparisons. Such analysis has not guided the decisions of the U.S. Congress and the administration regarding these large withdrawals. The problem of comparing social values derived from alternative uses is complicated by the fact that in the absence of exploration we do not know the potential mineral value in particular areas, and after the withdrawal of lands from mineral use we may never know. For example, the social value of the mineral output of a few hundred square miles of the Alaskan interior containing rich uranium deposits or petroleum reserves may be many times greater than any conceivable social cost of withdrawing these acres from a wilderness status. In dealing with this problem, it might be possible to permit limited exploration over large areas and then, if a decision is made against intensive exploration or exploitation at certain sites in view of the environmental costs, the mining firms could be fully compensated for their work if commercial deposits were found. Conceivably, at a later date it might be decided that the social benefits of exploitation of the minerals would outweigh the environmental costs, at which time the government could license the exploitation and recover its payment for the exploration cost.[46]

[44] See Thomas N. Walthier, "The Shrinking World of Exploration," *Mining Engineering* (April and May 1976); see also Gary Bennethum and L. C. Lee, "Is Our Account Overdrawn?" *Mining Congress Journal* (September 1975).

[45] According to the U.S. Bureau of Mines, only 0.16 percent of the total land area of the United States has been utilized by the mining industry during 1930–71. U.S. Bureau of Mines, *Land Utilization and Reclamation in the Mining Industry, 1930–1971*, Information Circular 1974.

[46] See Raymond F. Mikesell, *The Rate of Discount for Evaluating Public Projects* (Washington, D.C., American Enterprise Institute, 1978) pp. 47–49, for a further discussion of this issue.

14

Summary and Conclusions

THIS CHAPTER presents the principal findings that emerge from our broad survey of the copper industry and brings them to bear on certain policy issues that have been raised in the foregoing chapters.

The Present State of the Copper Industry

The past several years have not been happy ones for the world copper industry. The threefold rise in the LME price of copper between early 1973 and April 1974, followed by an equally precipitous decline and the maintenance of low prices in the face of rapidly rising producing costs throughout the 1975–78 period have created serious dislocations in the industry, including periods of low earnings or of losses for many mining firms, and serious balance-of-payments deficits for those developing countries that are heavily dependent upon copper exports. By the fourth quarter of 1977 both U.S. producers' prices and the LME price of copper in constant 1957 dollars were at their lowest levels since 1963 (table 4-1). These prices did not cover operating costs for some firms, and few firms, if any, covered their full costs, including an adequate return on capital. In view of the sharp increase in capital costs for new capacity, 1977–78 copper prices were well below long-run marginal costs.

U.S. copper producers were subject to government price controls until May 1974, followed by increasingly costly pollution abatement regulations and uncertainties regarding their application. Much of the foreign producing capacity of international mining companies was nationalized during the 1960s and 1970s, and a poor investment climate in most developing countries has discouraged foreign mining activities in these countries. Rapidly rising capital and production costs in the face of low prices and demand uncertainties have made planning capacity for future growth of the industry exceedingly hazardous. The advances in technology in both copper producing and consuming industries (reviewed in chapter 2) have added to these uncertainties.

Copper inventories remained large throughout the 1975–77 period, about one-fourth of annual consumption, and the output of existing mines in the United States and other industrial countries was cut back in the face of the low prices during 1977. However, this period of copper glut is likely to give way to one of capacity shortage and excessively high prices in relation to long-run costs unless there is an appropriate expansion in copper producing capacity over the next few years. On the basis of some demand forecasts and of present plans for expanding both mine and smelter producing capacity which are likely to be realized in the next few years, it is quite possible that the sharp rise in copper prices that took place in 1973–74 will be repeated by the mid-1980s. Such gyrations in prices serve no economic function and are harmful to both consumers and producers. It is not surprising, therefore, that both copper exporting and importing countries have become interested in devising measures for mitigating these price fluctuations and in achieving a better balance over time between the growth of consumption and the expansion of productive capacity.

Some part of the problem of world imbalance in the copper industry may arise from the existing market organization described in chapter 3 and from U.S. government price controls prior to mid-1974. Although during most periods the differential between U.S. producers' prices and the LME price has been fairly narrow, there have been long periods during which one of these prices has been 30 to 50 percent higher than the other. Such differentials are undoubtedly destabilizing for the world market as a whole and lead U.S. consumers to accumulate inventories rather than meet their future requirements through the forward markets. The two-price system limits the ability of consumers to hedge their purchases from primary producers on the commodity exchanges since forward markets for copper sold at producers' prices do not exist, and producers' prices do not, over the short run at least, move in line with LME or Comex futures prices. It has been argued that if all consumers contracted for their copper supplies at free market prices rather than at producers' prices (coupled at times with rationing of supplies of producers' copper), spot and forward prices on the free market for copper would adjust more smoothly to fundamental demand and supply conditions. An opposing argument by those who favor the producers' price system is that this system avoids sharp short-term price fluctuations while permitting producers' prices to adjust to fundamental demand and supply forces over the longer run. (This controversy is somewhat analogous to that between those favoring an adjustable par value foreign exchange system and those favoring freely fluctuating exchange rates with no central bank intervention in the exchange markets.)

The argument for a domestic producers' price system might be more convincing if it did not at times lead to the rationing of producers' copper, an event that often generates heavy demand on the open markets for copper and instability in prices of fabricated products. In periods of reduced demand, the maintenance of domestic producers' prices depends upon the willingness of producers to cut back production or produce for inventory. However, as we have seen, significantly lower prices on the open markets for copper have put substantial pressure on U.S. producers' prices. The decision of both Kennecott and Anaconda in 1978 to base their prices on daily quotations on the Comex suggests that the two-price system for U.S. primary copper may be breaking down.

A world producers' price system in which all major primary copper producers would sell at producers' prices more or less in line with one another seems unlikely to be achieved in the near future. In any event, it would be rash to argue that the unification of the world's copper markets, either on the basis of a world producers' price or on the basis of a system of integrated free copper exchanges, would provide an adequate solution to the problem of wildly gyrating copper prices.

Costs and Prices

Our historical review of copper prices and costs in chapter 4 provided evidence that in most years during the period 1957–68 the deflated U.S. producers' price for copper was reasonably close to the upper range of Herfindahl's long-run equilibrium price prevailing over the 1926–57 period. This suggests that the real cost of producing copper had not risen significantly since the 1920s. After 1968, copper prices were, in most years, well above Herfindahl's estimate of the long-run equilibrium price (cost) of copper, but following the sharp increase in 1973–74, real copper prices declined and were at times below the upper range of Herfindahl's estimated long-run equilibrium price. In view of the substantial increases in *real* costs of production and in *real* capital costs for new copper producing capacity during the 1970s, it seems clear that 1977–78 copper prices were well below the long-run equilibrium level as determined by full production costs.

The analysis of the structure of the world copper industry in chapter 4 supported Herfindahl's conclusion that the world copper industry is basically competitive. There is considerable evidence that the interna-

tional copper companies' loss of ownership and control of copper producing capacity in the developing countries has substantially reduced
their market power. Moreover, as was noted in chapter 1, there has been
a substantial shift in the geographical distribution of copper mine production and smelting in favor of the developing countries in recent
years. Although the U.S. primary copper industry is oligopolistic in the
sense that the major primary copper producers are price *makers* rather
than price *takers*, they are unable to maintain prices above those quoted
on the commodity exchanges for more than short periods of time. Moreover, in most years since 1963, the LME copper price has been above the
average U.S. producers' prices. This phenomenon is difficult to rational-
ize in terms of the economic interests of the U.S. primary producers,
although for a considerable period of time it can be explained by the
imposition of U.S. government price controls.

Copper Modeling

Chapters 5 and 6 examine the methodology of constructing econometric
models for analyzing the complex interactions of demand and supply
in the copper industry. Such models are useful tools for handling the
large number of variables and their interrelationships for an understanding of the dynamics of the copper industry and for dealing with
such questions as: (1) the effect on copper prices of changes in prices of
substitutes for copper, or of new technological developments in copper
consuming industries; (2) the nature and decision rules for a copper
buffer stock program designed to promote price stability; or (3) the
impact of various government regulations on the future output of the
U.S. copper industry.

As more information becomes available on the various sectors of the
industries supplying and using copper and on the behavioral patterns of
decision makers in various sectors of the industry, econometric models
will undoubtedly do a better job of portraying the operations of the
copper market. However, our examination of the leading copper models
shows rather wide discrepancies in their estimates of short- and long-run
price elasticities of demand, of demand elasticities with respect to the
index of durable manufactures, and of cross-price elasticities with respect to substitutes for copper, such as aluminum. In addition, the track
record of current models for projecting copper prices has been notori-
ously poor. This has been due in part to difficulties with the models
themselves in estimating equations from historical data, and in part
from the fact that projections must be based on projected exogenous

variables, such as industrial production, which rarely conform to expectations.

The modeling of copper supply is full of difficulties. In the short run producers may cut back output, produce for inventory, or continue producing at capacity in response to a reduction in price. Given a period of a year or so it is possible to expand capacity somewhat by installing additional units at certain stages of production or delay partial curtailment of production for normal maintenance. Long-run supply involving a major expansion of existing mines or smelters, or of developing new mines, or delaying plans for new productive capacity is not simply a function of current or expected price at some point in time, but of a host of factors governing investment decisions and the opportunities for new investment as determined by discoveries of reserves and the political and other constraints on exploiting them. Some models have used announced plans for additions to capacity as the basis for long-run supply projections, but plans are continually revised for reasons that cannot be anticipated.

Recognition of the shortcomings of existing econometric models and the obstacles to improving them should not be interpreted as a recommendation that work in this area be abandoned or that models are incapable of producing useful results. Progress in quantitative analysis offers the hope of increasing our knowledge of the copper industry and of providing the empirical basis for problem solving and policy determination.

International Price Stabilization

In chapter 7 we examined current proposals for an international stabilization agreement in copper and concluded that the outlook for an agreement was not encouraging because of apparently irreconcilable differences between Third World governments and the governments of the industrialized countries on both the objectives of an agreement and the mechanisms to be employed. There is a danger that any arrangement agreed upon might try to support a price above the long-run equilibrium level, with serious consequences for the future economic welfare of the industry. Nevertheless, it is not concluded that a well-managed international buffer copper stock, adequately supported with both financial resources and copper stocks, would be incapable of moderating future price fluctuations and of facilitating the growth in world copper producing capacity in line with the expansion of consumer demand. The essential conditions for a successful buffer stock operation include adequate funding, flexibility in adjusting upper and lower price support levels, political independence, and a high degree of competence of the buffer stock manager; but there are serious political barriers to the realization of these conditions.

Our analysis in chapter 7 of the potential market power of an international producers' cartel consisting of members of CIPEC (perhaps joined by other developing countries) concluded that such a cartel would not be capable of improving the export earnings of its members by means of export restrictions for more than a year or so. Over a longer period both demand elasticities and elasticities of supply of sources outside the cartel are sufficiently high to render a cartel operation unprofitable. In the longer run, individual CIPEC members are in competition with one another for shares of the world market and are unlikely to agree on limiting the growth of their productive capacities. Even if they were able to do so, they might encourage the expansion of copper producing capacity in the United States, Canada, and other countries outside the cartel, since the developed countries are relatively well endowed with copper resources and their reserves continue to expand with new discoveries.

Finally it was concluded in chapter 7 that recent U.S. legislative proposals, supported by some mining industry spokesmen, for the creation of a U.S. government copper stockpile would provide U.S. producers little, if any, benefits. Such action would be inappropriate while the U.S. government is participating in international negotiations on a copper buffer stock agreement. Moreover, the high degree of U.S. self-sufficiency in copper scarcely warrants the inclusion of copper in a national strategic mineral reserve.

The Investment Decision in the Mining Industry

In chapter 8 we reexamined Herfindahl's basic question of whether aggregate investment in the copper industry responds systematically to expected returns, or whether investment is haphazard because of accidental finds and the inability of firms to predict the relationship between investment and returns. Herfindahl concluded that investment in the copper industry did respond systematically to expected profit signals and, therefore, it is possible to develop a long-run supply function for copper relating output or capacity to cost of production and to copper prices. Although sufficient information is not available for a satisfactory test of Herfindahl's hypothesis for the period since 1957, there is considerable evidence that for the major U.S. copper companies the mining business is not a lottery. Major U.S. companies have grown more or less steadily over the past two decades with average after-tax profits comparable to those in the manufacturing industry.

Investment decisions are involved at each stage in the copper production process, beginning with the initial phases of exploration through the feasibility study and the final decision to construct a mine. This process, which is analyzed in chapter 8, has become quite sophisticated in terms of probability and cash flow analysis at each stage where a decision on further investment must be made.

Large international mining companies can undertake a number of investments in various regions of the world, and if they have done a competent job in calculating the probability coefficients for the expected financial outcomes of each investment, they should over time earn a rate of return approximating the opportunity cost of the equity and loan capital employed. Although some firms may experience long periods of disappointing or higher than expected returns, a large, diversified and well-managed mining firm should be subject to less risk on total investment and enjoy a higher average rate of return on invested capital than the average rate of return for a collection of smaller firms. Unfortunately, it is difficult to test this proposition in the mining industry because there are insufficient data on the number of small firms that emerge and disappear or are merged with larger firms. In addition, large copper mining firms are diversified into other minerals and engage in downstream activities, and large petroleum companies have diversified into mining. Hence, it is often difficult to separate rates of return on investment in different sectors for the same firm.

Foreign Investment in the Copper Industry

As was noted in chapter 1, the nationalization or partial nationalization of the copper industries in developing countries, together with the shift in copper mine production and smelting in favor of the developing regions, has greatly reduced the concentration of ownership and control of world copper production. Although foreign investment in the developing countries continues to be significant, there have been marked changes in the pattern of ownership and control in the copper industries of the developing countries.

The decline in foreign investment in the mining industry in recent years, engendered in large part by the expropriation of foreign properties and by the generally unfavorable investment climate, has raised the question of whether the production of nonfuel minerals in the developing countries will expand at a rate warranted by the quality and quantity of the mineral resources of these countries. Although this is a problem for the industrialized countries, especially in the case of minerals such as tin and bauxite, which are not found in substantial quantities in the developed countries, it may be an even more serious problem for the mineral-rich developing countries. This problem for the latter group of countries is particularly important in the case of copper since there are substantial copper resources in the developed countries. The failure of developing countries to expand their copper producing capacity at a rate warranted by the quality and quantity of their reserves will, therefore, encourage the development of lower grade resources in the United States and other developed countries.

The issue posed above raises a number of questions which are addressed in chapters 9, 10, and 11. These include: (1) What are the special contributions of foreign investment to the mining industries of the Third World and can the inputs of traditional foreign investment be supplied to the developing countries in other ways? (2) How can the constraints on foreign investment arising from conflicts between international mining companies and host governments be resolved? (3) What are the tradeoffs for developing countries in choosing between foreign investment and domestic exploitation of their resources? (4) What are the economic considerations facing developing countries in deciding on the rate at which their resources should be developed?

A major finding in dealing with these questions is that foreign investment does play a vital role in mobilizing the managerial and technical skills and the equity and debt financing for realizing the mineral producing potential of the developing countries. It is also argued that foreign investment in the resource industries can be compatible with the national economic objectives of developing countries, although it may run counter to their political objectives. Finally, it is believed that in most cases developing countries will not increase their welfare by deliberately retarding the rate at which their resources are exploited in order to reap higher returns in the future, or to transfer income to future generations.

On the basis of these findings, it is clearly in the interest of both the developing countries and the international mining firms to find ways of resolving conflicts and of establishing conditions that will promote foreign investment. Our analysis of the constraints on foreign investment suggests that more imaginative and comprehensive mine development agreements offer considerable promise in resolving conflicts between foreign investors and host governments. This conclusion is supported in chapter 10 by a review of recent contract negotiations between foreign investors and host governments for the development of copper resources, which have apparently dealt satisfactorily with many of the obstacles to investment in the past and with resolving problems that may arise in the future. Among the more important features of recently negotiated mine development agreements are tax formulas that insure the foreign investor will be permitted to earn a minimum DCF rate over the life of the contract, and provisions which guarantee the right of managerial control and a veto over certain policy decisions in cases where the foreign investor has a minority equity interest.

Although the current outlook for a substantial expansion of foreign investment in the Third World by U.S. and European mining companies is not favorable, there are indications of changing attitudes on the part of mining officials regarding such issues as majority equity ownership, joint mining ventures with domestic and foreign partners, promoting national economic and social objectives, and sharing control in certain areas with the host government. There is at the same time an increasing realization on the part of governments of the conditions necessary to attract foreign investors and a greater degree of technical sophistication in contract negotiations.[1]

International Action

There is increasing interest in international action for promoting investment in the mineral industries of the developing countries, but the approaches of the Third World countries and of the industrialized countries diverge widely. Former Secretary Kissinger's proposal for an International Resources Bank put forward at the May 1976 UNCTAD conference in Nairobi, Kenya was rejected by the Third World countries, mainly because of its emphasis on foreign private investment. In contrast, the proposal for an International Minerals Investment Trust contained in a May 1977 report by the UN Committee on Natural Resources (summarized in chapter 12) was oriented to government mining enterprises and almost ignored foreign equity investment. At the time of writing it seems unlikely that any new international agency for promoting mineral investment in the developing countries will be established.

The UN Fund for Natural Resources Exploration created by the UN General Assembly in 1974 has been unable to attract sufficient

---

[1] The above statements are based on interviews by the author with a number of officials of U.S. and European mining firms and with officials of host governments, together with first-hand knowledge of recent contract negotiations.

seed capital from the industrialized countries to undertake more than a handful of exploration projects. Moreover, the UNDP, which has been conducting mineral projects for several years, does not have sufficient funds to undertake more than a small fraction of the geological survey and exploration work that should be carried on in the developing countries. Neither of these organizations is incompatible with foreign private investment in exploration and development of mineral resources, but they have found no support in the private international mining community.

In assessing the role of international development agencies such as the World Bank Group (chapter 12), it was concluded that these institutions could make a significant contribution to the flow of equity and loan capital to the mineral industries in Third World countries with only modest financial participation. Foreign equity investors could be given greater confidence in the observance of contract provisions if international development agencies were parties to the agreements. Considering the enormous amount of external financial resources required to carry out warranted expansions of productive capacity of nonfuel minerals in developing countries over the next two decades—well over a billion dollars a year in 1977 dollars for copper alone, and five billion a year for all of the major metals—international development agencies could not be expected to provide more than 10 percent of these requirements. On the other hand, participation in loan financing, including the evaluation of feasibility studies and perhaps the use of cross-default loan arrangements, could serve as a catalyst for providing the bulk of the loan capital from the private international financial markets.

Scrap

The world's supply of copper depends not only on newly mined copper, but on the growing volume of old scrap. There are, however, severe limitations on the contribution of scrap to the supply of copper in any given year. The quantity of copper that can be recovered at any date in the future is a function of the quantity that went into service an average component lifetime earlier. If the average component life of copper is twenty-six years, even complete recovery of all the copper produced in 1950 (2.5 million mt) would provide only 32 percent of that produced in 1976 (7.9 million mt). Complete recycling is physically impossible and the cost of recovery for a considerable portion of the potentially recoverable copper is prohibitive. Despite the world's large and growing pool of potentially recoverable copper—the volume of which is subject to a wide variety of estimates based on indirect evidence—most investigators do not project a significant increase in the current ratio of scrap recovery to total copper consumption over the next couple of decades. (In the United States, the ratio of old scrap utilized to total copper consumption has averaged about 17 percent during the past decade.) However, this projection could turn out to be wrong if economic and governmental incentives favored greater scrap recovery.

Adequate information is lacking on scrap collection and on the potential for larger scrap utilization through changes in government policies and waste disposal programs. Since copper recycling is a part of the broader issue of minerals recycling, action will not be taken with respect to copper alone. Moreover, in a period of low metal prices and perceived abundance of nonfuel mineral resources, economic incentives for recycling programs may not be favorable.

Outlook for World Copper Demand and Primary Producing Capacity

The disappointing rate of economic expansion in the industrialized countries and the large copper inventories have led to a reduction in the rate of growth in demand for copper since 1974, and most analysts foresee a lower rate of growth for the remainder of the twentieth century than the 4.2 percent rate for the 1964–75 period. Estimated annual rates of growth in world demand beyond 1980 range from less than 3 percent to over 4 percent. Moreover, the UN forecast of a 4.3 percent growth rate in world demand for the period 1976–90 was heavily influenced by an expected high annual rate of growth in consumption (10.3 percent) by the developing countries, as contrasted with a projected annual rate of growth of 2.9 percent for the developed countries.

Projections of copper producing capacity for the market economies for 1980, based on plans for capacity expansion that were made in 1977, differ by as much as a million metric tons. Hence, it is hazardous to project the balance between mine capacity and the demand for primary copper for 1980 or 1981. Nevertheless, in view of the large inventories it is difficult to believe that there will be a shortfall of copper supply which would warrant a sharp increase in the real price of copper by 1980. Beyond 1980 the outlook is less clear. Much depends upon the expansion of productive capacity in the developing countries. Although publicly announced plans for increased capacity for 1985 indicate substantial additions, only two large mines in the developing countries, namely La Caridad in Mexico and Sar Cheshmeh in Iran, are likely to come on-stream between 1978 and 1985. For most of the other announced large projects, the feasibility studies have not been completed nor the financing arranged. However, an expansion of several large mines in the developed countries could take place within two years if market conditions were favorable.

Investment requirements for additions to copper production capacity in the market economies for the period 1977–2000 are estimated to average about $2.7 billion per year in 1977 dollars (see table 12-5), and if the developing countries are to maintain their share of world copper production, at least half of the investment expenditures should go for projects in these countries. There should be little problem in mobilizing the financial resources for investments in the developed countries, but, for reasons already indicated, the mobilization of $1.3 billion per year for copper projects in the developing countries, of which about $1 billion per year will be required from foreign sources, will depend on the outlook for foreign investment.

In time, production of copper from the seabed nodules may contribute significantly to the world's supply of primary copper, but this source is unlikely to provide more than 5 percent of the world's demand for copper by 1990.

As was discussed in chapter 13, there may be a problem of providing sufficient copper smelting capacity, particularly in the United States. Part of the problem lies in the uncertainties regarding pollution abatement requirements. Failure to expand copper smelting capacity in the United States could also retard the growth of U.S. mine producing capacity, since it probably would not be economical for the U.S. to ship concentrates abroad for processing. Undoubtedly there will be a shift in smelter output from the developed countries to the copper producing countries in the Third World that seem willing to accept more pollution in order to increase their value-added from copper production. Whether the copper smelters will be built in line with demand depends again on the flow of financial and other resources to the developing countries.

Index

Adams, F. Gerard, 191*n*, 199*n*, 204*n*
ADB. *See* Asian Development Bank
ADL. *See* Little, Arthur D.
Africa: Copper production in, 8; expropriation of investments in, 1; mineral exploration in, 8–9. *See also* individual African countries
Agarwal, J. C., 353*n*
Air conditioners, substitution of aluminum for copper in, 162
Air pollution, 67, 68. *See also* Environmental pollution; Pollution abatement
Alfonza, J. P. Perez, 307*n*
Allende, Salvador, 253, 272*n*, 303, 336
Alloys, copper: aluminum as substitute for, 132, 163; market for, 144; as substitute for copper, 146
Aluminum: deposits of, 45; production of, 111; as substitute for copper, 110, 119, 145, 149–150, 156, 160–161, 212–213
AMAX. *See* American Metal Climax
American Metal Climax (AMAX), 27, 29, 32, 35, 43, 87*n*; affiliates of, 38; mining operations of, 109; sale of copper interests to Zambia, 262
American Metal Market, 86
American Smelting and Refining Company (ASARCO), 27, 29, 32, 34, 80, 87*n*, 107; affiliates of, 39–40; equity in Mexico, 36; exploration activities by, 55; mining operations of, 39, 109; sale of copper interests to foreign governments, 261; shaft furnace of, 71

American Society for Testing Materials (ASTM), 79, 85
Amortization, of invested captial, 266–268
Anaconda, 8, 29*n*, 32, 33, 34, 38, 39; affiliates of, 39; aluminum production by, 111; Chilean expropriation of mines of, 221, 336; exploration activities by, 221, 229; hydrometallurgical plant of, 357; merger with Atlantic Richfield, 219; rate of return on equity, 219; sale of copper interests to foreign governments, 260, 261; share of copper market by, 109
Anamax Mining Company, 38, 39
Andean Pact, 263
Andina mine, Chile, 33
Anglo-American Corporation of South Africa, 8, 27, 35; affiliates of, 43–44; sale of copper interests to Zambia, 262
Arbiter process, 66–67, 357, 359
Arbitrage transactions, 83, 85, 144
ARCO. *See* Atlantic Richfield Co.
ASARCO. *See* American Smelting and Refining Co.
ASARCO Mexicana, 36, 39
Asian Development Bank (ADB), 334
ASTM. *See* American Society for Testing Materials
Atlantic Richfield Company (ARCO), 31*n*, 33, 39
Atlas Consolidated, 29*n*, 35
Australia: copper exports, 19; copper production, 9; exploration for copper, 54–55; foreign ownership

Philippines (continued)
tion for copper, 54–55; foreign investor relationships in, 246; organization of copper industry in, 35–
36; projected copper mine capacity
of, 323; smelters of, 26
Physical properties of copper, 132
Pierce-Smith converter, 64
Plastics, as substitute for copper, 110,
145, 146, 212–213
PNG. See Papua New Guinea
Poland, mine output, 29, 323
Pollution abatement: capital for, 327;
and expansion of mining capacity,
166; impact on copper industry,
178, 179–180, 186; international
implications of, 362; and production costs, 127, 360–362
Polymetallic nodules: copper in, 13,
350–351; cost of exploiting, 353–
354; effect on copper market of,
354–355; feasibility of exploiting,
351; mining of, 352–353; mining
consortium involved with, 355–356;
projected copper production from,
375
Porphyry deposits, 6, 47; block caving for mining, 56; open-pit mining of, 57, 59; U.S. production
from, 7
Power plants, substitution of aluminum for copper in, 162
Prain, Ronald, 5n, 6n, 13n, 29, 59
122n, 128, 146
Preston, Lee E., 222n
Prices, copper, 1; cartels and, 103–
104; commodity exchange, 80–85;
demand and, 144, 185–186; environmental regulations and, 361–
362; and exploration for copper,
166; government control over, 104,
105, 111, 203, 364; hedging on, 82,
84, 89; international contracts
based on, 89–90; inventories and,
183; long-run equilibrium in, 119,

120–121, 202; maintenance of low,
109; in merchants markets, 85–86;
oligopoly, 89; refined, 79; and recoverable reserves, 166, 317, 320,
321; scrap, 86, 87; targets for, 195–
196, 202; world producers', 205–
206, 366. See also LME price; New
York Commodity Exchange; Price
stabilization; Producers' price system; Two-tier pricing system
Price stabilization, 2; arguments for,
189–193, 204; and buffer stock
operations, 188; criticism of, 203–
204; effect on long-run equilibrium
price, 193–194, 196–197; explanation of, 187; through export quotas
adjustment, 188, 202; international
agreements on, 204–207, 368–369;
inventories and, 197; production
efficiency from, 194; statistical
measures of, 187–188
Primary copper industry, 79–80; barriers to entry to, 108–109; market
power of, 106–108; percent of copper supply for, 182
Producers' price system, U.S., 80;
average annual, 119–121; under
government controls, 104, 105; and
LME price, 81–82, 86–87, 102, 111–
113, 215, 364, 365; and rationing,
114–115; and supply of copper, 65.
See also Two-tier pricing system
Production, copper: financing of
future, 326–332; by major country
and region, 9–11; by mines, 29–30;
projected capacity from, 321–322,
374–375; from scrap, 17, 79, 342–
347; stages of, 16–17, 116; world,
6, 9, 17–19, 125. See also Production costs
Production costs: fixed versus variable, 116–117; Herfindahl hypothesis for, 118–119, 121, 122,
124, 125; increase in, 126–129;
marginal, 122–123; for new copper

Tariffs, 74, 119
Taxation, of foreign investors, 119n;
contract provisions for, 276–277;
direct versus indirect, 265; exemption from, 266; flat rate for, 280;
Garnaut–Clunies-Ross formula for,
280–281, 295–297
Technology, for copper industry:
early development of, 5; hydrometallurgical, 65–67; and LRS,
150; and production costs, 119;
refining and smelting, 6, 70
Telegeoloc technique. *See* Remote
sensing
Tenke-Fungurume mine, Zaire, 34,
260
Texasgulf, 29n; agreement with
Panama, 286–288; smelting process,
65
Theil, Henri, 151n, 153n, 154n
Thiebach, G., 330n
Third World. *See* Less developed
countries
Tilton, John E., 77n, 194n, 319n, 341,
344n, 348n
Tims, Wouter, 180n, 182n
Tinsley, C. R., 353n
Toquepala mine, Peru, 34, 123, 259
Trade, copper: contracts for, 27; factors influencing, 26–27; world, 17,
19. *See also* Exports, copper; Imports, copper
Transportation: copper used in, 74;
cost of copper, 26, 123
Tsumeb Corporation, 38, 41
Turnovsky, S. J., 191n
Two-tier pricing system: criticism of,
115; history of, 111–112; operation
of, 112–113; rationale for, 114–116;
and rationing, 114, 115, 157n

Udall, Morris K., 215
UNCTAD. *See* United Nations
Conference on Trade and Development
Underground mining, 56–57

UNDP. *See* United Nations Development Program
Union Miniere du Haut-Katanga, 8
United Kingdom: copper consumption 13, copper imports, 24; copper
production, 5; copper refining, 70;
copper scrap exports, 342; report
on scrap collection by, 348–349
United Nations: projected copper
mine capacity by, 322; projected
world copper demand by, 324–325;
proposed investment code by, 335;
study of copper reserves by, 50–51,
317–318
United Nations Committee on Natural Resources, 333
United Nations Conference on Trade
and Development (UNCTAD), 1,
106, 187, 354n; estimates of target
prices for buffer stock operations,
198–199; integrated program for
commodities, 189, 202, 205, 214,
215
United Nations Development Program (UNDP), aid for copper exploration, 55, 230, 253–254, 305,
373
United Nations Revolving Fund for
Natural Resources Exploration,
253–254, 305, 372
United States: concentration in copper industry of, 31–33; copper consumption, 13, 14, 16, 132–136;
copper exports, 19; copper imports,
24, 32; copper prices, 79–80; copper production, 7, 9, 124–125;
copper production costs, 122–123;
copper refining, 70–71; copper
scrap exports, 342; copper supply,
169–170; decline in mining activity
in developing countries by, 250–
251; domestic mining company expenditures of, 251; exploration for
copper, 54–55; grade of copper reserves in, 318; hydrometallurgical
processes in, 66–67; leaching

Library of Congress Cataloging in Publication Data

Mikesell, Raymond Frech.
   The world copper industry.

   1. Copper industry and trade.   2. Copper
industry and trade—Finance.   I. Resources for
the Future.   II. Title.
HD9539.C6M54   338.2'7'43   79-4581
ISBN 8-8018-2257-2 cloth
ISBN 0-8018-2270-X paperback